OCP

Oracle® Certified Professional al
Java® SE 11 Developer
Practice Tests

Exam 1Z0-819 and Upgrade
Exam 1Z0-817

OCP
Oracle® Certified Professional Java® SE 11 Developer Practice Tests

Exam 1Z0-819 and Upgrade Exam 1Z0-817

Scott Selikoff

Jeanne Boyarsky

For my wife Patti—you put up with me.
—Scott

To Chris for being the first person on earth who knew I'd write a book or seven.
—Jeanne

Acknowledgments

Scott and Jeanne would like to thank numerous individuals for their contribution to this book. Thank you to David Clark for guiding us through the process and making the book better in so many ways. Thank you to Janeice DelVecchio for being our technical editor as we wrote this book. Janeice pointed out many subtle errors in addition to the big ones. And thank you to Elena Felder for being our technical proofreader and finding the errors that we managed to sneak by Janeice. This book also wouldn't be possible without many people at Wiley, including Kenyon Brown, Pete Gaughan, Christine O'Connor, Saravanan Dakshinamurthy, Kim Wimpsett, Evelyn Wellborn, and so many others.

Scott could not have reached this point without his wife, Patti, and family, whose love and support make this book possible. He would like to thank his twin daughters, Olivia and Sophia, and youngest daughter, Elysia, for their patience and understanding, especially when it was "time for Daddy to work in his office!" Scott would like to extend his gratitude to his wonderfully patient co-author, Jeanne, on this, their seventh book. He doesn't know how she's able to work with him for months at a time, but he's glad she does and thrilled at the quality of books we produce. A big thanks to Matt Dalen, who has been a great friend, sounding board, and caring father to Olivia, Adeline, and newborn Henry. Finally, Scott would like to thank his mother and retired teacher, Barbara Selikoff, for teaching him the value of education, and his father, Mark Selikoff, for instilling in him the benefits of working hard.

Jeanne would personally like to thank everyone who kept her sane during the COVID-19 pandemic, especially Dani, Elena, Janeice, Norm, Rodridgo, Scott, and Wendy. Scott was a great co-author, improving everything Jeanne wrote while writing his own chapters. A big thank-you to everyone at CodeRanch.com who asked and responded to questions and comments about our books. Another big thank-you to the NYJavaSig as it transitioned to online. Finally, Jeanne would like to thank all of the new programmers at CodeRanch.com and FIRST robotics teams FRC 694, FTC 310, FTC 479, and FTC 8365 for the reminders of how new programmers and technologists think.

Scott and Jeanne would like to give a big thank-you to the readers of all our books. Hearing from all of you who enjoyed the book and passed the exam is a great feeling. We'd also like to thank those who pointed out errors and made suggestions for improvements in our Java 11 Study Guides. As of October 2020, the top three were Jos Roseboom, Tomasz Kasprzyk, and Oksana Cherniavskaia. We'd also like to thank Campbell Ritchie for replying to so many reader comments on CodeRanch.com.

About the Authors

Scott Selikoff is a professional software consultant, author, and owner of Selikoff Solutions, LLC, which provides software development solutions to businesses in the tri-state New York City area. Skilled in a plethora of software languages and platforms, Scott specializes in full-stack database-driven systems, cloud-based applications, microservice architectures, and service-oriented architectures.

A native of Toms River, New Jersey, Scott achieved his Bachelor of Arts degree from Cornell University in Mathematics and Computer Science in 2002, after three years of study. In 2003, he received his Master of Engineering degree in Computer Science, also from Cornell University. As someone with a deep love of education, Scott has always enjoyed teaching others new concepts. He's given lectures at Cornell University and Rutgers University, as well as conferences including Oracle Code One and The Server Side Java Symposium.

Scott lives in New Jersey with his loving wife, Patti; three amazing daughters, twins Olivia and Sophia and little Elysia; two very playful dogs, Webby and Georgette; and three curious kittens, Snowball, Sugar, and Minnie Mouse. You can find out more about Scott at `www.linkedin.com/in/selikoff` or follow him on Twitter @ScottSelikoff.

Jeanne Boyarsky was selected as a Java Champion in 2019. She has worked as a Java developer for more than 18 years at a bank in New York City where she develops, mentors, and conducts training. Besides being a senior moderator at `CodeRanch.com` in her free time, she works on the forum code base and is a leader of the NYJavaSIG. Jeanne also mentors the programming division of a FIRST robotics team where she works with students just getting started with Java. She also speaks at several conferences each year.

Jeanne got her Bachelor of Arts degree in 2002 and her Master's in Computer Information Technology in 2005. She enjoyed getting her Master's degree in an online program while working full-time. This was before online education was cool! Jeanne is also a Distinguished Toastmaster and a Scrum Master. You can find out more about Jeanne at `www.jeanneboyarsky.com` or follow her on Twitter @JeanneBoyarsky.

Jeanne and Scott are both moderators on the `CodeRanch.com` forums and can be reached there for questions and comments. They also co-author a technical blog called Down Home Country Coding at `www.selikoff.net`.

In addition to this book, Scott and Jeanne are also the authors of the following best-selling Java 11 certification books: *OCP Java SE 11 Programmer I Study Guide* (Sybex, 2019), *OCP Java SE 11 Programmer II Study Guide* (Sybex, 2020), and *Java SE 11 Developer Complete Study Guide* (Sybex, 2020). They also wrote the three best-selling Java 8 certification books.

Contents at a Glance

Contents

Introduction

This book is intended for those who want become a Java 11 Oracle Certified Professional (OCP) by taking either the 1Z0-819 Exam or the 1Z0-817 Upgrade Exam, as well as those who want to test their knowledge of Java 11. If you are new to Java 11, we strongly recommend you start with a study guide to learn all of the facets of the language and come back to this book once you are thinking of taking the exam.

We recommend the best-selling *OCP Java SE 11 Developer Complete Study Guide* (Sybex, 2020), which we happen to be the authors of, to start in your studies. This book is also available as two separate volumes if you prefer to carry around a paper book: *OCP Java SE 11 Programmer I Study Guide* (Sybex, 2019) and *OCP Java SE 11 Programmer II Study Guide* (Sybex, 2020). Whether you purchase the Complete Guide, or the Programmer I and Programmer II books, the material is the same and will properly prepare you for the exams.

Regardless of which study guide you used to prepare, you can use this book to hone your skills, since it is based on topics on the actual exams.

Unlike the questions in our study guides, which are designed to be harder than the real exam, the questions in this book mirror the exam format. All the questions in this book tell you how many answers are correct. They will say "Choose two" or "Choose three" if more than one answer is correct.

Choosing an Exam

If you don't hold any previous Java certifications, then you should take the 1Z0-819 Java SE 11 Developer Exam. It is a very broad exam, covering subjects from basic Java concepts and syntax to more advanced topics and APIs. Some libraries you may use every day, while others you may not be familiar with in your career, such as the concurrency, annotations, and NIO.2 APIs. The exam also includes a lot of topics around the new Java module platform.

If you already hold a recent Java Professional certification, then you are eligible to take the upgrade exam. Table I.1 lists who is able to take each exam. This book will help you prepare for both the 1Z0-819 Exam and the 1Z0-817 Upgrade Exam.

TABLE I.1   Java 11 Professional Certification Exams

Exam Code	Name	Who Should Take
1Z0-819	*Java SE 11 Developer*	Everyone can take this exam.
1Z0-817	*Upgrade OCP Java 6, 7, & 8 to Java SE 11 Developer*	Holders of any of the following: • Sun Certified Programmer for the Java Platform, SE 6 (SCJP6) • Oracle Certified Professional, Java SE 6 Programmer (OCJP6) • Oracle Certified Professional, Java SE 7 Programmer (OCJP7) • Oracle Certified Professional, Java SE 8 Programmer (OCJP8)

What Happened to the 1Z0-815 and 1Z0-816 Exams?

When Oracle released the Java 11 certification in March 2019, it was originally obtained by taking two exams: the Programmer I 1Z0-815 Exam, which focused on core Java structures, and the Programmer II 1Z0-816 Exam, which focused on broad topics and APIs.

In October 2020, Oracle retired these two exams and replaced them with a combined 1Z0-819 Exam. The authors of this book were instrumental in working directly with Oracle to ensure the new exam did not introduce a lot of new material that was not on the previous two exams.

We mentioned this in case you pick up one of our Java 11 Study Guides and notice the 1Z0-815 or 1Z0-816 Exam titles on the cover. Don't panic! These books can definitely be used for the 1Z0-819 exam! The material is nearly identical. Please visit our blog for more details:

`www.selikoff.net/ocp11-819`

The 1Z0-819 Exam

The 1Z0-819 Exam is a 90-minute exam with 50 questions and requires a passing score of 68 percent. For those who may be familiar with the previous Java 7 and 8 certifications exams, the 1Z0-819 Exam combines material from what was previously two exams into a much broader exam with fewer questions. This means that each question may cover a variety of objectives and the time you have on each question is more constrained.

To study for the 1Z0-819 Exam, we recommend a study plan that uses our *OCP Oracle Certified Professional Java SE 11 Developer Complete Study Guide* along with this book. As mentioned, this book is available in two parts if you prefer an easier to carry around option, *OCP Java SE 11 Programmer I Study Guide* and *OCP Java SE 11 Programmer II Study Guide*.

We also recommend reading our blog about some of the changes made to the 1Z0-819 Exam after these study guides were published.

www.selikoff.net/ocp11-819

The 1Z0-817 Upgrade Exam

The 1Z0-817 Upgrade Exam is a 180-minute exam with 80 questions and requires a passing score of 61 percent. It is designed for those who already hold a Java 6 or higher Sun or Oracle Professional Certification. Those with only Java Associate certification titles or older Java certifications are not eligible for this exam.

For the 1Z0-817 Upgrade Exam, we recommend a study plan that uses either our *OCP Oracle Certified Professional Java SE 11 Developer Complete Study Guide* or *OCP Oracle Certified Professional Java SE 11 Programmer II Study Guide*, along with this book.

While either our Complete Study Guide or Programmer II Study Guide will help you pass the exam and make you a better programmer, you do not need to read the entire book. Table I.2 lists the chapters that will prepare you for the 1Z0-817 Upgrade Exam.

TABLE I.2   Study Guide Chapters for the 1Z0-817 Upgrade Exam

Book	Chapters To Review
Java 11 Complete Study Guide	2, 6, 11, 12, 14, 15, 16, 17, 18, 20
Java 11 Programmer II Study Guide	1, 3, 4, 5, 6, 7, 9, Appendix

You can still use the practice exams in Chapters 14, 15, and 16 of this book to prepare for the 1Z0-817 Upgrade Exam. You can just skip any questions on the topics that are not on the upgrade exam and calculate your score with the remaining questions.

Which Exam Should I Take?

If you hold an eligible certification title, you are free to take either the 1Z0-819 Exam or the 1Z0-817 Upgrade Exam. Which you take is completely up to you. Having taken both, we tend to believe the 1Z0-817 Upgrade Exam is less challenging, in part because the number of topics is not nearly as broad as the 1Z0-819 Exam. You also have more time to read each question on the exam.

Who Should Buy This Book

If you are looking to become a Java 11 Oracle Certified Professional, then this book is for you. Regardless of which exam you plan to take, make sure to always keep your study guide handy. This book is about honing your knowledge of Java 11, while your study guide is about building it.

How This Book Is Organized

This book consists of 13 objective-based chapters followed by 3 full-length mock practice exams. There are some subtle differences between the objective-based chapters and practice exam chapters that you should be aware of while reading this book.

Using the Objective-Based Chapters

An objective-based chapter is composed of questions that correspond to an objective set, as defined by Oracle on the 1Z0-819 Exam. We designed the structure and style of each question in the objective-based chapters to reflect a more positive learning experience, allowing you to spend less time on each question but covering a broader level of material. For example, you may see two questions that look similar within a chapter but contain a subtle difference that has drastic implications on whether the code compiles or what output it produces.

Just like the review questions in our study guide, these questions are designed so that you can answer them many times. While these questions may be easier than exam questions, they will reinforce concepts if you keep taking them on a topic you don't feel strongly on.

In our study guides, we often group related topics into chapters or split them for understanding. For example, in our study guides we presented parallel streams as part of the concurrency chapter since these concepts are often intertwined, whereas the 1Z0-819 Exam splits concurrency and parallel streams across two separate objectives. In this book, though, the chapters are organized around Oracle's objectives so you can test your skills. While you don't need to read an entire study guide before using an objective-based chapter in this book, you do need to study the relevant objectives.

Table I.3 shows what chapters you need to have read in our Java 11 study guides at a minimum before practicing with the questions in this book. Remember that the Java 11 Programmer I and II Study Guides contain the same material as the combined Java 11 Complete Study Guide.

TABLE I.3 Oracle Objectives and Related Study Guide Chapters

Chapter in This Book	Objectives	Complete Study Guide Chapter	OCP Programmer I Chapter	OCP Programmer II Chapter
1	Working with Java Data Types	3, 4, 5, 6, and 12	3, 4, 5, and 6	1
2	Controlling Program Flow	4	4	
3	Java Object-Oriented Approach	2, 7, 8, 9, and 12	2, 7, 8, and 9	1
4	Exception Handling	10 and 16	10	5
5	Working with Arrays and Collections	5 and 14	5	3
6	Working with Streams and Lambda Expressions	6, 15, and 18	6	4 and 7
7	Java Platform Module System	11 and 17	11	6
8	Concurrency	18		7
9	Java I/O API	19 and 20		8 and 9
10	Secure Coding in Java SE Application	22		11
11	Database Applications with JDBC	21		10
12	Localization	16		5
13	Annotations	13		2

Some of our chapters have a lot of questions. For example, Chapter 3 contains more than 200 questions. This is based on how Oracle chose to organize its objectives. We recommend doing these larger chapters in batches of 30–50 questions at a time. That way you can reinforce your learning before doing more questions. This also lets you practice with sets of questions that are closer to the length of the exam.

Taking the Practice Exams

Chapters 14, 15, and 16 of this book contain three full-length practice exams. The questions in these chapters are quite different from the objective-based chapters in a number of important ways. These practice exam questions tend to be harder because they are designed to test your cumulative knowledge rather than reinforcing your existing skill set. In other words, you may get a question that tests two discrete topics at the same time.

Like the objective chapters, we do indicate exactly how many answers are correct in the practice exam chapters, as is done on the real exam. All three practice exam chapters are designed to be taken within 90 minutes and have a passing score of 68 percent. That means you need to answer at least 34 questions correctly. Remember not to take the practice exam until you feel ready. There are only so many practice exams available, so you don't want to waste a fresh attempt.

While an objective-based chapter can be completed over the course of a few days, the practice exam chapters were each designed to be completed in one sitting. You should try simulating the exam experience as much as possible. This means setting aside 90 minutes, grabbing a whiteboard or scrap paper, and answering every question even if you aren't sure of the answer. Remember, there is no penalty for guessing, and the more incorrect answers you can eliminate the better.

Reviewing Exam Changes

Oracle does change the number of questions, passing score, and time limit from time to time. Scott and Jeanne maintain a blog that tracks updates to the real exams, as quickly as Oracle updates them.

    www.selikoff.net/ocp11-pt

We recommend you read this page before you take the real exam, in case any of the information since the time this book was published has changed. Although less common, Oracle does add, remove, or reword objectives. When this happens, we offer free supplemental material on our website as blog entries.

Ready to Take the Exam

If you can score above 70 percent consistently on all of the chapters related to the exam you want to take, including above a 70 percent on the simulated practice exam, then you are probably ready to take the real exam. Just remember there's a big difference between taking a practice test by yourself in your own home, versus spending hundreds of dollars to take a real proctored exam.

Although a lot of people are inclined to cram as much material as they can in the hours leading up to the exam, most studies have shown that this is a poor test-taking strategy. The best thing we can recommend that you do before the exam is to get a good night's rest!

Need More Help Preparing?

Both of the authors are moderators at CodeRanch.com, a very large and active programming forum that is very friendly toward Java beginners. See the OCP Forum.

coderanch.com/f/24

If you don't understand a question, even after reading the explanation, feel free to ask about it in one of those forums. You'll get an answer from a knowledgeable Java programmer. It might even be one of us.

Good luck on the exam and happy studies!

Interactive Online Learning Environment and Test Bank

To access the interactive online learning environment and test bank, simply visit www.wiley.com/go/sybextestprep, register to receive your unique PIN, and instantly gain one year of FREE access after activation to the interactive test bank with 3 practice exams and hundreds of domain-by-domain questions. Over 1,000 questions total!

Chapter

1

Working with Java Data Types

THE OCP EXAM TOPICS COVERED IN THIS PRACTICE TEST INCLUDE THE FOLLOWING:

✓ **Working with Java Data Types**

- Use primitives and wrapper classes, including, operators, parentheses, type promotion and casting

- Handle text using String and StringBuilder classes

- Use local variable type inference, including as lambda parameters

1. Which of the following are not valid variable names? (Choose two.)

    A. _

    B. _blue

    C. 2blue

    D. blue$

    E. Blue

2. What is the value of `tip` after executing the following code snippet?

    ```
    int meal = 5;
    int tip = 2;
    var total = meal + (meal>6 ? tip++ : tip--);
    ```

    A. 1

    B. 2

    C. 3

    D. 7

    E. None of the above

3. Which is equivalent to `var q = 4.0f;`?

    A. `float q = 4.0f;`

    B. `Float q = 4.0f;`

    C. `double q = 4.0f;`

    D. `Double q = 4.0f;`

    E. `Object q = 4.0f;`

4. What is the output of the following?

    ```
    12: var b = "12";
    13: b += "3";
    14: b.reverse();
    15: System.out.println(b.toString());
    ```

    A. 12

    B. 123

    C. 321

    D. The code does not compile.

5. What is the output of the following?

    ```
    5: var line = new StringBuilder("-");
    6: var anotherLine = line.append("-");
    7: System.out.print(line == anotherLine);
    ```

```
8: System.out.print(" ");
9: System.out.print(line.length());
```

A. false 1
B. false 2
C. true 1
D. true 2
E. It does not compile.

6. Given the following Venn diagram and the boolean variables, apples, oranges, and bananas, which expression most closely represents the filled-in region of the diagram?

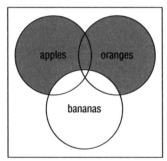

A. apples && oranges && !bananas
B. orange || (oranges && !bananas)
C. (apples || bananas) && oranges
D. oranges && apples
E. (apples || oranges) && !bananas
F. apples ^ oranges

7. What is the output of the following?

```
5: var line = new String("-");
6: var anotherLine = line.concat("-");
7: System.out.print(line == anotherLine);
8: System.out.print(" ");
9: System.out.print(line.length());
```

A. false 1
B. false 2
C. true 1
D. true 2
E. Does not compile

8. Which can fill in the blank? (Choose two.)

```
public void math() {
    _____ pi = 3.14;
}
```

A. byte

B. double

C. float

D. short

E. var

9. Fill in the blanks: The operators !=, _____, _____, _____, and ++ are listed in the same or increasing level of operator precedence. (Choose two.)

A. ==, *, !

B. /, %, *

C. *, --, /

D. !, *, %

E. +=, &&, *

F. *, <, /

10. How many of these compile?

```
18: Comparator<String> c1 = (j, k) -> 0;
19: Comparator<String> c2 = (String j, String k) -> 0;
20: Comparator<String> c3 = (var j, String k) -> 0;
21: Comparator<String> c4 = (var j, k) -> 0;
22: Comparator<String> c5 = (var j, var k) -> 0;
```

A. 0

B. 1

C. 2

D. 3

E. 4

F. 5

11. The author of this method forgot to include the data type. Which of the following reference types can best fill in the blank to complete this method?

```
public static void secret(_____ mystery) {
    char ch = mystery.charAt(3);
    mystery = mystery.insert(1, "more");
    int num = mystery.length();
}
```

   A. String
   B. StringBuilder
   C. Both
   D. Neither

12. What is the output of the following?

```
var teams = new StringBuilder("333");
teams.append(" 806");
teams.append(" 1601");
System.out.print(teams);
```

   A. 333
   B. 333 806 1601
   C. The code compiles but outputs something else.
   D. The code does not compile.

13. Which of the following declarations does not compile?
   A. double num1, int num2 = 0;
   B. int num1, num2;
   C. int num1, num2 = 0;
   D. int num1 = 0, num2 = 0;
   E. All of the above
   F. None of the above

14. Given the file `Magnet.java` shown, which of the marked lines can you independently insert the line `var color;` into and still have the code compile?

```
// line a1
public class Magnet {
   // line a2
   public void attach() {
      // line a3
   }
   // line a4
}
```

   A. a2
   B. a3
   C. a2 and a3
   D. a1, a2, a3, and a4
   E. None of the above

15. Which is one of the lines output by this code?

```
10: var list = new ArrayList<Integer>();
11: list.add(10);
12: list.add(9);
13: list.add(8);
14:
15: var num = 9;
16: list.removeIf(x -> {int keep = num; return x != keep;});
17: System.out.println(list);
18:
19: list.removeIf(x -> {int keep = num; return x == keep;});
20: System.out.println(list);
```

A. []
B. [8, 10]
C. [8, 9, 10]
D. [10, 8]
E. The code does not compile.

16. Which of the following can fill in the blank so the code prints `true`?

```
var happy = " :) - (: ";
var really = happy.trim();
var question = _____;
System.out.println(really.equals(question));
```

A. happy.substring(0, happy.length() - 1)
B. happy.substring(0, happy.length())
C. happy.substring(1, happy.length() - 1)
D. happy.substring(1, happy.length())

17. How many of the following lines contain a compiler error?

```
double num1 = 2.718;
double num2 = 2._718;
double num3 = 2.7_1_8;
double num4 = _2.718;
```

A. 0
B. 1
C. 2
D. 3
E. 4

18. What is the output of the following application?

```java
public class Airplane {
    static int start = 2;
    final int end;
    public Airplane(int x) {
        x = 4;
        end = x;
    }
    public void fly(int distance) {
        System.out.print(end-start+" ");
        System.out.print(distance);
    }
    public static void main(String... start) {
        new Airplane(10).fly(5);
    }
}
```

A. 2 5

B. 8 5

C. 6 5

D. The code does not compile.

E. None of the above.

19. What is the output of the following class?

```java
1: package rocket;
2: public class Countdown {
3:     public static void main(String[] args) {
4:         var builder = "54321";
5:         builder = builder.substring(4);
6:         System.out.println(builder.charAt(2));
7:     }
8: }
```

A. 2

B. 3

C. 4

D. None of the above

20. What is the output of the following application?

```java
package transporter;
public class Rematerialize {
    public static void main(String[] input) {
        int init = 11;
        int split = 3;
        int partA = init / split;
        int partB = init % split;
        int result = split * (partB + partA);
        System.out.print(result);
    }
}
```

A. 9

B. 11

C. 12

D. 15

E. The code does not compile.

F. None of the above.

21. What is the result of the following code?

```java
var sb = new StringBuilder("radical")
    .insert(sb.length(), "robots");
System.out.println(sb);
```

A. radicarobots

B. radicalrobots

C. The code does not compile.

D. The code compiles but throws an exception at runtime.

22. Given the following code snippet, what is the value of dinner after it is executed?

```java
int time = 9;
int day = 3;
var dinner = ++time >= 10 ? day-- <= 2
    ? "Takeout" : "Salad" : "Leftovers";
```

A. Takeout

B. Leftovers

C. Salad

D. The code does not compile but would compile if parentheses were added.

E. None of the above.

23. What is the output of the following?

```java
var teams = new String("694");
teams.concat(" 1155");
teams.concat(" 2265");
teams.concat(" 2869");
System.out.println(teams);
```

　　A. 694

　　B. 694 1155 2265 2869

　　C. The code compiles but outputs something else.

　　D. The code does not compile.

24. How many of the following lines compile?

```java
bool b = null;
Bool bl = null;
int i = null;
Integer in = null;
String s = null;
```

　　A. None

　　B. One

　　C. Two

　　D. Three

　　E. Four

　　F. Five

25. What is the output of the following code snippet?

```java
int height = 2, length = 3;
boolean w = height > 1 | --length < 4;
var x = height!=2 ? length++ : height;
boolean z = height % length == 0;
System.out.println(w + "-" + x + "-" + z);
```

　　A. true-2-true

　　B. false-2-false

　　C. true-2-false

　　D. true-3-false

　　E. true-3-true

　　F. false-3-false

26. What is the output of the following?

```
1: public class Legos {
2:    public static void main(String[] args) {
3:        var sb = new StringBuilder();
4:        sb.append("red");
5:        sb.deleteCharAt(0);
6:        sb.delete(1, 2);
7:        System.out.println(sb);
8:    }
9: }
```

A. e

B. d

C. ed

D. None of the above

27. Which is a true statement?

A. If s.contains("abc") is true, then s.equals("abc") is also true.

B. If s.contains("abc") is true, then s.startsWith("abc") is also true.

C. If s.startsWith("abc") is true, then s.equals("abc") is also true.

D. If s.startsWith("abc") is true, then s.contains("abc") is also true.

28. What is the output of the following code snippet?

```
boolean carrot = true;
Boolean potato = false;
var broccoli = true;
carrot = carrot & potato;
broccoli = broccoli ? !carrot : potato;
potato = !broccoli ^ carrot;
System.out.println(carrot + "," + potato + "," + broccoli);
```

A. true,false,true

B. true,true,true

C. false,false,false

D. false,true,true

E. false,false,true

F. The code does not compile.

29. What does this code output?

```
var babies = Arrays.asList("chick", "cygnet", "duckling");
babies.replaceAll(x -> { var newValue = "baby";
   return newValue; });
System.out.println(babies);
```

A. [baby]

B. [baby, baby, baby]

C. [chick, cygnet, duckling]

D. None of the above.

E. The code does not compile.

30. What is the output of the following class?

```
1: package rocket;
2: public class Countdown {
3:    public static void main(String[] args) {
4:       var builder = new StringBuilder("54321");
5:       builder.substring(2);
6:       System.out.println(builder.charAt(1));
7:    }
8: }
```

A. 1

B. 2

C. 3

D. 4

E. Does not compile

Chapter

2

Controlling Program Flow

THE OCP EXAM TOPICS COVERED IN THIS PRACTICE TEST INCLUDE THE FOLLOWING:

✓ **Controlling Program Flow**

- Create and use loops, if/else, and switch statements

1. Variables declared as which of the following are never permitted in a `switch` statement? (Choose two.)

   A. `var`

   B. `double`

   C. `int`

   D. `String`

   E. `char`

   F. `Object`

2. What happens when running the following code snippet?

```
3: var gas = true;
4: do (
5:     System.out.println("helium");
6:     gas = gas ^ gas;
7:     gas = !gas;
8: ) while (!gas);
```

   A. It completes successfully without output.

   B. It outputs helium once.

   C. It outputs helium repeatedly.

   D. Line 6 does not compile.

   E. None of the above.

3. What is output by the following?

```
10: int m = 0, n = 0;
11: while (m < 5) {
12:     n++;
13:     if (m == 3)
14:         continue;
15:
16:     switch (m) {
17:         case 0:
18:         case 1:
19:             n++;
20:         default:
21:             n++;
22:     }
23:     m++;
24: }
25: System.out.println(m + " " + n);
```

A. 3 10

B. 3 12

C. 5 10

D. 5 12

E. The code does not compile.

F. None of the above.

4. Given the following, which can fill in the blank and allow the code to compile? (Choose three.)

```java
var quest = _____;
for(var zelda : quest) {
    System.out.print(zelda);
}
```

A. 3

B. `new int[] {3}`

C. `new StringBuilder("3")`

D. `List.of(3)`

E. `new String[3]`

F. `"Link"`

5. Which of the following rules about a `default` branch in a `switch` statement are correct? (Choose two.)

A. A `switch` statement is required to declare a `default` statement.

B. A `default` statement must be placed after all `case` statements.

C. A `default` statement can be placed between any `case` statements.

D. Unlike a `case` statement, a `default` statement does not take a parameter value.

E. A `switch` statement can contain more than one `default` statement.

F. A `default` statement can be used only when at least one `case` statement is present.

6. What does the following method output?

```java
void dance() {
    var singer = 0;
    while (singer)
        System.out.print(singer++);
}
```

A. The code does not compile.

B. The method completes with no output.

C. The method prints 0 and then terminates.

D. The method enters an infinite loop.

E. None of the above.

7. Which are true statements comparing for-each and traditional `for` loops? (Choose two.)

   A. Both can iterate through an array starting with the first element.

   B. Only the for-each loop can iterate through an array starting with the first element.

   C. Only the traditional `for` loop can iterate through an array starting with the first element.

   D. Both can iterate through an array starting from the end.

   E. Only the for-each loop can iterate through an array starting from the end.

   F. Only the traditional `for` loop can iterate through an array starting from the end.

8. What is the output of the following application?

```
package planning;
public class ThePlan {
    public static void main(String[] input) {
        var plan = 1;
        plan = plan++ + --plan;
        if(plan==1) {
            System.out.print("Plan A");
        } else { if(plan==2) System.out.print("Plan B");
        } else System.out.print("Plan C"); }
    }
}
```

   A. `Plan A`

   B. `Plan B`

   C. `Plan C`

   D. The class does not compile.

   E. None of the above.

9. What is true about the following code? (Choose two.)

```
23: var race = "";
24: loop:
25: do {
26:     race += "x";
27:     break loop;
28: } while (true);
29: System.out.println(race);
```

   A. It outputs x.

   B. It does not compile.

   C. It is an infinite loop.

   D. With lines 25 and 28 removed, it outputs x.

   E. With lines 25 and 28 removed, it does not compile.

   F. With lines 25 and 28 removed, it is an infinite loop.

10. Which of the following can replace the body of the `perform()` method to produce the same output on any nonempty input? (Choose two.)

```
public void perform(String[] circus) {
    for (int i=circus.length-1; i>=0; i--)
        System.out.print(circus[i]);
}
```

A.

```
for (int i=circus.length; i>0; i--)
    System.out.print(circus[i-1]);
```

B.

```
for-reversed (String c = circus)
    System.out.print(c);
```

C.

```
for (var c : circus)
    System.out.print(c);
```

D.

```
for(var i=0; i<circus.length; i++)
    System.out.print(circus[circus.length-i-1]);
```

E.

```
for (int i=circus.length; i>0; i--)
    System.out.print(circus[i+1]);
```

F.

```
for-each (String c circus)
    System.out.print(c);
```

11. What does the following code snippet output?

```
var bottles = List.of("glass", "plastic", "can");
for (int type = 1; type < bottles.size();) {
    System.out.print(bottles.get(type) + "-");
    if(type < bottles.size()) break;
}
System.out.print("end");
```

A. `glass-end`

B. `glass-plastic-can-end`

C. `plastic-end`

D. `plastic-can-end`

E. The code does not compile.

F. None of the above.

12. What is the result of executing the following code snippet?

```
final var GOOD = 100;
var score = 10;
switch (score) {
   default:
   1 : System.out.print("1-");
   -1 : System.out.print("2-"); break;
   4,5 : System.out.print("3-");
   6 : System.out.print("4-");
   9 : System.out.print("5-");
}
```

   A. 1-

   B. 1-2-

   C. 2-

   D. 3-

   E. 4-

   F. None of the above

13. What is the output of the following application?

```
package dinosaur;
public class Park {
   public final static void main(String... arguments) {
      int pterodactyl = 8;
      long triceratops = 3;
      if(pterodactyl % 3 > 1 + 1)
         triceratops++;
         triceratops--;
      System.out.print(triceratops);
   }
}
```

   A. 2

   B. 3

   C. 4

   D. The code does not compile.

   E. The code compiles but throws an exception at runtime.

14. What variable type of `red` allows the following application to compile?

```
package tornado;
public class Kansas {
   public static void main(String[] args) {
      int colorOfRainbow = 10;
      _____ red = 5;
      switch(colorOfRainbow) {
         default:
            System.out.print("Home");
            break;
         case red:
            System.out.print("Away");
      }
   }
}
```

A. long

B. double

C. int

D. var

E. String

F. None of the above

15. How many lines of the `magic()` method contain compilation errors?

```
10: public void magic() {
11:    do {
12:       int trick = 0;
13:       LOOP: do {
14:          trick++;
15:       } while (trick < 2--);
16:       continue LOOP;
17:    } while (1 > 2);
18:    System.out.println(trick);
19: }
```

A. Zero

B. One

C. Two

D. Three

E. Four

16. How many of these statements can be inserted after the `println` to have the code flow follow the arrow in this diagram?

```
break;
break letters;
break numbers;
continue;
continue letters;
continue numbers;
```

```
letters: for (char ch = 'a'; ch <= 'z'; ch++) {
    numbers: for (int n = 0; n<=10; n++) {
        System.out.print(ch);
```

```
    }
}
```

A. One

B. Two

C. Three

D. Four

E. Five

F. None of above

17. What is the output of the following application?

```
package dessert;
public class IceCream {
    public final static void main(String... args) {
        var flavors = 30;
        int eaten = 0;
        switch(flavors) {
            case 30: eaten++;
            case 40: eaten+=2;
            default: eaten--;
        }
        System.out.print(eaten);
    }
}
```

A. 1

B. 2

C. 3

D. The code does not compile because `var` cannot be used in a `switch` statement.

E. The code does not compile for another reason.

F. None of the above.

18. Which of the following statements compile and create infinite loops at runtime? (Choose two.)

    A. `while (!false) {}`

    B. `do {}`

    C. `for( : ) {}`

    D. `do {} while (true);`

    E. `while {}`

    F. `for( ; ; ) {}`

19. Which of the following iterates a different number of times than the others?

    A. `for (int k=0; k < 5; k++) {}`

    B. `for (int k=1; k <= 5; k++) {}`

    C. `int k=0; do { } while(k++ < 5);`

    D. `int k=0; while (k++ < 5) {}`

    E. All of these iterate the same number of times.

20. What is the output of the following code snippet?

    ```
    int count = 0;
    var stops = new String[] { "Washington", "Monroe",
        "Jackson", "LaSalle" };
    while (count < stops.length)
        if (stops[++count].length() < 8)
            break;
        else continue;
    System.out.println(count);
    ```

    A. 0

    B. 1

    C. 2

    D. 3

    E. The code does not compile.

    F. None of the above.

21. What is the output of the following code snippet?

```
int hops = 0;
int jumps = 0;
jumps = hops++;
if(jumps)
    System.out.print("Jump!");
else
    System.out.print("Hop!");
```

A. Jump!

B. Hop!

C. The code does not compile.

D. The code compiles but throws an exception at runtime.

E. None of the above.

22. Which of the following best describes the flow of execution in this for loop if beta always returns false?

```
for (alpha; beta; gamma) {
  delta;
}
```

A. alpha

B. alpha, beta

C. alpha, beta, gamma

D. alpha, gamma

E. alpha, gamma, beta

F. None of the above

23. What is the output of the following code snippet?

```
boolean balloonInflated = false;
do {
    if (!balloonInflated) {
        balloonInflated = true;
        System.out.print("inflate-");
    }
} while (! balloonInflated);
System.out.println("done");
```

A. done

B. inflate-done

C. The code does not compile.

D. This is an infinite loop.

E. None of the above.

24. Which of these code snippets behaves differently from the others?

A.

```
if (numChipmunks == 1)
    System.out.println("One chipmunk");
if (numChipmunks == 2)
    System.out.println("Two chipmunks");
if (numChipmunks == 3)
    System.out.println("Three chipmunks");
```

B.

```
switch (numChipmunks) {
    case 1:  System.out.println("One chipmunk");
    case 2:  System.out.println("Two chipmunks");
    case 3:  System.out.println("Three chipmunks");
}
```

C.

```
if (numChipmunks == 1)
    System.out.println("One chipmunk");
else if (numChipmunks == 2)
    System.out.println("Two chipmunks");
else if (numChipmunks == 3)
    System.out.println("Three chipmunks");
```

D. All three code snippets do the same thing.

25. Which statements about loops are correct? (Choose three.)

A. A do/while loop requires a body.

B. A while loop cannot be exited early with a `return` statement.

C. A while loop requires a conditional expression.

D. A do/while loop executes the body (if present) at least once.

E. A do/while loop cannot be exited early with a `return` statement.

F. A while loop executes the body (if present) at least once.

26. Given the following enum and class, which option fills in the blank and allows the code to compile?

```
enum Season { SPRING, SUMMER, WINTER }
public class Weather {
    public int getAverageTemperate(Season s) {
        switch (s) {
            default:
                _____ return 30;
        }
    }
}
```

A. case Season.WINTER:

B. case WINTER, SPRING:

C. case SUMMER | WINTER:

D. case SUMMER ->

E. case FALL:

F. None of the above

27. Fill in the blank with the line of code that causes the application to compile and print exactly one line at runtime.

```
package nyc;
public class TourBus {
    public static void main(String... args) {
        var nycTour = new String[] { "Downtown", "Uptown",
            "Brooklyn" };
        var times = new String[] { "Day", "Night" };
        for (_____ i<nycTour.length && j<times.length;
             i++, j++)
            System.out.println(nycTour[i] + "-" + times[j]);
    }
}
```

A. int i=1; j=1;

B. int i=0, j=1;

C. int i=1; int j=0;

D. int i=1, int j=0;

E. int i=1, j=0;

F. None of the above

28. The code contains six pairs of curly braces. How many pairs can be removed without changing the behavior?

```
12: public static void main(String[] args) {
13:     int secret = 0;
14:     for (int i = 0; i < 10; i++) {
15:         while (i < 10) {
16:             if (i == 5) {
17:                 System.out.println("if");
18:             } else {
19:                 System.out.println("in");
20:                 System.out.println("else");
21:             }
22:         }
23:     }
24:     switch (secret) {
25:         case 0:  System.out.println("zero");
26:     }
27: }
```

- **A.** One
- **B.** Two
- **C.** Three
- **D.** Four
- **E.** Five
- **F.** Six

29. Which of the following can replace the body of the `travel()` method to produce the same output on any nonempty input?

```
public void travel(List<Integer> roads) {
   for (int w = 1; w <= roads.size(); w++)
      System.out.print(roads.get(w-1));
}
```

A.
```
for (int r = 0; r < roads.size(); r += 1)
   System.out.print(roads.get(0));
```

B.
```
for(var z : roads)
   System.out.print(z);
```

C.

```java
for (int t = roads.size(); t > 0; t--)
   System.out.print(roads.get(t));
```

D.

```java
for (var var : roads)
   System.out.print(roads);
```

E.

```java
for (int q = roads.size(); q >= 0; q++)
   System.out.print(roads.get(q));
```

F.   None of the above

30. Which statement about the following code snippet is correct?

```java
3: final var javaVersions = List.of(9,10,11);
4: var exams = List.of("1Z0-811", "1Z0-819");
5: V: for (var e1 : javaVersions) {
6:    E: for (String e2 : exams)
7:        System.out.println(e1 + "_" + e2);
8:        break;
9: }
```

A.   One line does not compile.

B.   Two lines do not compile.

C.   Three lines do not compile.

D.   It compiles and prints two lines at runtime.

E.   It compiles and prints three lines at runtime.

F.   None of the above.

Chapter

3

Java Object-Oriented Approach

THE OCP EXAM TOPICS COVERED IN THIS PRACTICE TEST INCLUDE THE FOLLOWING:

✓ **Java Object-Oriented Approach**

- Declare and instantiate Java objects including nested class objects, and explain objects' lifecycles (including creation, dereferencing by reassignment, and garbage collection)

- Define and use fields and methods, including instance, static and overloaded methods

- Initialize objects and their members using instance and static initialiser statements and constructors

- Understand variable scopes, apply encapsulation and make objects immutable

- Create and use subclasses and superclasses, including abstract classes

- Utilize polymorphism and casting to call methods, differentiate object type versus reference type

- Create and use interfaces, identify functional interfaces, and utilize private, static, and default methods

- Create and use enumerations

1. What is the output of the following application?

```java
package dnd;
final class Story {
    void recite(int chapter) throws Exception {}
}
public class Adventure extends Story {
    final void recite(final int chapter) {   // g1
        switch(chapter) {                     // g2
            case 2: System.out.print(9);
            default: System.out.print(3);
        }
    }
    public static void main(String... u) {
        var bedtime = new Adventure();
        bedtime.recite(2);
    }
}
```

   A. 3
   B. 9
   C. 93
   D. The code does not compile because of line g1.
   E. The code does not compile because of line g2.
   F. None of the above.

2. Which of the following lines of code are not permitted as the first line of a Java class file? (Choose two.)
   A. `import widget.*;`
   B. `// Widget Manager`
   C. `int facilityNumber;`
   D. `package sprockets;`
   E. `/** Author: Cid **/`
   F. `void produce() {}`

3. Which of the following modifiers can be applied to an abstract method? (Choose two.)
   A. `final`
   B. `private`
   C. `public`
   D. `default`
   E. `protected`
   F. `concrete`

4. What is the result of compiling and executing the following class?

```
1: public class ParkRanger {
2:     int birds = 10;
3:     public static void main(String[] data) {
4:         var trees = 5;
5:         System.out.print(trees+birds);
6:     }
7: }
```

A. It compiles and outputs 5.

B. It compiles and outputs 15.

C. It does not compile.

D. It compiles but throws an exception at runtime.

5. Fill in the blanks: The _____ access modifier allows access to everything the _____ access modifier does and more.

A. package-private, `protected`

B. `private`, package-private

C. `private`, `protected`

D. `private`, `public`

E. `public`, `private`

F. None of the above

6. Which set of modifiers, when added to a `default` method within an interface, prevents it from being overridden by a class implementing the interface?

A. `const`

B. `final`

C. `static`

D. `private`

E. `private static`

F. None of the above

7. Given the following application, fill in the missing values in the table starting from the top and going downward.

```
package competition;
public class Robot {
    static String weight = "A lot";
    double ageMonths = 5, ageDays = 2;
    private static boolean success = true;

    public void main(String[] args) {
        final String retries = "1";
```

```
        // P1
    }
}
```

Variable Type	Number of Variables Accessible at P1
Class	_____
Instance	_____
Local	_____

A. 2, 0, 1

B. 2, 2, 1

C. 1, 0, 1

D. 0, 2, 1

8. Given the following code, what values inserted, in order, into the blank lines allow the code to compile? (Choose two.)

```
_____ agent;
public _____ Banker {
    private static _____ getMaxWithdrawal() {
        return 10;
    }
}
```

A. package, new, int

B. package, class, long

C. import, class, null

D. //, class, int

E. import, interface, void

F. package, class, void

9. Which of the following are correct? (Choose two.)

```
public class Phone {
    private int size;

    // insert constructor here

    public static void sendHome(Phone p, int newSize) {
        p = new Phone(newSize);
        p.size = 4;
    }
    public static final void main(String... params) {
        final var phone = new Phone(3);
```

```
        sendHome(phone,7);
        System.out.print(phone.size);
    }
}
```

A. The following is a valid constructor:

```
public static Phone create(int size) {
    return new Phone(size);
}
```

B. The following is a valid constructor:

```
public static Phone newInstance(int size) {
    return new Phone();
}
```

C. The following is a valid constructor:

```
public Phone(int size) {
    this.size=size;
}
```

D. The following is a valid constructor:

```
public void Phone(int size) {
    this.size=size;
}
```

E. With the correct constructor, the output is 3.

F. With the correct constructor, the output is 7.

10. Given the following class structures, which lines can be inserted into the blank independently that would allow the class to compile? (Choose two.)

```
public class Dinosaur {
    class Pterodactyl extends Dinosaur {}
    public void roar() {
        var dino = new Dinosaur();
        _____;
    }
}
```

A. dino.Pterodactyl()

B. Dinosaur.new Pterodactyl()

C. dino.new Pterodactyl()

D. new Dino().new Pterodactyl()

E. new Dinosaur().Pterodactyl()

F. new Dinosaur.Pterodactyl()

11. What is the output of the Computer program?

```
class Laptop extends Computer {
    public void startup() {
        System.out.print("laptop-");
    }
}
public class Computer {
    public void startup() {
        System.out.print("computer-");
    }
    public static void main(String[] args) {
        Computer computer = new Laptop();
        Laptop laptop = new Laptop();
        computer.startup();
        laptop.startup();
    }
}
```

A. computer-laptop-

B. laptop-computer-

C. laptop-laptop-

D. The code does not compile.

E. None of the above.

12. What access modifier is used to mark class members package-private?

A. default

B. friend

C. protected

D. private

E. None of the above

13. How many lines does the following code output?

```
public class Cars {
    private static void drive() {
        static {
            System.out.println("static");
        }
        System.out.println("fast");
        { System.out.println("faster"); }
```

```
    }
    public static void main(String[] args) {
        drive();
        drive();
    }
}
```

- **A.** One.
- **B.** Two.
- **C.** Three.
- **D.** Four.
- **E.** None of the above. The code does not compile.

14. Which statements about `static` interface methods are correct? (Choose three.)

- **A.** A `static` interface method can be `final`.
- **B.** A `static` interface method can be declared `private`.
- **C.** A `static` interface method can be package-private.
- **D.** A `static` interface method can be declared `public`.
- **E.** A `static` interface method can be declared `protected`.
- **F.** A `static` interface method can be declared without an access modifier.

15. Fill in the blanks with the only option that makes this statement false: A(n) _____ can access _____ of the enclosing class in which it is defined.

- **A.** `static` nested class, `static` members
- **B.** `static` nested class, instance members
- **C.** member inner class, `static` members
- **D.** member inner class, instance members
- **E.** local class, instance members from within an instance method
- **F.** anonymous class, instance members from within an instance method

16. What is the result of executing the following program?

```
public class Canine {
    public String woof(int bark) {
        return "1"+bark.toString();
    }

    public String woof(Integer bark) {
        return "2"+bark.toString();
    }
```

```
    public String woof(Object bark) {
       return "3"+bark.toString();
    }

    public static void main(String[] a) {
       System.out.println(woof((short)5));
    }
}
```

A. 15

B. 25

C. 35

D. One line does not compile.

E. Two lines do not compile.

F. The program compiles but throws an exception at runtime.

17. What statement best describes the notion of effectively final in Java?

A. A local variable that is marked `final`

B. A `static` variable that is marked `final`

C. A local variable whose primitive value or object reference does not change after it is initialized

D. A local variable whose primitive value or object reference does not change after a certain point in the method

E. None of the above

18. What is the output of the `Turnip` class?

```
package animal;
interface GameItem {
   int sell();
}
abstract class Vegetable implements GameItem {
   public final int sell() { return 5; }
}
public class Turnip extends Vegetable {
   public final int sell() { return 3; }
   public static void main(String[] expensive) {
      System.out.print(new Turnip().sell());
   }
}
```

A. 3

B. 5

C. The code does not compile.

D. The code compiles but throws an exception at runtime.

E. None of the above.

19. What is the output of the following application?

```
package holiday;
enum DaysOff {
    Thanksgiving, PresidentsDay, ValentinesDay
}
public class Vacation {
    public static void main(String... unused) {
        final DaysOff input = DaysOff.Thanksgiving;
        switch(input) {
            default:
            case DaysOff.ValentinesDay:
                System.out.print("1");
            case DaysOff.PresidentsDay:
                System.out.print("2");
        }
    }
}
```

A. 1

B. 2

C. 12

D. The code does not compile.

E. The code compiles but throws an exception at runtime.

F. None of the above.

20. Which statements about instance keywords are correct? (Choose two.)

A. The that keyword can be used to read public members in the direct parent class.

B. The this keyword can be used to read all members declared within the class.

C. The super keyword can be used to read all members declared in a parent class.

D. The that keyword can be used to read members of another class.

E. The this keyword can be used to read public members in the direct parent class.

F. The super keyword can be used in static methods.

21. Fill in the blanks: A class _____ an interface and _____ an `abstract` class. An interface _____ another interface.

   A. `extends, extends, implements`

   B. `extends, implements, extends`

   C. `extends, implements, implements`

   D. `implements, extends, extends`

   E. `implements, extends, implements`

   F. `implements, implements, extends`

22. Suppose you have the following code. Which of the images best represents the state of the references `c1`, `c2`, and `c3`, right before the end of the `main()` method, assuming garbage collection hasn't run? In the diagrams, each box represents a `Chicken` object with a number of `eggs`.

```
1:  public class Chicken {
2:      private Integer eggs = 2;
3:      { this.eggs = 3; }
4:      public Chicken(int eggs) {
5:          this.eggs = eggs;
6:      }
7:      public static void main(String[] r) {
8:          var c1 = new Chicken(1);
9:          var c2 = new Chicken(2);
10:         var c3 = new Chicken(3);
11:         c1.eggs = c2.eggs;
12:         c2 = c1;
13:         c3.eggs = null;
14:     } }
```

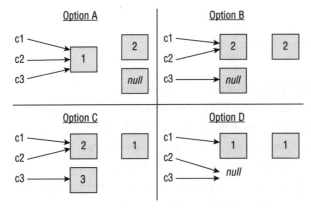

   A. Option A.

   B. Option B.

C. Option C.

D. Option D.

E. The code does not compile.

F. None of the above.

23. What is the output of the following application?

```
package musical;
interface Speak { default int talk() { return 7; } }
interface Sing { default int talk() { return 5; } }
public class Performance implements Speak, Sing {
    public int talk(String... x) {
        return x.length;
    }
    public static void main(String[] notes) {
        System.out.print(new Performance().talk());
    }
}
```

A. 7

B. 5

C. The code does not compile.

D. The code compiles without issue, but the output cannot be determined until runtime.

E. None of the above.

24. What is the output of the following application?

```
package ai;

interface Pump {
    void pump(double psi);
}
interface Bend extends Pump {
    void bend(double tensileStrength);
}
public class Robot {
    public static final void apply(
        Bend instruction, double input) {
        instruction.bend(input);
    }
    public static void main(String... future) {
        final Robot r = new Robot();
```

```
    r.apply(x -> System.out.print(x+" bent!"), 5);
    }
}
```

A. 5 bent!

B. 5.0 bent!

C. The code does not compile because Bend is not a functional interface.

D. The code does not compile because of the apply() method declaration.

E. None of the above.

25. Which statement is true about encapsulation while providing the broadest access allowed?

   A. Variables are private, and methods are private.

   B. Variables are private, and methods are public.

   C. Variables are public, and methods are private.

   D. Variables are public, and methods are public.

   E. None of the above.

26. Fill in the blanks: The _____ access modifier allows access to everything the _____ access modifier does and more.

   A. package-private, private

   B. private, protected

   C. protected, public

   D. private, package-private

   E. None of the above

27. Which statement about the following interface is correct?

```
public interface Swimming {
    String DEFAULT = "Diving!";       // k1
    abstract int breath();
    private static void stroke() {
        if(breath()==1) {             // k2
            System.out.print("Go!");
        } else {
            System.out.print(dive());  // k3
        }
    }
    static String dive() {
        return DEFAULT;                // k4
    }
}
```

    A. The code compiles without issue.

    B. The code does not compile because of line k1.

    C. The code does not compile because of line k2.

    D. The code does not compile because of line k3.

    E. The code does not compile because of line k4.

    F. None of the above.

28. Which is the first line to fail to compile?

```
class Tool {
    private void repair() {}            // r1
    void use() {}                       // r2
}

class Hammer extends Tool {
    private int repair() { return 0; } // r3
    private void use() {}               // r4
    public void bang() {}               // r5
}
```

    A. r1

    B. r2

    C. r3

    D. r4

    E. r5

    F. None of the above

29. Which modifier can be applied to an abstract interface method?

    A. final

    B. interface

    C. protected

    D. void

    E. None of the above

30. What is the output of the Plant program?

```
class Bush extends Plant {
    String type = "bush";
}
public class Plant {
    String type = "plant";
    public static void main(String[] args) {
```

```
        Plant w1 = new Bush();
        Bush w2 = new Bush();
        Plant w3 = w2;
        System.out.print(w1.type+","+w2.type+","+w3.type);
    }
}
```

A. plant,bush,plant

B. plant,bush,bush

C. bush,plant,bush

D. bush,bush,bush

E. The code does not compile.

F. None of the above.

31. Which statements can accurately fill in the blanks in this table? (Choose two.)

Variable Type	Can Be Called Within the Class from What Type of Method?
Instance	Blank 1: _____
static	Blank 2: _____

A. Blank 1: an instance method only

B. Blank 1: a static method only

C. Blank 1: an instance or static method

D. Blank 2: an instance method only

E. Blank 2: a static method only

F. Blank 2: an instance or static method

32. What is the correct order of statements for a Java class file?

A. import statements, package statement, class declaration

B. package statement, class declaration, import statements

C. class declaration, import statements, package statement

D. package statement, import statements, class declaration

E. import statements, class declaration, package statement

F. class declaration, package statement, import statements

33. What is true of the following code? (Choose three.)

```
1: class Penguin {
2:     enum Baby { EGG }
3:     static class Chick {
4:         enum Baby { EGG }
```

```
5:      }
6:      public static void main(String[] args) {
7:          boolean match = false;
8:          Baby egg = Baby.EGG;
9:          switch (egg) {
10:            case EGG:
11:                match = true;
12:         }
13:      }
14: }
```

A. It compiles as is.

B. It does not compile as is.

C. Removing line 2 would create an additional compiler error.

D. Removing line 2 would not create an additional compiler error.

E. Removing the `static` modifier on line 3 would create an additional compiler error.

F. Removing the `static` modifier on line 3 would not create an additional compiler error.

34. Which are true of the following? (Choose two.)

```
package beach;
public class Sand {
   private static int numShovels;
   private int numRakes;

   public static int getNumShovels() {
      return numShovels;
   }
   public static int getNumRakes() {
      return numRakes;
   }
   public Sand() {
      System.out.print("a");
   }
   public void Sand() {
      System.out.print("b");
   }
   public void run() {
      new Sand();
      Sand();
   }
```

```
    public static void main(String... args) {
        new Sand().run();
    }
}
```

A. The code compiles.

B. One line doesn't compile.

C. Two lines don't compile.

D. If any constructors and/or methods that do not compile are removed, the remaining code prints a.

E. If the code compiles or if any constructors/methods that do not compile are removed, the remaining code prints ab.

F. If the code compiles or if any constructors/methods that do not compile are removed, the remaining code prints aab.

35. Which of the following class types cannot be marked `final` or `abstract`?

A. `static` nested class.

B. Local class.

C. Anonymous class.

D. Member inner class.

E. All of the above can be marked `final` or `abstract`.

36. Fill in the blanks: The _____ access modifier allows access to everything the _____ access modifier does and more. (Choose three.)

A. package-private, `protected`

B. package-private, `public`

C. `protected`, package-private

D. `protected`, `public`

E. `public`, package-private

F. `public`, `protected`

37. Which is the first line containing a compiler error?

```
var title = "Weather";      // line x1
var hot = 100, var cold = 20;  // line x2
var f = 32, int c = 0;      // line x3
```

A. x1

B. x2

C. x3

D. None of the above

38. How many of the following members of `Telephone` interface are `public`?

```
public interface Telephone {
    static int call() { return 1; }
    default void dial() {}
    long answer();
    String home = "555-555-5555";
}
```

A. Zero.

B. One.

C. Two.

D. Three.

E. Four.

F. The code does not compile.

39. Which best describes what the new keyword does?

A. Creates a copy of an existing object and treats it as a new one.

B. Creates a new primitive.

C. Instantiates a new object.

D. Switches an object reference to a new one.

E. The behavior depends on the class implementation.

40. How many lines will not compile?

```
12: public void printVarargs(String... names) {
13:     System.out.println(Arrays.toString(names));
14: }
15: public void printArray(String[] names) {
16:     System.out.println(Arrays.toString(names));
17: }
18: public void stormy() {
19:     printVarargs("Arlene");
20:     printVarargs(new String[]{"Bret"});
21:     printVarargs(null);
22:     printArray ("Cindy");
23:     printArray (new String[]{"Don"});
24:     printArray (null);
25: }
```

A. Zero

B. One

   C. Two

   D. Three

   E. Four

   F. Five

41. Which of the following can include a `static` method in its definition? (Choose three.)

   A. Interface

   B. Anonymous class

   C. Abstract class

   D. Member inner class

   E. Local class

   F. `static` nested class

42. What is the minimum number of lines that need to be removed to make this code compile?

```
@FunctionalInterface
public interface Play {
    public static void baseball() {}
    private static void soccer() {}
    default void play() {}
    void fun();
}
```

   A. 1.

   B. 2.

   C. 3.

   D. 4.

   E. The code compiles as is.

43. Fill in the blanks: A class that defines an instance variable with the same name as a variable in the parent class is referred to as _____ a variable, while a class that defines a `static` method with the same signature as a `static` method in a parent class is referred to as _____ a method.

   A. hiding, overriding

   B. overriding, hiding

   C. masking, masking

   D. hiding, masking

   E. replacing, overriding

   F. hiding, hiding

44. What change is needed to make `Secret` well encapsulated?

```
import java.util.*;

public class Secret {

    private int number = new Random().nextInt(10);
    public boolean guess(int candidate) {
       return number == candidate;
    }
}
```

A. Change `number` to use a `protected` access modifier.

B. Change `number` to use a `public` access modifier.

C. Declare a `private` constructor.

D. Declare a `public` constructor.

E. Remove the `guess` method.

F. None. It is already well encapsulated.

45. Which of the following are the best reasons for creating a `public static` interface method? (Choose two.)

A. Allow `static` methods to access instance methods.

B. Allow an interface to define a method at the class level.

C. Provide an implementation that a class implementing the interface can override.

D. Improve code reuse within the interface.

E. Add backward compatibility to existing interfaces.

F. Improve encapsulation of the interface.

46. What is the output of the following application?

```
package space;
public class Bottle {
   public static class Ship {
      private enum Sail {          // w1
         TALL {protected int getHeight() {return 100;}},
         SHORT {protected int getHeight() {return 2;}};
         protected abstract int getHeight();
      }
      public Sail getSail() {
         return Sail.TALL;
      }
   }
```

```
public static void main(String[] stars) {
    var bottle = new Bottle();
    Ship q = bottle.new Ship();   // w2
    System.out.print(q.getSail());
}
}
```

A. TALL

B. The code does not compile because of line w1.

C. The code does not compile because of line w2.

D. The code does not compile for another reason.

E. The code compiles, but the application does not produce any output at runtime.

F. None of the above.

47. Which of the following is not a valid order for elements within a class?

A. Constructor, instance variables, method declarations

B. Instance variables, `static` initializer constructor, method declarations

C. Method declarations, instance variables, constructor

D. Instance initializer, constructor, instance variables, constructor

E. None of the above

48. Which line of code, inserted at line p1, causes the application to print 5?

```
package games;
public class Jump {
    private int rope = 1;
    protected boolean outside;

    public Jump() {
        // line p1
        outside = true;
    }

    public Jump(int rope) {
        this.rope = outside ? rope : rope+1;
    }

    public static void main(String[] bounce) {
        System.out.print(new Jump().rope);
    }
}
```

A. `this(4);`

B. `new Jump(4);`

C. `this(5);`

D. `rope = 4;`

E. `super(4);`

F. `super(5);`

49. Which of the following is not a reason to use encapsulation when designing a class? (Choose two.)

   A. Improve security.

   B. Increase concurrency and improve performance.

   C. Maintain class data integrity of data elements.

   D. Prevent users from modifying the internal attributes of a class.

   E. Prevent variable state from changing.

   F. Promote usability by other developers.

50. Which statement about the following program is correct? (Choose two.)

```
package ballroom;

class Leader {}
class Follower {}
abstract class Dancer {
   public Leader getPartner() { return new Leader(); }
   abstract public Leader getPartner(int count);   // u1
}

public abstract class SwingDancer extends Dancer {
   public Leader getPartner(int x) { return null; }
   public Follower getPartner() {                    // u2
      return new Follower();                         // u3
   }
   public static void main(String[] args) {
      new SwingDancer().getPartner();                // u4
   }
}
```

   A. The code does not compile because of line u1.

   B. The code does not compile because of line u2.

   C. The code does not compile because of line u3.

   D. The code does not compile because of line u4.

   E. At least three of the classes compile without issue.

   F. All of the classes compile without issue.

51. Which is not a true statement given this diagram? Assume all classes are public.

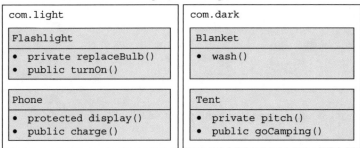

A. Instance methods in the `Blanket` class can call the `Flashlight` class's `turnOn()`.

B. Instance methods in the `Flashlight` class can call the `Flashlight` class's `replaceBulb()`.

C. Instance methods in the `Phone` class can call the `Blanket` class's `wash()`.

D. Instance methods in the `Tent` class can call the `Tent` class's `pitch()`.

E. None of the above.

52. Given the diagram in the previous question, how many of the classes shown in the diagram can call the `display()` method?

A. Zero

B. One

C. Two

D. Three

E. Four

53. Which of the following statements are correct? (Choose two.)

A. Java allows multiple inheritance using two abstract classes.

B. Java allows multiple inheritance using two interfaces.

C. Java does not allow multiple inheritance.

D. An interface can extend another interface.

E. An interface can implement another interface.

54. Which statement about the following code is correct?

```java
public class Dress {
    int size = 10;
    default int getSize() {
        display();
        return size;
    }
    static void display() {
        System.out.print("What a pretty outfit!");
    }
```

```
        private int getLength() {
            display();
            return 15;
        }
        private static void tryOn() {
            display();
        }
    }
```

A. The code contains an invalid constant.

B. The method `getSize()` does not compile.

C. The method `getLength()` does not compile.

D. The method `tryOn()` does not compile.

E. The code compiles.

F. None of the above.

55. What is the output of the following application?

```
package ocean;
abstract interface CanSwim {
    public void swim(final int distance);
}
public class Turtle {
    final int distance = 2;
    public static void main(String[] seaweed) {
        final int distance = 3;
        CanSwim seaTurtle = {
            final int distance = 5;
            @Override
            public void swim(final int distance) {
                System.out.print(distance);
            }
        };
        seaTurtle.swim(7);
    }
}
```

A. 2

B. 3

C. 5

D. 7

E. The code does not compile.

F. None of the above.

56. What is the output of the following application?

```
package pet;
public class Puppy {
   public static int wag = 5;   // q1
   public void Puppy(int wag) { // q2
      this.wag = wag;
   }
   public static void main(String[] tail) {
      System.out.print(new Puppy(2).wag); // q3
   }
}
```

A. 2

B. 5

C. The first line with a compiler error is line q1.

D. The first line with a compiler error is line q2.

E. The first line with a compiler error is line q3.

57. Given the following method signature, which classes can call it?

```
void run(String government)
```

A. Classes in other packages

B. Classes in the same package

C. Subclasses in a different package

D. All classes

E. None of the above

58. Which is the first declaration to not compile?

```
package desert;

interface CanBurrow {
   public abstract void burrow();
}

@FunctionalInterface interface HasHardShell
   extends CanBurrow {}

abstract class Tortoise implements HasHardShell {
   public abstract int toughness();
}
```

```
public class DesertTortoise extends Tortoise {
    public int toughness() { return 11; }
}
```

A. The `CanBurrow` interface does not compile.

B. The `HasHardShell` interface does not compile.

C. The `Tortoise` interface does not compile.

D. The `DesertTortoise` interface does not compile.

E. All of the interfaces compile.

59. Which is the first line to not compile?

```
interface Building {
    default Double getHeight() { return 1.0; }        // m1
}
interface Office {
    public default String getHeight() { return null; } // m2
}
abstract class Tower implements Building, Office {}    // m3
public class Restaurant extends Tower {}               // m4
```

A. Line m1

B. Line m2

C. Line m3

D. Line m4

E. None of the above

60. What is the output of the following code snippet?

```
String tree = "pine";
int count = 0;
if (tree.equals("pine")) {
    int height = 55;
    count = count + 1;
}
System.out.print(height + count);
```

A. 1

B. 55

C. 56

D. It does not compile.

61. Which of the following are valid comments in Java? (Choose three.)

   A. `/****** TODO */`

   B. `# Fix this bug later`

   C. `' Error closing pod bay doors`

   D. `/ Invalid record /`

   E. `/* Page not found */`

   F. `// IGNORE ME`

62. Which of the following modifiers can both be applied to a method? (Choose three.)

   A. `private` and `final`

   B. `abstract` and `final`

   C. `static` and `private`

   D. `private` and `abstract`

   E. `abstract` and `static`

   F. `static` and `protected`

63. Given the following class, what should be inserted into the two blanks to ensure the class data is properly encapsulated?

```
package storage;
public class Box {
    public String stuff;
    _____ String _____() {
       return stuff;
    }

    public void setStuff(String stuff) {
       this.stuff = stuff;
    }
}
```

   A. `private` and `getStuff`

   B. `private` and `isStuff`

   C. `public` and `getStuff`

   D. `public` and `isStuff`

   E. None of the above

64. How many rows of the following table contain an error?

Interface member	Membership type	Requires method body?
Static method	Class	Yes
Private non-static method	Class	Yes
Abstract method	Instance	No
Default method	Instance	No
Private static method	Class	Yes

- **A.** Zero
- **B.** One
- **C.** Two
- **D.** Three
- **E.** Four

65. Fill in the blanks: _____ is used to call a constructor in the parent class, while _____ is used to reference a member of the parent class.

- **A.** super and this()
- **B.** super and super()
- **C.** super() and this
- **D.** super() and super
- **E.** None of the above

66. What is the output of the Watch program?

```
1:  class SmartWatch extends Watch {
2:      private String getType() { return "smart watch"; }
3:      public String getName(String suffix) {
4:          return getType() + suffix;
5:      }
6:  }
7:  public class Watch {
8:      private String getType() { return "watch"; }
9:      public String getName(String suffix) {
10:         return getType() + suffix;
11:     }
12:     public static void main(String[] args) {
13:         var watch = new Watch();
14:         var smartWatch = new SmartWatch();
15:         System.out.print(watch.getName(","));
16:         System.out.print(smartWatch.getName(""));
```

```
17:    }
18: }
```

A. `smart watch,watch`
B. `watch,smart watch`
C. `watch,watch`
D. The code does not compile.
E. An exception is printed at runtime.
F. None of the above.

67. What is the output of the `Movie` program?

```
package theater;
class Cinema {
    private String name = "Sequel";
    public Cinema(String name) {
        this.name = name;
    }
}
public class Movie extends Cinema {
    private String name = "adaptation";
    public Movie(String movie) {
        this.name = "Remake";
    }
    public static void main(String[] showing) {
        System.out.print(new Movie("Trilogy").name);
    }
}
```

A. `Sequel`
B. `Trilogy`
C. `Remake`
D. `Adaptation`
E. `null`
F. None of the above

68. Where can a `final` instance variable be assigned a value? (Choose three.)
A. Instance initializer
B. `static` initializer
C. Instance method
D. On the line it is declared
E. Class constructor
F. `static` method

69. What is the output of the following code?

```java
public class Bunny {
    static interface Rabbit { }
    static class FlemishRabbit implements Rabbit { }

    private static void hop(Rabbit r) {
        System.out.print("hop");
    }
    private static void hop(FlemishRabbit r) {
        System.out.print("HOP");
    }
    public static void main(String[] args) {
        Rabbit r1 = new FlemishRabbit();
        FlemishRabbit r2 = new FlemishRabbit();
        hop(r1);
        hop(r2);
    }
}
```

- **A.** hophop
- **B.** HOPhop
- **C.** hopHOP
- **D.** HOPHOP
- **E.** The code does not compile.

70. Which of the following results is not a possible output of this program?

```java
package sea;
enum Direction { north, south, east, west; };
public class Ship {
    public static void main(String[] compass) {
        System.out.print(Direction.valueOf(compass[0]));
    }
}
```

- **A.** WEST is printed.
- **B.** south is printed.
- **C.** An `ArrayIndexOutOfBoundsException` is thrown at runtime.
- **D.** An `IllegalArgumentException` is thrown at runtime.
- **E.** All of the above are possible.

71. Which statement about encapsulation is not true?

   A. Encapsulation allows putting extra logic in the getter and setter methods.

   B. Encapsulation can use immutable instance variables in the implementation.

   C. Encapsulation causes two classes to be more tightly tied together.

   D. Encapsulation makes it easier to change the instance variables in the future.

   E. All of the above are true.

72. What is the output of the following application?

```
package radio;
public class Song {
    public void playMusic() {
        System.out.print("Play!");
    }
    private static void playMusic() {
        System.out.print("Music!");
    }
    private static void playMusic(String song) {
        System.out.print(song);
    }
    public static void main(String[] tracks) {
        new Song().playMusic();
    }
}
```

   A. `Play!`

   B. `Music!`

   C. The code does not compile.

   D. The code compiles, but the answer cannot be determined until runtime.

73. Which of the following statements about overriding a method are correct? (Choose three.)

   A. The return types must be covariant.

   B. The access modifier of the method in the child class must be the same or narrower than the method in the superclass.

   C. The return types must be the same.

   D. A checked exception thrown by the method in the parent class must be thrown by the method in the child class.

   E. A checked exception thrown by a method in the child class must be the same or narrower than the exception thrown by the method in the parent class.

   F. The access modifier of the method in the child class must be the same or broader than the method in the superclass.

74. How lines of the following code do not compile?

```
10: interface Flavor {
11:     public default void happy() {
12:         printFlavor("Rocky road");
13:     }
14:     private static void excited() {
15:         printFlavor("Peanut butter");
16:     }
17:     private void printFlavor(String f) {
18:         System.out.println("Favorite Flavor is: "+f);
19:     }
20:     public static void sad() {
21:         printFlavor("Butter pecan");
22:     }
23: }
24: public class IceCream implements Flavor {
25:     @Override public void happy() {
26:         printFlavor("Cherry chocolate chip");
27:     } }
```

- **A.** None, they all compile
- **B.** One
- **C.** Two
- **D.** Three
- **E.** Four
- **F.** Five or more

75. Of the following four modifiers, choose the one that is not implicitly applied to all interface variables.

- **A.** final
- **B.** abstract
- **C.** static
- **D.** public

76. Given the following method, what is the first line that does not compile?

```
public static void main(String[] args) {
    int Integer = 0;        // k1
    Integer int = 0;        // k2
    Integer ++;             // k3
    int++;                  // k4
```

```
    int var = null;            // k5
}
```

A. k1

B. k2

C. k3

D. k4

E. k5

77. What is the result of compiling and executing the following class?

```
public class Tolls {
    private static int yesterday = 1;
    int tomorrow = 10;

    public static void main(String[] args) {
        var tolls = new Tolls();
        int today = 20, tomorrow = 40;   // line x
        System.out.print(
            today + tolls.tomorrow + tolls.yesterday); // line y
    }
}
```

A. The code does not compile due to line x.

B. The code does not compile due to line y.

C. 31

D. 61

78. What is the output of the following application?

```
package weather;
public class Forecast {
    public enum Snow {
        BLIZZARD, SQUALL, FLURRY
        @Override public String toString() { return "Sunny"; }
    }

    public static void main(String[] modelData) {
        System.out.print(Snow.BLIZZARD.ordinal() + " ");
        System.out.print(Snow.valueOf("flurry".toUpperCase()));
    }
}
```

A. 0 FLURRY

B. 1 FLURRY

C. 0 Sunny

D. 1 Sunny

E. The code does not compile.

F. None of the above.

79. Which of the following is not a true statement?

    A. The first line of every constructor is a call to the parent constructor via the `super()` command.

    B. A class is not required to have a constructor explicitly defined.

    C. A constructor may pass arguments to the parent constructor.

    D. A `final` instance variable whose value is not set when it is declared or in an initialization block should be set by the constructor.

    E. None of the above.

80. What can fill in the blank so the `play()` method can be called from all classes in the `com.mammal` and `com.mammal.eland` package, but not the `com.mammal.gopher` package?

```
package com.mammal;

public class Enrichment {
    _____ void play() {}
}
```

    A. Leave it blank.

    B. `private`

    C. `protected`

    D. `public`

    E. None of the above.

81. What is the output of the `Rocket` program?

```
package transport;

class Ship {
    protected int weight = 3;
    private int height = 5;
    public int getWeight() { return weight; }
    public int getHeight() { return height; }
}

public class Rocket extends Ship {
```

```
        public int weight = 2;
        public int height = 4;
        public void printDetails() {
            System.out.print(super.getWeight()+","+super.height);
        }
        public static final void main(String[] fuel) {
            new Rocket().printDetails();
        }
    }
```

A. 2,5

B. 3,4

C. 5,2

D. 3,5

E. The code does not compile.

F. None of the above.

82. Imagine you are working with another team to build an application. You are developing code that uses a class that the other team has not finished writing yet. You want to allow easy integration once the other team's code is complete. Which statements would meet this requirement? (Choose two.)

   A. An abstract class is best.

   B. An interface is best.

   C. Either of an abstract class or interface would meet the requirement.

   D. The methods should be `protected`.

   E. The methods should be `public`.

   F. The methods should be `static`.

83. Fill in the blank with the line of code that allows the program to compile and print 10 at runtime.

```
interface Speak {
    public default int getVolume() { return 20; }
}
interface Whisper {
    public default int getVolume() { return 10; }
}
public class Debate implements Speak, Whisper {
    public int getVolume() { return 30; }
    public static void main(String[] a) {
        var d = new Debate();
```

```
        System.out.println(_____);
    }
}
```

A. `Whisper.d.getVolume()`

B. `d.Whisper.getVolume()`

C. `Whisper.super.getVolume()`

D. `d.Whisper.super.getVolume()`

E. The code does not compile regardless of what is inserted into the blank.

F. None of the above.

84. Which of the following properties of an enum can be marked `abstract`?

    A. The enum type definition

    B. An enum method

    C. An enum value

    D. An enum constructor

    E. None of the above

85. How many lines does the following code output?

```
public class Cars {
   static {
       System.out.println("static");
   }
   private static void drive() {
       System.out.println("fast");
   }
   { System.out.println("faster"); }
   public static void main(String[] args) {
       drive();
       drive();
   }
}
```

    A. One.

    B. Two.

    C. Three.

    D. Four.

    E. Five.

    F. None of the above. The code does not compile.

86. Suppose `foo` is a reference to an instance of a class `Foo`. Which of the following is not possible about the variable reference `foo.bar`?

A. `bar` is an instance variable.

B. `bar` is a `static` variable.

C. `bar` is a local variable.

D. It can be used to read from `bar`.

E. It can be used to write to `bar`.

F. All of the above are possible.

87. The following diagram shows two reference variables pointing to the same Bunny object in memory. The reference variable myBunny is of type Bunny, while unknownBunny is a valid but unknown data type. Which statements about the reference variables are true? Assume the instance methods and variables shown in the diagram are marked `public`. (Choose three.)

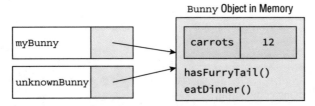

A. The reference type of unknownBunny must be Bunny or a supertype of Bunny.

B. The reference type of unknownBunny cannot be cast to a reference type of Bunny.

C. The reference type of unknownBunny must be Bunny or a subclass of Bunny.

D. If the reference type of unknownBunny is Bunny, it has access to all of the same methods and variables as myBunny.

E. The reference type of unknownBunny could be an interface, class, or abstract class.

F. If the reference type of unknownBunny is `Object`, it has access to all of the same methods and variables as myBunny without a cast.

88. Which of the following interface methods are inherited by classes that implement the interface? (Choose two.)

A. `private` methods

B. `private static` methods

C. `default` methods

D. `static` methods

E. `abstract` methods

F. `final` methods

89. Which of these are functional interfaces?

```
interface Lion {
    public void roar();
    default void drink() {}
```

```
    String toString();
}

interface Tiger {
    public void roar();
    default void drink() {}
    int hashCode();
}
```

A. Lion

B. Tiger

C. Both Lion and Tiger

D. Neither is a functional interface.

E. The code does not compile.

90. Given the following code, which lines when placed independently in the blank allow the code to compile and print bounce? (Choose two.)

```
public class TennisBall {
    public TennisBall() {
        System.out.println("bounce");
    }
    public static void main(String[] slam) {

        _____

    }
}
```

A. `var new = TennisBall;`

B. `TennisBall();`

C. `var var = new TennisBall();`

D. `new TennisBall;`

E. `new TennisBall();`

91. How many of these methods compile?

```
public class Singing {
    private void sing(String key) { }
    public void sing_do(String key, String... harmonies) {
        this.sing(key);
    }
    public void sing_re(int note, String... sound, String key) {
        this.sing(key);
    }
```

```
    public void sing_me(String... keys, String... pitches) {
        this.sing(key);
    }
    public void sing_far(String key, String... harmonies) {
        this.Singing.sing(key);
    }
    public void sing_so(int note, String... sound, String key) {
        this.Singing.sing(key);
    }
    public void sing_la(String... keys, String... pitches) {
        this.Singing.sing(key);
    }
}
```

A. Zero

B. One

C. Two

D. Three

E. Four

F. Five

92. What is the output of the following application?

```
package world;
public class Matrix {
    private int level = 1;
    class Deep {
        private int level = 2;
        class Deeper {
            private int level = 5;
            public void printReality(int level) {
                System.out.print(this.level+" ");
                System.out.print(Matrix.Deep.this.level+" ");
                System.out.print(Deep.this.level);
            }
        }
    }
    public static void main(String[] bots) {
        Matrix.Deep.Deeper simulation = new Matrix()
            .new Deep().new Deeper();
```

```
        simulation.printReality(6);
    }
}
```

A. 1 1 2

B. 5 2 2

C. 5 2 1

D. 6 2 2

E. 6 2 1

F. The code does not compile.

93. Given that `Integer` and `Long` are direct subclasses of `Number`, what type can be used to fill in the blank in the following class to allow it to compile?

```
package orchestra;
interface MusicCreator { public Number play(); }
abstract class StringInstrument {
    public Long play() {return 3L;}
}
public class Violin extends StringInstrument
        implements MusicCreator {
    public _____ play() {
        return null;
    }
}
```

A. `Long`

B. `Integer`

C. `Long` or `Integer`

D. `Long` or `Number`

E. `Long`, `Integer`, or `Number`

F. None of the above

94. What is the output of the `RightTriangle` program?

```
package shapes;

abstract class Triangle {
    abstract String getDescription();
}
abstract class IsoRightTriangle extends RightTriangle { // g1
    public String getDescription() { return "irt"; }
}
```

```
public class RightTriangle extends Triangle {
    protected String getDescription() { return "rt"; }   // g2
    public static void main(String[] edges) {
        final var shape = new IsoRightTriangle();          // g3
        System.out.print(shape.getDescription());
    }
}
```

A. rt

B. irt

C. The code does not compile due to line g1.

D. The code does not compile due to line g2.

E. The code does not compile due to line g3.

F. None of the above.

95. What is the output of the following program?

```
interface Dog {
    private void buryBone() { chaseTail(); }
    private static void wagTail() { chaseTail(); }
    public default String chaseTail() { return "So cute!"; }
}
public class Puppy implements Dog {
    public String chaseTail() throws IllegalArgumentException {
        throw new IllegalArgumentException("Too little!");
    }
    public static void main(String[] t) {
        var p = new Puppy();
        System.out.print(p.chaseTail());
    }
}
```

A. So cute!

B. An exception is thrown with a Too little! message.

C. A different exception is thrown.

D. The code does not compile because buryBone() is not used.

E. The code does not compile because chaseTail() cannot declare any exceptions in the Puppy class.

F. None of the above.

96. Which of the following are advantages of using enumerated types in Java, rather than `static` constant values? (Choose three.)

  A. Improve performance.

  B. Provide access to fixed set of constants whose values do not change during the course of the application.

  C. Provide a caller with a list of available values for a parameter within a method.

  D. Ensure consistency of data across an application.

  E. Add support for concurrency.

  F. Offer ability to create new enumerated values at runtime.

97. How do you force garbage collection to occur at a certain point?

  A. Calling `System.forceGc()`

  B. Calling `System.gc()`

  C. Calling `System.requireGc()`

  D. Calling `GarbageCollection.clean()`

  E. None of the above

98. Which changes made to the following class would help to properly encapsulate the data in the class?

```
package shield;
public class Protect {
    private String material;
    protected int strength;

    public int getStrength() {
        return strength;
    }
    public void setStrength(int strength) {
        this.strength = strength;
    }
}
```

  A. Add a getter method for `material`.

  B. Add a setter method for `material`.

  C. Change the access modifier of material to `protected`.

  D. Change the access modifier of `strength` to `private`.

  E. None of the above.

99. Which are true statements about referencing variables from a lambda? (Choose two.)

   A. Instance and `static` variables can be used regardless of whether effectively final.

   B. Instance and local variables can be used regardless of whether effectively final.

   C. Instance variables and method parameters must be effectively final to be used.

   D. Local variables and method parameters must be effectively final to be used.

   E. Local and `static` variables can be used regardless of whether effectively final.

   F. Method parameters and `static` variables can be used regardless of whether effectively final.

100. Given the following two classes, each in a different package, which line inserted into the code allows the second class to compile?

```
package commerce;
public class Bank {
    public void withdrawal(int amountInCents) {}
    public void deposit(int amountInCents) {}
}
```

```
package employee;
// INSERT CODE HERE
public class Teller {
    public void processAccount(int deposit, int withdrawal) {
        withdrawal(withdrawal);
        deposit(deposit);
    }
}
```

   A. `import static commerce.Bank.*;`

   B. `import static commerce.Bank;`

   C. `static import commerce.Bank.*;`

   D. `static import commerce.Bank;`

   E. None of the above

101. Given the following structure, which snippets of code return `true`? (Choose three.)

```
interface Friendly {}
abstract class Dolphin implements Friendly {}
class Animal implements Friendly {}
class Whale extends Object {}
public class Fish {}
class Coral extends Animal {}
```

A. `new Coral() instanceof Friendly`

B. `null instanceof Object`

C. `new Coral() instanceof Object`

D. `new Fish() instanceof Friendly`

E. `new Whale() instanceof Object`

F. `new Dolphin() instanceof Friendly`

102. What is true of the following code?

```java
public class Eggs {
    enum Animal {
        CHICKEN(21), PENGUIN(75);

        private int numDays;
        private Animal(int numDays) {
            this.numDays = numDays;
        }
        public int getNumDays() {
            return numDays;
        }
        public void setNumDays(int numDays) {
            this.numDays = numDays;
        }
    }
    public static void main(String[] args) {
        Animal chicken = Animal.CHICKEN;
        chicken.setNumDays(20);

        System.out.print(chicken.getNumDays());
        System.out.print(" ");
        System.out.print(Animal.CHICKEN.getNumDays());
        System.out.print(" ");
        System.out.print(Animal.PENGUIN.getNumDays());
    }
}
```

A. It prints 20 20 20

B. It prints 20 20 75

C. It prints 20 21 75

D. It prints 21 21 75

E. It does not compile due to `setNumDays()`.

F. It does not compile for another reason.

103. What statement about the following interface is correct?

```
1: public interface Thunderstorm {
2:     float rain = 1;
3:     char getSeason() { return 'W'; }
4:     boolean isWet();
5:     private static void hail() {}
6:     default String location() { return "Home"; }
7:     private static int getTemp() { return 35; }
8: }
```

A. Line 2 does not compile.

B. Line 3 does not compile.

C. Line 4 does not compile.

D. Line 5 does not compile.

E. Line 6 does not compile.

F. Line 7 does not compile.

G. All of the lines compile.

104. What is the output of the following application?

```
package finance;

enum Currency {
    DOLLAR, YEN, EURO
}
abstract class Provider {
    protected Currency c = Currency.EURO;
}
public class Bank extends Provider {
    protected Currency c = Currency.DOLLAR;
    public static void main(String[] pennies) {
        int value = 0;
        switch(new Bank().c) {
            case 0:
                value--; break;
            case 1:
                value++; break;
        }
        System.out.print(value);
    }
}
```

A. -1

B. 0

C. 1

D. The `Provider` class does not compile.

E. The `Bank` class does not compile.

F. None of the above.

105. How many lines need to be removed for this code to compile?

```
1:  package figures;
2:  public class Dolls {
3:      public int num() { return 3.0; }
4:      public int size() { return 5L; }
5:
6:      public void nested() { nested(2,true); }
7:      public int nested(int w, boolean h) { return 0; }
8:      public int nested(int level) { return level+1; }
9:
10:     public static void main(String[] outOfTheBox) {
11:         System.out.print(new Dolls().nested());
12:     }
13: }
```

A. Zero

B. One

C. Two

D. Three

E. Four

F. Five

106. Fill in the blanks: A class may be assigned to a(n) _____ reference variable automatically but requires an explicit cast when assigned to a(n) _____ reference variable.

A. subclass, outer class

B. superclass, subclass

C. concrete class, subclass

D. subclass, superclass

E. abstract class, concrete class

107. Which statement about functional interfaces is incorrect?

   A. A functional interface can have any number of `static` methods.

   B. A functional interface can have any number of `default` methods.

   C. A functional interface can have any number of `private static` methods.

   D. A functional interface can have any number of `abstract` methods.

   E. A functional interface can have any number of `private` methods.

   F. All of the above are correct.

108. What are possible outputs of the following given that the comment on line X can be replaced by code?

```
// Mandrill.java
public class Mandrill {
    public int age;
    public Mandrill(int age) {
        this.age = age;
    }
    public String toString() {
        return "" + age;
    }
}


// PrintAge.java
public class PrintAge {
    public static void main (String[] args) {
        var mandrill = new Mandrill(5);

        // line X

        System.out.println(mandrill);
    }
}
```

   A. 0

   B. 5

   C. Either 0 or 5

   D. Any `int` value

   E. Does not compile

109. How many of the `String` objects are eligible for garbage collection right before the end of the `main()` method?

```
public static void main(String[] ohMy) {
    String animal1 = new String("lion");
    String animal2 = new String("tiger");
    String animal3 = new String("bear");

    animal3 = animal1;
    animal2 = animal3;
    animal1 = animal2;
}
```

A. None
B. One
C. Two
D. Three
E. None of the above

110. Suppose Panther and Cub are interfaces and neither contains any `default` methods. Which statements are true? (Choose two.)

A. If Panther has a single `abstract` method, Cub is guaranteed to be a functional interface.
B. If Panther has a single `abstract` method, Cub may be a functional interface.
C. If Panther has a single `abstract` method, Cub cannot be a functional interface.
D. If Panther has two `abstract` methods, Cub is guaranteed to be a functional interface.
E. If Panther has two `abstract` methods, Cub may be a functional interface.
F. If Panther has two `abstract` methods, Cub cannot be a functional interface.

111. A local class can access which type of local variables? (Choose two.)
A. `final`
B. `private`
C. effectively final
D. `static`
E. `default`
F. `const`

112. What does the following output?

```
1:  public class InitOrder {
2:      public String first = "instance";
3:      public InitOrder() {
4:          first = "constructor";
5:      }
6:      { first = "block";  }
7:      public void print() {
8:          System.out.println(first);
9:      }
10:     public static void main(String... args) {
11:         new InitOrder().print();
12:     }
13: }
```

A. block

B. constructor

C. instance

D. The code does not compile.

E. None of the above.

113. Which statement about the following interface is correct?

```
public interface Tree {
    public static void produceSap() {
        growLeaves();
    }
    public abstract int getNumberOfRings() {
        return getNumberOfRings();
    }
    private static void growLeaves() {
        produceSap();
    }
    public default int getHeight() {
        return getHeight ();
    }
}
```

A. The code compiles.

B. The method produceSap() does not compile.

C. The method getNumberOfRings() does not compile.

D. The method growLeaves() does not compile.

E. The method `getHeight()` does not compile.

F. The code does not compile because it contains a cycle.

114. Which statements about a variable with a type of `var` are true? (Choose two.)

A. The variable can be assigned `null` at any point in the program.

B. The variable can be assigned `null` only after initial initialization.

C. The variable can never be assigned `null`.

D. Only primitives can be used with the variable.

E. Only objects can be used with the variable.

F. Either a primitive or an object can be used with the variable.

115. Assume there is a class `Bouncer` with a `protected` variable. Methods in which class can access this variable?

A. Any subclass of `Bouncer` or any class in the same package as `Bouncer`

B. Any superclass of `Bouncer`

C. Only subclasses of `Bouncer`

D. Only classes in the same package as `Bouncer`

E. None of the above

116. What is the output of the following application?

```java
package forest;
public class Woods {
    static class Tree {}
    public static void main(String[] leaves) {
        int heat = 2;
        int water = 10-heat;
        final class Oak extends Tree {  // p1
            public int getWater() {
                return water;           // p2
            }
        }
        System.out.print(new Oak().getWater());
        water = 0;
    }
}
```

A. 8

B. Line p1 contains a compiler error.

C. Line p2 contains a compiler error.

D. Another line of code contains a compiler error.

E. None of the above.

117. Which can fill in the blank to make the code compile? (Choose two.)

```
interface Australian {}
interface Mammal {}
_____ Australian, Mammal {}
```

   A. `class Quokka extends`
   B. `class Quokka implements`
   C. Neither A nor B. Only one interface can be specified.
   D. `interface Quokka extends`
   E. `interface Quokka implements`
   F. Neither D nor E. Only one interface can be specified.

118. What is true of the following method?

```
public void setColor(String color) {
    color = color;
}
```

   A. It is a correctly implemented accessor method.
   B. It is a correctly implemented mutator method.
   C. It is an incorrectly implemented accessor method.
   D. It is an incorrectly implemented mutator method.
   E. None of the above.

119. Which of the following statements about calling `this()` in a constructor are true? (Choose three.)
   A. If arguments are provided to `this()`, then there must be a constructor in the class able to take those arguments.
   B. If arguments are provided to `this()`, then there must be a constructor in the super-class able to take those arguments.
   C. If the no-argument `this()` is called, then the class must explicitly implement the no-argument constructor.
   D. If `super()` and `this()` are both used in the same constructor, `super()` must appear on the line immediately after `this()`.
   E. If `super()` and `this()` are both used in the same constructor, `this()` must appear on the line immediately after `super()`.
   F. If `this()` is used, it must be the first line of the constructor.

120. What is the result of compiling and executing the following class?

```
public class RollerSkates {
    static int wheels = 1;
    int tracks = 5;
    public static void main(String[] arguments) {
        RollerSkates s = new RollerSkates();
```

```
        int feet=4, tracks = 15;
        System.out.print(feet + tracks + s.wheels);
    }
}
```

A. The code does not compile.

B. 4

C. 5

D. 10

E. 20

121. Which statements about the following program are correct? (Choose two.)

```
package vessel;

class Problem extends Exception {}
abstract class Danger {
    protected abstract void isDanger() throws Problem; // m1
}
public class SeriousDanger extends Danger { // m2
    protected void isDanger() throws Exception { // m3
        throw new RuntimeException(); // m4
    }
    public static void main(String[] w) throws Throwable { // m5
        var sd = new SeriousDanger().isDanger(); // m6
    }
}
```

A. The code does not compile because of line m1.

B. The code does not compile because of line m2.

C. The code does not compile because of line m3.

D. The code does not compile because of line m4.

E. The code does not compile because of line m5.

F. The code does not compile because of line m6.

122. Which statements about top-level and member inner classes are correct? (Choose three.)

A. Both can be marked `protected`.

B. Only top-level classes can be declared `final`.

C. Both can declare constructors.

D. Member inner classes cannot be marked `private`.

E. Member inner classes can access `private` variables of the top-level class in which it is defined.

F. Both can be marked `abstract`.

123. What is required to define a valid Java class file?

    A. A `class` declaration

    B. A `package` statement

    C. An `import` statement

    D. A `class` declaration and `package` statement

    E. A `class` declaration and at least one `import` statement

    F. The `public` modifier

124. How many objects are eligible for garbage collection right before the end of the `main()` method?

```
1:  public class Person {
2:      public Person youngestChild;
3:
4:      public static void main(String... args) {
5:          Person elena = new Person();
6:          Person janeice = new Person();
7:          elena.youngestChild = janeice;
8:          janeice = null;
9:          Person zoe = new Person();
10:         elena.youngestChild = zoe;
11:         zoe = null;
12:     } }
```

    A. None.

    B. One.

    C. Two.

    D. Three.

    E. The code does not compile.

125. What is the output of the following application?

```
package race;
interface Drive {
   int SPEED = 5;
   default int getSpeed() { return SPEED; }
}
interface Hover {
   int MAX_SPEED = 10;
   default int getSpeed() { return MAX_SPEED; }
}
public class Car implements Drive, Hover {
   public static void main(String[] gears) {
```

```
       class RaceCar extends Car {
           @Override public int getSpeed() { return 15; }
       };
       System.out.print(new RaceCar().getSpeed());
    } }
```

A. 5

B. 10

C. 15

D. The code does not compile.

E. The answer cannot be determined with the information given.

126. What is the output of the following application? (Choose two.)

```
1:  public class ChooseWisely {
2:      public ChooseWisely() { super(); }
3:      public int choose(int choice) { return 5; }
4:      public int choose(short choice) { return 2; }
5:      public int choose(long choice) { return 11; }
6:      public int choose(double choice) { return 6; }
7:      public int choose(Float choice) { return 8; }
8:      public static void main(String[] path) {
9:          ChooseWisely c = new ChooseWisely();
10:         System.out.println(c.choose(2f));
11:         System.out.println(c.choose((byte)2+1));
12:     }
13: }
```

A. 2

B. 3

C. 5

D. 6

E. 8

127. Fill in the blanks: It is possible to extend a(n) _____ but not a(n) _____.
(Choose two.)

A. interface, abstract class

B. anonymous class, `static` nested class

C. abstract class, enum

D. enum, interface

E. abstract class, interface

F. local class, anonymous class

128. How many lines of the following program do not compile?

```
1: public enum Color {
2:     RED(1,2) { void toSpectrum() {} },
3:     BLUE(2) { void toSpectrum() {} void printColor() {} },
4:     ORANGE() { void toSpectrum() {} },
5:     GREEN(4);
6:     public Color(int... color) {}
7:     abstract void toSpectrum();
8:     final void printColor() {}
9: }
```

A. Zero

B. One

C. Two

D. Three

E. More than three

129. What is the output of the Square program?

```
package shapes;

abstract class Trapezoid {
    private int getEqualSides() {return 0;}
}
abstract class Rectangle extends Trapezoid {
    public static int getEqualSides() {return 2;}  // x1
}
public final class Square extends Rectangle {
    public int getEqualSides() {return 4;}          // x2
    public static void main(String[] corners) {
        final Square myFigure = new Square();       // x3
        System.out.print(myFigure.getEqualSides());
    }
}
```

A. 0

B. 2

C. 4

D. The code does not compile due to line x1.

E. The code does not compile due to line x2.

F. The code does not compile due to line x3.

130. What can fill in the blank so the `play()` method can be called from all classes in the `com.mammal` package, but not the `com.mammal.gopher` package?

```
package com.mammal;

public class Enrichment {
    _____ void play() {}
}
```

A. Leave it blank.

B. `private`

C. `protected`

D. `public`

E. None of the above.

131. How many cells in the following table are incorrect?

Type	Allows abstract methods?	Allows constants?	Allows constructors?
Abstract class	Yes	Yes	No
Concrete class	Yes	Yes	Yes
Interface	Yes	Yes	Yes

A. Zero

B. One

C. Two

D. Three

E. Four

132. Which statements are true about a functional interface? (Choose three.)

A. It may contain any number of `abstract` methods.

B. It must contain a single `abstract` method.

C. It may contain any number of `private` methods.

D. It must contain a single `private` method.

E. It may contain any number of `static` methods.

F. It must contain a single `static` method.

133. Which variables have a scope limited to a method?

A. Interface variables

B. Class variables

C. Instance variables

D. Local variables

134. What is a possible output of the following application?

```java
package wrap;
public class Gift {
    private final Object contents;
    protected Object getContents() {
        return contents;
    }
    protected void setContents(Object contents) {
        this.contents = contents;
    }
    public void showPresent() {
        System.out.print("Your gift: "+contents);
    }
    public static void main(String[] treats) {
        Gift gift = new Gift();
        gift.setContents(gift);
        gift.showPresent();
    }
}
```

A. Your gift: wrap.Gift@29ca2745

B. Your gift: Your gift:

C. It does not compile.

D. It compiles but throws an exception at runtime.

135. Which of the following are the best reasons for creating a `default` interface method? (Choose two.)

A. Allow interface methods to be overloaded.

B. Add backward compatibility to existing interfaces.

C. Give an interface the ability to create `final` methods.

D. Allow an interface to define a method at the class level.

E. Improve code reuse among classes that implement the interface.

F. Improve encapsulation of the interface.

136. How many compiler errors does the following code contain?

```java
package animal;
interface CanFly {
    public void fly() {}
}
final class Bird {
    public int fly(int speed) {}
}
public class Eagle extends Bird implements CanFly {
```

```java
    public void fly() {}
}
```

A. None

B. One

C. Two

D. Three

E. Four

137. Which of the following statements is not true?

A. An instance of one class may access an instance of another class's attributes if it has a reference to the instance and the attributes are declared `public`.

B. An instance of one class may access package-private attributes in a parent class, provided the parent class is not in the same package.

C. An instance of one class may access an instance of another class's attributes if both classes are located in the same package and marked `protected`.

D. Two instances of the same class may access each other's `private` attributes.

E. All of the above are true.

138. What is the output of the following code?

```java
public class Bunny {
    static class Rabbit {
        void hop() {
            System.out.print("hop");
        }
    }
    static class FlemishRabbit extends Rabbit {
        void hop() {
            System.out.print("HOP");
        }
    }
    public static void main(String[] args) {
        Rabbit r1 = new FlemishRabbit();
        FlemishRabbit r2 = new FlemishRabbit();
        r1.hop();
        r2.hop();
    }
}
```

A. hophop

B. HOPhop

C. hopHOP

D. HOPHOP

E. The code does not compile.

139. Which of the following are valid class declarations? (Choose three.)

   A. `class _ {}`

   B. `class river {}`

   C. `class Str3@m {}`

   D. `class Pond2$ {}`

   E. `class _var_ {}`

   F. `class 50cean {}`

140. What is the output of the `InfiniteMath` program?

```
class Math {
    public final double secret = 2;
}
class ComplexMath extends Math {
    public final double secret = 4;
}
public class InfiniteMath extends ComplexMath {
    public final double secret = 8;
    public static void main(String[] numbers) {
        Math math = new InfiniteMath();
        System.out.print(math.secret);
    }
}
```

   A. `2.0`

   B. `4.0`

   C. `8.0`

   D. The code does not compile.

   E. The code compiles but prints an exception at runtime.

   F. None of the above.

141. Given the following application, which diagram best represents the state of the `mySkier`, `mySpeed`, and `myName` variables in the `main()` method after the call to the `slalom()` method?

```
package slopes;
public class Ski {
    private int age = 18;
    private static void slalom(Ski racer,
        int[] speed, String name) {

        racer.age = 18;
```

```java
        name = "Wendy";
        speed = new int[1];
        speed[0] = 11;
        racer = null;
    }

    public static void main(String... mountain) {
        final var mySkier = new Ski();
        mySkier.age = 16;
        final int[] mySpeed = new int[1];
        final String myName = "Rosie";
        slalom(mySkier,mySpeed,myName);
    }
}
```

A.

B.

C.

D.

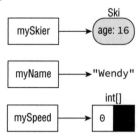

142. What is the output of the following application?

```
package zoo;
public class Penguin {
    private int volume = 1;
    private class Chick {
        private static int volume = 3;
        void chick() {
            System.out.print("Honk("+Penguin.this.volume+")!");
        }
    }
    public static void main(String... eggs) {
        Penguin pen = new Penguin();
        final Penguin.Chick littleOne = pen.new Chick();
        littleOne.chick();
    }
}
```

A. Honk(1)!

B. Honk(3)!

C. The code does not compile.

D. The code compiles, but the output cannot be determined until runtime.

E. None of the above.

143. Which can implement a functional interface?

A. An anonymous class

B. A top-level class

C. A lambda expression

D. An anonymous class or a top-level class

E. A top-level class or a lambda expression

F. An anonymous class, a top-level class, or a lambda expression

144. Fill in the blank with the line of code that allows the program to compile and print E at runtime.

```java
interface Fruit {
   public default char getColor() { return 'F'; }
}
interface Edible  {
   public default char getColor() { return 'E'; }
}
public class Banana implements Fruit, Edible {
   public char getColor() { return _____; }
   public static void main(String[] a) {
      var d = new Banana();
      System.out.println(d.getColor());
   }
}
```

A. `Edible.getColor()`

B. `Edible.super.getColor()`

C. `super.Edible.getColor()`

D. `super.getColor()`

E. The code does not compile regardless of what is inserted into the blank.

F. None of the above.

145. Given the following two classes, each in a different package, which line inserted into the code allows the second class to compile?

```java
package clothes;
public class Store {
   public static String getClothes() { return "dress"; }
}
```

```java
package wardrobe;
// INSERT CODE HERE
public class Closet {
   public void borrow() {
      System.out.print("Borrowing clothes: "+getClothes());
   }
}
```

A. `static import clothes.Store.getClothes;`

B. `import clothes.Store.*;`

C. `import static clothes.Store.getClothes;`

D. `import static clothes.Store;`

146. What is the output of the `ElectricCar` program?

```java
package vehicles;
class Automobile {
    private final String drive() { return "Driving vehicle"; }
}
class Car extends Automobile {
    protected String drive() { return "Driving car"; }
}
public class ElectricCar extends Car {
    public final String drive() { return "Driving electric car"; }
    public static void main(String[] wheels) {
        final Automobile car = new ElectricCar();
        var v = (Car)car;
        System.out.print(v.drive());
    }
}
```

A. Driving vehicle

B. Driving electric car

C. Driving car

D. The code does not compile.

E. The code compiles but produces a `ClassCastException` at runtime.

F. None of the above.

147. What is the output of the following program?

```java
public class Music {
    { System.out.print("do-"); }
    static { System.out.print("re-"); }
    { System.out.print("mi-"); }
    static { System.out.print("fa-"); }

    public Music() {
        System.out.print("so-");
    }

    public Music(int note) {
        System.out.print("la-");
    }
```

```
    public static void main(String[] sound) {
        System.out.print("ti-");
        var play = new Music();
    }
}
```

A. re-fa-ti-do-mi-so-

B. do-re-mi-fa-ti-so-

C. ti-re-fa-do-mi-so-

D. re-fa-la-mi-ti-do-

E. do-re-mi-fa-so-ti

F. The code does not compile.

G. None of the above.

148. Given the following class declaration, which options correctly declare a local variable containing an instance of the class?

```
public class Earth {
    private abstract class Sky {
        void fall() {
            var e = _____
        }
    }
}
```

A. new Sunset() extends Sky {};

B. new Sky();

C. new Sky() {}

D. new Sky() { final static int blue = 1; };

E. The code does not compile regardless of what is placed in the blank.

F. None of the above.

149. What is the output of the Encyclopedia program?

```
package paper;
abstract class Book {
    protected static String material = "papyrus";
    public Book() {}
    abstract String read() {}
    public Book(String material) {this.material = material;}
}
```

```java
public class Encyclopedia extends Book {
    public static String material = "cellulose";
    public Encyclopedia() {super();}
    public String read() { return "Reading is fun!"; }
    public String getMaterial() {return super.material;}

    public static void main(String[] pages) {
        System.out.print(new Encyclopedia().read());
        System.out.print("-" + new Encyclopedia().getMaterial());
    }
}
```

A. Reading is fun!-papyrus

B. Reading is fun!-cellulose

C. null-papyrus

D. null-cellulose

E. The code does not compile.

F. None of the above.

150. What does the following print?

```java
interface Vehicle {}
class Bus implements Vehicle {}

public class Transport {
    public static void main(String[] args) {
        Bus bus = new Bus();
        boolean n = null instanceof Bus;
        boolean v = bus instanceof Vehicle;
        boolean b = bus instanceof Bus;
        System.out.println(n + " " + v + " " + b);
    }
}
```

A. false false false

B. false false true

C. false true true

D. true false true

E. true true false

F. true true true

151. How many rows of the following table contain an error?

Interface member	Optional modifier(s)	Required modifier(s)
Private method	`private`	–
Default method	`public`	`default`
Static method	`public static`	–
Abstract method	`public`	`abstract`

- **A.** Zero
- **B.** One
- **C.** Two
- **D.** Three
- **E.** Four

152. What is the output of the following program?

```java
public class Dwarf {
    private final String name;

    public Dwarf() {
        this("Bashful");
    }

    public Dwarf(String name) {
        name = "Sleepy";
    }

    public static void main(String[] sound) {
        var d = new Dwarf("Doc");
        System.out.println(d.name);
    }
}
```

- **A.** Sleepy
- **B.** Bashful
- **C.** Doc
- **D.** The code does not compile.
- **E.** An exception is thrown at runtime.

153. What is the output of the following application?

```
package pocketmath;
interface AddNumbers {
    int add(int x, int y);
    static int subtract(int x, int y) { return x-y; }
    default int multiply(int x, int y) { return x*y; }
}
public class Calculator {
    protected void calculate(AddNumbers n, int a, int b) {
        System.out.print(n.add(a, b));
    }
    public static void main(String[] moreNumbers) {
        final var ti = new Calculator() {};
        ti.calculate((k,p) -> p+k+1, 2, 5);  // j1
    }
}
```

A. 8

B. The code does not compile because AddNumbers is not a functional interface.

C. The code does not compile because of line j1.

D. The code does not compile for a different reason.

E. None of the above.

154. Which of the following variables are always in scope for the entire program once defined?

A. Package variables

B. Class variables

C. Instance variables

D. Local variables

155. What is the command to call one constructor from another constructor in the same class?

A. construct()

B. parent()

C. super()

D. this()

E. that()

156. Which of the following statements about no-argument constructors and inheritance are correct? (Choose two.)

A. The compiler cannot insert a no-argument constructor into an abstract class.

B. If a parent class does not include a no-argument constructor, a child class cannot declare one.

C. If a parent class declares constructors but each of them take at least one parameter, then a child class must declare at least one constructor.

D. The no-argument constructor is sometimes inserted by the compiler.

E. If a parent class declares a no-argument constructor, a child class must declare a no-argument constructor.

F. If a parent class declares a no-argument constructor, a child class must declare at least one constructor.

157. Fill in the blanks: _____ allow Java to support multiple inheritance, and anonymous classes can _____ of them.

A. Abstract classes, extend at most one

B. Abstract classes, extend any number

C. Interfaces, implement at most one

D. Interfaces, implement any number

E. Concrete classes, extend at most one

F. None of the above

158. What is the result of executing the `Grasshopper` program?

```
// Hopper.java
package com.animals;

public class Hopper {
   protected void hop() {
      System.out.println("hop");
   }
}
```

```
// Grasshopper.java
package com.insect;
import com.animals.Hopper;

public class Grasshopper extends Hopper {
   public void move() {
      hop();   // p1
   }
   public static void main(String[] args) {
      var hopper = new Grasshopper();
      hopper.move();   // p2
      hopper.hop();    // p3
   }
}
```

A. The code prints hop once.

B. The code prints hop twice.

C. The first compiler error is on line p1.

    D. The first compiler error is on line p2.

    E. The first compiler error is on line p3.

159. What is the minimum number of lines that need to be removed to make this code compile?

```
@FunctionalInterface
public interface Play {
    public static void baseball() {}
    private static void soccer() {}
    default void play() {}
    void fun();
    void game();
    void toy();
}
```

    A. 1

    B. 2

    C. 3

    D. 4

    E. The code compiles as is.

160. Which of the following are the best reasons for creating a `private` interface method? (Choose two.)

    A. Add backward compatibility to existing interfaces.

    B. Provide an implementation that a class implementing the interface can override.

    C. Increase code reuse within the interface.

    D. Allow interface methods to be inherited.

    E. Improve encapsulation of the interface.

    F. Allow `static` methods to access instance methods.

161. What is the result of executing the Sounds program?

```
// Sheep.java
package com.mammal;

public class Sheep {
    private void baa() {
        System.out.println("baa!");
    }
    private void speak() {
        baa();
    }
}
```

```
// Sounds.java
package com.animals;
import com.mammal.Sheep;

public class Sounds {
    public static void main(String[] args) {
        var sheep = new Sheep();
        sheep.speak();
    }
}
```

A. The code runs and prints baa!.

B. The Sheep class does not compile.

C. The Sounds class does not compile.

D. Neither class compiles.

162. What is the output of the following application?

```
package stocks;
public class Bond {
    private static int price = 5;
    public boolean sell() {
        if(price<10) {
            price++;
            return true;
        } else if(price>=10) {
            return false;
        }
    }
    public static void main(String[] cash) {
        new Bond().sell();
        new Bond().sell();
        new Bond().sell();
        System.out.print(price);
    }
}
```

A. 5

B. 6

C. 8

D. The code does not compile.

163. Given the following class declaration, what expression can be used to fill in the blank so that 88 is printed at runtime?

```java
final public class Racecar {
    final private int speed = 88;
    final protected class Engine {
        private final int speed = 100;
        public final int getSpeed() {
            return _____;
        }
    }
    final Engine engine = new Engine();
    final public static void main(String[] feed) {
        System.out.print(new Racecar().engine.getSpeed());
    }
}
```

   A. Racecar.speed
   B. this.speed
   C. this.Racecar.speed
   D. Racecar.Engine.this.speed
   E. Racecar.this.speed
   F. The code does not compile regardless of what is placed in the blank.

164. Which statements about `static` initializers are correct? (Choose three.)
   A. They cannot be used to create instances of the class they are contained in.
   B. They can assign a value to a `static final` variable.
   C. They are executed at most once per program.
   D. They are executed each time an instance of the class is created from a local cache of objects.
   E. They are executed each time an instance of the class is created using the new keyword.
   F. They may never be executed.

165. What is the output of the `BlueCar` program?

```java
package race;
abstract class Car {
    static { System.out.print("1"); }
    public Car(String name) {
        super();
        System.out.print("2");
    }
```

```
         { System.out.print("3"); }
    }
    public class BlueCar extends Car {
        { System.out.print("4"); }
        public BlueCar() {
            super("blue");
            System.out.print("5");
        }
        public static void main(String[] gears) {
            new BlueCar();
        }
    }
```

A. 23451

B. 12345

C. 14523

D. 13245

E. The code does not compile.

F. None of the above.

166. Given the following class declaration, which value cannot be inserted into the blank line that would allow the code to compile?

```
package mammal;
interface Pet {}
public class Canine implements Pet {
    public _____ getDoggy() {
        return this;
    }
}
```

A. Canine

B. List

C. Object

D. Pet

E. All of the above can be inserted.

167. Which statement about the following interface is correct?

```
public interface Movie {
    String pass = "TICKET";
    private void buyPopcorn() {
        purchaseTicket();
```

```
   }
   public static int getDrink() {
      buyPopcorn();
      return 32;
   }
   private static String purchaseTicket() {
      getDrink();
      return pass;
   }
}
```

A. The code compiles.

B. The code contains an invalid constant.

C. The method buyPopcorn() does not compile.

D. The method getDrink() does not compile.

E. The method purchaseTicket() does not compile.

F. The code does not compile for a different reason.

168. Which methods compile?

```
private static int numShovels;
private int numRakes;

public int getNumShovels() {
   return numShovels;
}

public int getNumRakes() {
   return numRakes;
}
```

A. Just getNumRakes()

B. Just getNumShovels()

C. Both methods

D. Neither method

169. How many lines of the following class contain compilation errors?

```
1: class Fly {
2:    public Fly Fly() { return Fly(); }
3:    public void Fly(int kite) {}
4:    public int Fly(long kite) { return 1; }
5:    public static void main(String[] a) {
6:       var f = new Fly();
```

```
7:        f.Fly();
8:    }
9: }
```

A. None.

B. One.

C. Two.

D. Three.

E. Four.

F. The answer cannot be determined with the information given.

170. How many of the classes in the figure can write code that references the `sky()` method?

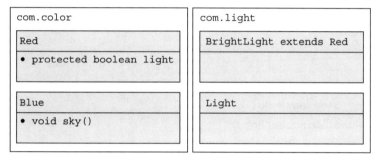

A. None

B. One

C. Two

D. Three

E. Four

171. For the diagram in the previous question, how many classes can write code that references the `light` variable?

A. None

B. One

C. Two

D. Three

E. Four

172. Given the following method signature, which classes cannot call it?

`protected void run(String government)`

A. All classes in other packages

B. All classes in the same package

C. Subclasses in a different package

D. Subclasses in the same package

173. What is the output of the following application?

```java
interface Toy { String play(); }
public class Gift {
   public static void main(String[] matrix) {
      abstract class Robot {}
      class Transformer extends Robot implements Toy {
         public String name = "GiantRobot";
         public String play() {return "DinosaurRobot";}   // y1
      }
      Transformer prime = new Transformer () {
         public String play() {return name;}                 // y2
      };
      System.out.print(prime.play()+" "+name);
   }
}
```

A. GiantRobot GiantRobot

B. GiantRobot DinosaurRobot

C. DinosaurRobot DinosaurRobot

D. The code does not compile because of line y1.

E. The code does not compile because of line y2.

F. None of the above.

174. What is the output of the HighSchool application?

```java
package edu;
import java.io.FileNotFoundException;
abstract class School {
   abstract Float getNumTeachers();
   public int getNumStudents() {
      return 10;
   }
}
public class HighSchool extends School {
   final Float getNumTeachers() { return 4f; }
   public int getNumStudents() throws FileNotFoundException {
      return 20;
   }
   public static void main(String[] s) throws Exception {
      var school = new HighSchool();
```

```
            System.out.print(school.getNumStudents());
    }
}
```

A. 10
B. 20
C. 4.0
D. One line of the program does not compile.
E. Two lines of the program do not compile.
F. None of the above.

175. What is the output of the following application?

```
package track;
interface Run {
    default CharSequence walk() {
        return "Walking and running!";
    }
}
interface Jog {
    default String walk() {
        return "Walking and jogging!";
    }
}
public class Sprint implements Run, Jog {
    public String walk() {
        return "Sprinting!";
    }
    public static void main(String[] args) {
        var s = new Sprint();
        System.out.println(s.walk());
    }
}
```

A. Walking and running!
B. Walking and jogging!
C. Sprinting!
D. The code does not compile.
E. The code compiles but prints an exception at runtime.
F. None of the above.

176. What is true of these two interfaces?

```
interface Crawl {
  void wriggle();
}
interface Dance {
    public void wriggle();
}
```

A. A concrete class can implement both, but must implement `wriggle()`.

B. A concrete class can implement both, but must not implement `wriggle()`.

C. A concrete class would only be able to implement both if the `public` modifier were removed but must implement `wriggle()`.

D. If the `public` modifier were removed, a concrete class can implement both, but must not implement `wriggle()`.

E. None of the above.

177. Which of these are functional interfaces?

```
interface Lion {
    public void roar();
    default void drink() {}
    boolean equals(Lion lion);
}

interface Tiger {
    public void roar();
    default void drink() {}
    String toString(String name);
}
```

A. `Lion`

B. `Tiger`

C. Both `Lion` and `Tiger`

D. Neither is a functional interface.

E. The code does not compile.

178. How many lines of the following class contain a compiler error?

```
1:  public class Dragon {
2:      boolean scaly;
3:      static final int gold;
4:      Dragon protectTreasure(int value, boolean scaly) {
```

```
5:        scaly = true;
6:        return this;
7:    }
8:    static void fly(boolean scaly) {
9:        scaly = true;
10:   }
11:   int saveTheTreasure(boolean scaly) {
12:       return this.gold;
13:   }
14:   static void saveTheDay(boolean scaly) {
15:       this.gold = 0;
16:   }
17:   static { gold = 100; }
18: }
```

A. None

B. One

C. Two

D. Three

E. More than three

179. What is true of the following method?

```
public String getColor() {
   return color;
}
```

A. It is a correctly implemented accessor method.

B. It is a correctly implemented mutator method.

C. It is an incorrectly implemented accessor method.

D. It is an incorrectly implemented mutator method.

E. None of the above.

180. Which statement is true?

A. You can always change a method signature from `call(String[] arg)` to `call(String... arg)` without causing a compiler error in the calling code.

B. You can always change a method signature from `call(String... arg)` to `call(String[] arg)` without causing a compiler error in the existing code.

C. Both of the above.

D. Neither of the above.

181. What are two motivations for marking a class `final`? (Choose two.)

    A. Guarantee behavior of a class

    B. Allow the class to be extended

    C. Improve security

    D. Support polymorphism

    E. Improve performance

    F. Ensure the contents of the class are immutable

182. Which statement about the following interface is correct?

```
public interface Planet {
    int circumference;
    public abstract void enterAtmosphere();
    public default int getCircumference() {
        enterAtmosphere();
        return circumference;
    }
    private static void leaveOrbit() {
        var earth = new Planet() {
            public void enterAtmosphere() {}
        };
        earth.getCircumference();
    }
}
```

    A. The code compiles.

    B. The method `enterAtmosphere()` does not compile.

    C. The method `getCircumference()` does not compile.

    D. The method `leaveOrbit()` does not compile.

    E. The code does not compile for a different reason.

    F. None of the above.

183. Fill in the blanks: _____ methods always have the same name but a different list of parameters, while _____ methods always have the same name and the same return type.

    A. Overloaded, overridden

    B. Inherited, overridden

    C. Overridden, overloaded

    D. Hidden, overloaded

    E. Overridden, hidden

    F. None of the above

184. What is the output of the following program?

```java
public class Husky {
    { this.food = 10; }
    { this.toy = 2; }
    private final int toy;
    private static int food;
    public Husky(int friend) {
        this.food += friend++;
        this.toy -= friend--;
    }
    public static void main(String... unused) {
        var h = new Husky(2);
        System.out.println(h.food+","+h.toy);
    }
}
```

A. 12,-1

B. 12,2

C. 13,-1

D. Exactly one line of this class does not compile.

E. Exactly two lines of this class do not compile.

F. None of the above.

185. Suppose you have the following code. Which of the images best represents the state of the references right before the end of the main() method, assuming garbage collection hasn't run?

```java
1:  public class Link {
2:      private String name;
3:      private Link next;
4:      public Link(String name, Link next) {
5:          this.name = name;
6:          this.next = next;
7:      }
8:      public void setNext(Link next) {
9:          this.next = next;
10:     }
11:     public Link getNext() {
12:         return next;
13:     }
14:     public static void main(String... args) {
```

```
15:        var apple = new Link("x", null);
16:        var orange = new Link("y", apple);
17:        var banana = new Link("z", orange);
18:        orange.setNext(banana);
19:        banana.setNext(orange);
20:        apple = null;
21:        banana = null;
22:    }
23: }
```

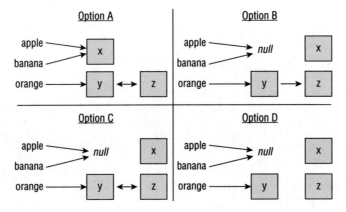

A. Option A.

B. Option B.

C. Option C.

D. Option D.

E. The code does not compile.

F. None of the above.

186. Which statement about a no-argument constructor is true?

A. The Java compiler will always insert a default no-argument constructor if you do not define a no-argument constructor in your class.

B. For a class to call super() in one of its constructors, its parent class must explicitly implement a no-argument constructor.

C. If a class extends another class that has only one constructor that takes a value, then the child class must explicitly declare at least one constructor.

D. A class may contain more than one no-argument constructor.

187. Which variable declaration is the first line not to compile?

```
public class Complex {
    class Building {}
```

```
class House extends Building{}

public void convert() {
    Building b1 =  new Building();
    House h1 = new House();
    Building b2 = new House();
    Building b3 = (House) b1;
    House h2 = (Building) h1;
    Building b4 = (Building) b2;
    House h3 = (House) b2;
}
}
```

A. b3

B. h2

C. b4

D. h3

E. All of the lines compile.

188. What is the output of the following application?

```
1:  interface Tasty {
2:     default void eat() {
3:        System.out.print("Spoiled!");
4:     } }
5:  public class ApplePicking {
6:     public static void main(String[] food) {
7:        var apple = new Tasty() {
8:           @Override
9:           void eat() {
10:             System.out.print("Yummy!");
11:          }
12:       }
13:    } }
```

A. Spoiled!

B. Yummy!

C. The application completes without printing anything.

D. One line of this application fails to compile.

E. Two lines of this application fail to compile.

F. None of the above.

189. Which of the following statements about functional interfaces is true?

A. It is possible to define a functional interface that returns two data types.

B. It is possible to define a primitive functional interface that uses `float`, `char`, or `short`.

C. All functional interfaces must take arguments or return a value.

D. None of the primitive functional interfaces includes generic arguments.

E. None of these statements is true.

190. What is the result of executing the `Tortoise` program?

```java
// Hare.java
package com.mammal;

public class Hare {
    void init() {
        System.out.print("init-");
    }
    protected void race() {
        System.out.print("hare-");
    }
}
```

```java
// Tortoise.java
package com.reptile;
import com.mammal.Hare;

public class Tortoise {
    protected void race(Hare hare) {
        hare.init();     // x1
        hare.race();     // x2
        System.out.print("tortoise-");
    }
    public static void main(String[] args) {
        var tortoise = new Tortoise();
        var hare = new Hare();
        tortoise.race(hare);
    }
}
```

A. `init-hare-tortoise`

B. `init-hare`

C. The first line with a compiler error is line `x1`.

D. The first line with a compiler error is line `x2`.

E. The code does not compile due to a different line.

F. The code throws an exception.

191. How many lines of the following program do not compile?

```java
interface Tool {
    void use(int fun);
}
abstract class Childcare {
    abstract void use(int fun);
}
final public class Stroller extends Childcare implements Tool {
    final public void use(int fun) {
        int width = 5;
        class ParkVisit {
            int getValue() { return width + fun; }
        }
        System.out.print(new ParkVisit().getValue());
    }
}
```

A. Zero

B. One

C. Two

D. Three

E. More than three

192. What is the result of executing the Sounds program?

```java
// Sheep.java
package com.mammal;

public class Sheep {
    default void baa() {
        System.out.println("baa!");
    }
    default void speak() {
        baa();
    }
}


// Sounds.java
package com.animals;
import com.mammal.Sheep;
```

```
public class Sounds {
    public static void main(String[] args) {
        var sheep = new Sheep();
        sheep.speak();
    }
}
```

A. The code runs and prints baa!.

B. The Sheep class does not compile.

C. The Sounds class does not compile.

D. Neither class compiles.

193. What is the best reason for marking an existing static method private within in an interface?

A. It allows the method to be overridden in a subclass.

B. It hides the secret implementation details from another developer using the interface.

C. It improves the visibility of the method.

D. It ensures the method is not replaced with an overridden implementation at runtime.

E. It allows the method to be marked abstract.

F. Trick question! All static methods are implicitly private within an interface.

194. What is the output of the following application?

```
package jungle;
public class RainForest extends Forest {
    public RainForest(long treeCount) {
        this.treeCount = treeCount+1;
    }
    public static void main(String[] birds) {
        System.out.print(new RainForest(5).treeCount);
    }
}
class Forest {
    public long treeCount;
    public Forest(long treeCount) {
        this.treeCount = treeCount+2;
    }
}
```

A. 5

B. 6

C. 8

D. The code does not compile.

195. What is the result of compiling and executing the following class?

```java
package sports;
public class Bicycle {
   String color = "red";
   private void printColor(String color) {
      color = "purple";
      System.out.print(color);
   }
   public static void main(String[] rider) {
      new Bicycle().printColor("blue");
   }
}
```

   A. red
   B. purple
   C. blue
   D. It does not compile.

196. Given that `Short` and `Integer` extend `Number` directly, what type can be used to fill in the blank in the following class to allow it to compile?

```java
package band;

interface Horn {
   public Integer play();
}
abstract class Woodwind {
   public Short play() {
      return 3;
   }
}
public final class Saxophone extends Woodwind implements Horn {
   public _____ play() {
      return null;
   }
}
```

   A. Object
   B. Integer
   C. Short
   D. Number
   E. None of the above

197. Which statements about abstract classes and methods are correct? (Choose three.)

A. An abstract class can be extended by a `final` class.

B. An abstract method can be overridden by a `final` method.

C. An abstract class can be extended by multiple classes directly.

D. An abstract class can extend multiple classes directly.

E. An abstract class cannot implement an interface.

F. An abstract class can extend an interface.

198. Given the following enum declaration, how many lines contain compilation errors?

```
public enum Proposition {
    TRUE(1) { String getNickName() { return "RIGHT"; }},
    FALSE(2) { public String getNickName() { return "WRONG"; }},
    UNKNOWN(3) { public String getNickName() { return "LOST"; }}
    public int value;
    Proposition(int value) {
        this.value = value;
    }
    public int getValue() {
        return this.value;
    }
    protected abstract String getNickName();
}
```

A. Zero

B. One

C. Two

D. Three

E. More than three

199. Which statements about Java classes are true? (Choose three.)

A. A Java class file may include more than one `package` statement.

B. A Java class file may include more than one `import` statement.

C. A Java class file may contain more than one comment.

D. Any instance fields within a class must be defined after the class name.

E. Any instance fields within a class must be defined before the class name.

F. Java supports macros, in which fragments of code within a class may be defined inside a Java file, separate from any top-level type declaration.

200. What is the result of executing the `HopCounter` program?

```
// Hopper.java
package com.animals;

public class Hopper {
    protected void hop() {
        System.out.println("hop");
    }
}
```

```
// Grasshopper.java
package com.insect;
import com.animals.Hopper;

public class Grasshopper extends Hopper {
    public void move() {
        hop();   // p1
    }
}
```

```
// HopCounter.java
package com.insect;

public class HopCounter {
    public static void main(String[] args) {
        var hopper = new Grasshopper();
        hopper.move();   // p2
        hopper.hop();    // p3
    }
}
```

A. The code prints hop once.

B. The code prints hop twice.

C. The first compiler error is on line p1.

D. The first compiler error is on line p2.

E. The first compiler error is on line p3.

201. Which of the following is not an attribute common to both abstract classes and interfaces?

A. They both can contain `abstract` methods.

B. They both can contain `public` methods.

C. They both can contain `protected` methods.

D. They both can contain `static` variables.

202. Given the following class, which method signature could be successfully added to the class as an overloaded version of the `findAverage()` method?

```
public class Calculations {
    public Integer findAverage(int sum) { return sum; }
}
```

A. `public Long findAverage(int sum)`

B. `public Long findAverage(int sum, int divisor)`

C. `public Integer average(int sum)`

D. `private void findAverage(int sum)`

203. Which of the following is a valid method name in Java? (Choose two.)

A. `Go_$Outside$2()`

B. `have-Fun()`

C. `new()`

D. `9enjoyTheWeather()`

E. `$sprint()`

F. `walk#()`

204. Fill in the blanks: A functional interface must contain or inherit _____ and may optionally include _____.

A. at least one `abstract` method, the `@Override` annotation

B. exactly one method, `static` methods

C. exactly one `abstract` method, the `@FunctionalInterface` annotation

D. at least one `static` method, at most one `default` method

E. None of the above

205. Fill in the blank with the line of code that allows the program to compile and print 15 at runtime.

```
package love;
interface Sport {
    private int play() { return 15; }
}
interface Tennis extends Sport {
    private int play() { return 30; }
}
public class Game implements Tennis {
```

```
public int play() { return _____; }
public static void main(String... ace) {
    System.out.println(new Game().play());
} }
```

A. `Sport.play()`

B. `Sport.super.play()`

C. `Sport.Tennis.play()`

D. `Tennis.Sport.super.play()`

E. The code does not compile regardless of what is inserted into the blank.

F. None of the above.

206. What is the output of the following program?

```
public class MoreMusic {
    {
        System.out.print("do-");
        System.out.print("re-");
    }

    public MoreMusic() {
        System.out.print("mi-");
    }
    public MoreMusic(int note) {
        this(null);
        System.out.print("fa-");
    }
    public MoreMusic(String song) {
        this(9);
        System.out.print("so-");
    }

    public static void main(String[] sound) {
        System.out.print("la-");
        var play = new MoreMusic(1);
    }
}
```

A. `la-do-re-mi-so-fa-`

B. `la-do-re-mi-fa-`

C. `do-re-mi-fa-so-la-`

D. `fa-re-do-mi-so-`

E. The code does not compile.

F. None of the above.

207. Given the following two classes in the same package, what is the result of executing the Hug program?

```
public class Kitten {
    /** private **/ float cuteness;
    /* public */ String name;
    // default double age;
    void meow() { System.out.println(name + " - "+cuteness); }
}

public class Hug {
    public static void main(String... friends) {
        var k = new Kitten();
        k.cuteness = 5;
        k.name = "kitty";
        k.meow();
    }
}
```

A. `kitty - 5.0`

B. The `Kitten` class does not compile.

C. The Hug class does not compile.

D. The `Kitten` and Hug classes do not compile.

E. None of the above.

208. Which expressions about enums used in `switch` statements are correct? (Choose two.)

A. The name of the enum type must not be used in each `case` statement.

B. A `switch` statement that takes a enum value may not use `ordinal()` numbers as `case` statement matching values.

C. The name of the enum type must be used in each `case` statement.

D. Every value of the enum must be present in a `case` statement.

E. A `switch` statement that takes a enum value can use `ordinal()` numbers as `case` statement matching values.

F. Every value of the enum must be present in a `case` statement unless a `default` branch is provided.

209. What is the output of the following application?

```
package prepare;
interface Ready {
    static int first = 2;
    final short DEFAULT_VALUE = 10;
    GetSet go = new GetSet();        // n1
}
```

```java
public class GetSet implements Ready {
   int first = 5;
   static int second = DEFAULT_VALUE;    // n2
   public static void main(String[] begin) {
      var r = new Ready() {};
      System.out.print(r.first);         // n3
      System.out.print(" " + second);    // n4
   }
}
```

A. 2 10

B. 5 10

C. The code does not compile because of line n1.

D. The code does not compile because of line n2.

E. The code does not compile because of line n3.

F. The code does not compile because of line n4.

210. What is the result of executing the Tortoise program?

```java
// Hare.java
package com.mammal;

public class Hare {
   public void init() {
      System.out.print("init-");
   }
   private void race() {
      System.out.print("hare-");
   }
}
```

```java
// Tortoise.java
package com.reptile;
import com.mammal.Hare;

public class Tortoise {
   protected void race(Hare hare) {
      hare.init();     // x1
      hare.race();     // x2
      System.out.print("tortoise-");
   }
   public static void main(String[] args) {
```

```
        var tortoise = new Tortoise();
        var hare = new Hare();
        tortoise.race(hare);
    }
}
```

A. `init-hare-tortoise`

B. `init-hare`

C. The first line with a compiler error is `line x1`.

D. The first line with a compiler error is `line x2`.

E. The code does not compile due to a different line.

F. The code throws an exception.

211. What is the result of executing the Sounds program?

```
// Sheep.java
package com.mammal;

public class Sheep {
    private void baa() {
        System.out.println("baa!");
    }
    private static void speak() {
        baa();
    }
}
```

```
// Sounds.java
package com.animals;
import com.mammal.Sheep;

public class Sounds {
    public static void main(String[] args) {
        var sheep = new Sheep();
        sheep.speak();
    }
}
```

A. The code runs and prints `baa!`.

B. The `Sheep` class does not compile.

C. The `Sounds` class does not compile.

D. Neither class compiles.

212. What is the output of the `Helicopter` program?

```
package flying;

class Rotorcraft {
   protected final int height = 5;
   abstract int fly();
}
interface CanFly {}
public class Helicopter extends Rotorcraft implements CanFly {
   private int height = 10;
   protected int fly() {
      return super.height;
   }
   public static void main(String[] unused) {
      Helicopter h = (Helicopter)new Rotorcraft();
      System.out.print(h.fly());
   }
}
```

A. 5

B. 10

C. The code does not compile.

D. The code compiles but produces a `ClassCastException` at runtime.

E. None of the above.

213. Which statements about the following `Twins` class are true? (Choose three.)

```
package clone;
interface Alex {
   default void write() { System.out.print("1"); }
   static void publish() {}
   void think();
   private int process() { return 80; }
}
interface Michael {
   default void write() { System.out.print("2"); }
   static void publish() {}
   void think();
   private int study() { return 100; }
}
public class Twins implements Alex, Michael {
```

```
    void write() { System.out.print("3"); }
    static void publish() {}
    void think() {
        System.out.print("Thinking...");
    }
}
```

A. The class fails to compile because of the `write()` method.

B. The class fails to compile because of the `publish()` method.

C. The class fails to compile because of the `think()` method.

D. All of the methods defined in the `Alex` interface are accessible in the `Twins` class.

E. All of the methods defined in the `Michael` interface are accessible in the `Twins` class.

F. The `Twins` class cannot be marked `abstract`.

214. Given the following program, what is the first line to fail to compile?

```
1: public class Electricity {
2:     interface Power {}
3:     public static void main(String[] light) {
4:         class Source implements Power {};
5:         final class Super extends Source {};
6:         var start = new Super() {};
7:         var end = new Source() { static boolean t = true; };
8:     }
9: }
```

A. Line 2

B. Line 4

C. Line 5

D. Line 6

E. Line 7

F. All of the lines compile

215. What is the output of the following application?

```
package prepare;
public class Ready {
    protected static int first = 2;
    private final short DEFAULT_VALUE = 10;
    private static class GetSet {
        int first = 5;
        static int second = DEFAULT_VALUE;
    }
    private GetSet go = new GetSet();
    public static void main(String[] begin) {
```

```
        Ready r = new Ready();
        System.out.print(r.go.first);
        System.out.print(", "+r.go.second);
    }
}
```

A. 2, 5

B. 5, 10

C. 2, 10

D. The code does not compile because of the GetSet class declaration.

E. The code does not compile for another reason.

216. Which of the following are true about the following code? (Choose two.)

```
public class Values {
    static ____ defaultValue = 8;
    static ____ DEFAULT_VALUE;

    public static void main(String[] args) {
        System.out.println(defaultValue + DEFAULT_VALUE);
    }
}
```

A. When you fill in both blanks with double, it prints 8.00.0

B. When you fill in both blanks with double, it prints 8.0

C. When you fill in both blanks with int, it prints 8

D. When you fill in both blanks with int, it prints 80

E. When you fill in both blanks with var, it prints 8

F. When you fill in both blanks with var, it prints 80

217. How many Gems objects are eligible for garbage collection right before the end of the main() method?

```
public class Gems {
    public String name;
    public Gems(String name) {
        this.name = name;
    }
    public static void main(String... args) {
        var g1 = Gems("Garnet");
        var g2 = Gems("Amethyst");
        var g3 = Gems("Pearl");
        var g4 = Gems("Steven");
        g2 = g3;
        g3 = g2;
```

```
        g1 = g2;
        g4 = null;
    }
}
```

A. None

B. One

C. Two

D. Three

E. Four

F. The code does not compile

218. How many lines of the following program contain compilation errors?

```
package sky;
public class Stars {
    private int inThe = 4;
    public void Stars() {
        super();
    }
    public Stars(int inThe) {
        this.inThe = this.inThe;
    }
    public static void main(String[] endless) {
        System.out.print(new sky.Stars(2).inThe);
    }
}
```

A. None

B. One

C. Two

D. Three

219. What is the output of the following application?

```
package sports;
abstract class Ball {
    protected final int size;
    public Ball(int size) {
        this.size = size;
    }
}
interface Equipment {}
public class SoccerBall extends Ball implements Equipment {
```

```
        public SoccerBall() {
            super(5);
        }
        public Ball get() { return this; }
        public static void main(String[] passes) {
            var equipment = (Equipment)(Ball)new SoccerBall().get();
            System.out.print(((SoccerBall)equipment).size);
        }
    }
```

A. 5

B. The code does not compile due to an invalid cast.

C. The code does not compile for a different reason.

D. The code compiles but throws a ClassCastException at runtime.

220. Which statement about the Elephant program is correct?

```
package stampede;
interface Long {
    Number length();
}
public class Elephant {
    public class Trunk implements Long {
        public Number length() { return 6; }    // k1
    }
    public class MyTrunk extends Trunk {         // k2
        public Integer length() { return 9; }   // k3
    }
    public static void charge() {
        System.out.print(new MyTrunk().length());
    }
    public static void main(String[] cute) {
        new Elephant().charge();                 // k4
    }
}
```

A. It compiles and prints 6.

B. The code does not compile because of line k1.

C. The code does not compile because of line k2.

D. The code does not compile because of line k3.

E. The code does not compile because of line k4.

F. None of the above.

Chapter

4

Exception Handling

THE OCP EXAM TOPICS COVERED IN THIS PRACTICE TEST INCLUDE THE FOLLOWING:

✓ **Exception Handling**

- Handle exceptions using try/catch/finally clauses, try-with-resource, and multi-catch statements
- Create and use custom exceptions

1. Fill in the blanks: The _____ keyword is used in method declarations, while the _____ keyword is used to send an exception to the surrounding process.

    A. throwing, catch

    B. throws, throw

    C. catch, throw

    D. throws, catch

    E. throw, throws

    F. catch, throwing

2. What is the result of compiling and executing the following application?

```
package mind;
import java.io.*;
public class Remember {
    public static void think() throws IOException {  // k1
        try {
            throw Exception();
        } catch (RuntimeException r) {}              // k2
    }
    public static void main(String... ideas) throws Exception {
        think();
    }
}
```

    A. The code compiles and runs without printing anything.

    B. The code compiles, but a stack trace is printed at runtime.

    C. The code does not compile because of line k1.

    D. The code does not compile because of line k2.

    E. None of the above.

3. Given the following keywords, in which order could they be used? (Choose two.)

    A. try, finally

    B. catch, try, finally

    C. try, catch, catch, finally

    D. finally, catch, try

    E. try, finally, catch

    F. try, catch, finally, finally

4. Fill in the blanks: A try statement _____ a catch or a finally block, while a try-with-resources statement _____.

    A. is not required to contain, is not required to contain either

    B. is not required to contain, must contain one of them

   C.   must contain, is not required to contain either

   D.   must contain, must contain a `catch` block

   E.   None of the above.

5. What is the output of the following application?

```
package park;
class LostBallException extends Exception {}
public class Ball {
    public void toss() throw LostBallException {
        var windUp = new int[0];
        System.out.println(windUp[0]);
    }
    public static void main(String[] bouncy) {
        try {
            new Ball().toss();
        } catch (Throwable e) {
            System.out.print("Caught!");
        }
    }
}
```

   A.   `0`

   B.   `Caught!`

   C.   The code does not compile because `LostBallException` is not handled or declared in the `main()` method.

   D.   The code does not compile because `ArrayIndexOutOfBoundsException` is not handled or declared in the `toss()` method.

   E.   The code does not compile for a different reason.

   F.   None of the above.

6. Assuming `Scanner` is a valid class that implements `AutoCloseable`, what is the expected output of the following code?

```
try (Scanner s = new Scanner(System.in)) {
    System.out.print(1);
    s.nextLine();
    System.out.print(2);
    s = null;
} catch (IllegalArgumentException | NullPointerException x) {
    s.nextLine();
    System.out.print(3);
} finally {
```

```
    s.nextLine();
    System.out.print(4);
}
System.out.print(5);
```

A. 1245

B. 125

C. 1234 followed by a stack trace

D. 124 followed by a stack trace

E. Does not compile

F. None of the above

7. How many constructors in `WhaleSharkException` compile in the following class?

```java
package friendly;
public class WhaleSharkException extends Exception {
    public WhaleSharkException() {
        super("Friendly shark!");
    }

    public WhaleSharkException(String message) {
        super(new Exception(new WhaleSharkException()));
    }

    public WhaleSharkException(Exception cause) {}
}
```

A. None

B. One

C. Two

D. Three

8. What is the output of the following application?

```java
package game;
public class Football {
    public static void main(String officials[]) {
        try {
            System.out.print('A');
            throw new ArrayIndexOutOfBoundsException();
        } catch (RuntimeException r) {
            System.out.print('B');
            throw r;
```

```
        } catch (Exception e) {
            System.out.print('C');
        } finally {
            System.out.print('D');
        }
    }
}
```

- **A.** ABC
- **B.** ABD
- **C.** ABC followed by a stack trace
- **D.** ABD followed by a stack trace
- **E.** AD followed by a stack trace
- **F.** None of the above

9. Which of the following types are not recommended to catch in your application? (Choose two.)

- **A.** Exception
- **B.** CheckedException
- **C.** Throwable
- **D.** RuntimeException
- **E.** UncheckedException
- **F.** Error

10. What is the output of the following program?

```
package buffet;
class Garden implements AutoCloseable {
    private final int g;
    Garden(int g) { this.g = g; }
    public void close() throws Exception {
        System.out.print(g);
    }
}
public class Salad {
    public static void main(String[] u) throws Exception {
        var g = new Garden(5);
        try (g;
                var h = new Garden(4);
                var i = new Garden(2)) {
        } finally {
```

```
            System.out.println(9);
         }
         g = null;
      }
   }
```

   A. 2459
   B. 9245
   C. 5429
   D. 9542
   E. The code does not compile.
   F. None of the above.

11. What is the output of the following application?

```
package paper;
import java.io.Closeable;
public class PrintCompany {
   class Printer implements Closeable {      // r1
      public void print() {
         System.out.println("This just in!");
      }
      public void close() {}
   }
   public void printHeadlines() {
      try {Printer p = new Printer()} {      // r2
         p.print();
      }
   }
   public static void main(String[] headlines) {
      new PrintCompany().printHeadlines();   // r3
   }
}
```

   A. This just in!
   B. The code does not compile because of line r1.
   C. The code does not compile because of line r2.
   D. The code does not compile because of line r3.
   E. The code does not compile for a different reason.
   F. None of the above.

12. How many of these custom exceptions are unchecked exceptions?

```
class ColoringException extends IOException {}
class CursiveException extends WritingException {}
class DrawingException extends IllegalStateException {}
class SketchingException extends DrawingException {}
class WritingException extends Exception {}
```

A. None
B. One
C. Two
D. Three
E. Four
F. Five

13. How many lines of text does the following program print?

```
package lighting;
import java.io.IOException;
public class Light {
    public static void main(String[] v) throws Exception {
        try {
            new Light().turnOn();
        } catch (RuntimeException v) {  // y1
            System.out.println(v);
            throw new IOException();     // y2
        } finally {
            System.out.println("complete");
        }
    }
    public void turnOn() throws IOException {
        new IOException("Not ready");    // y3
    }
}
```

A. One.
B. Two.
C. The code does not compile because of line y1.
D. The code does not compile because of line y2.
E. The code does not compile because of line y3.
F. None of the above.

14. Which statements about try-with-resources are false? (Choose two.)

   A.   If more than one resource is used, the resources are closed in the order they were created.

   B.   Parentheses are used for the resource declaration section, even if more than one resource is used.

   C.   If the `try` block and `close()` method both throw an exception, then the one thrown by the `close()` method is suppressed.

   D.   A resource may be declared before it is used in a try-with-resources statement.

   E.   Resources declarations are separated by commas.

   F.   A `catch` block is not required.

15. How many lines of text does the following program print?

```
package bee;
class SpellingException extends RuntimeException {}
public class SpellChecker {
    public final static void main(String... participants) {
        try {
            if(!"cat".equals("kat")) {
                new SpellingException();
            }
        } catch (SpellingException | NullPointerException e) {
            System.out.println("Spelling problem!");
        } catch (Exception e) {
            System.out.println("Unknown Problem!");
        } finally {
            System.out.println("Done!");
        }
    }
}
```

   A.   One.

   B.   Two.

   C.   Three.

   D.   The code does not compile.

   E.   None of the above.

16. Which of the following exception types must be handled or declared by the method in which they are thrown? (Choose three.)

   A.   `FileNotFoundException`

   B.   `ClassCastException`

   C.   `Error`

D. `IOException`

E. `NullPointerException`

F. `Exception`

17. What is the output of the following application?

```
package bed;
public class Sleep {
   public static void snore() {
      try {
         String sheep[] = new String[3];
         System.out.print(sheep[3]);
      } catch (RuntimeException | Error e) {
         System.out.print("Awake!");
      } finally {
         throw new Exception();                 // x1
      }
   }
   public static void main(String... sheep) {   // x2
      new Sleep().snore();                       // x3
   }
}
```

A. `Awake!`

B. `Awake!` followed by a stack trace

C. Does not compile because of line x1

D. Does not compile because of line x2

E. Does not compile because of line x3

F. None of the above

18. What is the output of the following code?

```
class ProblemException extends Exception {
   ProblemException(Exception e) { super(e); }
}
class MajorProblemException extends ProblemException {
   MajorProblemException(String message) { super(message); }
}
public class Unfortunate {
   public static void main(String[] args) throws Exception {
      try {
         System.out.print(1);
```

```
        throw new MajorProblemException("Uh oh");
    } catch (ProblemException | RuntimeException e) {
        System.out.print(2);
        try {
            throw new MajorProblemException("yikes");
        } finally {
            System.out.print(3);
        }
    } finally {
        System.out.print(4);
    }
  }
}
```

A. 123

B. 123 followed by an exception stack trace.

C. 1234

D. 1234 followed by an exception stack trace.

E. The code does not compile.

F. None of the above.

19. Which statement best describes how a class that implements the `AutoCloseable` interface should be written? (Choose two.)

A. The `close()` method is optional since the `AutoCloseable` interface defines a `default` implementation.

B. The `close()` method should avoid modifying data after it has been run once.

C. The `close()` method should not throw any exceptions.

D. The `close()` method should throw an exception if there is a problem closing the resource.

E. The `close()` method should return a status code.

20. Which of the following diagrams of `java.lang` classes shows the inheritance model properly?

A.

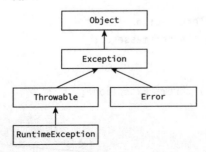

B.

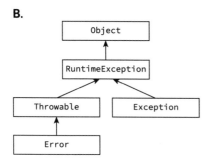

C.

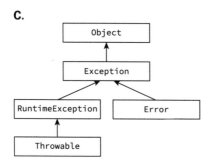

D.

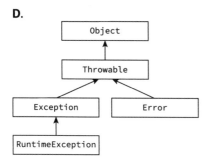

21. Which exception classes, when inserted into the blank in the `Problems` class, allow the code to compile?

```
class MissingMoneyException {}
class MissingFoodException {}
public class Problems {
    public void doIHaveAProblem()
            throws MissingMoneyException, MissingFoodException {
        System.out.println("No problems");
    }
    public static void main(String[] s) throws _____ {
        try {
```

```
          final Problems p = new Problems();
          p.doIHaveAProblem();
       } catch (Exception e) {
          throw e;
       } } }
```

A. Exception

B. RuntimeException

C. MissingFoodException

D. MissingMoneyException, MissingFoodException

E. MissingMoneyException

F. None of the above

22. Which statements about Closeable and AutoCloseable are true? (Choose two.)

   A. AutoCloseable extends Closeable.

   B. Closeable extends AutoCloseable.

   C. The close() method in a class that implements AutoCloseable cannot throw an IOException.

   D. The close() method in a class that implements Closeable cannot throw an Exception.

   E. There is no difference; one was added for backward compatibility.

   F. Both have a generic return type.

23. Which expressions, when inserted into the blank in the following class, allow the code to compile? (Choose two.)

```
package sun;
import java.io.*;
public class Beach {
   class TideException extends Exception {}
   public void surf() throws RuntimeException {
      try {
         throw new TideException();
      } catch (_____) {}
   }
}
```

   A. Exception a | RuntimeException f

   B. IllegalStateException | TideException t

   C. TideException | IOException i

   D. TideException | Exception x

   E. Error e

   F. Exception z

24. Which of the following are the best scenarios in which to use and catch an exception? (Choose two.)

    A. The computer caught fire.

    B. A network connection goes down.

    C. A caller passes invalid data to a method.

    D. The code does not compile.

    E. A method finishes sooner than expected.

    F. The program runs out of memory.

25. Which statement about the following program is correct?

```
1:  package dogpark;
2:  public class Fetch {
3:      public int play(String name) throws RuntimeException {
4:          try {
5:              throw new RuntimeException(name);
6:          } catch (Throwable e) {
7:              throw new RuntimeException(e);
8:          }
9:      }
10:     public static final void main(String[] ball)
11:             throws RuntimeException {
12:         new Fetch().play("Webby");
13:         new Fetch().play("Georgette");
14:     }
15: }
```

    A. One exception is thrown to the caller at runtime.

    B. Two exceptions are thrown to the caller at runtime.

    C. More than two exceptions are thrown to the caller at runtime.

    D. The class does not compile because of the `play()` method.

    E. The class does not compile because of the `main()` method.

    F. None of the above.

26. What is the output of the following application?

```
package body;
import java.io.IOException;
class Organ {
    public void operate() throws IOException {
        throw new RuntimeException("Not supported");
    }
```

```
    }
public class Heart extends Organ {
    public void operate() throws Exception {
        System.out.print("beat");
    }
    public static void main(String... c) throws Exception {
        try {
            new Heart().operate();
        } finally {
            System.out.print("!");
        }
    }
}
```

A. beat

B. beat!

C. Not supported

D. The code does not compile.

E. The code compiles, but a stack trace is printed at runtime.

F. None of the above.

27. Which of the following are not true of using a try-with-resources statement? (Choose two.)

A. It shortens the amount of code a developer must write.

B. It is possible to close a resource before the end of the `try` block.

C. Associated `catch` blocks are run before the declared resources have been closed.

D. It is compatible with all classes that implement the `Closeable` interface.

E. It is compatible with all classes that implement the `AutoCloseable` interface.

F. It cannot be used with a `finally` block.

28. What is the result of compiling and executing the following class?

```
package wind;
public class Storm {
    public static void main(String... rain) throws Exception {
        var weatherTracker = new AutoCloseable() {
            public void close() throws RuntimeException {
                System.out.println("Thunder");
            }
        };
        try (weatherTracker) {
            System.out.println("Tracking");
```

```
        } catch (Exception e) {
            System.out.println("Lightning");
        } finally {
            System.out.println("Storm gone");
            weatherTracker.close();
        }
    } }
```

A. It prints one line.

B. It prints two lines.

C. It prints three lines.

D. It prints four lines.

E. It does not compile due to an error in the declaration of the `weatherTracker` resource.

F. It does not compile for a different reason.

29. How many of the following are valid exception declarations?

```
class Error extends Exception {}
class _X extends IllegalArgumentException {}
class 2BeOrNot2Be extends RuntimeException {}
class NumberException<Integer> extends NumberFormatException {}
interface Worry implements NumberFormatException {}
```

A. Zero

B. One

C. Two

D. Three

E. Four

F. Five

30. If a `try` statement has `catch` blocks for both `ClassCastException` and `RuntimeException`, then which of the following statements is correct?

A. The `catch` blocks for these two exception types can be declared in any order.

B. A `try` statement cannot be declared with these two `catch` block types because they are incompatible.

C. The `catch` block for `ClassCastException` must appear before the `catch` block for `RuntimeException`.

D. The `catch` block for `RuntimeException` must appear before the `catch` block for `ClassCastException`.

E. None of the above.

31. Assuming Scanner is a valid class that implements AutoCloseable, what is the expected output of the following application?

```
package castles;
import java.util.Scanner;
public class Fortress {
    public void openDrawbridge() throws Exception {  // p1
        try {
            throw new Exception("Circle");           // p2
        } catch (Exception | Error e) {
            System.out.print("Opening!");
        } finally {
            System.out.print("Walls");
        }
    }
    public static void main(String[] moat) {
        try (var e = new Scanner(System.in)) {
            new Fortress().openDrawbridge();          // p3
        }
    }
}
```

A. Opening!Walls

B. The code does not compile because of line p1.

C. The code does not compile because of line p2.

D. The code does not compile because of line p3.

E. The code compiles, but a stack trace is printed at runtime.

F. None of the above.

32. What is the output of the following application?

```
package game;
public class BasketBall {
    public static void main(String[] dribble) {
        try {
            System.out.print(1);
            throw new ClassCastException();
        } catch (ArrayIndexOutOfBoundsException ex) {
            System.out.print(2);
        } catch (Throwable ex) {
```

```
            System.out.print(3);
        } finally {
            System.out.print(4);
        }
        System.out.print(5);
    }
}
```

A. 145

B. 1345

C. 1235

D. The code does not compile.

E. The code compiles but throws an exception at runtime.

F. None of the above.

33. Which of the following statements about `finally` blocks are true? (Choose two.)

    A. Every line of the `finally` block is guaranteed to be executed.

    B. The `finally` block is executed only if the related `catch` block is also executed.

    C. The `finally` statement requires curly braces, {}.

    D. A `finally` block cannot throw an exception.

    E. The first line of a `finally` block is guaranteed to be executed.

    F. A `finally` block can only throw unchecked exceptions.

34. What is the output of the following application?

```
package signlanguage;
import java.io.Closeable;
class ReadSign implements Closeable {
    public void close() {}
    public String get() {return "Hello";}
}
class MakeSign implements AutoCloseable {
    public void close() {}
    public void send(String message) {
        System.out.print(message);
    }
}
public class Translate {
    public static void main(String... hands) {
        try (ReadSign r = new ReadSign();
```

```
            MakeSign w = new MakeSign();) {
            w.send(r.get());
        }
    }
}
```

A. `Hello`

B. The code does not compile because of the `ReadSign` class.

C. The code does not compile because of the `MakeSign` class.

D. The code does not compile because of the `Translate` class.

E. The code docs not compile because of the try-with-resources statement.

F. None of the above.

35. What is the output of the following application?

```
package what;
class FunEvent implements AutoCloseable {
    private final int value;
    FunEvent(int value) { this.value = value; }
    public void close() {
        System.out.print(value);
    }
}
public class Happening {
    public static void main(String... lots) {
        FunEvent e = new FunEvent(1);
        try (e; var f = new FunEvent(8)) {
            System.out.print("2");
            throw new ArithmeticException();
        } catch (Exception x) {
            System.out.print("3");
        } finally {
            System.out.print("4");
        }
    } }
```

A. 24

B. 21834

C. 23418

D. 23481

E. 28134

F. The code does not compile.

36. What is the output of the following application?

```java
package office;
import java.io.*;
public class Printer {
   public void print() {
      try {
         throw new FileNotFoundException();
      } catch (Exception | RuntimeException e) {
         System.out.print("Z");
      } catch (Throwable f) {
         System.out.print("X");
      } finally {
         System.out.print("Y");
      }
   }

   public static void main(String... ink) {
      new Printer().print();
   }
}
```

A. Y

B. XY

C. ZY

D. The code does not compile.

E. The code compiles, but a stack trace is printed at runtime.

F. None of the above.

37. What is the output of the following code?

```java
class ProblemException extends Exception {
   ProblemException(Exception e) { super(e); }
}
class MajorProblemException extends ProblemException {
   MajorProblemException(Exception e) { super(e); }
}
public class Unfortunate {
   public static void main(String[] args) throws Exception {
      try {
         System.out.print(1);
         throw new MajorProblemException(
            new IllegalStateException());
```

```
    } catch (ProblemException | RuntimeException e) {
        System.out.print(2);
        try {
            throw new MajorProblemException(e);
        } finally {
            System.out.print(3);
        }
    } finally {
        System.out.print(4);
    }
}
}
```

A. 123

B. 123 followed by an exception stack trace

C. 1234

D. 1234 followed by an exception stack trace

E. Does not compile

F. None of the above

38. What is the output of the following application?

```
1:  package robot;
2:  public class Computer {
3:      public void compute() throws Exception {
4:          throw new NullPointerException("Does not compute!");
5:      }
6:      public static void main(String[] b) throws Exception {
7:          try {
8:              new Computer().compute();
9:          } catch (RuntimeException e) {
10:             System.out.print("zero");
11:             throw e;
12:         } catch (Exception e) {
13:             System.out.print("one");
14:             throw e;
15:         }
16:     }
17: }
```

A. zero

B. one

C. zero followed by a stack trace

    D. one followed by a stack trace

    E. Does not compile

    F. None of the above

39. Given the following class diagram, which two classes are missing in the hierarchy at positions 1 and 2?

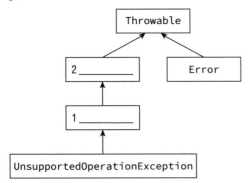

    A. `IOException` at position 1, `Exception` at position 2

    B. `Exception` at position 1, `RuntimeException` at position 2

    C. `IllegalArgumentException` at position 1, `RuntimeException` at position 2

    D. `IllegalStateException` at position 1, `RuntimeException` at position 2

    E. `Exception` at position 1, `FileNotFoundException` at position 2

    F. None of the above

40. What is the output of the following application?

```
package vortex;
class TimeException extends Exception {}
class TimeMachine implements AutoCloseable {
    int v;
    public TimeMachine(int v) {this.v = v;}
    public void close() throws Exception {
        System.out.print(v);
    } }
public class TimeTraveler {
    public static void main(String[] twelve) {
        try (var timeSled = new TimeMachine(1);
                var delorean = new TimeMachine(2);
                var tardis = new TimeMachine(3)) {
        } catch (TimeException e) {
            System.out.print(4);
        } finally {
```

```
        System.out.print(5);
      }
  } }
```

A. 1235

B. 3215

C. 5123

D. 5321

E. The code does not compile.

F. None of the above.

41. Which of the following are common reasons to add a checked exception to a method signature? (Choose three.)

A. To alert developers that the state of the JVM has been corrupted

B. To force a caller to handle or declare potential problems

C. To ensure that exceptions never cause the application to terminate

D. To notify the caller of potential types of problems

E. To give the caller a chance to recover from a problem

F. To annoy other developers

42. Which statement about the following application is correct?

```
package highway;
import java.io.*;
class CarCrash extends RuntimeException {
   CarCrash(Exception e) {}                                    // w1
}
public class Car {
   public static void main(String[] s) throws Exception { // w2
      try {
         throw new IOException("Auto-pilot error");
      } catch (Exception | CarCrash e) {                     // w3
         throw e;
      } catch (Exception a) {                                // w4
         throw a;
      }
   }
}
```

A. The code does not compile because of line w1.

B. The code does not compile because of line w2.

C. The code does not compile because of line w3.

D. The code does not compile because of line w4.

E. The code compiles and prints a stack trace at runtime.

F. None of the above.

43. Which of the following exception classes must be handled or declared in the method in which they are thrown? (Choose three.)

```
public class Happy extends IOException {}
public class Dopey extends Grumpy {}
public class Sleepy extends IllegalStateException {}
public class Sneezy extends UnsupportedOperationException {}
public class Doc extends AssertionError {}
public class Grumpy extends SQLException {}
```

A. Happy

B. Dopey

C. Sleepy

D. Sneezy

E. Doc

F. Grumpy

44. What is the output of the following application?

```
package pond;
abstract class Duck {
    protected int count;
    public abstract int getDuckies();
}
public class Ducklings extends Duck {
    private int age;
    public Ducklings(int age) { this.age = age; }
    public int getDuckies() { return this.age/count; }
    public static void main(String[] pondInfo) {
        Duck itQuacks = new Ducklings(5);
        System.out.print(itQuacks.getDuckies());
    }
}
```

A. 0

B. 1

C. 5

D. The code does not compile.

E. The code compiles but throws an exception at runtime.

F. None of the above.

45. Which statements about the following line of code are correct? (Choose three.)

```
throw new IllegalArgumentException ();
```

A. The method where this is called must declare a compatible exception.

B. The code where this is called can include a try-with-resources block that handles this exception.

C. This exception should not be handled or declared.

D. The code where this is called can include a `try/catch` block that handles this exception.

E. This exception should be thrown only at the start of a method.

F. This exception does not need to be handled by the method in which it is called.

46. What is the output of the following application?

```java
package storage;
import java.io.*;
public class Backup {
    public void performBackup() {
        try {
            throw new IOException("Disk not found");   // z1
        } catch (Exception e) {
            try {
                throw new FileNotFoundException("File not found");
            } catch (FileNotFoundException e) {        // z2
                System.out.print("Failed");
            }
        }
    }
    public static void main(String... files) {
        new Backup().performBackup();                  // z2
    }
}
```

A. `Failed`

B. The application compiles, but a stack trace is printed at runtime.

C. The code does not compile because of line z1.

D. The code does not compile because of line z2.

E. The code does not compile because of line z3.

F. None of the above.

47. What is the output of the following?

```java
package com.tps;
import java.io.IOException;
public class IncidentReportException extends RuntimeException {
```

```
   public static void main(String[] args) throws Exception {
      try {
         throw new IncidentReportException(new IOException());
      } catch (RuntimeException e) {
         System.out.println(e.getCause());
      }
   }
}
```

A. `com.tps.IncidentReportException`

B. `java.lang.IOException`

C. The code does not compile because `IOException` is a checked exception.

D. The code does not compile due to the declaration of `IncidentReportException`.

E. None of the above.

48. Which expression, when inserted into the blank in the following class, allows the code to compile?

```
package music;
import java.sql.*;
public class Bells {
   class Player implements AutoCloseable {
      @Override public void close() throws RingException {}
   }
   class RingException extends Exception {
      public RingException(String message) {}
   }
   public static void main(String[] notes) throws Throwable {
      try (Player p = null) {
         throw new Exception();
      } catch (Exception e) {
      } catch (_____) {
      }
   }
}
```

A. `Error r`

B. `IllegalStateException b`

C. `RingException q`

D. `SQLException p`

E. `RuntimeException r`

F. The code does not compile regardless of the expression used.

49. What is the output of the following application?

```
package zoo;
class BigCat {
    void roar(int level) throw RuntimeException {
        if(level<3) throw new IllegalArgumentException();
        System.out.print("Roar!");
    }
}
public class Lion extends BigCat {
    public void roar() {
        System.out.print("Roar!!!");
    }
    void roar(int sound) {
        System.out.print("Meow");
    }
    public static void main(String[] cubs) {
        final BigCat kitty = new Lion();
        kitty.roar(2);
    }
}
```

A. Meow

B. Roar!

C. Roar!!!

D. MeowRoar!

E. A stack trace is printed at runtime.

F. None of the above.

50. Which statement about the following program is true?

```
package tag;
class MissedCallException extends Exception {}
public class Phone {
    static void makeCall() throws RuntimeException {
        throw new ArrayIndexOutOfBoundsException("Call");
    }
    public static void main(String[] messages) {
        try {
            makeCall();
        } catch (MissedCallException e) {
            throw new RuntimeException("Voicemail");
```

```
      } finally {
         throw new RuntimeException("Text");
      }
   }
}
```

A. An exception is printed at runtime with `Call` in the message.

B. An exception is printed at runtime with `Voicemail` in the message.

C. An exception is printed at runtime with `Text` in the message.

D. The code does not compile.

E. None of the above.

51. If a try statement has `catch` blocks for both `IllegalArgumentException` and `NullPointerException`, then which of the following statements is correct?

A. The `catch` blocks for these two exception types can be declared in any order.

B. A `try` statement cannot be declared with these two `catch` block types because they are incompatible.

C. The catch block for `IllegalArgumentException` must appear before the catch block for `NullPointerException`.

D. The `catch` block for `NullPointerException` must appear before the catch block for `IllegalArgumentException`.

E. None of the above.

52. What is the output of the following application?

```
package furniture;
class Chair {
   public void sit() throws IllegalArgumentException {
      System.out.print("creek");
      throw new RuntimeException();
   }
}
public class Stool extends Chair {
   public void sit() throws RuntimeException {
      System.out.print("thud");
   }
   public static void main(String... c) throws Exception {
      try {
         new Stool().sit();
      } finally {
         System.out.print("?");
      }
   }
}
```

A. creek

B. thud

C. thud?

D. The code does not compile.

E. The code compiles, but a stack trace is printed at runtime.

F. None of the above.

53. What is the output of the following application?

```java
import java.io.*;
import java.sql.*;
public class DatabaseHelper {
    static class MyDatabase implements Closeable {
        public void close() throws SQLException {
            System.out.print("2");
        }
        public void write(String data) {}
        public String read() {return null;}
    }
    public static void main(String... files) throws Exception {
        try (MyDatabase myDb = new MyDatabase()) {
            // TODO: Decide what to read/rite
        } finally {
            System.out.print("1");
        }
    }
}
```

A. 12

B. 21

C. The code does not compile because of the `MyDatabase` nested class.

D. The code does not compile because of the try-with-resources statement.

E. The code does not compile for a different reason.

54. What constructors are capable of being called on a custom exception class that directly extends the `Exception` class?

A. One that takes a single `Exception`

B. One that takes a single `String`

C. Both of these

D. Neither of these

55. What is the result of compiling and running the following application?

```java
package dinner;
public class Pizza {
    Exception order(RuntimeException e) {        // h1
        throw e;                                  // h2
    }
    public static void main(String... u) {
        var p = new Pizza();
        try {
            p.order(new IllegalArgumentException()); // h3
        } catch(RuntimeException e) {              // h4
            System.out.print(e);
        }
    }
}
```

- **A.** `java.lang.IllegalArgumentException` is printed.
- **B.** The code does not compile because of line h1.
- **C.** The code does not compile because of line h2.
- **D.** The code does not compile because of line h3.
- **E.** The code does not compile because of line h4.
- **F.** The code compiles, but a stack trace is printed at runtime.

56. Given an application that hosts a website, which of the following would most likely result in a `java.lang.Error` being thrown? (Choose two.)

- **A.** A user tries to sign in too many times.
- **B.** Two users try to register an account at the same time.
- **C.** An order update page calls itself infinitely.
- **D.** The application temporarily loses connection to the network.
- **E.** A user enters their password incorrectly.
- **F.** The connections to a database are never released and keep accumulating.

57. How many lines of text does the following program print?

```java
package tron;
class DiskPlayer implements AutoCloseable {
    public void close() {}
}
```

```
public class LightCycle {
    public static void main(String... bits) {
        try (DiskPlayer john = new DiskPlayer()) {
            System.out.println("ping");
            john.close();
        } finally {
            System.out.println("pong");
            john.close();
        }
        System.out.println("return");
    }
}
```

A. One.

B. Two.

C. Three.

D. The code does not compile because of the DiskPlayer class.

E. The code does not compile for a different reason.

F. None of the above.

58. What is the output of the following?

```
package com.tps;
import java.io.IOException;
public class IncidentReportException extends RuntimeException {
    public IncidentReportException(Exception e) {
        super(e);
    }
    public static void main(String[] args) throws Exception {
        try {
            throw new IncidentReportException(new IOException());
        } catch (RuntimeException e) {
            System.out.println(e.getCause());
        }
    }
}
```

A. com.tps.IncidentReportException

B. java.lang.IOException

C. The code does not compile because IOException is a checked exception.

D. The code does not compile due to the declaration of IncidentReportException.

E. None of the above.

59. Given the following application, what is the name of the class printed at line e1?

```
package canyon;
final class FallenException extends Exception {}
final class HikingGear implements AutoCloseable {
    @Override public void close() throws Exception {
        throw new FallenException();
    }
}
public class Cliff {
    public final void climb() throws Exception {
        try (HikingGear gear = new HikingGear()) {
            throw new RuntimeException();
        }
    }
    public static void main(String... rocks) {
        try {
            new Cliff().climb();
        } catch (Throwable t) {
            System.out.println(t);   // e1
        }
    }
}
```

   A. `canyon.FallenException`
   B. `java.lang.RuntimeException`
   C. The code does not compile.
   D. The code compiles, but the answer cannot be determined until runtime.
   E. None of the above.

60. Given the following application, which specific type of exception will be printed in the stack trace at runtime?

```
package carnival;
public class WhackAnException {
    public static void main(String... hammer) {
        try {
            throw new ClassCastException();
        } catch (IllegalArgumentException e) {
            throw new IllegalArgumentException();
        } catch (RuntimeException e) {
            throw new NullPointerException();
        } finally {
```

```
        throw new RuntimeException();
    }
  }
}
```

A. ClassCastException

B. IllegalArgumentException

C. NullPointerException

D. RuntimeException

E. The code does not compile.

F. None of the above.

Chapter

5

Working with Arrays and Collections

THE OCP EXAM TOPICS COVERED IN THIS PRACTICE TEST INCLUDE THE FOLLOWING:

✓ **Working with Arrays and Collections**

- Use generics, including wildcards

- Use a Java array and List, Set, Map and Deque collections, including convenience methods

- Sort collections and arrays using Comparator and Comparable interfaces

1. What is the output of the following?

```
List<String> museums = new ArrayList<>(1);
museums.add("Natural History");
museums.add("Science");
museums.add("Art");
museums.remove(2);
System.out.println(museums);
```

    A. [Natural History, Science]

    B. [Natural History, Art, Science]

    C. The code does not compile.

    D. The code compiles but throws an exception at runtime.

2. How many of the following are legal declarations?

```
[]String lions = new String[];
String[] tigers = new String[1] {"tiger"};
String bears[] = new String[] {};
String ohMy [] = new String[0] {};
```

    A. None

    B. One

    C. Two

    D. Three

    E. Four

3. Which of the following can fill in the blank to make the code compile?

```
public class News<_____> {}
```

    A. ? only

    B. N only

    C. ? and N

    D. News, and Object

    E. N, News, and Object

    F. None of the above

4. What is true of this code? (Choose two.)

```
26: List<String> strings = new ArrayList<?>();
27: var ints = new HashSet<Integer>();
28: Double dbl = 5.0;
29: ints.add(2);
30: ints.add(null);
```

    A. The code compiles as is.

    B. One line needs to be removed for the code to compile.

    C. Two lines need to be removed for the code to compile.

    D. One line of code uses autoboxing.

    E. Two lines of code use autoboxing.

    F. Three lines of code use autoboxing.

5. Which of the following creates an empty two-dimensional array with dimensions 2×2?

    A. `int[][] blue = new int[2, 2];`

    B. `int[][] blue = new int[2], [2];`

    C. `int[][] blue = new int[2][2];`

    D. `int[][] blue = new int[2 x 2];`

    E. None of the above

6. What is the output of the following?

```
var q = new ArrayDeque<String>();
q.offer("snowball");
q.offer("minnie");
q.offer("sugar");

System.out.println(q.peek() + " " + q.peek() + " " + q.size());
```

    A. `sugar sugar 3`

    B. `sugar minnie 1`

    C. `snowball minnie 1`

    D. `snowball snowball 3`

    E. The code does not compile.

    F. None of the above.

7. We are running a library. Patrons select books by name. They get at the back of the checkout line. When they get to the front, they scan the book's ISBN, a unique identification number. The checkout system finds the book based on this number and marks the book as checked out. Of these choices, which data structures best represent the line to check out the book and the book lookup to mark it as checked out, respectively?

    A. `ArrayList, HashSet`

    B. `ArrayList, TreeMap`

    C. `ArrayList, TreeSet`

    D. `LinkedList, HashSet`

    E. `LinkedList, TreeMap`

    F. `LinkedList, TreeSet`

8. What is the result of running the following program?

```
1:   package fun;
2:   public class Sudoku {
3:       static int[][] game;
4:
5:       public static void main(String[] args) {
6:           game[3][3] = 6;
7:           Object[] obj = game;
8:           game[3][3] = "X";
9:           System.out.println(game[3][3]);
10:      }
11: }
```

A. X

B. The code does not compile.

C. The code compiles but throws a `NullPointerException` at runtime.

D. The code compiles but throws a different exception at runtime.

9. Suppose we want to implement a `Comparator<String>` so that it sorts the longest strings first. You may assume there are no `null` values. Which method could implement such a comparator?

A.

```
public int compare(String s1, String s2) {
   return s1.length() - s2.length();
}
```

B.

```
public int compare(String s1, String s2) {
   return s2.length() - s1.length();
}
```

C.

```
public int compare(Object obj1, Object obj2) {
   String s1 = (String) obj1;
   String s2 = (String) obj2;
   return s1.length() - s2.length();
}
```

D.

```
public int compare(Object obj1, Object obj2) {
   String s1 = (String) obj1;
   String s2 = (String) obj2;
   return s2.length() - s1.length();
}
```

E.   None of the above

10. How many lines does the following code output?

```
var days = new String[] { "Sunday", "Monday", "Tuesday",
   "Wednesday", "Thursday", "Friday", "Saturday" };

for (int i = 1; i < days.length; i++)
      System.out.println(days[i]);
```

A.   Zero.

B.   Six.

C.   Seven.

D.   The code does not compile.

E.   The code compiles but throws an exception at runtime.

11. Which cannot fill in the blank for this code to compile?

```
var c = new _____<String>();
c.add("pen");
c.remove("pen");
System.out.println(c.isEmpty());
```

A.   `ArrayList`

B.   `LinkedList`

C.   `TreeMap`

D.   `TreeSet`

E.   All of these can fill in the blank.

12. What is true of the following code? (Choose two.)

```
private static void sortAndSearch(String... args) {
   var one = args[0];
   Arrays.sort(args);
   _____ result = Arrays.binarySearch(args, one);
   System.out.println(result);
}
```

```
public static void main(String[] args) {
   sortAndSearch("seed", "flower");
}
```

- **A.** If the blank contains `int`, then the code outputs 0.
- **B.** If the blank contains `int`, then the code outputs 1.
- **C.** If the blank contains `int`, then the does not compile.
- **D.** If the blank contains `String`, then the code outputs `flower`.
- **E.** If the blank contains `String`, then the code outputs `seed`.
- **F.** If the blank contains `String`, then the code does not compile.

13. How many of the following are legal declarations?

```
public void greek() {
   [][]String alpha;
   []String beta;
   String[][] gamma;
   String[] delta[];
   String epsilon[][];
   var[][] zeta;
}
```

- **A.** One
- **B.** Two
- **C.** Three
- **D.** Four
- **E.** Five
- **F.** Six

14. What is the result of the following?

```
var list = new ArrayList<Integer>();
list.add(56);
list.add(56);
list.add(3);
var set = new TreeSet<Integer>(list);
System.out.print(set.size());
System.out.print(" ");
System.out.print(set.iterator().next());
```

- **A.** 2 3
- **B.** 2 56

C. 3 3

D. 3 56

E. None of the above

15. What is true of the code when run as `java Copier.java`? (Choose two.)

```
1:  import java.util.Arrays;
2:
3:  public class Copier {
4:      public static void main(String... original) {
5:          String... copy = original;
6:          Arrays.linearSort(original);
7:          Arrays.search(original, "");
8:          System.out.println(original.size()
9:              + " " + original[0]);
10:     }
11: }
```

A. One line contains a compiler error.

B. Two lines contain a compiler error.

C. Three lines contain a compiler error.

D. Four lines contain a compiler error.

E. If the compiler errors were fixed, the code would throw an exception.

F. If the compiler errors were fixed, the code would run successfully.

16. What is the output of the following? (Choose three.)

```
20: var chars = new _____<Character>();
21: chars.add('a');
22: chars.add(Character.valueOf('b'));
23: chars.set(1, 'c');
24: chars.remove(0);
25: System.out.print(chars.size() + " " + chars.contains('b'));
```

A. When inserting `ArrayList` into the blank, the code prints `1 false`.

B. When inserting `ArrayList` into the blank, the code does not compile.

C. When inserting `HashMap` into the blank, the code prints `1 false`.

D. When inserting `HashMap` into the blank, the code does not compile.

E. When inserting `HashSet` into the blank, the code prints `1 false`.

F. When inserting `HashSet` into the blank, the code does not compile.

17. What is the output of the following?

```java
class Magazine {
    private String name;
    public Magazine(String name) {
        this.name = name;
    }
    public int compareTo(Magazine m) {
        return name.compareTo(m.name);
    }
    public String toString() {
        return name;
    }
}
public class Newsstand {
    public static void main(String[] args) {
        var set = new TreeSet<Magazine>();
        set.add(new Magazine("highlights"));
        set.add(new Magazine("Newsweek"));
        set.add(new Magazine("highlights"));
        System.out.println(set.iterator().next());
    }
}
```

A. highlights

B. Newsweek

C. null

D. The code does not compile.

E. The code compiles but throws an exception at runtime.

18. Which is the first line to prevent this code from compiling and running without error?

```java
char[][] ticTacToe = new char[3][3];                      // r1
ticTacToe[1][3] = 'X';                                    // r2
ticTacToe[2][2] = 'X';
ticTacToe[3][1] = 'X';
System.out.println(ticTacToe.length + " in a row!"); // r3
```

A. Line r1

B. Line r2

C. Line r3

D. None of the above

19. What is the first line with a compiler error?

```
class Mammal {}
class Bat extends Mammal {}
class Cat extends Mammal {}
class Sat {}

class Fur<T extends Mammal> {      // line R

    void clean() {
        var bat = new Fur<Bat>();  // line S
        var cat = new Fur<Cat>();  // line T
        var sat = new Fur<Sat>();  // line U
    }
}
```

A. Line R

B. Line S

C. Line T

D. Line U

E. None of the above

20. What is a possible result of this code?

```
17: var nums = new HashSet<Long>();
18: nums.add((long) Math.min(5, 3));
19: nums.add(Math.round(3.14));
20: nums.add((long) Math.pow(4,2));
21: System.out.println(nums);
```

A. [3]

B. [16]

C. [16, 3]

D. [16, 3, 3]

E. None of the above

21. What is the output of the following?

```
5: var x = new LinkedList<Integer>();
6: x.offer(18);
7: x.offer(5);
8: x.push(13);
9: System.out.println(x.poll() + " " + x.poll());
```

A. 13 5

B. 13 18

    C. 18 5

    D. 18 13

    E. The code does not compile.

    F. The code compiles, but prints something else.

22. Suppose we want to store `JellyBean` objects. Which of the following require `JellyBean` to implement the `Comparable` interface or create a `Comparator` to add them to the collection? (Choose two.)

    A. `ArrayList`

    B. `HashMap`

    C. `HashSet`

    D. `SortedArray`

    E. `TreeMap`

    F. `TreeSet`

23. Which of the following references the first and last elements in a nonempty array?

    A. `trains[0]` and `trains[trains.length]`

    B. `trains[0]` and `trains[trains.length - 1]`

    C. `trains[1]` and `trains[trains.length]`

    D. `trains[1]` and `trains[trains.length - 1]`

    E. None of the above

24. Which of the following fills in the blank so this code compiles?

```
public static void throwOne(Collection<_____> coll) {
    var iter = coll.iterator();
    if (iter.hasNext())
        throw iter.next();
}
```

    A. `?`

    B. `? extends RuntimeException`

    C. `? super RuntimeException`

    D. None of the above

25. Which of these four array declarations produces a different array than the others?

    A. `int[][] nums = new int[2][1];`

    B. `int[] nums[] = new int[2][1];`

    C. `int[] nums[] = new int[][] { { 0 }, { 0 } };`

    D. `int[] nums[] = new int[][] { { 0, 0 } };`

26. What does the following output?

```
var linux = new String[] { "Linux", "Mac", "Windows" };
var mac = new String[] { "Mac", "Linux", "Windows" };

var search = Arrays.binarySearch(linux, "Linux");
var mismatch1 = Arrays.mismatch(linux, mac);
var mismatch2 = Arrays.mismatch(mac, mac);

System.out.println(search + " " + mismatch1 + " " + mismatch2);
```

A. -1 0 -1

B. -1 -1 0

C. 0 -1 0

D. 0 0 -1

E. The output is not defined.

F. The code does not compile.

27. Which line in the `main()` method doesn't compile or points to a class that doesn't compile?

```
1:  interface Comic<C> {
2:     void draw(C c);
3:  }
4:  class ComicClass<C> implements Comic<C> {
5:     public void draw(C c) {
6:        System.out.println(c);
7:     }
8:  }
9:  class SnoopyClass implements Comic<Snoopy> {
10:    public void draw(Snoopy c) {
11:       System.out.println(c);
12:    }
13: }
14: class SnoopyComic implements Comic<Snoopy> {
15:    public void draw(C c) {
16:       System.out.println(c);
17:    }
18: }
19: public class Snoopy {
20:    public static void main(String[] args) {
21:       Comic<Snoopy> c1 = c -> System.out.println(c);
22:       Comic<Snoopy> c2 = new ComicClass<>();
```

```
23:        Comic<Snoopy> c3 = new SnoopyClass();
24:        Comic<Snoopy> c4 = new SnoopyComic();
25:    }
26: }
```

A. Line 21.
B. Line 22.
C. Line 23.
D. Line 24.
E. None of the above. All of the code compiles.

28. Fill in the blank to make this code compile:

```
public class Truck implements Comparable<Truck> {
    private int id;
    public Truck(int id) {
        this.id = id;
    }
    @Override
    public int _____ {
        return id - t.id;
    }
}
```

A. compare(Truck t)
B. compare(Truck t1, Truck t2)
C. compareTo(Truck t)
D. compareTo(Truck t1, Truck t2)
E. None of the above

29. How many lines does the following code output?

```
var days = new String[] { "Sunday", "Monday", "Tuesday",
    "Wednesday", "Thursday", "Friday", "Saturday" };

for (int i = 0; i < days.length; i++)
    System.out.println(days[i]);
```

A. Six.
B. Seven.
C. The code does not compile.
D. The code compiles but throws an exception at runtime.

30. Which of the following fill in the blank to print out `true`? (Choose two.)

```
String[] array = {"Natural History", "Science"};
var museums = _____;
museums.set(0, "Art");
System.out.println(museums.contains("Art"));
```

A. `Arrays.asList(array)`

B. `Arrays.asList("Natural History, Science")`

C. `List.of(array)`

D. `List.of("Natural History", "Science")`

E. `new ArrayList<String>("Natural History", "Science")`

F. `new List<String>("Natural History", "Science")`

31. Which option cannot fill in the blank to print `Clean socks`?

```
class Wash<T> {
    T item;
    public void clean(T item) {
        System.out.println("Clean " + item);
    }
}
public class LaundryTime {
    public static void main(String[] args) {
        _____
        wash.clean("socks");
    }
}
```

A. `var wash = new Wash<String>();`

B. `var wash = new Wash<>();`

C. `Wash wash = new Wash();`

D. `Wash wash = new Wash<String>();`

E. `Wash<String> wash = new Wash<>();`

F. All of these can fill in the blank.

32. Which of the options in the graphic best represent the `blocks` variable?

```
char[][] blocks = new char[][] {
    { 'a', 'b', 'c' }, { 'd' }, { 'e', 'f' } };
```

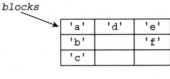

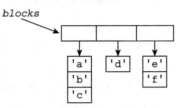

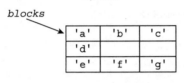

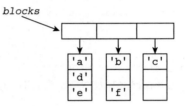

A. Option A

B. Option B

C. Option C

D. Option D

33. Fill in the blank so the code prints gamma. (Choose two.)

```
var list = Arrays.asList("alpha", "beta", "gamma");
Collections.sort(list, _____);
System.out.println(list.get(0));
```

A. `(s, t) -> s.compareTo(t)`

B. `(s, t) -> t.compareTo(s)`

C. `Comparator.comparing((String s) -> s.charAt(0))`

D. `Comparator.comparing((String s) -> s.charAt(0)).reverse()`

E. `Comparator.comparing((String s) -> s.charAt(0)).reversed()`

34. How many of the following are legal declarations?

```
float[] lion = new float[];
float[] tiger = new float[1];
float[] bear = new[] float;
float[] ohMy = new[1] float;
```

A. None
B. One
C. Two
D. Three
E. Four

35. Which is the first line of code that causes an `ArrayIndexOutOfBoundsException`?

```
var matrix = new String[1][2];
matrix[0][0] = "Don't think you are, know you are.";      // m1
matrix[0][1] = "I'm trying to free your mind Neo";        // m2
matrix[1][0] = "Is all around you ";                      // m3
matrix[1][1] = "Why oh why didn't I take the BLUE pill?"; // m4
```

A. m1
B. m2
C. m3
D. m4
E. The code does not compile.
F. None of the above.

36. Suppose we have `list` of type `List<Integer>`. Which method allows you to pass a `List` and returns an immutable `Set` containing the same elements?

A. `List.copyOf(list)`
B. `List.of(list)`
C. `Set.copyOf(list);`
D. `Set.of(list);`
E. None of the above

37. What does the following output? (Choose two.)

```
var os = new String[] { "Mac", "Linux", "Windows" };
Arrays.sort(os);

System.out.println(Arrays.binarySearch(os, "RedHat"));
System.out.println(Arrays.binarySearch(os, "Mac"));
```

A. -1
B. -2
C. -3
D. 0
E. 1
F. 2

38. What does the following output?

```
var names = new HashMap<String, String>();
names.put("peter", "pan");
names.put("wendy", "darling");
var first = names.entrySet();          // line x1
System.out.println(first.getKey());    // line x2
```

A. peter

B. wendy

C. Does not compile due to line x1

D. Does not compile due to line x2

E. Does not compile due to another reason

F. Throws an exception at runtime

39. Which of these elements are in the output of the following? (Choose three.)

```
var q = new ArrayDeque<String>();
q.offerFirst("snowball");
q.offer("sugar");
q.offerLast("minnie");

System.out.println(q.poll());
System.out.println(q.removeFirst());
System.out.println(q.size());
```

A. sugar

B. minnie

C. snowball

D. 1

E. 2

F. 3

40. Which of these four pairs of declarations can point to an array that is different from the others?

A. `int[][][][] nums1a, nums1b;`

B. `int[][][] nums2a[], nums2b;`

C. `int[][] nums3a[][], nums3b[][];`

D. `int[] nums4a[][][], numbs4b[][][];`

41. Which of the following does not behave the same way as the others?

A. `var set = new HashSet<>();`

B. `var set = new HashSet<Object>();`

C. `HashSet<> set = new HashSet<Object>();`

D. `HashSet<Object> set = new HashSet<>();`

E. `HashSet<Object> set = new HashSet<Object>();`

42. What is true about the output of the following code?

```
var ints = new int[] {3,1,4};
var others = new int[] {2,7,1,8};
System.out.println(Arrays.compare(ints, others));
```

A. It is negative because `ints` has fewer elements.

B. It is 0 because the arrays can't be compared.

C. It is positive because the first element is larger.

D. It is undefined.

E. The code does not compile.

43. Fill in the blank so the code prints `beta`.

```
var list = List.of("alpha", "beta", "gamma");
Collections.sort(list, _____);
System.out.println(list.get(0));
```

A. `(s, t) -> s.compareTo(t)`

B. `(s, t) -> t.compareTo(s)`

C. `Comparator.comparing(String::length)`

D. `Comparator.comparing(String::length).reversed()`

E. None of the above

44. How many of these lines have a compiler error?

```
20: var list = List.of('a', 'c', 'e');
21: Char letter1 = list.get(0);
22: char letter2 = list.get(0);
23: int letter3 = list.get(0);
24: Integer letter4 = list.get(0);
25: Object letter5 = list.get(0);
```

A. 0

B. 1

C. 2

D. 3

E. 4

F. 5

45. How many dimensions does the array reference `moreBools` allow?

```
boolean[][] bools[], moreBools;
```

A. One dimension

B. Two dimensions

C. Three dimensions

D. None of the above

46. What is the result of the following?

```
Comparator<Integer> c = (x, y) -> y - x;
var ints = Arrays.asList(3, 1, 4);
Collections.sort(ints, c);
System.out.println(Collections.binarySearch(ints, 1));
```

A. -1

B. 0

C. -1

D. The code does not compile.

E. The result is not defined.

47. Which statement most accurately represents the relationship between searching and sorting with respect to the `Arrays` class?

A. If the array is not sorted, calling `Arrays.binarySearch()` will be accurate, but slower than if it were sorted.

B. The array does not need to be sorted before calling `Arrays.binarySearch()` to get an accurate result.

C. The array must be sorted before calling `Arrays.binarySearch()` to get an accurate result.

D. None of the above.

48. Which statement is true about the following figure while ensuring the code continues to compile? (Choose two.)

```
List  balloons = new ArrayList ();
     ↑                          ↑
     P                          Q


var  air = new ArrayList ();
    ↑                     ↑
    R                     S
```

A. `<>` can be inserted at positions P and R without making any other changes.

B. `<>` can be inserted at positions Q and S without making any other changes.

C. `<>` can be inserted at all four positions.

D. Both variables point to an `ArrayList<String>`.

E. Only one variable points to an `ArrayList<String>`.

F. Neither variable points to an `ArrayList<String>`.

49. What is the result of the following when called as `java Binary.java`? (Choose two.)

```
1: import java.util.*;
2: public class Binary {
3:
4:     public static void main(String... args) {
5:         Arrays.sort(args);
6:         System.out.println(Arrays.toString(args));
7:         System.out.println(args[0]);
8:     } }
```

A. `null`

B. `[]`

C. `Binary`

D. The code throws an `ArrayIndexOutOfBoundsException`.

E. The code throws a `NullPointerException`.

F. The code does not compile.

50. What is the first line with a compiler error?

```
class Mammal {}
class Bat extends Mammal {}
class Cat extends Mammal {}
class Sat {}

class Fur<? extends Mammal> {     // line R

    void clean() {
        var bat = new Fur<Bat>();  // line S
        var cat = new Fur<Cat>();  // line T
        var sat = new Fur<Sat>();  // line U
    }
}
```

A. Line R

B. Line S

C. Line T

D. Line U

E. None of the above

51. What is the result of running the following program?

```
1:  package fun;
2:  public class Sudoku {
3:     static int[][] game = new int[6][6];
4:
5:     public static void main(String[] args) {
6:        game[3][3] = 6;
7:        Object[] obj = game;
8:        obj[3] = "X";
9:        System.out.println(game[3][3]);
10:    }
11: }
```

A. 6

B. X

C. The code does not compile.

D. The code compiles but throws a `NullPointerException` at runtime.

E. The code compiles but throws a different exception at runtime.

52. How many of these allow inserting null values: ArrayList, LinkedList, HashSet, and TreeSet?

A. 0

B. 1

C. 2

D. 3

E. 4

53. What is the output of the following?

```
var threes = Arrays.asList("3", "three", "THREE");
Collections.sort(threes);
System.out.println(threes);
```

A. [3, three, THREE]

B. [3, THREE, three]

C. [three, THREE, 3]

D. [THREE, three, 3]

E. None of the above

54. How many dimensions does the array reference `moreBools` allow?

```
boolean[][][] bools, moreBools;
```

A. One dimension

B. Two dimensions

C. Three dimensions

D. None of the above

55. What is the output of the following?

```
20: List<Character> chars = new ArrayList<>();
21: chars.add('a');
22: chars.add('b');
23: chars.clear();
24: chars.remove(0);
25: System.out.print(chars.isEmpty() + " " + chars.length());
```

A. false 0

B. true 1

C. 2

D. The code does not compile.

E. The code throws an exception at runtime.

56. Which fills in the blank in the method signature to allow this code to compile?

```
import java.util.*;
public class ExtendingGenerics {
    private static <_____ , U> U add(T list, U element) {
        list.add(element);
        return element;
    }
    public static void main(String[] args) {
        var values = new ArrayList<String>();
        add(values, "duck");
        add(values, "duck");
        add(values, "goose");
        System.out.println(values);
    }
}
```

A. ? extends Collection<U>

B. ? implements Collection<U>

C. T extends Collection<U>

D. T implements Collection<U>

E. None of the above

57. What does the following output?

```
String[] os = new String[] { "Mac", "Linux", "Windows" };
System.out.println(Arrays.binarySearch(os, "Linux"));
```

A. 0

B. 1

C. 2

D. The output is not defined.

58. Which is the first line to prevent this code from compiling and running without error?

```
char[][] ticTacToe = new char[3,3];                     // r1
ticTacToe[1][3] = 'X';                                  // r2
ticTacToe[2][2] = 'X';
ticTacToe[3][1] = 'X';
System.out.println(ticTacToe.length + " in a row!"); // r3
```

A. Line r1

B. Line r2

C. Line r3

D. None of the above

59. What is the result of the following?

```
var list = new ArrayList<String>();
list.add("Austin");
list.add("Boston");
list.add("San Francisco");
list.removeIf(a -> a.length() > 10);
System.out.println(list.size());
```

A. 1

B. 2

C. 3

D. None of the above

60. What happens when calling the following method with a non-null and non-empty array?

```
public static void addStationName(String[] names) {
    names[names.length] = "Times Square";
}
```

A. It adds an element to the array the value of which is Times Square.

B. It replaces the last element in the array with the value Times Square.

    C. It does not compile.

    D. It throws an exception.

    E. None of the above.

61. Which is not a true statement about an array?

    A. An array expands automatically when it is full.

    B. An array is allowed to contain duplicate values.

    C. An array understands the concept of ordered elements.

    D. An array uses a zero index to reference the first element.

62. Which of the following cannot fill in the blank to make the code compile?

```
private void output(_____<?> x) {
   x.forEach(System.out::println);
}
```

    A. `Collection`

    B. `LinkedList`

    C. `TreeMap`

    D. None of these can fill in the blank.

    E. All of these can fill in the blank.

63. Which of the following fills in the blank so this code compiles?

```
public static void getExceptions(Collection<_____> coll) {
   coll.add(new RuntimeException());
   coll.add(new Exception());
}
```

    A. `?`

    B. `? extends RuntimeException`

    C. `? super RuntimeException`

    D. None of the above

64. What is the output of the following? (Choose two.)

```
35: var mags = new HashMap<String, Integer>();
36: mags.put("People", 1974);
37: mags.put("Readers Digest", 1922);
38: mags.put("The Economist", 1843);
39:
40: Collection<Integer> years = mags.values();
41:
42: List<Integer> sorted = new ArrayList<>(years);
```

```
43: Collections.sort(sorted);
44:
45: int first = sorted.get(0);
46: System.out.println(first);
47:
48: Integer last = sorted.get(sorted.size());
49: System.out.println(last);
```

A. 1843

B. 1922

C. 1974

D. The code compiles but throws an exception at runtime.

65. How do you access the array element with the value of `"z"`?

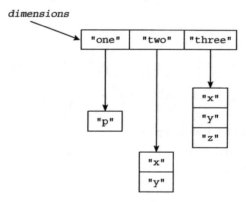

A. `dimensions["three"][2]`

B. `dimensions["three"][3]`

C. `dimensions[2][2]`

D. `dimensions[3][3]`

66. What is the output of the following?

```
class Magazine implements Comparable<Magazine> {
    private String name;
    public Magazine(String name) {
        this.name = name;
    }
    @Override
    public int compareTo(Magazine m) {
        return name.compareTo(m.name);
    }
```

```
      @Override
      public String toString() {
         return name;
      }
   }
   public class Newsstand {
      public static void main(String[] args) {
         var set = new TreeSet<Magazine>();
         set.add(new Magazine("highlights"));
         set.add(new Magazine("Newsweek"));
         set.add(new Magazine("highlights"));
         System.out.println(set.iterator().next());
      }
   }
```

   A. highlights

   B. Newsweek

   C. The code does not compile.

   D. The code compiles but throws an exception at runtime.

67. Which options can fill in the blanks to print `Cleaned 2 items`?

```
   import java.util.*;
   class Wash<T _____ Collection> {
      T item;
      public void clean(T items) {
         System.out.println("Cleaned " + items.size() + " items");
      }
   }
   public class LaundryTime {
      public static void main(String[] args) {
         Wash<List> wash = new Wash<_____>();
         wash.clean(List.of("sock", "tie"));
      }
   }
```

   A. extends, ArrayList

   B. extends, List

   C. super, ArrayList

   D. super, List

   E. None of the above

68. How many lines does the following code output?

```
var days = new String[] { "Sunday", "Monday", "Tuesday",
    "Wednesday", "Thursday", "Friday", "Saturday" };
for (int i = 1; i <= days.length; i++)
    System.out.println(days[i]);
```

- **A.** Six.
- **B.** Seven.
- **C.** The code does not compile.
- **D.** The code compiles but throws an exception at runtime.

69. What is the output of the following?

```
var listing = new String[][] {
    { "Book" }, { "Game", "29.99" } };
System.out.println(listing.length + " " + listing[0].length);
```

- **A.** 1 2
- **B.** 2 1
- **C.** 2 2
- **D.** The code does not compile.
- **E.** The code compiles but throws an exception at runtime.

70. What is the output of the following?

```
Queue<String> q = new ArrayDeque<>();
q.add("snowball");
q.addLast("sugar");
q.addFirst("minnie");

System.out.println(q.peek() + " " + q.peek() + " " + q.size());
```

- **A.** sugar sugar 3
- **B.** sugar minnie 1
- **C.** minnie minnie 3
- **D.** minnie snowball 1
- **E.** The code does not compile.
- **F.** None of the above.

71. What is the result of the following?

```
13: var numbers = Arrays.asList(3, 1, 4);
14: numbers.set(1, null);
15: int first = numbers.get(0);
```

```
16: int middle = numbers.get(1);
17: int last = numbers.get(3);
18: System.out.println(first + " " + middle + " " + last);
```

A. The code does not compile.

B. Line 14 throws an exception.

C. Line 15 throws an exception.

D. Line 16 throws an exception.

E. Line 17 throws an exception.

F. 3null4

72. Fill in the blank so the code prints gamma.

```
var list = Arrays.asList("alpha", "beta", "gamma");
Collections.sort(list, _____);
System.out.println(list.get(0));
```

A.

```
Comparator.comparing(String::length)
    .andCompare(s -> s.charAt(0))
```

B.

```
Comparator.comparing(String::length)
   .thenCompare(s -> s.charAt(0))
```

C.

```
Comparator.comparing(String::length)
   .thenComparing(s -> s.charAt(0))
```

D.

```
Comparator.comparing(String::length)
    .andCompare(s -> s.charAt(0))
    .reversed()
```

E.

```
Comparator.comparing(String::length)
   .thenCompare(s -> s.charAt(0))
   .reversed()
```

F.

```
Comparator.comparing(String::length)
   .thenComparing(s -> s.charAt(0))
   .reversed()
```

73. What is the output of the following when run as `java FirstName Wolfie`? (Choose two.)

```
public class FirstName {
    public static void main(String... names) {
        System.out.println(names[0]);
        System.out.println(names[1]);
    }
}
```

A. `FirstName`

B. `Wolfie`

C. The code throws an `ArrayIndexOutOfBoundsException`.

D. The code throws a `NullPointerException`.

E. The code throws a different exception.

74. What does the following output?

```
11: var pennies = new ArrayList<>();
12: pennies.add(1);
13: pennies.add(2);
14: pennies.add(Integer.valueOf(3));
15: pennies.add(Integer.valueOf(4));
16: pennies.remove(2);
17: pennies.remove(Integer.valueOf(1));
18: System.out.println(pennies);
```

A. `[1, 2]`

B. `[1, 4]`

C. `[2, 4]`

D. `[2, 3]`

E. `[3, 4]`

F. The code does not compile.

75. What is true of the following code? (Choose two.)

```
private static void sortAndSearch(String... args) {
    var one = args[1];
    Comparator<String> comp = (x, y) -> _____;
    Arrays.sort(args, comp);
    var result = Arrays.binarySearch(args, one, comp);
    System.out.println(result);
}
```

```
public static void main(String[] args) {
   sortAndSearch("seed", "flower");
}
```

A. If the blank contains -x.compareTo(y), then the code outputs 0.

B. If the blank contains -x.compareTo(y), then the code outputs -1.

C. If the blank contains x.compareTo(y), then the code outputs 0.

D. If the blank contains -y.compareTo(x), then the code outputs 0.

E. If the blank contains -y.compareTo(x), then the code outputs -1.

F. If the blank contains y.compareTo(x), then the code outputs 0.

G. If the blank contains y.compareTo(x), then the code outputs -1.

76. What does this code output?

```
String[] nums = new String[] { "1", "9", "10" };
Arrays.sort(nums);
System.out.println(Arrays.toString(nums));
```

A. [1, 9, 10]

B. [1, 10, 9]

C. [9, 1, 10]

D. [9, 10, 1]

E. [10, 1, 9]

F. [10, 9, 1]

77. Which is the first line to prevent this code from compiling and running without error?

```
char[][] ticTacToe = new char[3][3];               // r1
ticTacToe[0][0] = 'X';                             // r2
ticTacToe[1][1] = 'X';
ticTacToe[2][2] = 'X';
System.out.println(ticTacToe.length + " in a row!"); // r3
```

A. Line r1

B. Line r2

C. Line r3

D. None of the above

78. What is true of the following code? (Choose three.)

```
36: var names = new HashMap<String, String>();
37: names.put("peter", "pan");
38: names.put("wendy", "darling");
39:
```

```
40: String w = names.getOrDefault("peter");
41: String x = names.getOrDefault("peter", "x");
42: String y = names.getOrDefault("john", "x");
```

A. One line does not compile.

B. Two lines do not compile.

C. If any lines that do not compile are removed, the String on line 40 is set to null.

D. If any lines that do not compile are removed, the String on line 41 is set to "pan".

E. If any lines that do not compile are removed, the String on line 41 is set to "x".

F. If any lines that do not compile are removed, the String on line 42 is set to "x".

79. What does the following output?

```
18: List<String> list = List.of(
19:    "Mary", "had", "a", "little", "lamb");
20: Set<String> set = new HashSet<>(list);
21: set.addAll(list);
22: for(String sheep : set)
23:    if (sheep.length() > 1)
24:        set.remove(sheep);
25: System.out.println(set);
```

A. [a, lamb, had, Mary, little]

B. [a]

C. [a, a]

D. The code does not compile.

E. The code throws an exception at runtime.

80. Which of the following fills in the blank so this code compiles?

```
public static void getExceptions(Collection<_____> coll) {
    coll.add(new RuntimeException());
    coll.add(new Exception());
}
```

A. ?

B. ? extends Exception

C. ? super Exception

D. None of the above

Chapter

6

Working with Streams and Lambda Expressions

THE OCP EXAM TOPICS COVERED IN THIS PRACTICE TEST INCLUDE THE FOLLOWING:

✓ **Working with Streams and Lambda Expressions**

- Implement functional interfaces using lambda expressions, including interfaces from the java.util.function package

- Use Java Streams to filter, transform and process data

- Perform decomposition and reduction, including grouping and partitioning on sequential and parallel streams

1. The following figure represents a stream pipeline. Given this, would the boxes X, Y, Z best represent?

   ```
   ┌───────┐          ┌───────┐          ┌───────┐
   │   X   │  ══════▶ │   Y   │  ══════▶ │   Z   │
   └───────┘          └───────┘          └───────┘
   ```

   A. Origin, intermediate operation, and final operation
   B. Origin, intermediate operation, and sink
   C. Origin, intermediate operation, and terminal operation
   D. Source, intermediate operation, and final operation
   E. Source, intermediate operation, and sink
   F. Source, intermediate operation, and terminal operation

2. Which of the following is required for all valid lambda expressions?

   A. ()
   B. ->
   C. {}
   D. Parameter data type(s)
   E. None of the above

3. Fill in the blanks: The _____ functional interface does not take any inputs, while the _____ functional interface does not return any data.

   A. IntConsumer, LongSupplier
   B. IntSupplier, Function
   C. Supplier, DoubleConsumer
   D. UnaryOperator, Consumer
   E. None of the above

4. What is the result of executing the following application multiple times?

   ```java
   package bears;
   import java.util.*;
   public class Bounce {
      public static void main(String... legend) {
         List.of(1,2,3,4).stream()
            .forEach(System.out::println);
         List.of(1,2,3,4).parallel()
            .forEach(System.out::println);
         List.of(1,2,3,4).parallel()
            .forEachOrdered(System.out::println);
      } }
   ```

   A. Only the first stream prints the same order every time.
   B. Only the first and second streams print the same order every time.

    C.   Only the first and third streams print the same order every time.

    D.   All of the streams print the same order every time.

    E.   None of the streams prints the same order every time.

    F.   None of the above.

5.   A lambda expression for which of the following functional interfaces could be used to return a Double value? (Choose two.)

    A.   `UnaryOperator`

    B.   `BiPredicate`

    C.   `BiOperator`

    D.   `BiConsumer`

    E.   `BiFunction`

    F.   `BiSupplier`

6.   What does the following output?

```
var list = new ArrayList<String>();
list.add("Austin");
list.add("Boston");
list.add("San Francisco");
var c = list.stream()
    .filter(a -> a.length() > 10)     // line x
    .count();
System.out.println(c + " " + list.size());
```

    A.   1 1

    B.   1 3

    C.   2 3

    D.   The code does not compile due to line x.

    E.   None of the above.

7.   Identify the correct functional interfaces to fill in this table correctly. (Choose three.)

Functional Interface	Possible Return Type
Interface X	`Boolean`
Interface Y	`int`
Interface Z	`Void`

    A.   Interface X is `Predicate`.

    B.   Interface X is `Supplier`.

    C.   Interface Y is `Comparator`.

    D.   Interface Y is `Supplier`.

    E.   Interface Z is `Consumer`.

    F.   Interface Z is `Supplier`.

8.   What is a common reason for a stream pipeline not to run?

    A.   The source doesn't generate any items.

    B.   There are no intermediate operations.

    C.   The terminal operation is missing.

    D.   The version of Java is too old.

    E.   None of the above.

9.   Which functional interface takes a `long` value as an input argument and has an `accept()` method?

    A.   `LongConsumer`

    B.   `LongFunction`

    C.   `LongPredicate`

    D.   `LongSupplier`

    E.   None of the above

10.   Given a parallel `Stream<T>`, which method would you use to obtain an equivalent serial `Stream<T>`?

    A.   `unordered()`

    B.   `reduce()`

    C.   `concat()`

    D.   `stream()`

    E.   `boxed()`

    F.   None of the above

11.   Which of the following is a valid lambda expression?

    A.   `r -> {return 1==2}`

    B.   `(q) -> true`

    C.   `(x,y) -> {int test; return test>0;}`

    D.   `a,b -> true`

    E.   None of the above

12.   Which are true of the following? (Choose two.)

```
var empty = Optional.empty();
var param = Optional.of(null);
var method = Optional.ofNullable(null);
```

    A.   All of these will run without error.

    B.   One of the lines fails to compile or throws an exception.

   C. Two of the lines fail to compile or throw an exception.

   D. None of these returns `true` when calling `opt.isPresent()`

   E. One of these returns `true` when calling `opt.isPresent()`

   F. Two of these return `true` when calling `opt.isPresent()`

13. Which of the following statements about `DoubleSupplier` and `Supplier<Double>` is not true?

   A. Both are functional interfaces.

   B. Both take zero parameters.

   C. Lambdas for both can return a `double` value.

   D. Lambdas for both cannot return a `null` value.

   E. One supports a generic type; the other does not.

   F. All of these are true.

14. What is the output of the following program?

```java
import java.util.stream.*;
public class Bull {
    void charge() {
        IntStream.range(1,6)
            .parallel()
            .forEachOrdered(System.out::print);
    }
    public static void main(String[] args) {
        var b = new Bull();
        b.charge();
    }
}
```

   A. 12345

   B. 54321

   C. The output cannot be determined ahead of time.

   D. The code does not compile.

   E. An exception is thrown at runtime.

   F. None of the above.

15. Fill in the blank with the functional interface from `java.util.function` that allows the code to compile and print 3 at runtime.

```java
_____ transformer = x -> x;

var prime = List.of(3,1,4,1,5,9)
```

```
        .stream()
        .limit(1)
        .peek(s -> {})
        .mapToInt(transformer)
        .peek(s -> {})
        .sum();
System.out.println(prime);
```

A. `Function<Integer,Integer>`
B. `UnaryOperator<Integer>`
C. `ToIntFunction<Integer>`
D. `IntUnaryOperator`
E. The code does not compile regardless of what functional interface is placed in the blank.
F. The code is capable of compiling, but since `prime` is an `OptionalInt` value, it cannot be 3 at runtime.

16. Which fills in the blank so the code is guaranteed to print 1?

```
var stream = Stream.of(1, 2, 3);
System.out.println(stream._____);
```

A. `anyMatch()`
B. `findAny()`
C. `first()`
D. `min()`
E. None of the above

17. What is the result of the following?

```
6:  var list = new ArrayList<String>();
7:  list.add("Monday");
8:  list.add(String::new);
9:  list.add("Tuesday");
10: list.remove(0);
11: System.out.println(list.get(0));
```

A. `null`
B. An empty String.
C. `Monday`
D. The code does not compile.
E. The code compiles but throws an exception at runtime.

18. Which functional interface, when filled into the blank, allows the class to compile?

```
package space;
import java.util.function.*;

public class Asteroid {
    public void mine(_____ lambda) {
        // IMPLEMENTATION OMITTED
    }
    public static void main(String[] debris) {
        new Asteroid().mine((s,p) -> s+p);
    }
}
```

- **A.** BiConsumer<Integer,Double>
- **B.** BiConsumer<Integer,Double,Double>
- **C.** BiFunction<Integer,Double,Double>
- **D.** BiFunction<Integer,Integer,Double>
- **E.** Function<Integer,Double>
- **F.** None of the above

19. What best describes a reduction?

- **A.** A source operation that creates a small value
- **B.** An intermediate operation where it filters the stream it receives
- **C.** An intermediate operation where it mathematically divides each element in the stream
- **D.** A terminal operation where a single value is generated by reading each element in the prior step in a stream pipeline
- **E.** A terminal operation where one element is returned from the prior step in a stream pipeline without reading all the elements

20. Which statements about the following application are correct? (Choose two.)

```
import java.util.concurrent.atomic.*;
import java.util.stream.*;
public class TicketTaker {
    long ticketsSold;
    final AtomicInteger ticketsTaken;
    public TicketTaker() {
        ticketsSold = 0;
        ticketsTaken = new AtomicInteger(0);
    }
    public void performJob() {
```

```
        IntStream.iterate(1, p -> p+1)
            .parallel()
            .limit(100)
            .forEach(i -> ticketsTaken.getAndIncrement());
        IntStream.iterate(1, q -> q+1)
            .parallel()
            .limit(500)
            .forEach(i -> ++ticketsSold);
        System.out.print(ticketsTaken+" "+ticketsSold);
    }
    public static void main(String[] matinee) {
        new TicketTaker().performJob();
    } }
```

A. The `TicketTaker` constructor does not compile.

B. The `performJob()` method does not compile.

C. The class compiles.

D. The first number printed is consistently `100`.

E. The second number printed is consistently `500`.

F. A `ConcurrentModificationException` is thrown at runtime.

21. Suppose you have a stream with one element and the code
    `stream.xxxx.forEach(System.out::println)`. Filling in xxxx from top to bottom
    in the table, how many elements can be printed out? Assume a valid lambda expression is
    passed to each method in the table.

Method	Number elements printed
`filter()`	?
`flatMap()`	?
`map()`	?

A. Zero or one, zero or more, exactly one

B. Zero or one, exactly one, zero or more

C. Zero or one, zero or more, zero or more

D. Exactly one, zero or more, exactly one

E. Exactly one, exactly one, zero or more

F. Exactly one, zero or more, zero or more

22. Assuming the proper generic types are used, which lambda expression can be assigned to a
    `ToDoubleBiFunction` functional interface reference? (Choose three.)

A. `(Integer a, Double b) -> {int c; return b;}`

B. `(h,i) -> (long)h`

C. `(String u, Object v) -> u.length()+v.length()`

D. `(x,y) -> {int z=2; return y/z;}`

E. `z -> z`

F. `(double y, double z) -> y + z`

23. Given a `Stream<T>`, which method would you use to obtain an equivalent parallel `Stream<T>`?

    A. `getParallelStream()`

    B. `parallelStream()`

    C. `parallel()`

    D. `getParallel()`

    E. `parallels()`

    F. None of the above

24. Rewrite this lambda that takes an `int` n using a constructor reference:

    `n -> new ArrayList<>(n)`

    A. `ArrayList::new`

    B. `ArrayList::new()`

    C. `ArrayList::new(n)`

    D. `ArrayList::new[n]`

    E. None of the above

25. On a `DoubleStream`, how many of the methods `average()`, `count()`, `max()`, and `sum()` return an `OptionalDouble`?

    A. None

    B. One

    C. Two

    D. Three

    E. Four

26. Which of the following is not a functional interface in the `java.util.function` package? (Choose two.)

    A. `BiPredicate`

    B. `DoubleUnaryOperator`

    C. `IntUnaryOperator`

    D. `ObjectDoubleConsumer`

    E. `ObjectIntConsumer`

    F. `ToLongFunction`

27. Five of the following six methods always produce the same result whether they are executed on an ordered serial or parallel stream. Which one does not?

   A. `findAny()`

   B. `findFirst()`

   C. `limit()`

   D. `skip()`

   E. `anyMatch()`

   F. `count()`

28. In a stream pipeline, which can return a value other than a `Stream`?

   A. Source

   B. Intermediate operation

   C. Terminal operation

   D. None of the above

29. When working with a `Stream<String>`, which of these types can be returned from the `collect()` terminal operator by passing arguments to `Collectors.groupingBy()`?

   A. Only `Map<Boolean, HashSet<String>>`

   B. Only `Map<Integer, List<String>>`

   C. Both `Map<Boolean, HashSet<String>>` and `Map<Integer, List<String>>`

   D. Only `List<Integer>`

   E. Only `List<String>`

   F. Both `List<Integer>` and `List<String>`

30. What does the following output?

```
12: Set<String> set = new HashSet<>();
13: set.add("tire-");
14: List<String> list = new LinkedList<>();
15: Deque<String> queue = new ArrayDeque<>();
16: queue.push("wheel-");
17: Stream.of(set, list, queue)
18:    .flatMap(x -> x)
19:    .forEach(System.out::print);
```

   A. `[tire-][wheel-]`

   B. `tire-wheel-`

   C. `[wheel-][tire-]`

   D. `wheel-tire-`

   E. None of the above.

   F. The code does not compile.

31. What is the result of executing the following?

```
var list = new LinkedList<>();
list.add("Archie");
list.add("X-Men");
Stream s = list.stream();  // line w
s.forEach(System.out::println);
s.forEach(System.out::println);
```

A. The code runs without exception and prints two lines.

B. The code runs without exception and prints four lines.

C. The code does not compile due to line w.

D. The code does not compile due to another line.

E. The code compiles but throws an exception at runtime.

32. What is the output of the following application?

```
package zoo;
import java.util.function.*;

public class TicketTaker {
    private static int AT_CAPACITY = 100;
    public int takeTicket(int currentCount,
        IntUnaryOperator<Integer> counter) {

        return counter.applyAsInt(currentCount);
    }
    public static void main(String...theater) {
        final TicketTaker bob = new TicketTaker();
        final int oldCount = 50;
        final int newCount = bob.takeTicket(oldCount,t -> {
            if(t>AT_CAPACITY) {
                throw new RuntimeException(
                    "Sorry, max has been reached");
            }
            return t+1;
        });
        System.out.print(newCount);
    }
}
```

A. 50

B. 51

   C. The code does not compile because of the lambda expression.

   D. The code does not compile for a different reason.

   E. The code compiles but prints an exception at runtime.

33. What are the three requirements for performing a parallel reduction with the `collect()` method, which takes a `Collector` argument. (Choose three.)

   A. The `Collector` argument is marked concurrent.

   B. The elements of the stream implement the `Comparable` interface.

   C. The stream is parallel.

   D. The stream is thread-safe.

   E. The stream or `Collector` is marked unordered.

   F. The stream is not a primitive stream.

34. What is true about the following code? (Choose two.)

```
27: public static void main(String[] s) {
28:     Predicate dash = c -> c.startsWith("-");
29:     System.out.println(dash.test("-"));
30:
31:     Consumer clear = x -> System.out.println(x);
32:     clear.accept("pink");
33:
34:     Comparator<String> c = (String s, String t) -> 0;
35:     System.out.println(c.compare("s", "t"));
36: }
```

   A. The code compiles successfully.

   B. One line does not compile.

   C. Two lines do not compile.

   D. Three lines do not compile.

   E. If any lines that do not compile are fixed, the output includes pink.

   F. If any lines that do not compile are fixed, the output does not include pink.

35. Which functional interface returns a primitive value?

   A. `BiPredicate`

   B. `CharSupplier`

   C. `LongFunction`

   D. `UnaryOperator`

   E. `TriDoublePredicate`

   F. None of the above

36. Given the following code snippet, which lambda expressions are the best choices for an accumulator? (Choose two.)

```
import java.util.*;
import java.util.function.*;
public class GoodAccumulator {
    int i = 0;
    List<String> words = new ArrayList<>();
    public void test() {
        BiFunction<Integer,Integer,Integer> x = _____;
        System.out.print(List.of(1,2,3,4,5)
            .parallelStream()
            .reduce(0,x,(s1, s2) -> s1 + s2));
    } }
```

   A. (a,b) -> (a-b)
   B. (a,b) -> 5
   C. (a,b) -> i++
   D. (a,b) -> {words.add("awesome"); return 0;}
   E. (a,b) -> {return 0;}
   F. (a,b) -> words.add("awesome")

37. Fill in the blanks so that both methods produce the same output for all inputs.

```
private static void longer(Optional<Boolean> opt) {
    if (opt._____())
        System.out.println("run: " + opt.get());
}
private static void shorter(Optional<Boolean> opt) {
    opt.map(x -> "run: " + x)
        ._____(System.out::println);
}
```

   A. isNotNull, isPresent
   B. ifPresent, isPresent
   C. isPresent, forEach
   D. isPresent, ifPresent
   E. None of the above

38. Rewrite this lambda using a method reference:

```
() -> Math.random()
```

   A. `Math.random`

   B. `Math::random`

   C. `Math::random()`

   D. `java.lang::Math.random`

   E. None of the above

39. Which operation can occur more than once in a stream pipeline?

   A. Origin

   B. Sink

   C. Source

   D. Intermediate operation

   E. Terminal operation

   F. None of the above

40. What is true of the following code?

```
21: var list = List.of('c', 'b', 'a');
22:
23: list.stream()
24:     .sorted()
25:     .findAny()
26:     .ifPresent(System.out::println);
27:
28: System.out.println(list.stream().sorted().findFirst());
```

   A. Both streams are guaranteed to print the single character a.

   B. Both streams will print a single character of a, b, or c.

   C. Only one stream is guaranteed to print the single character a.

   D. Only one stream will print a single character of a, b, or c.

   E. The code does not compile.

41. Which functional interface, when entered into the following blank, allows the class to compile?

```
package groceries;
import java.util.*;
import java.util.function.*;

public class Market {
    private static void checkPrices(List<Double> prices,
            _____ scanner) {
```

```
        prices.forEach(scanner);
    }
    public static void main(String[] right) {
        List<Double> prices = List.of(1.2, 6.5, 3.0);
        checkPrices(prices,
            p -> {
                String result = p<5 ? "Correct" : "Too high";
                System.out.println(result);
            });
    }
}
```

A. Consumer

B. Consumer<Integer>

C. DoubleConsumer

D. Supplier<Double>

E. None of the above

42. Which of the following is not a valid lambda expression?

A. (Integer j, k) -> 5

B. (p,q) -> p+q

C. (Integer x, Integer y) -> x*y

D. (left,right) -> {return "null";}

E. All of these are valid.

43. What is the output of the following application?

```
package exercise;
import java.util.*;
public class Concat {
    public String concat1(List<String> values) {
        return values.parallelStream()
            .reduce("a",
                (x,y)->x+y,
                String::concat);
    }
    public String concat2(List<String> values) {
        return values.parallelStream()
            .reduce((w,z)->z+w).get();
    }
    public static void main(String... questions) {
```

```
        Concat c = new Concat();
        var list = List.of("Cat","Hat");
        String x = c.concat1(list);
        String y = c.concat2(list);
        System.out.print(x+" "+y);
    } }
```

 A. CatHat CatHat

 B. aCataHat HatCat

 C. The code does not compile because the stream in concat1() returns an Optional.

 D. The code does not compile for a different reason.

 E. An exception is printed at runtime.

 F. None of the above.

44. Which of the following three functional interfaces is not equivalent to the other two?

 A. BiFunction<Double,Double,Double>

 B. BinaryOperator<Double>

 C. DoubleFunction<Double>

 D. None of the above. All three are equivalent.

45. Given the following code snippet, what changes should be made for the JVM to correctly process this as a concurrent reduction? (Choose two.)

```
var w = Stream.of("c","a","t")
    .collect(HashSet::new, Set::add, Set::addAll);
System.out.println(w);
```

 A. Replace HashSet with LinkedHashSet.

 B. Mark the stream parallel.

 C. Remove the second argument of the collect() method.

 D. Remove the third argument of the collect() method.

 E. Replace HashSet with ConcurrentSkipListSet.

 F. Mark the stream unordered.

46. Fill in the blank so this code outputs three lines:

```
var list = new ArrayList<String>();
list.add("Atlanta");
list.add("Chicago");
list.add("New York");
list.stream()
    .filter(_____)
    .forEach(System.out::println);
```

A. `String::isEmpty`

B. `!String::isEmpty`

C. `String::! isEmpty`

D. `String::isNotEmpty`

E. None of the above

47. What does the following output?

```
var chars = Stream.generate(() -> 'a');
chars.filter(c -> c < 'b')
     .sorted()
     .findFirst()
     .ifPresent(System.out::print);
```

A. a

B. The code runs successfully without any output.

C. The code does not complete.

D. The code compiles but throws an exception at runtime.

48. What is the expected output of the following code snippet?

```
Stream.iterate(1, x -> x + 1)
   .limit(5)
   .skip(2)
   .peek(System.out::print)
   .collect(Collectors.toList())
   .forEach(System.out::print);
```

A. It does not compile.

B. It throws an exception at runtime.

C. It does not print any output at runtime.

D. 345345

E. 334455

F. The behavior of the code snippet cannot be determined until runtime.

49. What is the output of the following program?

```
package ai;
import java.util.function.*;

public class Android {
   public void wakeUp(Supplier supplier) {            // d1
      supplier.get();
   }
```

```
    public static void main(String... electricSheep) {
        Android data = new Android();
        data.wakeUp(() -> System.out.print("Started!")); // d2
    }
}
```

A. Started!

B. The code does not compile because of line d1 only.

C. The code does not compile because of line d2 only.

D. The code does not compile because of both lines d1 and d2.

50. Given the following code snippet, what statement about the values printed on lines p1 and p2 is correct?

```
var db = Collections.synchronizedList(new ArrayList<>());
IntStream.range(1,6)
    .parallel()
    .map(i -> {db.add(i); return i;})
    .forEachOrdered(System.out::print);   // p1
System.out.println();
db.forEach(System.out::print);           // p2
```

A. They are always the same.

B. They are sometimes the same.

C. They are never the same.

D. The code does not compile.

E. The code will produce a ConcurrentModificationException at runtime.

F. None of the above.

51. Fill in the blanks so this code prints *8.0-8.0*? (Choose two.)

```
var ints = IntStream.of(6, 10);
var longs = ints.mapToLong(i -> i);
var first = longs._____;


var moreLongs = LongStream.of(6, 10);
var stats = moreLongs.summaryStatistics();
var second = _____;
System.out.println("*" + first + "-" + second + "*");
```

A. averageAsDouble() in the first blank

B. average().getAsDouble() in the first blank

C. getAverage().get() in the first blank

D. stats.average() in the second blank

   E. `stats.average().get()` in the second blank

   F. `stats.getAverage()` in the second blank

52. Starting with `DoubleConsumer` and going downward, fill in the missing values for the table.

Functional Interface	# Parameters in Method Signature
DoubleConsumer	
IntFunction	
LongSupplier	
ObjDoubleConsumer	

   A. 0, 1, 1, 1

   B. 0, 1, 0, 2

   C. 0, 2, 1, 2

   D. 1, 1, 0, 2

   E. 1, 1, 1, 1

   F. None of the above

53. Starting with `DoubleConsumer` and going downward, fill in the values for the table. For the following choices, assume R is a generic type.

Functional Interface	Return Type
DoubleConsumer	
IntFunction	
LongSupplier	
ObjDoubleConsumer	

   A. double, int, long, R

   B. double, R, long, R

   C. R, int, long, R

   D. R, int, long, void

   E. void, int, R, void

   F. void, R, long, void

54. What is a possible output of the following application?

```
package salvage;
import java.util.*;
import java.util.stream.*;
public class Car {
```

```
private String model;
private int year;
@Override public String toString() {return model;}
// Constructor/Getters/Setters Omitted

public static void main(String... make) {
    var cars = new ArrayList<Car>();
    cars.add(new Car("Mustang",1967));
    cars.add(new Car("Thunderbird",1967));
    cars.add(new Car("Escort",1975));
    var map = cars
      .stream()
      .collect(
        Collectors.groupingByConcurrent(Car::getYear));
    System.out.print(map);
  }
}
```

A. `{1975=[Escort], 1967=[ Mustang, Thunderbird]}`

B. `{Escort=[1975], Thunderbird=[1967], Mustang=[1967]}`

C. The code does not compile.

D. The code hangs indefinitely at runtime.

E. The application throws an exception at runtime because the stream is not parallel.

F. None of the above.

55. How many lines does this code output?

```
var list = new LinkedList<String>();
list.add("Archie");
list.add("X-Men");
list.stream().forEach(System.out.println);
list.stream().forEach(System.out.println);
```

A. Two.

B. Four.

C. The code does not compile.

D. The code compiles but throws an exception at runtime.

56. Which lambda expression can replace the instance of `new BiologyMaterial()` in the `Scientist` class and produce the same results under various inputted values?

```
package university;
```

```
@FunctionalInterface interface Study {
    abstract int learn(String subject, int duration);
}

class BiologyMaterial implements Study {
    @Override public int learn(String subject, int duration) {
        if(subject == null)
            return duration;
        else
            return duration+1;
    }
}

public class Scientist {
    public static void main(String[] courses) {
        final Study s = new BiologyMaterial();
        System.out.print(s.learn(courses[0],
            Integer.parseInt(courses[1])));
    }
}
```

A. `(p,q) -> q==null ? p : p+1`

B. `(c,d) -> {int d=1; return c!=null ? d+1 : d;}`

C. `(x,y) -> {return x==null ? y : y+1;}`

D. `(a,b) -> 1`

E. None of the above

57. What is true of the following? (Choose two.)

```
var s = Stream.of("speak", "bark", "meow", "growl");
BinaryOperator<String> merge = (a, b) -> a;
var map = s.collect(toMap(String::length, k -> k, merge));
System.out.println(map.size() + " " + map.get(4));
```

A. The output is 2 bark.

B. The output is 2 meow.

C. The output is 4 bark.

D. The output is 4 meow.

E. If "meow" was replaced by a null reference, the output would remain the same.

F. If "meow" was replaced by a null reference, the output would change.

58. Which statement about a source in a `Stream` is true?

   A. The source is mandatory in a stream pipeline.

   B. The source is only allowed to return primitives.

   C. The source must be retrieved by calling the `stream()` method.

   D. The source must return a finite number of elements.

   E. None of the above.

59. Given an `IntStream`, which method would you use to obtain an equivalent parallel `Stream<T>`?

   A. `parallel()`

   B. `parallelStream()`

   C. `parallels()`

   D. `getParallel()`

   E. `getParallelStream()`

   F. None of the above

60. Which can fill in the blank to have the code print `true`?

```
var stream = Stream.iterate(1, i -> i+1);
var b = stream._____(i -> i > 5);
System.out.println(b);
```

   A. `anyMatch`

   B. `allMatch`

   C. `noneMatch`

   D. None of the above

61. Which of the following fills in the blank so that the code outputs one line but uses a poor practice?

```
import java.util.*;

public class Cheater {
   int count = 0;
   public void sneak(Collection<String> coll) {
      coll.stream()._____;
   }

   public static void main(String[] args) {
      var c = new Cheater();
      c.sneak(Arrays.asList("weasel"));
   }
}
```

A. peek(System.out::println)

B. peek(System.out::println).findFirst()

C. peek(r -> System.out.println(r)).findFirst()

D. peek(r -> {count++; System.out.println(r); }).findFirst()

E. None of the above compile.

F. None of these are bad practice.

62. What is the output of the following application?

```
package nesting;
import java.util.function.*;

public class Doll {
   private int layer;
   public Doll(int layer) {
      super();
      this.layer = layer;
   }

   public static void open(
      UnaryOperator<Doll> task, Doll doll) {

      while((doll = task.accept(doll)) != null) {
         System.out.print("X");
      }
   }

   public static void main(String[] wood) {
      open(s -> {
         if(s.layer<=0) return null;
         else return new Doll(s.layer--);
      }, new Doll(5));
   }
}
```

A. XXXXX

B. The code does not compile because of the lambda expression.

C. The code does not compile for a different reason.

D. The code compiles, but produces an infinite loop at runtime.

E. The code compiles, but throws an exception at runtime.

63. What is the expected output of the following code snippet?

```
Random r = new Random();
Stream.generate(r::nextDouble)
    .skip(2)
    .limit(4)
    .sorted()
    .peek(System.out::println)
    .forEach(System.out::println);
```

   A. It does not compile.

   B. It throws an exception at runtime.

   C. It does not print any output at runtime.

   D. It prints four numbers twice each.

   E. It can print up to eight distinct numbers.

   F. The behavior of the code snippet cannot be determined until runtime.

64. Which statements about the `findAny()` method applied to a stream are correct? (Choose three.)

   A. It always returns the first element on an ordered serial stream.

   B. It may return any element on an ordered serial stream.

   C. It always returns the first element on an unordered stream.

   D. It may return any element on an unordered stream.

   E. It always returns the first element on an ordered parallel stream.

   F. It may return any element on an ordered parallel stream.

65. Which functional interface has a `get()` method?

   A. `Consumer`

   B. `Function`

   C. `Supplier`

   D. `UnaryOperator`

   E. None of the above

66. Why can't `String::charAt` be used as a method reference within a `Function`?

   A. Method references can only be used on `static` methods.

   B. The `charAt()` method takes an `int` rather than `Integer` parameter.

   C. The method reference is not compatible with `Function`.

   D. The method reference syntax is illegal.

   E. There is no `charAt()` method in the `String` class.

   F. None of the above.

67. Given the following independent stream operations, which statements are correct? (Choose three.)

```
List.of(2,4,6,8)
   .parallel()
   .parallelStream()
   .forEach(System.out::print);

List.of(2,4,6,8)
   .parallelStream()
   .parallel()
   .forEach(System.out::print);

List.of(2,4,6,8)
   .parallelStream()
   .parallel().parallel().parallel()
   .forEach(System.out::print);
```

- **A.** The first stream operation compiles.
- **B.** The second stream operation compiles.
- **C.** The third stream operation compiles.
- **D.** None of the stream operations that compile produce an exception at runtime.
- **E.** At least one of the stream operations that compiles produces at exception at runtime.
- **F.** The output of the stream operations that compile is consistent between executions.

68. Which method reference can replace the lambda on the first line so the output is the same?

```
BiPredicate<String, String> pred = (a, b) -> a.contains(b);
System.out.println(pred.test("fish", "is"));
```

- **A.** `a::contains(b)`
- **B.** `a::contains`
- **C.** `String::contains(b)`
- **D.** `String::contains`
- **E.** The supplied code does not compile.
- **F.** None of the above.

69. What is the result of the following?

```
import static java.util.stream.Collectors.*;
import java.util.stream.Stream;

class Ballot {
```

```
      private String name;
      private int judgeNumber;
      private int score;

      public Ballot(String name, int judgeNumber, int score) {
         this.name = name;
         this.judgeNumber = judgeNumber;
         this.score = score;
      }
      // all getters and setters
   }

   public class Speaking {
      public static void main(String[] args) {
         Stream<Ballot> ballots = Stream.of(
            new Ballot("Mario", 1, 10),
            new Ballot("Christina", 1, 8),
            new Ballot("Mario", 2, 9),
            new Ballot("Christina", 2, 8)
         );

         var scores = ballots.collect(
            groupingBy(Ballot::getName,
            summingInt(Ballot::getScore)));
         System.out.println(scores.get("Mario"));
      }
   }
```

A. 2

B. 18

C. 19

D. 110

E. The code does not compile.

70. Which of the following can fill in the blank to have the code print 44?

```
var stream = Stream.of("base", "ball");
stream.____(s -> s.length()).forEach(System.out::print);
```

A. Only map

B. Only mapToInt

C. Only mapToObject

D. Both map and `mapToInt`

E. Both map and `mapToObject`

F. `map`, `mapToInt`, and `mapToObject`

71. What does the following do? (Choose two.)

```
public class Shoot {
    interface Target {
        boolean needToAim(double angle);
    }
    static void prepare(double angle, Target t) {
        boolean ready = t.needToAim(angle);  // k1
        System.out.println(ready);
    }
    public static void main(String[] args) {
        prepare(45, d -> d > 5 || d < -5);    // k2
    }
}
```

A. If any compiler errors are fixed, it prints `true`.

B. If any compiler errors are fixed, it prints `false`.

C. It compiles without issue.

D. It doesn't compile due to line `k1`.

E. It doesn't compile due to line `k2`.

72. Which statements about the following code are correct?

```
var data = List.of(1,2,3);
int f = data.parallelStream()
    .reduce(1, (a,b) -> a+b, (a,b) -> a+b);
System.out.println(f);
```

A. It consistently prints 6.

B. It consistently prints 7.

C. It consistently prints another value.

D. It does not consistently print the same value on every execution.

E. It compiles but throws an exception at runtime.

F. None of the above.

73. What is the result of the following?

```
11: var s1 = IntStream.empty();
12: System.out.print(s1.average().getAsDouble());
13:
```

```
14: var s2 = IntStream.of(-1,0, 1);
15: System.out.print(s2.average().getAsDouble());
```

A. Both statements print 0.

B. Both statements print 0.0.

C. The statements print different values.

D. The code does not compile.

E. The code compiles but throws an exception at runtime.

74. Which lambdas can replace the method references in this code? (Choose two.)

```
Stream.of("fish", "mammal", "amphibian")
    .map(String::length)
    .findFirst()
    .ifPresent(System.out::println);
```

A. `x.length()`

B. `x -> x.length()`

C. `x -> x::length`

D. `System.out.println(s)`

E. `s -> System.out.println(s)`

F. `s -> System.out::println`

75. What collector can turn the stream at left to the Map at right?

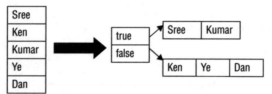

A. Only `grouping()`

B. Only `groupingBy()`

C. Only `partitioning()`

D. Only `partitioningBy()`

E. Both `grouping()` and `partitioning()`

F. Both `groupingBy()` and `partitioningBy()`

76. Which expression is compatible with the `IntSupplier` functional interface?

A. `() -> 1<10 ? "3" : 4`

B. `() -> {return 1/0;}`

C. `() -> return 4`

D. `System.out::print`

E. None of the above

77. What is the output of the following application?

```
package beach;
import java.util.function.*;

class Tourist {
   public Tourist(double distance) {
      this.distance = distance;
   }
   public double distance;
}
public class Lifeguard {
   private void saveLife(Predicate<Tourist> canSave,
      Tourist tourist) {

      System.out.print(canSave.test(tourist)
         ? "Saved" : "Too far");
   }
   public final static void main(String... sand) {
      new Lifeguard().saveLife(s -> s.distance<4,
         new Tourist(2));
   }
}
```

- **A.** Saved
- **B.** Too far
- **C.** The code does not compile because of the main() method.
- **D.** The code does not compile because of the saveLife() method.
- **E.** None of the above.

78. Given a LinkedList<E>, which method would you call to obtain a parallel stream that uses it as a data source?

- **A.** getParallel()
- **B.** parallels()
- **C.** getParallelStream()
- **D.** parallel()
- **E.** parallelStream()
- **F.** None of the above

79. How many lines does the following code output?

```
import java.util.*;
class Blankie {
   String color;
```

```
      String getColor() {
         return color;
      }
   }
   public class PreSchool {
      public static void main(String[] args) {
         var b1 = new Blankie();
         var b2 = new Blankie();
         b1.color = "pink";
         List<Blankie> list = Arrays.asList(b1, b2);
         list.stream()
            .filter(Blankie::getColor)        // line x
            .forEach(System.out::println);    // line y
      }
   }
```

   A. One.

   B. Two.

   C. The code does not compile due to line x.

   D. The code does not compile due to line y.

   E. The code compiles but throws an exception at runtime.

80. Which are true statements? (Choose two.)

   A. A source cannot return an infinite stream.

   B. A source may return an infinite stream.

   C. A source must return an infinite stream.

   D. An intermediate operation cannot return an infinite stream.

   E. An intermediate operation may return an infinite stream.

   F. An intermediate operation must return an infinite stream.

81. How many of these lines have compiler errors?

```
14: Consumer<Object> c1 = ArrayList::new;
15: Consumer<Object> c2 = String::new;
16: Consumer<Object> c3 = System.out::println;
17: var c4 = ArrayList::new;
18: var c5 = String::new;
19: var c6 = System.out::println;
```

   A. One.

   B. Two.

C. Three.

D. Four.

E. Five.

F. The code compiles as is.

82. What is the output of the following program?

```
var p = List.of(new StringBuilder("hello"),
   new StringBuilder("goodbye"));
var q = p.parallelStream().reduce(0,
   (w,x) -> w.length() + x.length(),
   (y,z) -> y.length() + z.length());
System.out.print(q);
```

A. 0

B. 12

C. 14

D. One line does not compile.

E. Two lines do not compile.

F. None of the above.

83. What is true of this code? (Choose two.)

```
var bools = Stream.of(Boolean.TRUE, null);
var map = bools
   .limit(1)    // line k
   .collect(partitioningBy(b -> b));
System.out.println(map);
```

A. It outputs {true=[true]}.

B. It outputs {false=null, true=[true]}.

C. It outputs {false=[], true=[true]}.

D. It outputs {false=[null], true=[true]}.

E. The output is the same if line k is removed.

F. The output is different after line k is removed.

84. What is the output of the following code snippet?

```
var apples = List.of(1, 2);
var oranges = List.of(1, 2);
final var count = Stream.of(apples, oranges)
   .flatMapToInt(List::stream)
   .peek(System.out::print)
```

```
    .count();
System.out.print(count);
```

A. 12124

B. 11224

C. 122

D. The code does not compile.

E. The code compiles but does not output anything at runtime.

F. None of the above.

85. Which functional interface, when filled into the blank, prevents the class from compiling?

```
package morning;
import java.util.function.*;

public class Sun {
    public static void dawn(_____ sunrise) {}
    public void main(String... rays) {
        dawn(s -> s+1);
    }
}
```

A. DoubleUnaryOperator

B. Function<String,String>

C. IntToLongFunction

D. UnaryOperator

E. All of the above allow the code to compile.

86. Which statements about applying forEachOrdered() to a parallel ordered stream instead of using forEach() are correct? (Choose two.)

A. The operation will likely be faster.

B. The operation will likely be slower.

C. There is no expected change in performance.

D. It forces some stream operations in the pipeline to be performed in a serial manner.

E. It forces all stream operations in the pipeline to be performed in a serial manner.

F. All stream operations will continue to be performed in a parallel manner.

87. What is the true of the following? (Choose two.)

```
IntegerSummaryStatistics stats = Stream.of(20, 40)
    .mapToInt(i -> i)
    .summaryStatistics();
long total = stats.getSum();
```

```
long count = stats.getCount();
long max = stats.getMax();
System.out.println(total + "-" + count + "-" + max);
```

A. The output is 60-0-40

B. The output is 60-2-40

C. The code does not compile for one reason.

D. The code does not compile for two reasons.

E. Correct code could be written without summary statistics using a single stream pipeline.

F. Correct code could not be written without summary statics using a single stream pipeline.

88. What is a difference between lambdas and method references?

A. Only one can take a method parameter.

B. Only one can reference an effectively final local variable.

C. Only one can make a method call where the method parameter is the hard-coded number 3.

D. Only one can use deferred execution.

E. None of the above.

89. Following the generate() method, which of the four method calls in this code can be removed and have the method still compile and run without error?

```
public static void main(String[] args) {
    Stream.generate(() -> 'a')
        .limit(5)
        .filter(c -> c < 'b')
        .sorted()
        .findFirst()
        .ifPresent(System.out::print);
}
```

A. filter()

B. sorted()

C. filter() and sorted()

D. filter() and ifPresent()

E. filter(), sorted(), and ifPresent()

F. filter(), sorted(), findFirst(), and ifPresent()

90. What is true of the following? (Choose three.)

```
import java.util.*;
public class Catch {
    public static void main(String[] args) {
```

```
        Optional opt = Optional.empty();
        var message = "";
        try {
            message = _____(opt);
        } catch (IllegalArgumentException e) {
            System.out.print("Caught it");
        }
        System.out.print(message);
    }
    private static String x(Optional<String> opt) {
        return opt.orElseThrow();
    }
    private static String y(Optional<String> opt) {
        return opt.orElseThrow(IllegalArgumentException::new);
    }
    private static String z(Optional<String> opt) {
        return opt.orElse("Caught it");
    }
}
```

A. If filling in the blank with method x, the code outputs Caught it.

B. If filling in the blank with method x, the code prints a stack trace.

C. If filling in the blank with method y, the code outputs Caught it.

D. If filling in the blank with method y, the code prints a stack trace.

E. If filling in the blank with method z, the code outputs Caught it.

F. If filling in the blank with method z, the code prints a stack trace.

91. Which statement is not true of Predicate?

A. A boolean is returned from the method it declares.

B. It is an interface.

C. The method it declares accepts two parameters.

D. The method it declares is named test.

E. All of the above are true.

92. Which functional interface does not have the correct number of generic arguments? (Choose two.)

A. BiFunction<T,U,R>

B. BinaryOperator<T, U>

C. DoubleFunction<T,R>

D. ToDoubleFunction<T>

E. ToIntBiFunction<T,U>

93. How many changes need to be made to the following stream operation to execute a parallel reduction?

```
var r = new Random();
var data = Stream.generate(() -> String.valueOf(r.nextInt()))
   .limit(50_000_000)
   .collect(Collectors.toSet());
var map = data.stream()
   .collect(Collectors.groupingBy(String::length));
```

A. None, it is already a parallel reduction.

B. One.

C. Two.

D. Three.

E. The code does not compile.

F. None of the above.

94. What is the output of this code?

```
Stream.of("one", "two", "bloat")
   .limit(1)
   .map(String::toUpperCase)       // line x
   .sorted()
   .forEach(System.out::println);
```

A. bloat

B. BLOAT

C. one

D. ONE

E. The code does not compile due to line x.

F. None of the above.

95. Which lambda expression can be passed to the `magic()` method?

```
package show;
import java.util.function.*;

public class Magician {
   public void magic(BinaryOperator<Long> lambda) {
      lambda.apply(3L, 7L);
   }
}
```

A. (a) -> a

B. (b,w) -> (long)w.intValue()

C. `(c,m) -> {long c=4; return c+m;}`

D. `(Integer d, Integer r) -> (Long)r+d`

E. None of the above

96. Fill in the blank: _____ is the only functional interface that does not involve `double`, `int`, or `long`.

    A. `BooleanSupplier`

    B. `CharPredicate`

    C. `FloatUnaryOperator`

    D. `ShortConsumer`

    E. None of the above

97. Which statements about parallel streams are correct? (Choose two.)

    A. A parallel stream is always faster than a serial stream.

    B. The JVM will automatically apply a parallel stream operation to an arbitrary stream in order to boost performance.

    C. A parallel stream synchronizes its operations so that they are atomic.

    D. All streams can be converted to a parallel stream.

    E. If a stream uses a reduction method, the result will be the same regardless of whether the stream is parallel or serial.

    F. Sometimes, a parallel stream will still operate in a single-threaded manner.

98. What is the output of the following?

```
var s = Stream.of("over the river",
    "through the woods",
    "to grandmother's house we go");

s.filter(n -> n.startsWith("t"))
    .sorted(Comparator::reverseOrder)
    .findFirst()
    .ifPresent(System.out::println);
```

    A. `over the river`

    B. `through the woods`

    C. `to grandmother's house we go`

    D. None of the above

99. Which can fill in the blank to have the code print the single digit 9?

```
var stream = LongStream.of(9);
stream._____(p -> p).forEach(System.out::print);
```

    A. Only `mapToDouble`

    B. Only `mapToInt`

    C. Only `mapToLong`

    D. Both `mapToDouble` and `mapToInt`

    E. `mapToDouble`, `mapToInt`, and `mapToLong`

    F. None of the above

100. What is the output of the following application?

```
package savings;
import java.util.function.*;

public class Bank {
    private int savingsInCents;
    private static class ConvertToCents {
        static DoubleToIntFunction f = p -> p*100;
    }
    public static void main(String... currency) {
        Bank creditUnion = new Bank();
        creditUnion.savingsInCents = 100;
        double deposit = 1.5;

        creditUnion.savingsInCents +=
            ConvertToCents.f.applyAsInt(deposit);  // j1
        System.out.print(creditUnion.savingsInCents);
    }
}
```

    A. 100

    B. 200

    C. 250

    D. The code does not compile because of line j1.

    E. None of the above.

101. Which statements about stateful lambda expressions are correct? (Choose two.)

    A. Stateful lambda expressions should be avoided on both serial and parallel streams.

    B. Stateful lambda expressions should be avoided on only serial streams.

    C. Stateful lambda expressions should be avoided on only parallel streams.

    D. One way to avoid modifying a `List` with a stateful lambda expression is to use a concurrent collection.

    E. One way to avoid modifying a `List` with a stateful lambda expression is to use a collector that outputs a `List`.

    F. One way to avoid modifying a `List` with a stateful lambda expression is to use a synchronized list.

102. Which method reference can replace the lambda on the second line so the output is the same?

```
var s = "fish";
Predicate<String> pred = (a) -> s.contains(a);
System.out.println(pred.test("fish", "is"));
```

  A. `a::contains(b)`

  B. `a::contains`

  C. `String::contains(b)`

  D. `String::contains`

  E. The supplied code does not compile.

  F. None of the above.

103. What is the best example of lazy evaluation?

  A. The pipeline can execute before seeing all the data.

  B. The pipeline does not begin until the terminal operation is executed.

  C. The pipeline executes all operations as quickly as possible.

  D. The pipeline loses data.

  E. The pipeline takes a nap.

104. Which method can be applied to an existing `Stream<T>` to return a stream with a different generic type?

  A. `distinct()`

  B. `iterate()`

  C. `peek()`

  D. `sorted()`

  E. `filter()`

  F. None of the above

105. The _____ functional interface has an `apply()` method, while the _____ functional interface has an `applyAsDouble()` method. (Choose two.)

  A. `BiConsumer`

  B. `BiFunction`

  C. `BiPredicate`

  D. `DoubleConsumer`

  E. `DoublePredicate`

  F. `DoubleUnaryOperator`

106. Given the following code snippet, what statement about the values printed on lines q1 and q2 is correct?

```
var mitchsWorkout = new CopyOnWriteArrayList<Integer>();
List.of(1,5,7,9).stream().parallel()
    .forEach(mitchsWorkout::add);
mitchsWorkout
    .forEachOrdered(System.out::print);  // q1
List.of(1,5,7,9).stream().parallel()
    .forEachOrdered(System.out::print);  // q2
```

- **A.** They are always the same.
- **B.** They are sometimes the same.
- **C.** They are never the same.
- **D.** The code does not compile.
- **E.** The code will produce a `ConcurrentModificationException` at runtime.
- **F.** None of the above.

107. Which of the following can fill in the blank to have the code print out *?

```
Stream.generate(() -> "*")
    .limit(3)
    .sorted(_____)
    .distinct()
    .forEach(System.out::println);
```

- **A.** `(s,t) -> s.length() - t.length()`
- **B.** `String::isEmpty`
- **C.** Both of these will produce the desired output.
- **D.** Neither of these will allow the code to compile.
- **E.** The code does not complete regardless of what goes in the blank.

108. Which statement about functional interfaces and lambda expressions is not true?

- **A.** A lambda expression may be compatible with multiple functional interfaces.
- **B.** A lambda expression must be assigned to a functional interface when it is declared.
- **C.** A method can return a lambda expression in the form of a functional interface instance.
- **D.** The compiler uses deferred execution to skip determining whether a lambda expression compiles or not.
- **E.** All of these are true.

109. Which can fill in the blank to have the code print `true`?

```
var stream = Stream.iterate(1, i -> i);
var b = stream._____(i -> i > 5);
System.out.println(b);
```

- **A.** `anyMatch`
- **B.** `allMatch`
- **C.** `noneMatch`
- **D.** None of the above

110. Given the following class, how many lines contain compilation errors?

```
1:  package showtimes;
2:  import java.util.*;
3:  import java.util.function.*;
4:  public class FindMovie {
5:      private Function<String> printer;
6:      protected FindMovie() {
7:          printer = s -> {System.out.println(s); return s;}
8:      }
9:      void printMovies(List<String> movies) {
10:         movies.forEach(printer);
11:     }
12:     public static void main(String[] screen) {
13:         List<String> movies = new ArrayList<>();
14:         movies.add("Stream 3");
15:         movies.add("Lord of the Recursion");
16:         movies.add("Silence of the Lambdas");
17:         new FindMovie().printMovies(movies);
18:     }
19: }
```

- **A.** None. The code compiles as is.
- **B.** One.
- **C.** Two.
- **D.** Three.
- **E.** Four.
- **F.** Five.

111. Which statements about the `findFirst()` method applied to a stream are correct? (Choose three.)

A. It always returns the first element on an ordered serial stream.

B. It may return any element on an ordered serial stream.

C. It always returns the first element on an unordered stream.

D. It may return any element on an unordered stream.

E. It always returns the first element on an ordered parallel stream.

F. It may return any element on an ordered parallel stream.

112. Which method reference can replace the lambda in the first line of the `main()` method to produce the same output?

```
interface Marsupial {
    void carryInPouch(int size);
}
public class Opossum {
    public static void main(String[] args) {
        Marsupial mar = x -> System.out.println("Carrying " + x);

        mar.carryInPouch(1);
    }
}
```

A. `System:out:println`

B. `System::out:println`

C. `System::out::println`

D. `System.out::println`

E. None of the above

113. What is true of the following code?

```
21: Stream<Integer> s1 = Stream.of(8, 2);
22: Stream<Integer> s2 = Stream.of(10, 20);
23: s2 = s1.filter(n -> n > 4);
24: s1 = s2.filter(n -> n < 1);
25: System.out.println(s1.count());
26: System.out.println(s2.count());
```

A. The code runs without error and prints 0.

B. The code runs without error and prints 1.

C. The code throws an exception on line 23.

D. The code throws an exception on line 24.

E. The code throws an exception on line 25.

F. The code throws an exception on line 26.

114. Which changes can be independently made to this code and have it still compile? (Choose three.)

```
Predicate<StringBuilder> p =
    (StringBuilder b) -> {return true;};
```

- **A.** Change `StringBuilder b` to var b.
- **B.** Change `StringBuilder b` to b.
- **C.** Remove `StringBuilder b`.
- **D.** Remove `->`.
- **E.** Remove `{` and `;}`.
- **F.** Remove `{ return` and `;}`.

115. What does this code output?

```
var babies = Arrays.asList("chick", "cygnet", "duckling");
babies.replaceAll(x -> { var newValue = "baby";
    return newValue; });
System.out.println(newValue);
```

- **A.** `baby`
- **B.** `chick`
- **C.** `cygnet`
- **D.** `duckling`
- **E.** The code does not compile.

116. Which lambda expression cannot be assigned to a `DoubleToLongFunction` functional interface?

- **A.** `a -> null==null ? 1 : 2L`
- **B.** `e -> (int)(10.0*e)`
- **C.** `(double m) -> {long p = (long)m; return p;}`
- **D.** `(Double s) -> s.longValue()`
- **E.** All of these can be assigned.

117. Given the following code snippet, which values of x will allow the call `divide(x)` to compile and provide predictable results at runtime? (Choose two.)

```
import java.util.stream.*;
public class Divide {
    static float divide(Stream<Float> s) {
        return s.reduce(1.0f, (a,b) -> a/b, (a,b) -> a/b);
    } }
```

- **A.** `Set.of(1f,2f,3f,4f).stream()`
- **B.** `List.of(1f,2f,3f,4f).stream()`

  C. `List.of(1f,2f,3f,4f).parallel()`

  D. `List.of(1f).parallelStream()`

  E. `List.of(1f,2f,3f,4f).parallelStream()`

  F. `List.of(1f).parallel()`

118. Which of the following produces different output than the others?

  A.

```
Stream.of("eeny", "meeny", "miny", "moe")
    .collect(partitioningBy(x -> x.charAt(0) == 'e'))
    .get(false)
    .stream()
    .collect(groupingBy(String::length))
    .get(4)
    .forEach(System.out::println);
```

  B.

```
Stream.of("eeny", "meeny", "miny", "moe")
    .filter(x -> x.charAt(0) != 'e')
    .collect(groupingBy(String::length))
    .get(4)
    .forEach(System.out::println);
```

  C.

```
Stream.of("eeny", "meeny", "miny", "moe")
    .collect(groupingBy(x -> x.charAt(0) == 'e'))
    .get(false)
    .stream()
    .collect(partitioningBy(String::length))
    .get(4)
    .forEach(System.out::println);
```

  D.

```
Stream.of("eeny", "meeny", "miny", "moe")
    .collect(groupingBy(x -> x.charAt(0) == 'e'))
    .get(false)
    .stream()
    .collect(groupingBy(String::length))
    .get(4)
    .forEach(System.out::println);
```

E.

```
Stream.of("eeny", "meeny", "miny", "moe")
    .collect(partitioningBy(x -> x.charAt(0) == 'e'))
    .get(false)
    .stream()
    .collect(partitioningBy(x -> x.length() == 4))
    .get(true)
    .forEach(System.out::println);
```

F. They all produce the same output.

119. Given an `IntStream`, which method would you use to obtain an equivalent parallel `IntStream`?

    A. `parallelStream()`

    B. `parallels()`

    C. `getParallelStream()`

    D. `parallel()`

    E. `getParallel()`

    F. None of the above

120. Which statement is true?

    A. All lambdas can be converted to method references, and vice versa.

    B. All lambdas can be converted to method references, but not vice versa.

    C. All method references can be converted to lambdas, but not vice versa.

    D. None of the above.

121. The following diagram shows input arguments being used in three functional interface methods of unknown type. Which three functional interfaces, inserted in order from left to right, could be used to complete the diagram?

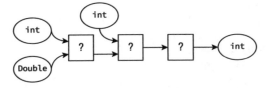

A.

```
DoubleBinaryOperator
ToDoubleBiFunction<Integer,Double>
UnaryOperator<Integer>
```

B.

```
BinaryOperator<Double>
BiFunction<Integer,Integer,Double>
UnaryOperator<Integer>
```

C.

```
Function<Double,Integer>
BiFunction<Integer,Integer,Double>
DoubleToIntFunction
```

D.

```
BiFunction<Integer,Double,Integer>
BinaryOperator<Integer>
IntUnaryOperator
```

E. None of the above

122. Which of the following is not a functional interface in the `java.util.function` package? (Choose two.)

A. `DoublePredicate`

B. `LongUnaryOperator`

C. `ShortSupplier`

D. `ToIntBiFunction`

E. `ToStringOperator`

123. What is the output of the following application?

```
package tps;
import java.util.*;

class Boss {
   private String name;
   public Boss(String name) {
      this.name = name;
   }
   public String getName() {return name.toUpperCase();}
   public String toString() {return getName();}
}
public class Initech {
   public static void main(String[] reports) {
      final List<Boss> bosses = new ArrayList(8);
      bosses.add(new Boss("Jenny"));
      bosses.add(new Boss("Ted"));
      bosses.add(new Boss("Grace"));
      bosses.removeIf(s -> s.equalsIgnoreCase("ted"));
      System.out.print(bosses);
   }
}
```

A. [JENNY, GRACE]

B. [ted]

C. [tps.Boss@4218224c, tps.Boss@815f19a]

D. The code does not compile because of the lambda expression.

E. The code does not compile for a different reason.

124. Which lambda can implement this functional interface?

```
public interface Serval {
    static void printName(String name) {}
    boolean cat(String name) { return true; }
}
```

A. () -> System.out.println()

B. n -> System.out.println(n)

C. () -> true

D. n -> true

E. None of the above

125. How many of these lines compile?

```
17: Comparator<String> c1 = s -> false;
18: Comparator<String, String> c2 = (s1, s2) -> false;
19: Predicate<String> p1 = String s -> false;
20: Predicate<String> p2 = (String s) -> false;
21: Supplier<String> s1 = String s -> false;
22: Supplier<String> s2 = (String s) -> false;
```

A. One

B. Two

C. Three

D. Four

E. Five

F. Six

126. Which method is not available on the IntSummaryStatistics class?

A. getCountAsLong()

B. getMax()

C. toString()

D. None of these methods is available.

E. All of these methods are available.

127. Which functional interface, when filled into the blank, allows the class to compile?

```java
package sleep;
import java.util.function.*;

class Sheep {}
public class Dream {
    int MAX_SHEEP = 10;
    int sheepCount;
    public void countSheep(_____ backToSleep) {
        while(sheepCount<MAX_SHEEP) {
            // TODO: Apply lambda
            sheepCount++;
        }
    }
    public static void main(String[] dark) {
        new Dream().countSheep(System.out::println);
    }
}
```

A. Consumer<Sheep>

B. Function<Sheep,void>

C. Supplier<Sheep>

D. UnaryOperator<Sheep>

E. None of the above

128. Given an instance of Stream s and Collection c, which of the following are valid ways of creating a parallel stream? (Choose three.)

A. c.parallel()

B. c.parallel().parallelStream()

C. c.parallelStream()

D. s.parallelStream()

E. c.parallelStream().parallel()

F. s.parallel()

129. What is true of the following code? (Choose two.)

```java
3:  public static void main(String[] args) {
4:      var prefix = "r";
5:      var pets = List.of("rabbit", "snake", "turtle");
6:
7:      // prefix = "t";
```

```
8:        pets.forEach(p -> {
9:            if (p.startsWith(prefix)) System.out.println(p); } );
10: }
```

A. As written, the code prints one line.

B. As written, the code prints two lines.

C. As written the code does not compile.

D. If line 7 is uncommented, the code prints one line.

E. If line 7 is uncommented, the code prints two lines.

F. If line 7 is uncommented, the code does not compile.

130. What is the output of the following code snippet?

```
10: var pears = List.of(1, 2, 3, 4, 5, 6);
11: final var sum = pears.stream()
12:     .skip(1)
13:     .limit(3)
14:     .flatMapToInt(s -> IntStream.of(s))
15:     .skip(1)
16:     .boxed()
17:     .mapToDouble(s -> s)
18:     .sum();
19: System.out.print(sum);
```

A. 6

B. 7.0

C. 6.0

D. 7

E. Exactly one line contains a compiler error.

F. More than one line contains a compiler error.

131. What is the minimum number of intermediate operations that can fill in each box [M, N, O, P] to have the pipeline complete given any intermediate operation?

Source	Intermediate Operation	Terminal Operation
Finite Stream Source	Box M	count()
Finite Stream Source	Box N	findFirst()
Infinite Stream Source	Box O	count()
Infinite Stream Source	Box P	findFirst()

A. `[0, 0, 0, 1]`

B. `[0, 0, 1, 0]`

C. `[0, 0, 1, 1]`

D. `[1, 1, 0, 1]`

E. `[1, 1 ,1, 0]`

F. `[1, 1, 1, 1]`

132. Given the table in the previous question, how many of the boxes in the *Intermediate Operation* column will have the pipeline complete regardless of which intermediate operation is placed in the box?

A. Zero

B. One

C. Two

D. Three

E. Four

133. Which of the following declares a `Comparator` where all objects are treated as equal?

A. `Comparator<Character> comp = (c1) -> 0;`

B. `Comparator<Character> comp = (c1) -> {0};`

C. `Comparator<Character> comp = (c1, c2) -> 0;`

D. `Comparator<Character> comp = (c1, c2) -> {0};`

E. None of the above

134. Which can fill in the blank so this code outputs `true`?

```
import java.util.function.*;
import java.util.stream.*;

public class HideAndSeek {
   public static void main(String[] args) {
      var hide = Stream.of(true, false, true);
      var found = hide.filter(b -> b)._____();
      System.out.println(found);
   }
}
```

A. Only `anyMatch`

B. Only `allMatch`

C. Both `anyMatch` and `allMatch`

D. Only `noneMatch`

E. The code does not compile with any of these options.

135. Which method reference can replace the lambda on the second line so the output is the same?

```
var s = "fish";
Predicate<String> pred = (a) -> s.contains(a);
System.out.println(pred.test("is"));
```

- **A.** `s::contains(a)`
- **B.** `s::contains`
- **C.** `String::contains(a)`
- **D.** `String::contains`
- **E.** The supplied code does not compile.
- **F.** None of the above.

136. How many of these lines compile?

```
Predicate<String> pred1 = (final String s) -> s.isEmpty();
Predicate<String> pred2 = (final s) -> s.isEmpty();
Predicate<String> pred3 = (final var s) -> s.isEmpty();
Predicate<String> pred4 = (String s) -> s.isEmpty();
Predicate<String> pred5 = (var s) -> s.isEmpty();
```

- **A.** 0
- **B.** 1
- **C.** 2
- **D.** 3
- **E.** 4
- **F.** 5

137. What is the output of the following application?

```
package pet;
import java.util.*;
import java.util.function.*;

public class DogSearch {
    void reduceList(List<String> names,
        Predicate<String> tester) {

        names.removeIf(tester);
    }
    public static void main(String[] treats) {
        int MAX_LENGTH = 2;
        DogSearch search = new DogSearch();
        List<String> names = new ArrayList<>();
```

```
        names.add("Lassie");
        names.add("Benji");
        names.add("Brian");
        search.reduceList(names, d -> d.length()>MAX_LENGTH);
        System.out.print(names.size());
    }
}
```

A. 0

B. 2

C. 3

D. The code does not compile because of the lambda expression.

E. The code does not compile for a different reason.

138. What is the output of the following program?

```
var p = List.of(1,3,5);
var q = p.parallelStream().reduce(0f,
    (w,x) -> w.floatValue() + x.floatValue(),
    (y,z) -> y.floatValue() + z.floatValue());
System.out.println(q);
```

A. 0.0

B. 9.0

C. 11.0

D. One line does not compile.

E. Two lines do not compile.

F. None of the above.

139. What does the following output?

```
Set<String> set = new HashSet<>();
set.add("tire-");
List<String> list = new LinkedList<>();
Deque<String> queue = new ArrayDeque<>();
queue.push("wheel-");
Stream.of(set, list, queue)
    .flatMap(x -> x.stream())
    .forEach(System.out::print);
```

A. [tire-][wheel-]

B. tire-wheel-

C. None of the above.

D. The code does not compile.

140. How many lines does this code output?

```
1:  import java.util.*;
2:
3:  public class PrintNegative {
4:      public static void main(String[] args) {
5:          List<String> list = new ArrayList<>();
6:          list.add("-5");
7:          list.add("0");
8:          list.add("5");
9:          list.removeIf(e -> e < 0);
10:         list.forEach(x -> System.out.println(x));
11:     }
12: }
```

A. One.

B. Two.

C. Three.

D. None. The code does not compile.

E. None. The code throws an exception at runtime.

141. How many of the following lines compile?

```
8:  IntFunction<Integer> f1 =(Integer f) -> f;
9:  IntFunction<Integer> f2 = (v) -> null;
10: IntFunction<Integer> f3 = s -> s;
11: IntFunction<Integer> f4 = () -> 5;
12: IntFunction<Integer> f5 = () -> Integer.valueOf(9);
```

A. None

B. One

C. Two

D. Three

E. Four

F. Five

142. Which statements about using a parallel stream instead of a serial stream are correct? (Choose three.)

A. The number of threads used is guaranteed to be higher.

B. It requires a stateful lambda expression.

C. The stream operation may execute faster.

D. The stream operation may execute slower.

    E.   The result of the stream operation will be the same.

    F.   The result of the stream operation may change.

143. Which is a possible output of the following code snippet?

```
var landmarks = Set.of("Eiffel Tower", "Statue of Liberty",
   "Stonehenge", "Mount Fuji");
var result = landmarks
   .stream()
   .collect(Collectors.partitioningBy(b -> b.contains(" ")))
   .entrySet()
   .stream()
   .flatMap(t -> t.getValue().stream())
   .collect(Collectors.groupingBy(s -> !s.startsWith("S")));
System.out.println(result);
```

    A. `{false=[Stonehenge, Statue of Liberty], true=[Eiffel Tower, Mount Fuji]}`

    B. `{false=[Stonehenge], true=[Mount Fuji, Eiffel Tower, Statue of Liberty]}`

    C. `{false=[Mount Fuji, Stonehenge], true=[Eiffel Tower, Statue of Liberty]}`

    D. Exactly one line contains a compiler error.

    E. More than one line contains a compiler error.

    F. None of the above.

144. Which can independently fill in the blank to output `No dessert today`?

```
import java.util.*;
public class Dessert {
  public static void main(String[] yum) {
    eatDessert(Optional.of("Cupcake"));
  }
  private static void eatDessert(Optional<String> opt) {
    System.out.println(opt._____);
  }
}
```

    A. `get("No dessert today")`

    B. `orElse("No dessert today")`

    C. `orElseGet(() -> "No dessert today")`

    D. `orElseThrow()`

    E. None of the above

145. What is the output of this code?

```
List.of("one", "two", "bloat")
   .limit(1)
   .map(String::toUpperCase)        // line x
   .sorted()
   .forEach(System.out::println);
```

A. bloat

B. BLOAT

C. one

D. ONE

E. The code does not compile due to line x.

F. None of the above.

146. Which is one of the lines output by this code?

```
10: var list = new ArrayList<Integer>();
11: list.add(10);
12: list.add(9);
13: list.add(8);
14:
15: var num = 9;
16: list.removeIf(x -> {int keep = num; return x == keep;});
17: System.out.println(list);
18:
19: num = 8;
20: list.removeIf(x -> {int keep = num; return x == keep;});
21: System.out.println(list);
```

A. []

B. [8]

C. [9]

D. [10]

E. The code does not compile.

147. What is the output of the following?

```
import java.util.Comparator;
import java.util.stream.Stream;

public class Compete {
   public static void main(String[] args) {
      Stream<Integer> is = Stream.of(8, 6, 9);
      Comparator<Integer> c = (a, b) -> a - b;
```

```
        is.sort(c).forEach(System.out::print);
    }
}
```

A. 689

B. 986

C. The code does not compile.

D. The code compiles but throws an exception at runtime.

148. What can a lambda implement?

A. All functional interfaces

B. Any interface

C. Only functional interfaces in the JDK

D. None of the above

149. What is the output of the following application?

```
package lot;
import java.util.function.*;

public class Warehouse {
    private int quantity = 40;
    private final BooleanSupplier stock;
    {
        stock = () -> quantity>0;
    }
    public void checkInventory() {
        if(stock.get())
            System.out.print("Plenty!");
        else {
            System.out.print("On Backorder!");
        }
    }
    public static void main(String... widget) {
        final Warehouse w13 = new Warehouse();
        w13.checkInventory();
    }
}
```

A. `Plenty!`

B. `On Backorder!`

C. The code does not compile because of the `checkInventory()` method.

D. The code does not compile for a different reason.

150. What is a possible output of the following application?

```java
import java.util.*;
import java.util.stream.*;
public class Thermometer {
    private String feelsLike;
    private double temp;
    @Override public String toString() { return feelsLike; }
    // Constructor/Getters/Setters Omitted

    public static void main(String... season) {
        var readings = List.of(new Thermometer("HOT!",72),
            new Thermometer("Too Cold!",0),
            new Thermometer("Just right!",72));
        readings
            .parallelStream()                   // k1
            .collect(Collectors.groupingByConcurrent(
                Thermometer::getTemp))          // k2
            .forEach(System.out::println);   // k3
} }
```

A. `{0.0=[Cold!], 72.0=[HOT!, Just right!]}`

B. `{0.0=[Cold!], 72.0=[Just right!] , 72.0=[HOT!]}`

C. The code does not compile because of line k1.

D. The code does not compile because of line k2.

E. The code does not compile because of line k3.

F. None of the above.

Chapter 7

Java Platform Module System

THE OCP EXAM TOPICS COVERED IN THIS PRACTICE TEST INCLUDE THE FOLLOWING:

✓ **Java Platform Module System**

- Deploy and execute modular applications, including automatic modules

- Declare, use, and expose modules, including the use of services

1. What is the name of a file that declares a module?

   A. `mod.java`

   B. `mod-data.java`

   C. `mod-info.java`

   D. `module.java`

   E. `module-data.java`

   F. `module-info.java`

2. Suppose you have a module that contains a class with a call to `exports(ChocolateLab.class)`. Which part of the module service contains this class?

   A. Consumer

   B. Service locator

   C. Service provider

   D. Service provider interface

   E. None of the above

3. Which are considered part of a service? (Choose two.)

   A. Consumer

   B. Service locator

   C. Service provider

   D. Service provider interface

4. Given the following diagram, how many of the following are named modules?

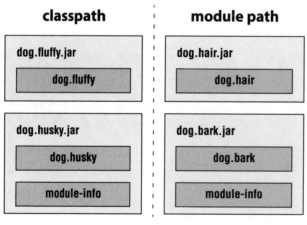

   A. 0

   B. 1

   C. 2

   D. 3

   E. 4

5. Given the diagram from the previous question, which is an automatic module?

   A. dog.bark

   B. dog.fluffy

   C. dog.hair

   D. dog.husky

   E. None of the above

6. Given the diagram from question 4, which is a default module?

   A. dog.bark

   B. dog.fluffy

   C. dog.hair

   D. dog.husky

   E. None of the above

7. Given the diagram from question 4, how many are unnamed modules?

   A. 0

   B. 1

   C. 2

   D. 3

   E. 4

8. Which of the following statements are true? (Choose two.)

   A. It is a good practice to add the --add-exports option to your java command.

   B. It is permitted, but not recommended, to add the --add-exports option to your java command.

   C. There is no --add-exports option on the java command.

   D. It is a good practice to add the --add-requires option to your java command.

   E. It is permitted, but not recommended, to add the --add-requires option to your java command.

   F. There is no --add-requires option on the java command.

9. How many of the following are legal module-info.java files?

```
module com.koala {
   exports cute;
}
module com-koala {
   exports cute;
}
public module com.koala {
   exports cute;
}
```

```
public module com-koala {
  exports cute;
}
```

A. None
B. One
C. Two
D. Three
E. Four

10. Which two would be best to combine into a single module?

    A. Consumer and service locator
    B. Consumer and service provider
    C. Consumer and service provider interface
    D. Service locator and service provider interface
    E. Service locator and service provider
    F. Service provider and service provider interface

11. What command could you run to print output like the following?

```
java.base@11.0.2
java.compiler@11.0.2
java.datatransfer@11.0.2
java.desktop@11.0.2
...
```

    A. java --all-modules
    B. java --describe-modules
    C. java --list-modules
    D. java --output-modules
    E. java --show-modules
    F. None of the above

12. Suppose we have an automatic module on the module path named dog-arthur2.jar and no Automatic-Module-Name specified? What module name should named modules use to reference it?

    A. dog-arthur
    B. dog-arthur2
    C. dog.arthur
    D. dog.arthur2
    E. None of the above

13. Given the dependencies in the diagram, which boxes represent the service provider interface and service provider, respectively?

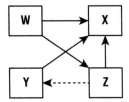

- **A.** W and X
- **B.** W and Z
- **C.** X and Y
- **D.** X and Z
- **E.** Y and Z
- **F.** None of the above

14. Using the diagram in the previous question, which boxes represent the consumer and service locator, respectively?

- **A.** W and X
- **B.** W and Z
- **C.** X and Y
- **D.** X and Z
- **E.** Y and Z
- **F.** None of the above

15. What is the minimum number of JAR files you need for a cyclic dependency?

- **A.** 0
- **B.** 1
- **C.** 2
- **D.** 3
- **E.** 4

16. Fill in the blank with code to look up and call a service.

```
String cheese = ServiceLoader.load(Mouse.class)
    .map(_____)
    .map(Mouse::favoriteFood)
    .findFirst()
    .orElse("");
```

- **A.** `Mouse.get()`
- **B.** `Mouse::get`
- **C.** `Provider.get()`
- **D.** `Provider::get`
- **E.** None of the above

17. Suppose we want to have two modules: `com.ny` and `com.sf`. Which is true about the placement of the `module-info.java` file(s)?

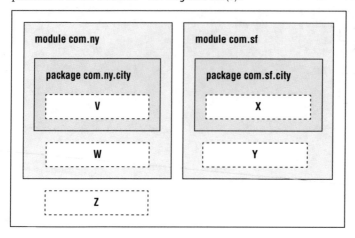

- **A.** One `module-info.java` file is required in position Z.
- **B.** Two `module-info.java` files are required, in positions V and X.
- **C.** Two `module-info.java` files are required, in positions W and Y.
- **D.** Three `module-info.java` files are required, in positions V, X, and Z.
- **E.** Three `module-info.java` files are required, in positions W, Y, and Z.
- **F.** None of the above.

18. Consider the modules in the previous diagram. Suppose we want the code in module `com.sf` to depend on code in module `com.ny`. Which of the following directives goes into module `com.sf`'s `module-info` file to configure that behavior?

- **A.** `export com.ny;`
- **B.** `exports com.ny;`
- **C.** `require com.ny;`
- **D.** `require com.ny.city;`
- **E.** `requires com.ny;`
- **F.** `requires com.ny.city;`

19. Consider the modules diagram in question 17. Suppose we want the code in module `com.sf` to depend on code in module `com.ny`. Which of the following directives goes into module `com.ny`'s `module-info` file to configure that behavior?

- **A.** `export com.ny;`
- **B.** `export com.ny.city;`
- **C.** `exports com.ny;`
- **D.** `exports com.ny.city;`
- **E.** `requires com.ny;`
- **F.** `requires com.ny.city;`

20. Suppose the consumer, service locator, service provider, and service provider interface are each in separate modules. Which of the following best describes the following `module-info` file?

```
module nature.tree {
   provides nature.sapling.Tree with nature.tree.Maple
}
```

   A. Consumer

   B. Service locator

   C. Service provider

   D. Service provider interface

   E. None of the above

21. Which options are commonly used when compiling a module?

   A. -d and -m

   B. -d and -p

   C. -m and -p

   D. -d, -m, and -p

   E. None of the above

22. Which of the following are modules supplied by the JDK? (Choose three.)

   A. `java.base`

   B. `java.basic`

   C. `java.desktop`

   D. `java.sdk`

   E. `java.sql`

   F. `java.swing`

23. Which best describes a top-down migration? (Choose two.)

   A. The first step is to move all the modules to the module path.

   B. The first step is to move a single module to the module path.

   C. Most steps consist of changing an automatic module to a named module.

   D. Most steps consist of changing an automatic module to a unnamed module.

   E. Most steps consist of changing an unnamed module to an automatic module.

   F. Most steps consist of changing an unnamed module to a named module

24. Suppose the consumer, service locator, service provider, and service provider interface are each in separate modules. Which of the following best describes the following `module-info` file?

```
module nature.tree {
   requires nature.sapling;
   requires nature.bush;
}
```

A.   Consumer

B.   Service locator

C.   Service provider

D.   Service provider interface

E.   None of the above

25. Suppose you have these two JARs from Java 8. Which steps, when taken together, would be the best way to make them modules? (Choose two.)

A.   Add a `module-info.java` to each.

B.   Add them to the classpath.

C.   Create a third module to contain the common code.

D.   Merge them into one module to break the cyclic dependency.

E.   Rename the modules to use dashes instead of dots.

26. Which command produces output such as the following?

```
animal.puppy -> animal.dog
```

A.   `jdeps -d zoo.animal.puppy.jar`

B.   `jdeps -s zoo.animal.puppy.jar`

C.   `jmod -d zoo.animal.puppy.jar`

D.   `jmod -s zoo.animal.puppy.jar`

E.   None of the above

27. Suppose the consumer, service locator, service provider, and service provider interface are each in separate modules. Which of the following best describes the following `module-info` file?

```
module nature.tree{
    requires nature.sapling;
    provides nature.sapling.Tree with nature.tree.Maple
}
```

A.   Consumer

B.   Service locator

C.   Service provider

D.   Service provider interface

E.   None of the above

28. Suppose we have module `com.bird` that contains package `com.bird.tweet` and class `Tweety` with a `main()` method. Which of the following can fill in the blank to run this program?

`java --module-path mods -module _____`

- **A.** `com.bird.Tweety`
- **B.** `com.bird.tweety.Tweety`
- **C.** `com.bird/Tweety`
- **D.** `com.bird.tweet/Tweety`
- **E.** `com.bird/com.bird.tweet.Tweety`
- **F.** `com.bird.tweet/com.bird.Tweety`

29. Which types of modules are required to contain a `module-info` file?

- **A.** Automatic only
- **B.** Named only
- **C.** Unnamed only
- **D.** Automatic and named
- **E.** Automatic and unnamed
- **F.** Named and unnamed

30. Suppose the consumer, service locator, service provider, and service provider interface are each in separate modules. Which of the following best describes the following `module-info` file?

```
module nature.tree{
   exports nature.tree.leaf;
   requires nature.sapling;
   uses nature.tree.Photosynthesis;
}
```

- **A.** Consumer
- **B.** Service locator
- **C.** Service provider
- **D.** Service provider interface
- **E.** None of the above

31. What is a benefit of using modules? (Choose two.)

- **A.** Better access control
- **B.** Custom Java builds
- **C.** Elimination of JAR files
- **D.** Fewer `.java` files needed in your application
- **E.** Not necessary to specify types of local variables
- **F.** Write once, run anywhere

32. Suppose the consumer, service locator, service provider, and service provider interface are each in separate modules. Which of the following best describes the following module-info file?

```
module nature.tree{
   requires nature.sapling;
}
```

- **A.** Consumer
- **B.** Service locator
- **C.** Service provider
- **D.** Service provider interface
- **E.** None of the above

33. Which types of modules are allowed to contain a module-info file?

- **A.** Automatic only
- **B.** Named only
- **C.** Unnamed only
- **D.** Automatic and named
- **E.** Automatic and unnamed
- **F.** Named and unnamed

34. Which of the following is true of the following module declaration?

```
1: class com.mammal {
2:     exports com.mammal.cat;
3:     exports cat.mammal.mouse to com.mice;
4:     uses com.animal;
5: }
```

- **A.** The first line that fails to compile is line 1.
- **B.** The first line that fails to compile is line 2.
- **C.** The first line that fails to compile is line 3.
- **D.** The first line that fails to compile is line 4.
- **E.** The code compiles.

35. How many of these keywords can be used in a module-info.java file: closes, export, import, require, and uses?

- **A.** None
- **B.** One

   C. Two

   D. Three

   E. Four

   F. Five

36. Suppose the consumer, service locator, service provider, and service provider interface are each in separate modules. Which of the following best describes the following `module-info` file?

```
module nature.tree{
   exports nature.tree.leaf;
}
```

   A. Consumer

   B. Service locator

   C. Service provider

   D. Service provider interface

   E. None of the above

37. Which of the following are modules supplied by the JDK? (Choose three.)

   A. `jdk.base`

   B. `jdk.basic`

   C. `jdk.desktop`

   D. `jdk.javadoc`

   E. `jdk.jdeps`

   F. `jdk.net`

38. Which are true statements about types of migration? (Choose three.)

   A. All modules are immediately moved to the module path in a bottom-up migration.

   B. All modules are immediately moved to the module path in a top-down migration.

   C. Modules migrate before the modules that depend on them in a bottom-up migration.

   D. Modules migrate before the modules that depend on them in a top-down migration.

   E. Modules that are not yet named modules are automatic modules in a bottom-up migration.

   F. Modules that are not yet named modules are automatic modules in a top-down migration

39. A class in which of the following parts of a module service should include a method call to `load(ChocolateLab.class)` that would allow callers to use it?

    A. Consumer

    B. Service locator

    C. Service provider

    D. Service provider interface

    E. None of the above

40. How many of these module declarations are valid?

```
module com.leaf {}
module com.leaf2 {}
module com-leaf { }
module LEAF {}
module leaf2 {}
```

    A. Zero

    B. One

    C. Two

    D. Three

    E. Four

    F. Five

41. Which is a benefit of `ServiceLoader`?

    A. It allows you to add functionality without recompiling the application.

    B. It allows you to load a service written in C++.

    C. It is an interface.

    D. When implementing a service, it references the `ServiceLoader`.

42. Which are true statements? (Choose two.)

    A. Code on the classpath can reference code in automatic, named, and unnamed modules.

    B. Code on the classpath can reference code in named modules, but not automatic and unnamed modules.

    C. Code on the classpath can reference code in automatic and named modules, but not unnamed modules.

    D. Code on the module path can reference code in automatic, named, and unnamed modules.

    E. Code on the module path can reference code in named modules, but not automatic and unnamed modules.

    F. Code on the module path can reference code in automatic and named modules, but not unnamed modules.

43. Suppose we have the packages in the diagram. What could we add to the module-info.java in com.duck to allow the com.park module to reference the Duckling class but not allow the com.bread module to do the same?

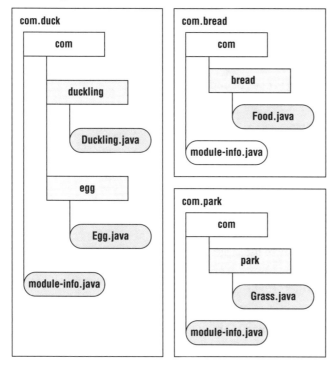

   A. exports com.duckling;

   B. exports com.duckling from com.park;

   C. exports com.duckling to com.park;

   D. exports com.park from com.duckling;

   E. exports com.park to com.duckling;

   F. None of the above

44. Given the diagram in the previous question, what could we add to module-info.java in com.duck to allow the com.park package to reference the Duckling class, but not allow the Egg class to reference the Duckling class?

   A. exports com.duckling;

   B. exports com.duckling from com.park;

   C. exports com.duckling to com.park;

   D. exports com.park from com.duckling;

   E. exports com.park to com.duckling;

   F. None of the above

45. Given the diagram in question 43 and the correct export statement to share only com. duckling, which of the following should be included in the module-info.java file of com.park to specify that com.park should have access to the com.duckling and com. bread packages, but not the com.egg package?

    A. require com.duck, com.bread;

    B. requires com.duck; com.bread;

    C. require com.duckling, com.bread;

    D. requires com.duckling; com.bread;

    E. None of the above

46. Which is both part of the service and has a provides directive?

    A. Consumer

    B. Service locator

    C. Service provider

    D. Service provider interface

    E. None of the above

47. What command is the simplest way to list suggestions for classes in jdk.unsupported?

    A. jdeps cookie.jar

    B. jdeps -s cookie.jar

    C. jdeps -jdkinternals cookie.jar

    D. jdeps --jdkinternals cookie.jar

    E. jdeps -jdkunsupported cookie.jar

    F. jdeps --jdkunsupported cookie.jar

48. Which modules are on the classpath?

    A. Automatic only

    B. Named only

    C. Unnamed only

    D. Automatic and named

    E. Automatic and unnamed

    F. Named and unnamed

49. Which line of code belongs in a service locator?

    A. ServiceLoader loader = ServiceLoader.load();

    B. ServiceLoader loader = ServiceLoader.load(Mouse.class);

    C. ServiceLoader<Mouse> loader = ServiceLoader.load();

    D. ServiceLoader<Mouse> loader = ServiceLoader.load(Mouse.class);

    E. Mouse loader = ServiceLoader.load();

    F. Mouse loader = ServiceLoader.load(Mouse .class);

50. Which is true about a service? (Choose two.)

    A. Changing the service provider interface always requires recompiling the service provider.

    B. Changing the service provider interface sometimes requires recompiling the service provider.

    C. Changing the service provider interface never requires recompiling the service provider.

    D. If the service provider interface references other classes in the method signatures, they are considered part of the service.

    E. If the service provider interface references other classes in the method signatures, they are not considered part of the service.

51. Which modules are on the module path?

    A. Automatic only

    B. Named only

    C. Unnamed only

    D. Automatic and named

    E. Automatic and unnamed

    F. Named and unnamed

52. The service locator and service provider interface share a module. Which boxes represent the consumer and service provider, respectively?

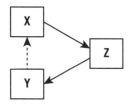

    A. X and Y

    B. X and Z

    C. Y and Z

    D. Z and Z

    E. Z and Y

    F. None of the above

53. What command is the simplest way to list what modules a JAR depends on without listing package names?

    A. `jdeps cookie.jar`

    B. `jdeps -s cookie.jar`

    C. `jdeps -jdkinternals cookie.jar`

    D. `jdeps --jdkinternals cookie.jar`

    E. `jdeps -jdk-unsupported cookie.jar`

    F. `jdeps --jdk-unsupported cookie.jar`

54. What is a benefit of using modules? (Choose three.)

 A. Ability to reuse code

 B. Clearer dependency management

 C. Improved performance

 D. Multithreading support

 E. Platform independence

 F. Unique package enforcement

55. Fill in the blanks to list a way of getting a lot of information useful in debugging modules:

_____ -m x -p y --_____

 A. `jar` and `-show-modules`

 B. `jar` and `-show-module-detail`

 C. `jar` and `-show-module-resolution`

 D. `java` and `-show-modules`

 E. `java` and `-show-module-detail`

 F. `java` and `-show-module-resolution`

56. Suppose you have the following interface in a module named `animal.insect.api`. What needs to be included in the `module-info` file for it to be a service provider interface?

```
package animal.insect.api.bugs;

public interface Bug {
    int crawl();
}
```

 A. `exports animal.insect.api;`

 B. `exports animal.insect.api.bugs;`

 C. `exports animal.insect.api.bugs.Bug;`

 D. `requires animal.insect.api;`

 E. `requires animal.insect.api.bugs;`

 F. `requires animal.insect.api.bugs.Bug;`

57. Suppose you have the following class in a module named `animal.insect.impl` and the service provider interface module from question 56. What needs to be included in the `module-info` for it to be a service provider? (Choose two.)

```
package animal.insect.impl;

import animal.insect.api.bugs.Bug;

public class Worm implements Bug {
```

```
    @Override
    public int crawl() {
       return 1;
    }
}
```

A. requires animal.insect.api.bugs;

B. requires animal.insect.lookup;

C. requires animal.printer;

D. provides animal.insect.impl.Worm;

E. provides animal.insect.api.bugs.Bug with animal.insect.impl. Worm;

F. provides animal.insect.impl.Worm with animal.insect.api.bugs. Bug;

58. Suppose you have the following class in a module named animal.insect.lookup, the service provider interface from question 56, and the service provider from question 57. What needs to be included in the module-info file besides an exports directive for it to be a service locator? (Choose two.)

```
package animal.insect.lookup;

import animal.insect.api.bugs.Bug;
import java.util.List;
import java.util.ServiceLoader;
import java.util.stream.Collectors;

public class InsectFinder {
   public static List<Bug> findAllBugs() {
      return ServiceLoader.load(Bug.class)
         .stream()
         .map(ServiceLoader.Provider::get)
         .collect(Collectors.toList());
   }
}
```

A. provides animal.insect.lookup;

B. provides animal.insect.lookup.InsectFinder;

C. requires animal.insect.api.bugs;

D. requires animal.insect.api.Bug;

E. uses animal.insect.api.bugs;

F. uses animal.insect.api.bugs.Bug;

59. Suppose you have the following class in a module named `animal.insect.printer`, the service provider interface from question 56, the service provider from question 57, and the service locator from question 58. What needs to be included in the `module-info` for it to be a consumer? (Choose two.)

```
package animal.printer;

import animal.insect.lookup.InsectFinder;

public class Print {
    public static void main(String[] args) {
        var bugs = InsectFinder.findAllBugs();
        bugs.forEach(System.out::println);
    }
}
```

   A. `requires animal.insect.api.bugs;`
   B. `requires animal.insect.lookup;`
   C. `requires animal.printer;`
   D. `uses animal.insect.api.bugs;`
   E. `uses animal.insect.api.bugs.Bug;`
   F. `uses animal.insect.lookup.InsectFinder;`

60. What command is the simplest way to list what modules a JAR depends on including package names?
   A. `jdeps cookie.jar`
   B. `jdeps -s cookie.jar`
   C. `jdeps -jdkinternals cookie.jar`
   D. `jdeps --jdkinternals cookie.jar`
   E. `jdeps -jdk-unsupported cookie.jar`
   F. `jdeps --jdk-unsupported cookie.jar`

61. How many modules are part of the cyclic dependency?

```
module com.light {
    exports com.light;
}
module com.animal {
    exports com.animal;
    requires com.light;
    requires com.plant;
}
module com.plant {
```

```
        exports com.plant;
        requires com.light;
        requires com.animal;
    }
    module com.worm {
        exports com.worm;
        requires com.light;
        requires com.animal;
        requires com.plant;
    }
```

   A. 0
   B. 1
   C. 2
   D. 3
   E. 4

62. What is true about the –d option?
    A. It can be used with the `jar` command, but not the `java` command.
    B. It can be used with the `java` command, but not the `jar` command.
    C. It can be used with the `jar` and `java` commands and serves the same purpose for both.
    D. It can be used with the `jar` and `java` commands, but means "directory" for the former and "describe module" for the later.
    E. None of the above.

63. Assuming all referenced files and directories exist and are correct, what does this code do?
```
javac –m mods –d mouse mouse/com/mouse/*.java
    mouse/module-info.java
jar –cvf mods/com.mouse.jar –C mouse/ .
```

    A. Creates a JAR file representing the com.mouse module
    B. Creates a JAR file that is not a module
    C. Fails on the `javac` command
    D. Fails on the `jar` command

64. What module is always in the `jdeps` output?
    A. `java.base`
    B. `java.lang`
    C. `java.self`
    D. `jdk.base`
    E. `jdk.lang`
    F. `jdk.self`

65. Which are valid modes on the `jmod` command? (Choose three.)

   A. `create`

   B. `list`

   C. `hash`

   D. `show`

   E. `verbose`

   F. `version`

66. This diagram shows the second step of a migration to modules. What type of migration is this?

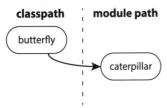

   A. Bottom-up.

   B. Side-to-side.

   C. Top-down.

   D. There is not enough information to determine which type it is.

67. Which are true statements about the diagram and scenario in the previous question? (Choose two.)

   A. `butterfly` is an automatic module.

   B. `butterfly` is a named module.

   C. `butterfly` is an unnamed module.

   D. `caterpillar` is an automatic module.

   E. `caterpillar` is a named module.

   F. `caterpillar` is an unnamed module.

68. Suppose we have the two JARs in the diagram on the module path and the `module-info` in the `com.magic` jar only `exports` one package: `com.magic.unicorn`. There is no `module-info` file in the `com.science` JAR. How many of the four packages in the diagram can a third module on the module path access?

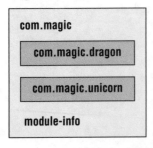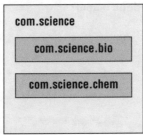

A.   0
B.   1
C.   2
D.   3
E.   4

69. Suppose the two JARs described in the previous question are on the classpath. How many of the four packages in the diagram can a module on the module path access?

A.   0
B.   1
C.   2
D.   3
E.   4

70. What is true about the following `module-info.java` file?

`module Book { }`

A.   It does not compile because it is empty.
B.   It does not compile because the module name is uppercase.
C.   It does not compile because the module name has only one component.
D.   It does not compile for another reason.
E.   It compiles.

71. When adding a new service provider, which of these do you need to recompile?

A.   Consumer
B.   Service locator
C.   Existing service providers
D.   Service provider interface
E.   None of the above

72. When working with modules, what option names are equivalent to -m and -s?

A.   `--module` and `--short`
B.   `--module` and `--statistics`
C.   `--module` and `--summary`
D.   `--module-path` and `--short`
E.   `--module-path` and `--statistics`
F.   `--module-path` and `--summary`

73. Which are considered part of a service?

A.   Classes referenced by the implementation, but not the interface
B.   Classes referenced by the interface, but not the implementation
C.   Classes referenced by either the implementation or the interface
D.   None of the above

74. Which commands have the options −m and −s to represent modules and summary, respectively?

- **A.** javac and jar
- **B.** javac and jdeps
- **C.** javac and jmod
- **D.** java and jar
- **E.** java and jdeps
- **F.** java and jmod

75. Suppose you have the following class in a module named animal.insect.impl. Which two most likely go in the module-info of the service locator? (Choose two.)

```
package animal.insect.impl;

import animal.insect.api.bugs.Bug;

public class Worm implements Bug {
    @Override
    public int crawl() {
        return 1;
    }
}
```

- **A.** requires animal.insect.api.bugs;
- **B.** requires animal.insect.api.bugs.Bug;
- **C.** requires animal.insect.impl;
- **D.** uses animal.insect.api.bugs;
- **E.** uses animal.insect.api.bugs.Bug;
- **F.** uses animal.insect.api.bugs.Bug with animal.insect.impl.Worm;

76. Which statements are true? (Choose two.)

- **A.** A bottom-up migration has more steps involving the classpath than a top-down migration.
- **B.** A top-down migration has more steps involving the classpath than a bottom-up migration.
- **C.** Both types of migration have the same number of steps involving the classpath.
- **D.** A bottom-up migration has unnamed modules on the module path
- **E.** A top-down migration has unnamed modules on the module path.
- **F.** Neither migration type has unnamed modules on the module path.

77. Fill in the blank with code to look up and call a service.

```
String cheese = ServiceLoader.load(Mouse.class)
    .stream()
```

```
    .map(_____)
    .map(Mouse::favoriteFood)
    .findFirst()
    .orElse("");
```

  A. `Mouse.get()`

  B. `Mouse::get`

  C. `Provider.get()`

  D. `Provider::get`

  E. None of the above

78. Given the diagram, what statements need to be in `module-info.java` for the `mammal` module? (Choose three.)

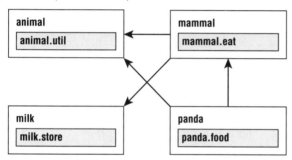

  A. `exports mammal;`

  B. `exports mammal.eat;`

  C. `requires animal;`

  D. `requires animal.util;`

  E. `requires milk;`

  F. `requires milk.store;`

79. Given the previous diagram and the following `module-info.java` for the panda module, what change can be made to the `requires` statement?

```
module panda {
    requires mammal;
}
```

  A. `exports transitive mammal;`

  B. `exports transitive mammal.eat;`

  C. `requires transitive animal;`

  D. `requires transitive animal.util;`

  E. `transitive requires animal;`

  F. `transitive requires animal.util;`

80. Given the diagram in question 78 and the following `module-info.java` for the panda module, what is the result of including line `m1`?

```
module panda {
    requires mammal;
    requires transitive mammal; // line m1
}
```

  A. Any modules that require `mammal` will automatically get `panda` as well.

  B. Any modules that require `panda` will automatically get `mammal` as well.

  C. There is no change in behavior.

  D. The code does not compile.

81. How many service providers are allowed to implement a service provider interface and have the consumer reference the first one?

  A. Exactly one

  B. Exactly two

  C. One or two

  D. One or more

  E. None of the above

82. Which of the following are modules supplied by the JDK? (Choose three.)

  A. `java.logging`

  B. `java.javadoc`

  C. `java.jdk`

  D. `java.management`

  E. `java.naming`

  F. `java.scripts`

83. Which are true of a JAR file that has only one `module-info.class` file, placed in the `META-INF` directory? (Choose two.)

  A. It is an automatic module if on the classpath.

  B. It is an automatic module if on the module path.

  C. It is a named module if on the classpath.

  D. It is a named module if on the module path.

  E. It is an unnamed module if on the classpath.

  F. It is an unnamed module if on the module path.

84. The service locator and service provider interface share a module. Which boxes represent the consumer and service provider, respectively?

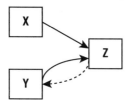

A. X and Y
B. X and Z
C. Y and Z
D. Z and Z
E. Z and Y
F. None of the above

85. What statements are most accurate about the `ServiceLoader` class? (Choose two.)

A. `load()` does not take any parameters.
B. `load()` takes the class type as a parameter.
C. When looping through the results of `load()`, you need to call the `get()` method on `Provider`.
D. When using the results of `load()` in a `Stream`, you need to call the `get()` method on `Provider`.

86. Suppose we have an automatic module on the module path named `lizard-^-cricket-^-1.0.0-SNAPSHOT.jar` and no `Automatic-Module-Name` specified. What module name should named modules use to reference it?

A. `lizard-cricket`
B. `lizard.cricket`
C. `lizard-cricket-SNAPSHOT`
D. `lizard-cricket.SNAPSHOT`
E. None of the above

87. What file formats are legal for a module to be distributed?

A. `jar`
B. `jmod`
C. `zip`
D. `jar` and `jmod`
E. `jar` and `zip`
F. `jmod` and `zip`

88. Why is this `module-info` incorrect for a service provider?

```
module plant.flower {
    exports plant.flower.impl;
    requires plant.flower.api;
    provides plant.flower.api.Petal
        with plant.flower.impl.PetalImpl;
}
```

A. The `exports` directive should be `export`.

B. The `exports` directive should not be present because all calls to the service provider should use the service locator.

C. The `provides` directive should be `uses` instead.

D. The `provides` directive has the implementation and interface in the wrong order.

E. The `requires` directive should be `exports` instead.

F. The `requires` directive should not be present because `provides` implies it.

89. How many modules are part of the cyclic dependency?

```
module.com.light {
    exports com.light;
}
module com.plant {
    exports com.plant;
    requires com.light;
    requires com.animal;
}
module com.animal {
    exports com.animal;
    requires com.light;
}
module com.worm {
    exports com.worm;
    requires com.light;
    requires com.animal;
    requires com.plant;
}
```

A. 0

B. 1

C. 2

D. 3

E. 4

90. What statements are true about `requires mandated java.base`? (Choose two.)

   A. This output is expected when running the `java --list-modules` command.

   B. This output is expected when running the `java --show-module-resolution` command.

   C. This output is expected when running the `jdeps` command.

   D. This output is expected when running the `jmod` command.

   E. All modules will include this in the output.

   F. Some modules will include this in the output.

Chapter

8

Concurrency

THE OCP EXAM TOPICS COVERED IN THIS PRACTICE TEST INCLUDE THE FOLLOWING:

✓ **Concurrency**

- Create worker threads using Runnable and Callable, and manage concurrency using an ExecutorService and java.util.concurrent API

- Develop thread-safe code, using different locking mechanisms and java.util.concurrent API

1. What is the output of the following code snippet?

```
Callable c = new Callable() {
    public Object run() {
        System.out.print("X");
        return 10;
    }
};
var s = Executors.newScheduledThreadPool(1);
for(int i=0; i<10; i++) {
    Future f = s.submit(c);
    f.get();
}
s.shutdown();
System.out.print("Done!");
```

A. XXXXXXXXXXDone!

B. Done!XXXXXXXXXX

C. The code does not compile.

D. The code hangs indefinitely at runtime.

E. The code throws an exception at runtime.

F. The output cannot be determined ahead of time.

2. Which of the following methods is not available on an `ExecutorService` instance? (Choose two.)

A. execute(Callable)

B. shutdownNow()

C. submit(Runnable)

D. exit()

E. submit(Callable)

F. execute(Runnable)

3. The following program simulates flipping a coin an even number of times. Assuming five seconds is enough time for all of the tasks to finish, what is the output of the following application?

```
import java.util.concurrent.*;
import java.util.concurrent.atomic.*;
public class Luck {
    private AtomicBoolean coin = new AtomicBoolean(false);
    void flip() {
        coin.getAndSet(!coin.get());
    }
```

```
   public static void main(String[] gamble) throws Exception {
      var luck = new Luck();
      ExecutorService s = Executors.newCachedThreadPool();
      for(int i=0; i<1000; i++) {
         s.execute(() -> luck.flip());
      }
      s.shutdown();
      Thread.sleep(5000);
      System.out.println(luck.coin.get());
   } }
```

A. false

B. true

C. The code does not compile.

D. The code hangs indefinitely at runtime.

E. The code throws an exception at runtime.

F. The output cannot be determined ahead of time.

4. Which of the following is a recommended way to define an asynchronous task?

   A. Create a `Callable` expression and pass it to an instance of an `Executor`.

   B. Create a class that extends `Thread` and override the `start()` method.

   C. Create a `Runnable` lambda expression and pass it to a `Thread` constructor.

   D. Create an anonymous `Runnable` class that overrides the `begin()` method.

   E. All of the above.

5. Given the following program, how many times is `Locked!` expected to be printed? Assume 100 milliseconds is enough time for each task created by the program to complete.

```
import java.util.concurrent.locks.*;
public class Padlock {
   private Lock lock = new ReentrantLock();
   public void lockUp() {
      if (lock.tryLock()) {
         lock.lock();
         System.out.println("Locked!");
         lock.unlock();
      }
   }
   public static void main(String... unused) throws Exception {
      var gate = new Padlock();
```

```
        for(int i=0; i<5; i++) {
            new Thread(() -> gate.lockUp()).start();
            Thread.sleep(100);
        }
    } }
```

A. One time.

B. Five times.

C. The code does not compile.

D. The code hangs indefinitely at runtime.

E. The code throws an exception at runtime.

F. The output cannot be determined ahead of time.

6. Given the `original` array, how many of the following `for` statements result in an exception at runtime, assuming each is executed independently?

```
var original = List.of(1,2,3,4,5);

var copy1 = new CopyOnWriteArrayList<Integer>(original);
for(Integer w : copy1)
    copy1.remove(w);

var copy2 = Collections.synchronizedList(original);
for(Integer w : copy2)
    copy2.remove(w);

var copy3 = new ArrayList<Integer>(original);
for(Integer w : copy3)
    copy3.remove(w);

var copy4 = new ConcurrentLinkedQueue<Integer>(original);
for(Integer w : copy4)
    copy4.remove(w);
```

A. Zero.

B. One.

C. Two.

D. Three.

E. Four.

F. The code does not compile.

7. Fill in the blanks: _____ is a special case of _____, in which two or more active threads try to acquire the same set of locks and are repeatedly unsuccessful.

    A. Deadlock, livelock

    B. Deadlock, resource starvation

    C. Livelock, resource starvation

    D. Resource starvation, race conditions

    E. Resource starvation, livelock

    F. None of the above

8. What is the output of the following application?

```
3:  public class TpsReport {
4:     public void submitReports() {
5:         var s = Executors.newCachedThreadPool();
6:         Future bosses = s.submit(() -> System.out.print("1"));
7:         s.shutdown();
8:         System.out.print(bosses.get());
9:     }
10:    public static void main(String[] memo) {
11:        new TpsReport().submitReports();
12:    }
13: }
```

    A. null

    B. 1null

    C. 1

    D. Line 6 does not compile.

    E. Line 8 does not compile.

    F. An exception is thrown at runtime.

9. Which of the following static methods does not exist in the Executors class? (Choose two.)

    A. newFixedScheduledThreadPool()

    B. newThreadPool()

    C. newFixedThreadPool(int)

    D. newSingleThreadExecutor()

    E. newScheduledThreadPool(int)

    F. newSingleThreadScheduledExecutor()

10. How many times does the following application print Ready at runtime?

```
package parade;
import java.util.concurrent.*;
public class CartoonCat {
    private void await(CyclicBarrier c) {
        try {
            c.await();
        } catch (Exception e) {}
    }
    public void march(CyclicBarrier c) {
        var s = Executors.newSingleThreadExecutor();
        for(int i=0; i<12; i++)
            s.execute(() -> await(c));
        s.shutdown();
    }
    public static void main(String... strings) {
        new CartoonCat().march(new CyclicBarrier(4,
                () -> System.out.println("Ready")));
    }
}
```

A. Zero.

B. One.

C. Three.

D. The code does not compile.

E. An exception is thrown at runtime.

11. Let's say you needed a thread executor to create tasks for a CyclicBarrier that has a barrier limit of five threads. Which static method in ExecutorService should you use to obtain it?

A. newSingleThreadExecutor()

B. newSingleThreadScheduledExecutor()

C. newCachedThreadPool()

D. newFixedThreadPool(2)

E. None of the above

12. The following diagrams represent the order of read/write operations of two threads sharing a common variable. Each thread first reads the value of the variable from memory and then writes a new value of the variable back to memory. Which diagram demonstrates proper synchronization?

A.

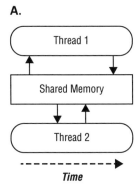

B.

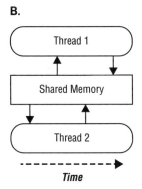

C.

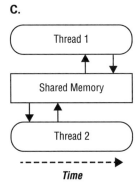

D.

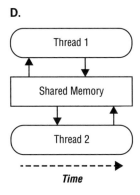

13. What is the output of the following application?

```java
import java.util.*;
import java.util.concurrent.*;
public class Race {
    ExecutorService service = Executors.newFixedThreadPool(8);
    public static int sleep() {
        try { Thread.sleep(1000); } catch (Exception e) {}
        return 1;
    }
    public void hare() {
        try {
            Callable<Integer> c = () -> sleep();
            final var r = List.of(c,c,c);
            var results = service.invokeAll(r);
            System.out.println("Hare won the race!");
        } catch (Exception e) {e.printStackTrace();}
    }
    public void tortoise() {
        try {
            Callable<Integer> c = () -> sleep();
            final var r = List.of(c,c,c);
            Integer result = service.invokeAny(r);
            System.out.println("Tortoise won the race!");
        } catch (Exception e) {e.printStackTrace();}
    }
    public static void main(String[] p) throws Exception {
        var race = new Race();
        race.service.execute(() -> race.hare());
        race.service.execute(() -> race.tortoise());
    }
}
```

A. Hare won the race! is printed first.

B. Tortoise won the race! is printed first.

C. The code does not compile.

D. The code hangs indefinitely at runtime.

E. The code throws an exception at runtime.

F. The output cannot be determined ahead of time.

14. Which of the following concurrent collections is sorted? (Choose two.)

- **A.** ConcurrentSkipList
- **B.** ConcurrentSkipListSet
- **C.** CopyOnWriteArrayList
- **D.** ConcurrentSkipListMap
- **E.** ConcurrentLinkedQueue
- **F.** LinkedBlockingQueue

15. What is the output of the following application?

```
package taxes;
import java.util.concurrent.*;
public class Accountant {
    public static void completePaperwork() {
        System.out.print("[Filing]");
    }
    public static double getPi() {
        return 3.14159;
    }
    public static void main(String[] args) throws Exception {
        ExecutorService x = Executors.newSingleThreadExecutor();
        Future<?> f1 = x.submit(() -> completePaperwork());
        Future<Object> f2 = x.submit(() -> getPi());
        System.out.print(f1.get()+" "+f2.get());
        x.shutdown();
    }
}
```

- **A.** [Filing]
- **B.** [Filing]3.14159
- **C.** [Filing]null 3.14159
- **D.** The declaration of f1 does not compile.
- **E.** The declaration of f2 does not compile.
- **F.** The output cannot be determined ahead of time.

16. Assuming 10 seconds is enough time for all of the tasks to finish, what statements about the following program are correct? (Choose two.)

```
import java.util.concurrent.*;
import java.util.concurrent.atomic.*;
public class Clock {
    private AtomicLong bigHand = new AtomicLong(0);
```

```
    void incrementBy10() {
        bigHand.getAndSet(bigHand.get() + 10);
    }
    public static void main(String[] c) throws Exception {
        var smartWatch = new Clock();
        ExecutorService s = Executors.newCachedThreadPool();
        for(int i=0; i<100; i++) {
            s.submit(() -> smartWatch.incrementBy10()).get();
        }
        s.shutdown();
        s.awaitTermination(10, TimeUnit.SECONDS);
        System.out.println(smartWatch.bigHand.get());
    } }
```

A. The code does not compile.

B. The `incrementBy10()` method is thread-safe.

C. The `incrementBy10()` method is not thread-safe.

D. The output is 1000 on every execution.

E. The output cannot be determined ahead of time.

F. The code hangs indefinitely at runtime.

17. What is the most likely result of executing the following application?

```
package jokes;
import java.util.concurrent.*;
public class Riddle {
    public void sleep() {
        try { Thread.sleep(5000); } catch (Exception e) {}
    }
    public String getQuestion(Riddle r) {
        synchronized {
            sleep();
            if(r != null) r.getAnswer(null);
            return "How many programmers does it take "
                    + "to change a light bulb?";
        }
    }
    public synchronized String getAnswer(Riddle r) {
        sleep();
        if(r != null) r.getAnswer(null);
        return "None, that's a hardware problem";
```

```
        }

        public static void main(String... ununused) {
            var r1 = new Riddle();
            var r2 = new Riddle();
            var s = Executors.newFixedThreadPool(2);
            s.submit(() -> r1.getQuestion(r2));
            s.execute(() -> r2.getAnswer(r1));
            s.shutdown();
        }
    }
```

A. A deadlock is produced at runtime.

B. A livelock is produced at runtime.

C. The application completes successfully.

D. The code does not compile.

E. The code hangs indefinitely at runtime.

F. The output cannot be determined ahead of time.

18. Which `ScheduledExecutorService` method can result in the same action being executed by two threads at the same time?

A. `scheduleAtFixedDelay()`

B. `scheduleAtFixedRate()`

C. `scheduleWithFixedDelay()`

D. `scheduleAtSameRate()`

E. `scheduleWithRate()`

F. None of the above

19. What is the output of the following application?

```
package olympics;
import java.util.concurrent.*;
public class Athlete {
    int stroke = 0;
    public synchronized void swimming() {
        stroke++;
    }
    private int getStroke() {
        synchronized(this) { return stroke; }
    }
    public static void main(String... laps) {
```

```
      ExecutorService s = Executors.newFixedThreadPool(10);
      Athlete a = new Athlete();
      for(int i=0; i<1000; i++) {
          s.execute(() -> a.swimming());
      }
      s.shutdown();
      System.out.print(a.getStroke());
   } }
```

A. A deadlock is produced at runtime.

B. A livelock is produced at runtime.

C. 1000

D. The code does not compile.

E. The result is unknown until runtime because `stroke` is not written in a thread-safe manner and a write may be lost.

F. None of the above.

20. Which of the following is most likely to be caused by a race condition?

    A. A thread perpetually denied access to a resource

    B. A program hanging indefinitely

    C. An `int` variable incorrectly reporting the number of times an operation was performed

    D. Two threads actively trying to restart a blocked process that is guaranteed to always end the same way

    E. Two threads endlessly waiting on each other to release shared locks

21. Which statement about the following class is correct?

```
package my;
import java.util.*;
public class ThreadSafeList {
    private List<Integer> data = new ArrayList<>();
    public synchronized void addValue(int value) {
        data.add(value);
    }
    public int getValue(int index) {
        return data.get(index);
    }
    public int size() {
        synchronized(ThreadSafeList.class) {
            return data.size();
        }
    }
}
```

A. The code compiles and is thread-safe.

B. The code compiles and is not thread-safe.

C. The code does not compile because of the `size()` method.

D. The code does not compile because of the `getValue()` method.

E. The code does not compile for another reason.

F. None of the above.

22. Which two method names, when filled into the `print2()` method, produce the same output as the `print1()` method? Assume the input arguments for each represent the same non-`null` numeric value.

```
public static synchronized void print1(int counter) {
    System.out.println(counter--);
    System.out.println(++counter);
}

public static synchronized void print2(AtomicInteger counter) {
    System.out.println(counter._____);
    System.out.println(counter._____);
}
```

A. `decrementAndGet()` and `getAndIncrement()`

B. `decrementAndGet()` and `incrementAndGet()`

C. `getAndDecrement()` and `getAndIncrement()`

D. `getAndDecrement()` and `incrementAndGet()`

E. None of the above

23. How many lines of the following code snippet contain compilation errors?

```
11: ScheduledExecutorService t = Executors
12:     .newSingleThreadScheduledExecutor();
13: Future result = t.execute(System.out::println);
14: t.invokeAll(null);
15: t.scheduleAtFixedRate(() -> {return;},5,TimeUnit.MINUTES);
```

A. None

B. One

C. Two

D. Three

E. None of the above

24. How many times does the following application print W at runtime?

```
package crew;
import java.util.concurrent.*;
import java.util.stream.*;
public class Boat {
    private void waitTillFinished(CyclicBarrier c) {
        try {
            c.await();
            System.out.print("W");
        } catch (Exception e) {}
    }
    public void row(ExecutorService s) {
        var cb = new CyclicBarrier(5);
        IntStream.iterate(1, i-> i+1)
            .limit(12)
            .forEach(i -> s.submit(() -> waitTillFinished(cb)));
    }
    public static void main(String[] oars) {
        ExecutorService service = null;
        try {
            service = Executors.newCachedThreadPool();
            new Boat().row(service);
        } finally {
            service.isShutdown();
        } } }
```

- **A.** 0
- **B.** 10
- **C.** 12
- **D.** The code does not compile.
- **E.** The output cannot be determined ahead of time.
- **F.** None of the above.

25. Using the Boat class from the previous question, what is the final state of the application?
- **A.** The application produces an exception at runtime.
- **B.** The application terminates successfully.
- **C.** The application hangs indefinitely because the ExecutorService is never shut down.
- **D.** The application produces a deadlock at runtime.
- **E.** None of the above.

26. Given the following program, how many times is TV Time expected to be printed? Assume 10 seconds is enough time for each task created by the program to complete.

```java
import java.util.concurrent.*;
import java.util.concurrent.locks.*;
public class Television {
    private static Lock myTurn = new ReentrantLock();
    public void watch() {
        try {
            if (myTurn.lock(5, TimeUnit.SECONDS)) {
                System.out.println("TV Time");
                myTurn.unlock();
            }
        } catch (InterruptedException e) {}
    }
    public static void main(String[] t) throws Exception {
        var newTv = new Television();
        for (int i = 0; i < 3; i++) {
            new Thread(() -> newTv.watch()).start();
            Thread.sleep(10*1000);
        }
    } }
```

A. One time.

B. Three times.

C. The code does not compile.

D. The code hangs indefinitely at runtime.

E. The code throws an exception at runtime.

F. The output cannot be determined ahead of time.

27. Given the original array, how many of the following for statements enter an infinite loop at runtime, assuming each is executed independently?

```java
var original = new ArrayList<Integer>(List.of(1,2,3));

var copy1 = new ArrayList<Integer>(original);
for(Integer q : copy1)
    copy1.add(1);

var copy2 = new CopyOnWriteArrayList<Integer>(original);
for(Integer q : copy2)
    copy2.add(2);

var copy3 = new LinkedBlockingQueue<Integer>(original);
```

```
for(Integer q : copy3)
   copy3.offer(3);

var copy4 = Collections.synchronizedList(original);
for(Integer q : copy4)
   copy4.add(4);
```

A. Zero.

B. One.

C. Two.

D. Three.

E. Four.

F. The code does not compile.

28. Which `ExecutorService` method guarantees all running tasks are stopped in an orderly fashion?

A. `shutdown()`

B. `shutdownNow()`

C. `halt()`

D. `shutdownAndTerminate()`

E. None of the above

29. Assuming 10 seconds is enough time for all of the tasks to finish, what is the output of the following application?

```
import java.util.concurrent.*;
public class Bank {
   static int cookies = 0;
   public synchronized void deposit(int amount) {
      cookies += amount;
   }
   public static synchronized void withdrawal(int amount) {
      cookies -= amount;
   }
   public static void main(String[] amount) throws Exception {
      var teller = Executors.newScheduledThreadPool(50);
      Bank bank = new Bank();
      for(int i=0; i<25; i++) {
         teller.submit(() -> bank.deposit(5));
         teller.submit(() -> bank.withdrawal(5));
      }
      teller.shutdown();
      teller.awaitTermination(10, TimeUnit.SECONDS);
```

```
            System.out.print(bank.cookies);
        } }
```

A. 0

B. 125

C. −125

D. The code does not compile.

E. The result is unknown until runtime.

F. An exception is thrown.

30. What is the output of the following application?

```
import java.util.*;
public class SearchList<T> {
    private List<T> data;
    private boolean foundMatch = false;
    public SearchList(List<T> list) {
        this.data = list;
    }
    public void exists(T v,int start, int end) {
        if(end-start==0) {}
        else if(end-start==1) {
            foundMatch = foundMatch || v.equals(data.get(start));
        } else {
            final int middle = start + (end-start)/2;
            new Thread(() -> exists(v,start,middle)).run();
            new Thread(() -> exists(v,middle,end)).run();
        }
    }
    public static void main(String[] a) throws Exception {
        List<Integer> data = List.of(1,2,3,4,5,6);
        SearchList<Integer> t = new SearchList<Integer>(data);
        t.exists(5, 0, data.size());
        System.out.print(t.foundMatch);
    } }
```

A. true

B. false

C. The code does not compile.

D. The result is unknown until runtime.

E. An exception is thrown.

F. None of the above.

Chapter

9

Java I/O API

THE OCP EXAM TOPICS COVERED IN THIS PRACTICE TEST INCLUDE THE FOLLOWING:

✓ **Java I/O API**

- Read and write console and file data using I/O Streams

- Implement serialization and deserialization techniques on Java objects

- Handle file system objects using java.nio.file API

1. The following code snippet results in an exception at runtime. Which of the following is the most likely type of exception to be thrown?

```
var oldHardDrivePath = Path.get("c://rodent/mouse.txt");
var newHardDrivePath = Path.get("d://rodent/rat.txt");
Files.move(oldHardDrivePath,newHardDrivePath,
    StandardCopyOption.REPLACE_EXISTING);
```

   A. AtomicMoveNotSupportedException

   B. DirectoryNotEmptyException

   C. FileAlreadyExistsException

   D. The code does not compile.

   E. None of the above.

2. What is the result of compiling and executing the following program?

```
package vacation;
import java.io.*;
import java.util.*;
public class Itinerary {
    private List<String> activities = new ArrayList<>();
    private static Itinerary getItinerary(String name) {
        return null;
    }
    public static void printItinerary() throws Exception {
        Console c = new Console();
        final String name = c.readLine("What is your name?");
        final var stuff = getItinerary(name);
        stuff.activities.forEach(s -> c.printf(s));
    }
    public static void main(String[] h) throws Exception {
        printItinerary();
    }
}
```

   A. The code does not compile.

   B. The code compiles and prints a NullPointerException at runtime.

   C. The code compiles but does not print anything at runtime.

   D. The code compiles and prints the value the user enters at runtime.

   E. The behavior cannot be determined until runtime.

   F. None of the above.

3. Assuming the file path referenced in the following class is accessible and writable, what is the output of the following program? (Choose two.)

```java
String fn = "icecream.txt";
try (var w = new BufferedWriter(new FileOutputStream(fn));
     var s = System.out) {
  w.write("ALERT!");
  w.flush();
  w.write('!');
  System.out.print("1");
} catch (IOException e) {
  System.out.print("2");
} finally {
  System.out.print("3");
}
```

A. 1

B. 23

C. 13

D. The code does not compile.

E. If the code compiles or the lines that do not compile are fixed, then the last value output is 3.

F. If the code compiles or the lines that do not compile are fixed, then the last value output is not 3.

4. What is the expected output of the following application? Assume the directories referenced in the class do not exist prior to the execution and that the file system is available and able to be written.

```java
package job;
import java.nio.file.*;
public class Resume {
    public void writeResume() throws Exception {
        var f1 = Path.of("/templates/proofs");
        f1.createDirectories();
        var f2 = Path.of("/templates");
        f2.createDirectory(); // k1
        try(var w = Files.newBufferedWriter(
                Path.of(f2.toString(), "draft.txt"))) {
            w.append("My dream job");
            w.flush();
        }
```

```
        f1.delete(f1);
        f2.delete(f2);          // k2
    }

    public static void main(String... leads) {
        try {
            new Resume().writeResume();
        } catch (Exception e) {
            e.printStackTrace();
        } } }
```

A. One line of this application does not compile.

B. Two lines of this application do not compile.

C. The code compiles, but line k1 triggers an exception at runtime.

D. The code compiles, but line k2 triggers an exception at runtime.

E. The code compiles and runs without printing an exception.

F. None of the above.

5. Which classes are least likely to be marked `Serializable`. (Choose two.)

A. A class that monitors the state of every thread in the application

B. A class that holds data about the amount of rain that has fallen in a given year

C. A class that manages the memory of running processes in an application

D. A class that stores information about apples in an orchard

E. A class that tracks the amount of candy in a gumball machine

F. A class that tracks which users have logged in

6. What is the output of the following code snippet? Assume that the current directory is the root path.

```
Path p1 = Path.of("./found/../keys");
Path p2 = Paths.get("/lost/blue.txt");
System.out.println(p1.resolve(p2));
System.out.println(p2.resolve(p1));
```

A. /lost/blue.txt and /lost/blue.txt/keys

B. /found/../keys/./lost/blue.txt and /lost/blue.txt/keys

C. /found/../keys/./lost/blue.txt and keys

D. /lost/blue.txt and /lost/blue.txt/./found/../keys

E. The code does not compile.

F. None of the above.

7. Fill in the blanks: `Writer` is a(n) _____ that related stream classes _____.

    A. concrete class, extend

    B. abstract class, extend

    C. abstract class, implement

    D. interface, extend

    E. interface, implement

    F. None of the above

8. Assuming `/away/baseball.txt` exists and is accessible, what is the expected result of executing the following code snippet?

```
var p1 = Path.of("baseball.txt");
var p2 = Path.of("/home");
var p3 = Path.of("/away");
Files.createDirectories(p2);
Files.copy(p3.resolve(p1),p2);
```

    A. A new file `/home/baseball.txt` is created.

    B. A new file `/home/away/baseball.txt` is created.

    C. The code does not compile.

    D. The code compiles, but an exception is printed at runtime.

    E. The output cannot be determined until runtime.

    F. None of the above.

9. Assuming the file referenced in the following snippet exists and contains five lines with the word `eggs` in them, what is the expected output?

```
var p = Path.of("breakfast.menu");
Files.readAllLines(p)
    .filter(s -> s.contains("eggs"))
    .collect(Collectors.toList())
    .forEach(System.out::println);
```

    A. No lines will be printed.

    B. One line will be printed.

    C. Five lines will be printed.

    D. More than five lines will be printed.

    E. The code does not compile.

    F. None of the above.

10. What is the output of the following program? Assume the file paths referenced in the class exist and are able to be written to and read from.

```java
import java.io.*;
public class Vegetable implements Serializable {
    private Integer size = 1;
    private transient String name = "Red";
    { size = 3; name = "Purple"; }
    public Vegetable() { this.size = 2; name = "Green"; }
    public static void main(String[] love) throws Throwable {
        try (var o = new ObjectOutputStream(
                new FileOutputStream("healthy.txt"))) {
            final var v = new Vegetable();
            v.size = 4;
            o.writeObject(v);
        }

        try (var o = new ObjectInputStream(
                new FileInputStream("healthy.txt"))) {
            var v = (Vegetable) o.readObject();
            System.out.print(v.size + "," + v.name);
        } } }
```

- **A.** 1,Red
- **B.** 2,Green
- **C.** 2,null
- **D.** 3,Purple
- **E.** 4,null
- **F.** null,null
- **G.** None of the above

11. Why does `Console readPassword()` return a `char` array rather than a `String`?

- **A.** It improves performance.
- **B.** It improves security.
- **C.** Passwords must be stored as a `char` array.
- **D.** `String` cannot hold the individual password characters.
- **E.** It adds encryption.
- **F.** None of the above.

12. Given the following class inheritance diagram, which two classes can be placed in the blank boxes?

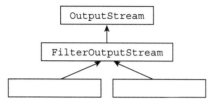

- **A.** `BufferedOutputStream` and `PrintStream`
- **B.** `BufferedOutputStream` and `PrintOutputStream`
- **C.** `ByteArrayOutputStream` and `Stream`
- **D.** `FileOutputStream` and `OutputStream`
- **E.** `ObjectOutputStream` and `PrintOutputStream`
- **F.** None of the above

13. How many lines of the following code contain compiler errors?

```
12: var path = Paths.get(new URI("ice.cool"));
13: var view = Files.readAttributes(path,
14:     BasicFileAttributes.class);
15: Files.createDirectories(Path.relativize(".backup"));
16: if(view.length() > 0 && view.isDirectory())
17:     view.setTimes(null,null,null);
18: System.out.println(Files.deleteIfExists(path));
```

- **A.** All of the lines compile
- **B.** One
- **C.** Two
- **D.** Three
- **E.** Four or more

14. What is the output of the following application?

```java
import java.io.*;
public class TaffyFactory {
    public int getPrize(byte[] luck) throws Exception {
        try (InputStream is = new ByteArrayInputStream(luck)) {
            is.read(new byte[2]);
            if (!is.markSupported()) return -1;
            is.mark(5);
            is.read(); is.read();
            is.skip(3);
```

```
            is.reset();
            return is.read();
        }
    }
    public static void main(String[] x) throws Exception {
        final TaffyFactory p = new TaffyFactory();
        final var luck = new byte[] { 1, 2, 3, 4, 5, 6, 7 };
        System.out.print(p.getPrize(luck));
    } }
```

A. -2

B. 2

C. 3

D. 5

E. 7

F. An exception is thrown at runtime.

15. What is the output of the following program? Assume the file paths referenced in the class exist and are able to be written to and read from.

```
package heart;
import java.io.*;
public class Valve implements Serializable {
    private int chambers = -1;
    private transient Double size = null;
    private static String color;
    public Valve() {
        this.chambers = 3;
        color = "BLUE";
    }
    public static void main(String[] love) throws Throwable {
        try (var o = new ObjectOutputStream(
                new FileOutputStream("scan.txt"))) {
            final Valve v = new Valve();
            v.chambers = 2;
            v.size = 10.0;
            v.color = "RED";
            o.writeObject(v);
        }
```

```
        new Valve();
        try (var o = new ObjectInputStream(
                new FileInputStream("scan.txt"))) {
            Valve v = (Valve)o.readObject();
            System.out.print(v.chambers+","+v.size+","+v.color);
        }
    }
    { chambers = 4; }
}
```

A. `2,null,RED`

B. `2,null,BLUE`

C. `3,10.0,RED`

D. `3,10.0,BLUE`

E. `0,null,null`

F. None of the above

16. Given the following file system diagram, in which `forward` is a symbolic link to the `java` directory, which values if inserted into the following code do not print `/java/Sort.java` at runtime? (Choose two.)

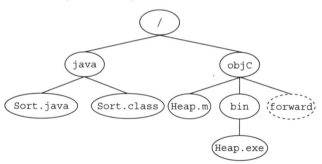

```
Path p = Path.of("/", "objC", "bin");
System.out.print(p.resolve("_____").toRealPath());
```

A. `objC/forward/Sort.java`

B. `../backwards/../forward/Sort.java`

C. `../forward/./Sort.java`

D. `../java/./forward/Sort.java`

E. `../../java/Sort.java`

F. `../././forward/Sort.java`

17. Which method defined in Reader can be used in place of calling skip(1)?

   A. jump()

   B. mark()

   C. markSupported()

   D. read()

   E. reset()

   F. None of the above

18. The Rose application is run with an input argument of /flower. The /flower directory contains five subdirectories, each of which contains five files. What is the result of executing the following program?

```java
import java.nio.file.*;
public class Rose {
    public void tendGarden(Path p) throws Exception {
        Files.walk(p,1)
            .map(q -> q.toRealPath())
            .forEach(System.out::println);
    }
    public static void main(String... thorns) throws Exception {
        new Rose().tendGarden(Paths.get(thorns[0]));
    }
}
```

   A. The program completes without outputting anything.

   B. One Path value is printed.

   C. Six Path values are printed.

   D. Twenty-five Path values are printed.

   E. Twenty-six Path values are printed.

   F. None of the above.

19. What may be the result of executing the following program?

```java
package test;
import java.io.*;
public class Turing {
    public static void main(String... robots) {
        Console c = System.console();
        final String response = c.readLine("Are you human?");
        System.err.print(response);
    }
}
```

A. The program asks the user a question and prints the results to the error stream.

B. The program throws a `NullPointerException` at runtime.

C. The program does not terminate.

D. All of the above.

E. The class does not compile.

20. What is the output of the following method applied to an `InputStream` that contains the first four prime numbers, stored as bytes: 2, 3, 5, 7?

```java
private void jumpAround(InputStream is) throws IOException {
    try (is) {
        is.skip(1);
        is.read();
        is.skip(1);
        is.mark(4);
        is.skip(1);
        is.reset();
        System.out.print(is.read());
    }
}
```

A. 5

B. 7

C. The code does not compile.

D. The code compiles but throws an exception at runtime.

E. The result cannot be determined until runtime.

F. None of the above.

21. Which statement about the following method is correct? Assume the directory `/tea/earlGrey/hot` exists and is able to be read.

```java
void order() throws Exception {
    var s = Path.of("/tea","earlGrey","hot");
    Files.find(s, (p,a) -> a.isDirectory());
}
```

A. It does not compile.

B. It compiles but does not print anything at runtime.

C. It compiles and prints `true` exactly once at runtime.

D. It compiles and prints `true` at least once.

E. The answer cannot be determined without knowing the contents of the directory.

F. None of the above.

22. Which method are classes that implement `java.io.Serializable` required to implement?

   A. `cereal()`

   B. `deserialize()`

   C. `serial()`

   D. `serialize()`

   E. `clone()`

   F. None of the above

23. What is the result of compiling and executing the following program? Assume the current directory is `/stock` and the path `/stock/sneakers` does not exist prior to execution.

```
package shoe;
import java.io.*;
import java.nio.file.*;
public class Sneaker {
    public void setupInventory(Path d) throws Exception {
        Path suggestedPath = Paths.get("sneakers");
        if(Files.isSameFile(suggestedPath, d)               // j1
            && !Files.exists(suggestedPath))
            Files.createDirectories(d);                      // j2
    }
    public static void main(String[] socks) throws Exception {
        Path w = new File("/stock/sneakers").toPath();  // j3
        new Sneaker().setupInventory(w);
    }
}
```

   A. The directory `/stock/sneakers` is created.

   B. Line `j1` does not compile or produces an exception at runtime.

   C. Line `j2` does not compile or produces an exception at runtime.

   D. Line `j3` does not compile or produces an exception at runtime.

   E. None of the above.

24. Assuming the absolute path referenced in the code exists and its contents are accessible, which statement about the following code snippet is correct?

```
Path p = Paths.get("/glasses/lens");

Files.walk(p)
    .map(z -> z.toAbsolutePath().toString())
    .filter(s -> s.endsWith(".java"))
    .collect(Collectors.toList()).forEach(System.out::println);
```

```
Files.find(p,Integer.MAX_VALUE,
      (w,a) -> w.toAbsolutePath().toString().endsWith(".java"))
   .collect(Collectors.toList()).forEach(System.out::println);
```

A. The first stream statement does not compile.

B. The second stream statement does not compile.

C. Neither statement compiles.

D. Both statements compile and produce the same result at runtime.

E. None of the above.

25. When reading file information, what is an advantage of using an NIO.2 attribute interface rather than reading the values individually using `Files` methods? (Choose two.)

A. Costs fewer round-trips to the file system

B. Guarantees performance improvement

C. Has support for symbolic links

D. Reduces memory leaks

E. Supports file-system dependent attributes

F. Reduces resource leaks

26. Suppose that you need to read data that consists of serialized `int`, `double`, `boolean`, and `String` values from a file. You also want the program to be performant on large files. Which three `java.io` stream classes can be chained together to best achieve this result? (Choose three.)

A. `BufferedInputStream`

B. `FileReader`

C. `ObjectInputStream`

D. `BufferedReader`

E. `BufferedStream`

F. `FileInputStream`

27. Which statement about the following method is correct? Assume the directory `coffee` exists and is able to be read.

```
void brew() throws Exception {
   final var m = Path.of("coffee");
   Files.walk(m)
      .filter(Files::isDirectory)
      .forEach(Files::isDirectory);
}
```

A. It does not compile.

B. It compiles but does not print anything at runtime.

C. It compiles and prints `true` exactly once at runtime.

D. It compiles and prints `true` at least once.

E. The answer cannot be determined without knowing the contents of the directory.

F. None of the above.

28. Assuming the file referenced in the `StudentManager` class exists and contains data, which statement about the following class is correct? (Choose two.)

```
package school;
import java.io.*;
class Student implements Serializable {
    transient int score = -1;
    String name;
    public String toString() { return name + ":" + score; }
}
public class StudentManager {
    public static void main(String[] grades) {
        try(var ios = new ObjectInputStream(
                new FileInputStream(new File("s.data")))) {
            Student record;
            while((record = (Student)ios.readObject()) != null)
                System.out.print(record);
        } catch (EOFException e) {
        } catch (Exception e) {
            throw new RuntimeException(e);
        }
    }
}
```

A. The code does not compile.

B. The code compiles but prints an exception at runtime.

C. The program runs and prints all students in the file.

D. The program runs but may only print some students in the files.

E. For any instance of `Student` that is correctly deserialized, the value of `score` will be −1.

F. For any instance of `Student` that is correctly deserialized, the value of `score` will not be −1.

29. Given an instance of `Console` c, which of the following two method calls are invalid ways of retrieving input from the user? (Choose two.)

A. `c.read()`

B. `c.reader().read()`

C. `c.reader().readLine()`

D. `c.readLine()`

E. `c.readPassword()`

30. What is the output of the following code snippet? Assume that the current directory is the root path /.

```
Path p1 = Paths.get("./locks");
Path p2 = Paths.get("/found/red.zip");
System.out.println(p1.relativize(p2));
```

```
System.out.println(p2.relativize(p1));
```

A. `../found/red.zip` and `../../locks`

B. `/found/red.zip` and `/found/red.zip/./locks`

C. `locks/../found/red.zip` and `../found/locks`

D. `../../locks` and `../found/red.zip`

E. `/found/red.zip` and `/found/red.zip/locks`

F. None of the above

31. Assuming the current working directory is `/home`, then what is the output of the following program?

```
1:  package magic;
2:  import java.nio.file.*;
3:  public class Magician {
4:      public String doTrick(Path path) {
5:          return path.subpath(2,3)
6:              .getName(1)
7:              .toAbsolutePath()
8:              .toString();
9:      }
10:     public static void main(String... cards) {
11:         final Magician m = new Magician();
12:         System.out.print(m.doTrick(
13:             Paths.get("/bag/of/tricks/.././disappear.txt")));
14:     } }
```

A. `/home/tricks`

B. `/home`

C. `tricks`

D. The code does not compile.

E. The code compiles but prints an exception at runtime.

F. None of the above.

32. Which statements about the `Files` methods `lines()` and `readAllLines()` are correct? (Choose two.)

A. They have different return types.

B. The `readAllLines()` method is always faster.

C. The `lines()` may require more memory.

D. They have the same return type.

E. The `lines()` method is always faster.

F. The `readAllLines()` method may require more memory.

33. Given the following application, in which a user enters bone twice, what is the expected result?

```
long start = System.currentTimeMillis();
var retriever = new BufferedReader(new
    InputStreamReader(System.in));
try(retriever; var husky = System.err) {
    var fetch = retriever.readLine();
    System.out.printf("%s fetched in %5.1f seconds",fetch, // v1
        (System.currentTimeMillis()-start)/1000.0);
}
var fetchAgain = retriever.readLine();
System.out.println(fetchAgain + " fetched again!");
```

A. The program completes after printing a message once.

B. The program completes after printing a message twice.

C. An IOException is thrown.

D. The program prints an exception because the format of the String on line v1 is invalid.

E. A NullPointerException is thrown since System.in may be unavailable.

F. None of the above as the code does not compile.

34. What is the expected result of calling deleteTree() on a directory? Assume the directory exists and is able to be modified.

```
import java.nio.file.*;
public class Exterminate {
    public void deleteTree(Path q) {
        if (!Files.isDirectory(q))
            Files.delete(q);
        else {
            Files.list(q).forEach(this::deleteTree);
            Files.delete(q);
        } } }
```

A. It will delete the directory itself only.

B. It will delete the directory and its file contents only.

C. It will delete the entire directory tree.

D. The code does not compile.

E. The code compiles but produces an exception at runtime.

F. None of the above.

35. Which code, if inserted into the method, will cause it to correctly copy any file passed to it that is accessible? (Choose two.)

```java
void copyFile(String source, String target) throws Exception {
    try (var is = new FileInputStream(source);
            OutputStream os = new FileOutputStream(target)) {
        byte[] data = new byte[123];
        int chirps;

        // INSERT CODE HERE
    }
}
```

A.
```java
while (is.read(data) > 0)
    os.write(data);
```
B.
```java
while ((chirps = is.read(data)) > 0)
    os.write(data, 0, chirps);
```
C.
```java
while ((chirps = is.read(data)) > 0)
    os.write(data);
```
D.
```java
while ((chirps = is.read(data)) > 0)
    os.write(data, chirps, data.length);
```
E.
```java
String line;
while ((line = is.readLine()) != null)
    os.write(line + "\n");
```
F.
```java
while ((chirps = is.read()) > 0)
    os.write(chirps);
```

36. Let's say we want to write an instance of `Cereal` to disk, having a `name` value of `CornLoops` and `sugar` value of 5. What is the value of `name` and `sugar` after this object has been read from disk using the `ObjectInputStream`'s `readObject()` method?

```java
package breakfast;
import java.io.Serializable;
class Bowl {
```

```
        boolean spoon = true;
        // Getters/Setters Omitted
    }
    public class Cereal implements Serializable {
        private String name = "CocoaCookies";
        private transient int sugar = 10;
        private Bowl bowl;
        public Cereal() {
            super();
            this.name = "CaptainPebbles";
            this.bowl = new Bowl();
            sugar = 2;
        }
        { name = "SugarPops"; }
        // Getters/Setters Omitted
    }
```

A. CaptainPebbles and 10

B. CornLoops and 0

C. SugarPops and 10

D. SugarPops and 2

E. CornLoops and -1

F. None of the above

37. What is the output of the following code snippet?

```
11: var halleysComet = Path.of("stars/./rocks/../m1.meteor")
12:     .subpath(1, 5).normalize();
13:
14: var lexellsComet = Paths.get("./stars/../solar/");
15: lexellsComet.subpath(1, 3)
16:     .resolve("m1.meteor").normalize();
17:
18: System.out.print(halleysComet.equals(lexellsComet) ?
19:     "Same!" : "Different!");
```

A. Same!

B. Different!

C. The code does not compile.

D. The class compiles but throws an exception at runtime.

E. None of the above.

38. During deserialization from an I/O stream, which element of the class can be used to assign a value to the deserialized object?

   A. Variable initializer

   B. Instance initializer

   C. Static initializer

   D. Constructor

   E. The `restoreObject()` method

   F. None of the above

39. Assuming there are no symbolic links involved and file `/nursery/sapling.seed` exists, which statements about the following code snippet are correct? (Choose three.)

```
Files.move(
    Paths.get("/nursery/sapling.seed"),
    Paths.get("/forest"),
    StandardCopyOption.ATOMIC_MOVE);
```

   A. The code may throw an exception at runtime.

   B. The code may complete without throwing an exception at runtime.

   C. After it runs, the new location of the file would be `/nursery/sapling.seed`

   D. After it runs, the new location of the file would be `/forest/sapling.seed`

   E. If a process is monitoring the move, it will not see an incomplete file.

   F. If a process is monitoring the move, it could see an incomplete file.

40. What is the output of the following application? Assume `/all-data` exists and is accessible within the file system.

```
1:  package sesame;
2:  import java.nio.file.*;
3:  import java.util.stream.*;
4:  public class TheCount {
5:      public static Stream<String> readLines(Path p) {
6:          try { return Files.lines(p); } catch (Exception e) {
7:              throw new RuntimeException(e);
8:          }
9:      }
10:     public static long count(Path p) throws Exception {
11:         return Files.list(p)
12:                 .filter(w -> Files.isRegularFile(w))
13:                 .flatMap(s -> readLines(s))
14:                 .count();
15:     }
```

```
16:    public static void main(String[] d) throws Exception {
17:        System.out.print(count(Paths.get("/all-data")));
18:    } }
```

A. The code does not compile.

B. The number of lines in all files in a directory tree.

C. The number of lines in all files in a single directory.

D. The code hangs indefinitely at runtime.

E. An exception is printed at runtime.

F. None of the above.

Chapter 10

Secure Coding in Java SE Application

THE OCP EXAM TOPICS COVERED IN THIS PRACTICE TEST INCLUDE THE FOLLOWING:

✓ **Secure Coding in Java SE Application**

- Develop code that mitigates security threats such as denial of service, code injection, input validation and ensure data integrity

- Secure resource access including filesystems, manage policies and execute privileged code

1. Which statement best describes this class?

```java
import java.util.*;
public final class Forest {
    private final int flora;
    private final List<String> fauna;

    public Forest() {
        this.flora = 5;
        this.fauna = new ArrayList<>();
    }

    public int getFlora() {
        return flora;
    }
    public List<String> getFauna() {
        return fauna;
    }
}
```

   A. It can be serialized.

   B. It is well encapsulated.

   C. It is immutable.

   D. It is both well encapsulated and immutable.

   E. None of the above as the code does not compile.

2. Fill in the blanks: The _____ class variable defines a whitelist of fields that should be serialized, while the _____ modifier is used to construct a blacklist of fields that should not be serialized. (Choose two.)

   A. `serialVersionUID` in the first blank

   B. `serialFields` in the first blank

   C. `serialPersistentFields` in the first blank

   D. `ignore` in the second blank

   E. `transient` in the second blank

   F. `skip` in the second blank

3. Which statement best describes the following method?

```java
public String findNewLego(String url, String type)
        throws SQLException {
    var query = "SELECT name FROM sets WHERE "
        + "type = " + type + " ORDER BY date DESC";
```

```
    var con = DriverManager.getConnection(url);
    try(con;
        var ps = con.createStatement();
        var rs = ps.executeQuery(query)) {

        if(rs.next()) return rs.getString(1);
    }
    throw new RuntimeException("None available, try  later");
}
```

A. It is not susceptible to any common attacks.

B. It is at risk of SQL injection attack only.

C. It is at risk of a denial of service attack only.

D. It is at risk of both SQL injection and denial of service attacks.

E. The method does not compile.

F. None of the above.

4. Fill in the blanks: _____ means the state of an object cannot be changed, while _____ means that it can.

A. Encapsulation, factory method

B. Immutability, mutability

C. Rigidity, flexibility

D. Static, instance

E. Tightly coupled, loosely coupled

F. None of the above

5. Which of the following best protect against denial of service attacks? (Choose three.)

A. Close resources with `catch` blocks.

B. Use `PreparedStatement` instead of `Statement`.

C. Close resources with try-with-resources statements.

D. Set a limit of the size of a file upload.

E. Set a limit on the size of a numeric input value.

F. Use immutable objects.

6. You ask to borrow one of your friend's recipe cards. Which statements about these cards, represented as Java policy file grants, are correct? (Choose two.)

```
grant {
    permission java.io.FilePermission
        "/dessert/icecream/rockyroad.yum", "read,write";
    permission java.io.FilePermission
```

```
        "/dessert/icecream/mintchip.yum", "read";
};
```

A. The policy syntax of the policy file is correct.

B. The policy syntax of the policy file is incorrect.

C. The policy is incorrect because `read` should not be included in the first permission.

D. The policy is incorrect because `write` should not be included in the first permission.

E. The policy is incorrect because `read` should not be included in the second permission.

F. The policy is incorrect because file permissions cannot be granted this way.

7. Which of the following best protect against inclusion attacks? (Choose two.)

A. Encrypt user passwords.

B. Use immutable objects.

C. Limit the recursive depth of ZIP files.

D. Apply a blacklist to the input data.

E. Turn the computer off when not in use.

F. Restrict the number of parse levels of XML files.

8. What changes, taken together, would make the `Tree` class immutable? (Choose three.)

```
1:  public class Tree {
2:      String species;
3:      public Tree(String species) {
4:          this.species = species;
5:      }
6:      public String getSpecies() {
7:          return species;
8:      }
9:      private final void setSpecies(String newSpecies) {
10:         species = newSpecies;
11:     }
12: }
```

A. Make all constructors `private`.

B. Change the access level of `species` to `private`.

C. Change the access level of `species` to `protected`.

D. Remove the `setSpecies()` method.

E. Mark the `Tree` class `final`.

F. Make a defensive copy of species in the `Tree` constructor.

9. Which techniques best prevent sensitive objects from being manipulated by an attacker who wants to create a malicious subclass? (Choose three.)

A. Add `final` to the class declaration.

B. Set `protected` as the access level for all method declarations.

C. Add `final` to all method declarations.

D. Add `final` to all instance variable declarations.

E. Add `final` to all constructors.

F. Set `private` as the access level for all constructors.

10. Which statement best describes the following method?

```
public String findNewLego(String url, int type)
        throws SQLException {
    var query = "SELECT name FROM sets WHERE "
        + "type = " + type + " ORDER BY date DESC";
    var con = DriverManager.getConnection(url);
    var ps = con.createStatement();
    try(con; ps; var rs = ps.executeQuery(query)) {
        if(rs.next()) return rs.getString(1);
    }
    throw new RuntimeException("None available, try  later");
}
```

A. It is not susceptible to any common attacks.

B. It is at risk of SQL injection attack only.

C. It is at risk of a denial of service attack only.

D. It is at risk of both SQL injection and denial of service attacks.

E. The method does not compile.

F. None of the above.

11. Which statements about executing the following program are correct? (Choose two.)

```
import java.security.*;
import java.util.*;

public class MagicTrick {
    private static final String WORD = "abracadabra";
    private static List<String> trick = new ArrayList<>();
    public static List<String> castSpell(String magic) {
        return AccessController.doPrivileged(
                new PrivilegedAction<List<String>>() {
            public List<String> run() {
```

```
            if (magic.equalsIgnoreCase(WORD)) {        // p1
                if(trick.isEmpty())
                    trick.add(System.getProperty(magic)); // p2
                return trick;                            // p3
            }
            throw new SecurityException("Incorrect code");
        }
    });
}
public static void main(String[] args) {
    if(args != null && args.length>0)
        System.out.print(MagicTrick.castSpell(args[0]));
} }
```

A. Line p1 makes the code susceptible to tainted inputs from the user.

B. Line p2 makes the code susceptible to tainted inputs from the user.

C. Line p3 makes the code susceptible to tainted inputs from the user.

D. The code is not susceptible to tainted inputs from the user.

E. Line p1 exposes sensitive information.

F. Line p2 exposes sensitive information.

G. Line p3 exposes sensitive information.

H. The code does not expose any sensitive information.

12. How do you change the value of an instance variable in an immutable class?

A. Call the setter method.

B. Remove the final modifier and set the instance variable directly.

C. Create a new instance with an inner class.

D. Use a method other than Option A, B, or C.

E. You can't.

13. Let's say you want to serialize the following class, but only want the flour quantity saved. What changes, if any, are required to the following class for this to occur?

```
import java.io.*;
public class Muffin {
    private Double flour;
    private Integer eggs;
    private Float sugar;
    private final ObjectStreamField[] serialPersistentFields =
        { new ObjectStreamField("flour", Double.class) };
}
```

A. No changes are required.

B. Mark `eggs` and `sugar` as `transient`.

C. Remove the `serialPersistentFields` variable.

D. Remove the `final` modifier from the `serialPersistentFields` variable.

E. Add a missing modifier to the `serialPersistentFields` variable.

F. None of the above.

14. Which are true about closing resources to guard against a denial of service attack? (Choose two.)

A. The NIO.2 `Files.lines()` method does not require closing a resource when it is used in a stream pipeline.

B. The NIO.2 `Files.lines()` method requires closing a resource when it is used in a stream pipeline.

C. When locking a resource using an instance of the concurrent `Lock` interface, the `unlock()` statement should be immediately before the `finally` block.

D. When locking a resource using an instance of the concurrent `Lock` interface, the `unlock()` statement should be in a `finally` block.

E. When locking a resource using an instance of the concurrent `Lock` interface, the `unlock()` statement should be immediately after the `finally` block.

15. Which type of attack requires more than one source to initiate?

A. Billion laughs attack

B. Million frowns attack

C. Distributed denial of service attack

D. SQL injection

E. Inclusion attack

F. Denial of service attack

16. What is this class an example of?

```
import java.util.*;
public class Nightclub {
    private List<String> approved = // IMPLEMENTATION OMITTED
    private List<String> rejected = // IMPLEMENTATION OMITTED
    public boolean checkAccess(String name) {
        var grantAccess = approved.contains(name)
            || rejected.contains(name);
        return grantAccess;
    } }
```

A. Turquoiselist

B. Whitelist

    C. Orangelist

    D. Blacklist

    E. Both blacklist and whitelist

    F. None of the above

17. Which statements about the `clone()` method are correct? (Choose two.)

    A. Calling `clone()` on a class that does not implement `Cloneable` results in a compiler error.

    B. Calling `clone()` on a class that does not implement `Cloneable` results in an exception at runtime.

    C. If a class implements `Cloneable` and does not override the `clone()` method, then the code does not compile.

    D. If a class implements `Cloneable` and does not override the `clone()` method, then an exception is thrown at runtime.

    E. Overriding the `clone()` method in a class that implements `Cloneable` guarantees at least a shallow copy will be performed.

    F. Overriding the `clone()` method in a class that implements `Cloneable` may result in a deep copy.

18. Which statements about securing confidential information are correct? (Choose three.)

    A. When writing to `System.out`, you should not include sensitive information.

    B. When reading sensitive data from a `Console,` you should use `readLine()`.

    C. When throwing an exception, it is acceptable to include sensitive information in the message.

    D. A `String` is not a good object type for sensitive data.

    E. A Java policy should only grant the permission `lock` to prevent a user from modifying the file.

    F. A Java policy should only grant the permission `read` to prevent a user from modifying the file.

19. What are the best scenarios for customizing the serialization process? (Choose two.)

    A. To prevent SQL injection.

    B. To shuffle data among users.

    C. It is the only way to prevent a sensitive field like birthdate from being written to disk.

    D. To improve performance by applying advanced optimization techniques.

    E. To encrypt a password before it is saved to disk.

    F. To customize the handling of certain user sensitive data like a Social Security number.

20. Select a good strategy for handling input validation failures?

    A. Use the `assert` statement.

    B. Throw an `Error`.

    C. Log an error but allow the user to continue.

    D. Throw an `Exception`.

E. Shut down the computer.

F. None of the above.

21. Which statements about executing the following program are correct? (Choose two.)

```java
import java.security.*;

public class PrintScores {
   private static final String CODE = "12345";
   private static final String SCORES = "test.scores";
   public static String getScores(String accessCode) {
      return AccessController.doPrivileged(
            new PrivilegedAction<String>() {
         public String run() {
            if(accessCode.equals(CODE))           // m1
               return System.getProperty(SCORES); // m2
            throw new SecurityException("Incorrect code");
         }
      });
   }

   public static void main(String[] args) {
      if(args != null && args.length>0)
         System.out.print(PrintScores.getScores(args[0]));
   } }
```

A. Line m1 makes the code susceptible to tainted inputs from the user.

B. Line m2 makes the code susceptible to tainted inputs from the user.

C. The code is not susceptible to tainted inputs from the user.

D. The code is susceptible to an injection attack.

E. The code is not susceptible to an injection attack.

F. The code is susceptible to an injection only if executed with a number as input.

22. Which can fill in the blank to make this code compile?

```java
import java.io.*;
public class Pony implements Serializable {
   private static final ObjectStreamField[]
      serialPersistentFields = { new ObjectStreamField("name",
         String.class) };
   private String name;
   private Integer age;
```

```
private void readObject(ObjectInputStream s)
    throws Exception {
  ObjectInputStream._____ fields = s.readFields();
  this.name = (String) fields.get("name", null);
} }
```

A. GetObject

B. ReadField

C. FetchItem

D. ReadItem

E. GetField

F. None of the above

23. Which statement about the following classes is correct?

```
import java.util.*;
public class Flower {
    private final String name;
    private final List<Integer> counts;
    public Flower(String name, List<Integer> counts) {
        this.name = name;
        this.counts = new ArrayList<>(counts);
    }
    public final String getName() { return name; }
    public final List<Integer> getCounts() {
        return new ArrayList<>(counts);
    } }

class Plant {
    private final String name;
    private final List<Integer> counts;
    public Plant(String name, List<Integer> counts) {
        this.name = name;
        this.counts = new ArrayList<>(counts);
    }
    public String getName() { return name; }
    public List<Integer> getCounts() {
        return new ArrayList<>(counts);
    } }
```

A. Only Flower is immutable.

B. Only Plant is immutable.

C. Both classes are immutable.

   D. Neither class is immutable.

   E. None of the above as one of the classes does not compile.

24. Which of the following can cause an injection attack? (Choose two.)

   A. Access control

   B. Command line input

   C. Constants in the program

   D. Mutable code

   E. Serialization

   F. XML parsing

25. Assuming this class is passed a valid non-negative integer, which statements best describe the following class? (Choose two.)

```java
public class Charity {
    private int numberRequests = 0;
    public synchronized int getNumberOfRequests() {
        return numberRequests;
    }

    private void callDatabaseToDonateADollar() {
        // IMPLEMENTATION OMITTED
    }

    public synchronized void donateDollar(int numDollars) {
        numberRequests++;
        for(int i=0; i<numDollars; i++) {
            callDatabaseToDonateADollar();
        }
    }

    public static void main(String[] args) {
        final var humanFund = new Charity();
        humanFund.donateDollar(Integer.valueOf(args[0]));
        System.out.print(humanFund.getNumberOfRequests());
    } }
```

   A. It is well encapsulated.

   B. It is susceptible to a denial of service attack.

   C. It creates an immutable object.

   D. It is susceptible to an inclusion attack.

   E. It is not thread-safe.

   F. It is susceptible to an exploit attack.

26. In which scenario is it appropriate for confidential information to be used?

   A. Writing to a log file

   B. Printing a stack trace

   C. Outputting to `System.err`

   D. Storing in a `String`

   E. Writing an unsecure email

   F. None of the above

27. What statements about the following method are correct? (Choose three.)

```java
public String checkAlarm(String connectionStr, boolean alarmed)
        throws SQLException {
    var query = "SELECT * FROM office WHERE alarmed = true";
    var con = DriverManager.getConnection(connectionStr);
    var stmt = con.createStatement();
    try (con;
            stmt;
            var rs = stmt.executeQuery(query)) {
        return rs.next() ? rs.getString("address") : null;
    } }
```

   A. It protects against a denial of service attack.

   B. It does not protect against denial of service attacks.

   C. It protects against SQL injection.

   D. It does not protect against SQL injection because it does not use a `PreparedStatement`.

   E. Even if the method completes without throwing an exception, a resource leak might occur.

   F. If the method completes without throwing an exception, then no resource leak can occur.

28. Which statement best describes this class?

```java
import java.util.*;
public final class Ocean {
    private final List<String> algae;
    private final double wave;
    private int sun;

    public Ocean(double wave) {
        this.wave = wave;
        this.algae = new ArrayList<>();
    }
```

```
    public int getSun() {
        return sun;
    }
    public void setSun(int sun) {
        sun = sun;
    }
    public double getWave() {
        return wave;
    }
    public List<String> getAlgae() {
        return new ArrayList<String>(algae);
    }
}
```

A. It can be serialized.

B. It is well encapsulated.

C. It is immutable.

D. It is both well encapsulated and immutable.

E. None of the above as the code does not compile.

29. Which are true about this class? (Choose three.)

```
import java.io.*;
import java.util.*;
public final class Forest implements Serializable {
    public final int flora;
    public final List<String> fauna;

    public Forest() {
        this.flora = 5;
        this.fauna = new ArrayList<>();
    }

    public int getFlora() {
        return flora;
    }
    public List<String> getFauna() {
        return new ArrayList<>(fauna);
    }
}
```

A. It is able to be serialized.

B. It is not able to be serialized.

   C. It is well encapsulated.

   D. It is not well encapsulated.

   E. It is immutable.

   F. It is not immutable.

30. You've been hired by Charlie Sweets to perform a security audit of their login system. After reviewing the following code, what recommendations would best improve the security of their system? (Choose three.)

```
1:  public class CandyFactory {
2:      boolean check(String username, String password) {
3:          // IMPLEMENTATION OMITTED
4:      }
5:      public void login() {
6:          var c = System.console();
7:          if(c != null) {
8:              var username = c.readLine("Username: ");
9:              var password = c.readLine("Password: ");
10:             System.out.println("["+username+","+password+"]");
11:             System.out.println(check(username,password)
12:                 ? "Here is your candy"
13:                 : "No candy for you");
14:      } } }
```

   A. Mark the `check()` method `final` on line 2.

   B. Remove the `null` check on line 7.

   C. Rewrite to not use `var` on lines 6, 8, and 9, as it is inherently unsafe.

   D. Rewrite to use `readPassword()` on line 8.

   E. Rewrite to use `readPassword()` on line 9.

   F. Change or remove line 10.

31. Fill in the blanks with the proper method names to serialize an object. (Choose two.)

```
import java.io.*;
public class DeliSandwich implements Serializable {
    public Object _____() throws ObjectStreamException {
        // IMPLEMENTATION OMITTED
    }

    private void _____(ObjectOutputStream out)
            throws IOException {
        // IMPLEMENTATION OMITTED
    }
}
```

A. `readResolve` in the first blank

B. `writeReplace` in the first blank

C. `writeObject` in the first blank

D. `writeObject` in the second blank

E. `readObject` in the second blank

F. `writeReplace` in the second blank

32. Your co-worker has called you in the middle of the night to report all the servers have been compromised and have run out of memory. After some debugging, it seems like the attacker exploited a file upload resource, but you aren't sure how since the endpoint has a small maximum file size limit. What is the most likely type of attack perpetrated against the system?

A. Denial of service attack

B. Inclusion attack

C. Distributed denial of service attack

D. Exploit attack

E. SQL injection

F. Injection attack

33. Which statements about the following class are correct? (Choose three.)

```java
import java.security.*;
import java.util.*;

public class UserProfile {
    private static class UserEntry {
        private final UserProfile value;
        private final Permission permission;
        // Constructors/Getters Omitted
    }

    public static Permission getPermission(String check) {
        // Implementation Omitted
    }

    private static Map<String,UserEntry> data = new HashMap<>();
    public static UserProfile getProfile(String check) {
        var securityRecord = data.get(check);
        if (securityRecord != null)
            return securityRecord.getValue();            // h1
```

```
    var permission = getPermission(check);
    var permCol = permission.newPermissionCollection();
    permCol.add(permission);
    var prof = AccessController.doPrivileged(          // h2
       new PrivilegedAction<UserProfile>() {
          public UserProfile run() {
             return new UserProfile();
       }},
       new AccessControlContext(
          new ProtectionDomain[] {
             new ProtectionDomain(null, permCol)
          }));
    data.put(check, new UserEntry(prof, permission)); // h3
    return prof;
} }
```

A. Line h1 properly validates security.

B. Line h1 presents an unacceptable security risk.

C. Line h2 elevates security privileges.

D. Line h2 does not elevate security privileges.

E. Line h3 violates security guidelines by allowing security information to be cached.

F. Line h3 does not violate security guidelines.

34. For which value of name will this code result in a successful SQL injection attack?

```
public Integer getScore(String connectionStr, String name)
      throws SQLException {
   var query = "SELECT score FROM records WHERE name = ?";
   var con = DriverManager.getConnection(connectionStr);
   try (con; var stmt = con.prepareStatement(query)) {
      stmt.setString(1, name);
      try(var rs = stmt.executeQuery()) {
         if(rs.next()) return rs.getInt("score");
      }
   }
   return null;
}
```

A. DELETE TABLE records;

B. 'Olivia'; DELETE TABLE records

C. 'Sophia; DELETE TABLE records

D. 'Elysia'; DELETE TABLE records

E. `?; DELETE TABLE records;`

F. None of the above

35. Which are requirements for a class to be immutable? (Choose three.)

A. A `private` constructor is provided.

B. Any instance variables are `private`.

C. Any instance variables are initialized in a constructor.

D. Methods cannot be overridden.

E. There are no setter methods.

F. Any instance variables are marked `final`.

36. Which of the following are not typically considered denial of service attacks? (Choose two.)

A. Downloading confidential information from a log file

B. Uploading a very large file

C. Performing SQL injection

D. Passing invalid numbers to trigger overflow or underflow

E. Exploiting a database resource leak

F. Uploading a zip bomb

37. The following code prints `false`. Which statements best describe the `Fruit` class? (Choose three.)

```
var original = new Fruit();
original.sweet = new ArrayList<>();
var cloned = (Fruit) original.clone();
System.out.print(original.sweet == cloned.sweet);
```

A. It does not implement `Cloneable`.

B. It performs a deep copy.

C. It performs a shallow copy.

D. It overrides `clone()`.

E. It implements `Cloneable`.

F. It does not override `clone()`.

38. What are the best ways to prevent SQL injection? (Choose two.)

A. Avoid SQL statements that take query parameters.

B. Log an error anytime a SQL injection attack is successful.

C. Avoid concatenating user input into a query string.

D. Ensure database resources are closed.

E. Always use a `PreparedStatement` instead of a `Statement`.

F. Do not use a relational database.

39. Given the following two classes, what change to the `StealSecret` class would allow it to read and email the password to a hacker?

```java
public class Secret {
   private String mySecret;
   public void setSecret(String secret) {
      mySecret = secret;
   }
   public void printSecret() {
      throw new UnsupportedOperationException("Nope!");
   }
   private void saveToDisk() {
      // IMPLEMENTATION OMITTED
   }
}


public class StealSecret extends Secret {
   // DO BAD STUFF
}
```

A. There are no changes, as the `Secret` class is secure.

B. Override the `mySecret` variable.

C. Override the `setSecret()` method.

D. Override the `printSecret()` method.

E. Override the `saveToDisk()` method.

F. Add a constructor.

40. Which statement about the following classes is correct?

```java
import java.util.*;
final class Faucet {
   private final String water;
   private final List<Double> pipes;
   public Faucet(String water, List<Double> pipes) {
      this.water = water;
      this.pipes = pipes;
   }
   public String getWater() { return water; }
   public List<Double> getPipes() { return pipes; } }

public final class Spout {
   private final String well;
```

```
   private final List<Boolean> buckets;
   public Spout(String well, List<Boolean> buckets) {
      this.well = well;
      this.buckets = new ArrayList<>(buckets);
   }
   public String getWell() { return well; }

   public List<Boolean> getBuckets() {
      return new ArrayList<>(buckets);
   } }
```

A. Only Faucet is immutable.

B. Only Spout is immutable.

C. Both classes are immutable.

D. Neither class is immutable.

E. None of the above as one of the classes does not compile.

Chapter

11

Database Applications with JDBC

THE OCP EXAM TOPICS COVERED IN THIS PRACTICE TEST INCLUDE THE FOLLOWING:

✓ **Database Applications with JDBC**

- Connect to and perform database SQL operations, process query results using JDBC API

1. How many of `Connection`, `Driver`, `DriverManager`, `PreparedStatement`, and `ResultSet` are JDBC interfaces included with the JDK?
   - **A.** None
   - **B.** One
   - **C.** Two
   - **D.** Three
   - **E.** Four
   - **F.** Five

2. Which is found in the `java.sql` package that come with the standard JDK?
   - **A.** Only `DerbyDriver`
   - **B.** Only `MySqlDriver`
   - **C.** Only `OracleDriver`
   - **D.** `DerbyDriver, MySqlDriver, OracleDriver`
   - **E.** Only `DerbyDriver` and `MySqlDriver`
   - **F.** None of these

3. What must be the first characters of a database URL?
   - **A.** `db,`
   - **B.** `db:`
   - **C.** `jdbc,`
   - **D.** `jdbc:`
   - **E.** None of the above

4. Which is responsible for getting a connection to the database?
   - **A.** `Driver`
   - **B.** `Connection`
   - **C.** `PreparedStatement`
   - **D.** `Statement`
   - **E.** `ResultSet`

5. Which of these obtains a `Connection`?
   - **A.** `Connection.getConnection(url)`
   - **B.** `Driver.getConnection(url)`
   - **C.** `DriverManager.getConnection(url)`
   - **D.** `new Connection(url)`
   - **E.** None of the above

6. Which method in `DriverManager` is overloaded to allow passing a username and password?

   A. `conn()`

   B. `connect()`

   C. `forName()`

   D. `getStatement()`

   E. `open()`

   F. None of the above

7. What is the output if the `clowns` database exists and contains an empty `clowns` table?

```
var url = "jdbc:derby:clowns;create=true";
var sql = "SELECT count(*) FROM clowns";
try (var conn = DriverManager.getConnection(url);
   var stmt = conn.prepareStatement(sql);
   var rs = stmt.executeQuery()) {

   System.out.println(rs.getInt(1));
}
```

   A. 0

   B. 1

   C. The code does not compile.

   D. The code compiles but throws an exception at runtime.

8. Consider the three methods `execute()`, `executeQuery()`, and `executeUpdate()`. Fill in the blanks: _____ of these methods is/are allowed to run a DELETE SQL statement while _____ of these methods is/are allowed to run an UPDATE SQL statement.

   A. None, one

   B. One, none

   C. One, one

   D. One, two

   E. Two, two

   F. Three, three

9. Suppose the `pandas` table has one row with the name `Mei Xiang` and the location DC. What does the following code output?

```
var url = "jdbc:derby:pandas";
var sql = "SELECT name FROM pandas WHERE location = 'DC'";
try (var conn = DriverManager.getConnection(url);     // s1
   var stmt = conn.prepareStatement(sql);             // s2
```

```
    var rs = stmt.executeQuery()) {

    if (rs.next())
        System.out.println(rs.getString("name"));
    else
        System.out.println("No match");
}
```

A. `Mei Xiang`

B. `No match`

C. The code does not compile due to line s1.

D. The code does not compile due to line s2.

E. The code does not compile due to another line.

F. The code throws an exception at runtime.

10. Suppose we have a `peacocks` table with two columns: `name` and `rating`. What does the following code output if the table is empty?

```
var url = "jdbc:derby:birds";
var sql = "SELECT name FROM peacocks WHERE name = ?";
try (var conn = DriverManager.getConnection(url);
    var stmt = conn.prepareStatement(sql)) {        // s1

    stmt.setString(1, "Feathers");
    stmt.setString(2, "Nice");

    boolean result = stmt.execute();                // s2

    System.out.println(result);
}
```

A. `false`

B. `true`

C. The code does not compile due to line s1.

D. The code does not compile due to line s2.

E. The code does not compile due to another line.

F. The code throws an exception at runtime.

11. Suppose we have an empty bunny table with two columns: `name` and `color`. What is the state of the table after running this code?

```
var url = "jdbc:derby:bunnies";
var sql = "INSERT INTO bunny(name, color) VALUES (?, ?)";
try (var conn = DriverManager.getConnection(url);
```

```
        var stmt = conn.prepareStatement(sql)) {  // s1

        stmt.setString(1, "Daisy");
        stmt.setString(2, "Brown");

        stmt.executeUpdate();

        stmt.setString(1, "Cinna");
        stmt.setString(2, "Brown");

        stmt.executeUpdate();
}
```

A. It has one row.

B. It has two rows, and the color is `Brown` in both.

C. The code does not compile due to line `s1`.

D. The code does not compile due to line `s2`.

E. The code does not compile due to another line.

F. The code throws an exception at runtime.

12. What is the name of a concrete class that implements `Statement` and is included in the core JDK?

A. `CallableStatement`

B. `PreparedStatement`

C. `StatementImpl`

D. Both A and B

E. None of the above

13. Given the table `books` in the figure and a `ResultSet` created by running the following SQL statement, which option prints the value 379?

title varchar(255)	num_pages integer
Beginning Java	379
Advanced Java	669

```
SELECT * FROM books WHERE title = 'Beginning Java'
```

A. `System.out.println(rs.getInt(1));`

B. `System.out.println(rs.getInt(2));`

C. `System.out.println(rs.getInteger(1));`

D. `System.out.println(rs.getInteger(2));`

14. Given the table books in the previous question and the following code, which lines would you add to successfully insert a row? (Choose two.)

```
var url = "jdbc:derby:books;create=true";
var sql = "INSERT INTO books (title,num_pages) VALUES(?,?)";
try (var conn = DriverManager.getConnection(url);
    var stmt = conn.prepareStatement(sql)) {

  // INSERT CODE HERE

  stmt.executeUpdate();
}
```

A. `stmt.setObject(0, "Intermediate Java");`

B. `stmt.setObject(1, "Intermediate Java");`

C. `stmt.setObject(1, 500);`

D. `stmt.setObject(2, 500);`

15. Given the table books from the previous two questions and a ResultSet created by running this SQL statement, which option prints Advanced Java?

```
SELECT title FROM books WHERE num_pages > 500
```

A. `System.out.println(rs.getString());`

B. `System.out.println(rs.getString("0"));`

C. `System.out.println(rs.getString("1"));`

D. `System.out.println(rs.getString("title"));`

E. None of the above

16. Which of the following could be valid JDBC URL formats for an imaginary driver named magic and a database named box?

```
String first = "jdbc:magic:127.0.0.1:1234/box";
String second = "jdbc:magic:box";
String third = "jdbc@magic:@127.0.0.1:1234";
```

A. Only first

B. Only second

C. Only third

D. Both first and second

E. Both first and third

F. All of these

17. Which is a benefit of `PreparedStatement` over `Statement`? (Choose two.)

A. Language independence

B. NoSQL support

C. Readability

D. Security

E. Supports stored procedures

18. Assuming the `clowns` database exists and contains one empty table named `clowns`, what is the output of the following?

```
var url = "jdbc:derby:clowns";
var sql = "SELECT * FROM clowns";
try (var conn = new Connection(url);        // s1
   var stmt = conn.prepareStatement(sql); // s2
   var rs = stmt.executeQuery()) {         // s3
   if (rs.next())
      System.out.println(rs.getString(1));
   }
}
```

A. The code terminates successfully without any output.

B. The code does not compile due to line s1.

C. The code does not compile due to line s2.

D. The code does not compile due to line s3.

E. None of the above.

19. What is the correct order to close database resources?

A. `Connection` then `PreparedStatement` then `ResultSet`

B. `Connection` then `ResultSet` then `PreparedStatement`

C. `PreparedStatement` then `Connection` then `ResultSet`

D. `PreparedStatement` then `ResultSet` then `Connection`

E. `ResultSet` then `PreparedStatement` then `Connection`

F. None of the above

20. Assuming the `clowns` database exists and contains one empty table named `clowns`, what is the output of the following?

```
var url = "jdbc:derby:clowns";
var sql = "SELECT * FROM clowns";
try (var conn = DriverManager.getConnection(url);   // s1
   var stmt = conn.prepareStatement(sql);          // s2
```

```
    var rs = stmt.executeQuery()) {                   // s3

    if (rs.next())
        System.out.println(rs.getString(1));
    }
}
```

A. The code terminates successfully without any output.

B. The code does not compile due to line s1.

C. The code does not compile due to line s2.

D. The code does not compile due to line s3.

E. None of the above.

21. Suppose we have a bunny table with two columns: name and color. What does the following code output if the table is empty?

```
var url = "jdbc:derby:bunnies";
var sql =
    "SELECT count(*) FROM bunny WHERE color = ? and name = ?";
try (var conn = DriverManager.getConnection(url);
    var stmt = conn.prepareStatement(sql)) {  // s1

    stmt.setString(1, "White");

    try (var rs = stmt.executeQuery()) {        // s2
        if (rs.next())
            System.out.println(rs.getInt(1));
    }
}
```

A. 0

B. 1

C. The code does not compile due to line s1.

D. The code does not compile due to line s2.

E. The code does not compile due to another line.

F. The code throws an exception at runtime.

22. Suppose the pandas table has one row with the name Mei Xiang and the location DC. What does the following code output?

```
var url = "jdbc:derby:pandas";
var sql = "SELECT name FROM pandas WHERE location = ?";
try (var conn = DriverManager.getConnection(url);  // s1
```

```
      var stmt = conn.prepareStatement(sql)) {        // s2

      stmt.setString(1, "DC");
      try (var rs = stmt.executeQuery()) {
         if (rs.next())
            System.out.println(rs.getString("name"));
         else
            System.out.println("No match");
      }
   }
```

A. `Mei Xiang`

B. `No match`

C. The code does not compile due to line `s1`.

D. The code does not compile due to line `s2`.

E. The code does not compile due to another line.

F. The code throws an exception at runtime.

23. Which statement is true about the JDBC core classes?

A. `Driver` is an implementation of `DriverManager`.

B. A general `Connection` implementation is included in the JDK.

C. A `PreparedStatement` uses bind variables.

D. None of the above.

24. Which is true if the `clowns` database exists and contains an empty `clowns` table?

```
var url = "jdbc:derby:clowns";
var sql = "SELECT COUNT(*) FROM clowns";
try (var conn = DriverManager.getConnection(url);
     var stmt = conn.prepareStatement(sql);
     var rs = stmt.executeQuery()) {

   rs.next();                            // r1
   System.out.println(rs.getInt(1));    // r2
}
```

A. The code compiles and prints `0` without error.

B. The code compiles and prints `1` without error.

C. The code does not compile.

D. The code compiles but throws an exception at runtime on line `r1`.

E. The code compiles but throws an exception at runtime on line `r2`.

25. Suppose we have an empty bunny table with two columns: name and color. What is the state of the table after running this code?

```
var url = "jdbc:derby:bunnies";
var sql = "INSERT INTO bunny(name, color) VALUES (?, ?)";
try (var conn = DriverManager.getConnection(url);
    var stmt = conn.prepareStatement(sql)) {  // s1

    stmt.setString(1, "Hoppy");
    stmt.setString(2, "Brown");

    stmt.executeUpdate();

    stmt.setString(1, "Daisy");

    stmt.executeUpdate();
}
```

  A. Only one row has the color Brown set.
  B. It has two rows, and the color is Brown in both.
  C. The code does not compile due to line s1.
  D. The code does not compile due to line s2.
  E. The code does not compile due to another line.
  F. The code throws an exception at runtime.

26. Which are true statements? (Choose two.)
  A. A PreparedStatement is generally faster than a Statement when each is run 100 times.
  B. A PreparedStatement is generally slower than a Statement when each is run 100 times.
  C. A PreparedStatement is generally the same speed as a Statement when each is run 100 times.
  D. PreparedStatement extends Statement
  E. Statement extends PreparedStatement
  F. PreparedStatement and Statement are not in the same inheritance hierarchy.

27. Which is true of a PreparedStatement?
  A. It has a method to change the bind variable to a different character other than ?.
  B. It can be used only for SELECT statements.
  C. It can be used only for UPDATE statements.
  D. All of these are true.
  E. None of these are true.

28. Suppose we have a `peacocks` table with two columns: `name` and `rating`. What does the following code output if the table is empty?

```
var url = "jdbc:derby:birds";
var sql = "SELECT name FROM peacocks WHERE name = ?";
try (var conn = DriverManager.getConnection(url);
    var stmt = conn.prepareStatement(sql)) {     // s1

    stmt.setString(1, "Feathers");

    System.out.println(stmt.executeUpdate());     // s2
}
```

A. `false`

B. `true`

C. The code does not compile due to line `s1`.

D. The code does not compile due to line `s2`.

E. The code does not compile due to another line.

F. The code throws an exception at runtime.

29. What is the most likely outcome of this code if the `people` table is empty?

```
6: var stmt = conn.prepareStatement("SELECT * FROM people");
7: var rs1 = stmt.executeQuery();
8: var rs2 = stmt.executeQuery();
9: System.out.println(rs1.next() + " " + rs2.next());
```

A. It prints `false false`.

B. It prints `true false`.

C. It does not terminate.

D. It throws a `SQLException`.

E. None of the above.

30. What is the most likely outcome of this code if the `bunnies` table is empty?

```
var url = "jdbc:derby:bunnies";
var sql = "INSERT INTO bunny(name, color) VALUES (?, ?)";
try (var conn = DriverManager.getConnection(url);
    var stmt = conn.createStatement()) {
```

```
    stmt.setString(1, "Hoppy");
    stmt.setString(2, "Brown");

    stmt.executeUpdate(sql);
}
```

A. One row is in the table.

B. Two rows are in the table.

C. The code does not compile.

D. The code throws a SQLException.

Chapter

12

Localization

✓ **Localization**

- Implement Localization using Locale, resource bundles, and Java APIs to parse and format messages, dates, and numbers

1. Which of the following are considered locales? (Choose three.)

    A. Cultural region

    B. Local address

    C. City

    D. Time zone region

    E. Political region

    F. Geographical region

2. Assuming the key green is in all five of the files referenced in the options, which file will the following code use for the resource bundle?

```
Locale.setDefault(new Locale("en", "US"));
var rb = ResourceBundle.getBundle("Colors", new Locale("fr"));
System.out.print(rb.getString("green"));
```

    A. `Colors_default.properties`

    B. `Colors.properties`

    C. `Colors_en.properties`

    D. `Colors_US.properties`

    E. `Colors_en_US.properties`

    F. None of the above

3. When localizing an application, which type of data varies in presentation depending on locale?

    A. Currencies

    B. Dates

    C. Both

    D. Neither

4. How do you find out the locale of the running program?

    A. `Locale.get("default")`

    B. `Locale.get(Locale.DEFAULT)`

    C. `Locale.of()`

    D. `Locale.now()`

    E. `Locale.getDefault()`

    F. None of the above

5. How long will the effects of calling `Locale.setDefault()` be active assuming no other calls to that method are made?

    A. Until the end of the method.

    B. Until the program exits.

    C. Until the next reboot of the computer.

    D. It persists after reboot.

    E. None of the above.

6. What is the output of the following code snippet?

```
var d = LocalDateTime.parse("2022-01-21T12:00:00",
    DateTimeFormatter.ISO_LOCAL_DATE_TIME);
System.out.print(d.format(DateTimeFormatter.ISO_LOCAL_DATE));
```

- **A.** `2022-00-21`
- **B.** `2022-00-22`
- **C.** `2022-01-21`
- **D.** `2022-01-22`
- **E.** The code does not compile.
- **F.** An exception is thrown at runtime.

7. What is the output if the `solveMystery()` method is applied to a `Properties` object loaded from `mystery.properties`?

mystery.properties
```
mystery=bag
type=paper
```

```
void solveMystery(Properties props) {
    var a = props.get("mystery");
    var b = props.get("more", null);
    var c = props.get("more", "trick");
    System.out.print(a + " " + b + " " + c);
}
```

- **A.** `bag ? trick`
- **B.** `bag ? null`
- **C.** `bag null null`
- **D.** `bag null trick`
- **E.** The code does not compile.
- **F.** An exception is thrown at runtime.

8. Fill in the blank with the option that allows the code snippet to compile and print a message without throwing an exception at runtime.

```
var x = LocalDate.of(2022, 3, 1);
var y = LocalDateTime.of(2022, 3, 1, 5, 55);
var f = DateTimeFormatter.ofPattern("MMMM' at 'h' o'clock'");
System.out.print(_____);
```

- **A.** `f.formatDate(x)`
- **B.** `f.formatDate(y)`
- **C.** `f.format(x)`
- **D.** `f.format(y)`

    E. The code does not compile regardless of what is placed in the blank.

    F. None of the above.

9. Which of the following are valid locale formats? (Choose two.)

    A. `hi`

    B. `hi_IN`

    C. `IN_hi`

    D. `in_hi`

    E. `HI_IN`

    F. `IN`

10. Assuming the key `indigo` is in all five of the files referenced in the options, which file will the following code use for the resource bundle?

```
Locale loc = new Locale("fr", "CH");
Locale.setDefault(new Locale("it", "CH"));
ResourceBundle rb = ResourceBundle.getBundle("Colors", loc);
rb.getString("Indigo");
```

    A. `Colors_default.properties`

    B. `Colors_en_US.properties`

    C. `Colors_CH.properties`

    D. `Colors_en.properties`

    E. `Colors_es.properties`

    F. None of the above

11. For currency, the US uses the $ symbol, the UK uses the £ symbol, and Germany uses the € symbol. Given this information, what is the expected output of the following code snippet?

```
Locale.setDefault(Locale.US);
Locale.setDefault(Category.FORMAT, Locale.GERMANY);
System.out.print(NumberFormat.getCurrencyInstance(Locale.UK)
    .format(1.1));
```

    A. `$1.10`

    B. `1,10€`

    C. `£1.10`

    D. The code does not compile.

    E. An exception is thrown at runtime.

    F. The output cannot be determined without knowing the locale of the system where it will be run.

12. Given the following four properties files, what does this code print?

Cars_en.properties
engine=engine horses=241

Cars.properties
engine=moteur country=earth road=highway

Cars_en_US.properties
country=US horses=45

Cars_fr_FR.properties
country=France road=autoroute

```
Locale.setDefault(new Locale("en"));
var rb = ResourceBundle.getBundle("Cars",
    new Locale("de", "DE"));
var r1 = rb.getString("engine");
var r2 = rb.getString("horses");
var r3 = rb.getString("country");
System.out.print(r1+ " " + r2 + " " + r3);
```

- **A.** null null null
- **B.** engine 241 US
- **C.** moteur 45 US
- **D.** engine 241 earth
- **E.** moteur 241 earth
- **F.** An exception is thrown at runtime.

13. Given the four properties files in question 12, what does this code print?

```
Locale.setDefault(new Locale("en", "US"));
var rb = ResourceBundle.getBundle("Cars",
    new Locale("fr", "FR"));
var s1 = rb.getString("country");
var s2 = rb.getString("horses");
var s3 = rb.getString("engine");
System.out.print(s1+ " " + s2 + " " + s3);
```

- **A.** France null engine
- **B.** France 241 moteur
- **C.** France 45 moteur
- **D.** France 241 engine
- **E.** France 45 engine
- **F.** An exception is thrown at runtime.

14. Given the four properties files in question 12, what does this code print?

```
Locale.setDefault(new Locale("ja","JP"));
var rb = ResourceBundle.getBundle("Cars",
    new Locale("fr", "FR"));
var t1 = rb.getString("engine");
var t2 = rb.getString("road");
var t3 = rb.getString("country");
System.out.print(t1+ " " + t2 + " " + t3);
```

A. moteur autoroute France

B. engine autoroute France

C. engine highway France

D. moteur highway France

E. moteur highway US

F. An exception is thrown at runtime.

15. Fill in the blank so the code correctly compiles and creates a `Locale` reference.

```
Locale loc = Locale._____;
```

A. get("Italian")

B. of(Locale.ITALIAN)

C. get(Locale.ITALIAN)

D. getLocale("Italian")

E. of("Italian")

F. None of the above

16. Assuming the key `turquoise` is in all five of the files referenced in the options, which file will the following code use for the resource bundle?

```
Locale loc = new Locale("zh", "CN");
Locale.setDefault(new Locale("en", "US"));
ResourceBundle rb = ResourceBundle.getBundle("Colors", loc);
rb.getString("turquoise");
```

A. Colors_en.properties

B. Colors_CN.properties

C. Colors.properties

D. Colors_default.properties

E. Colors_en_CN.properties

F. None of the above

17. How many lines does the following print out?

```
3: Locale.setDefault(Locale.KOREAN);
4: System.out.println(Locale.getDefault());
5: Locale.setDefault(new Locale("en", "AU"));
6: System.out.println(Locale.getDefault());
7: Locale.setDefault(new Locale("EN"));
8: System.out.println(Locale.getDefault());
```

   A. Only an exception is printed.
   B. One, followed by an exception.
   C. Two, followed by an exception.
   D. Three.
   E. It does not compile.

18. Assuming the key `red` is in all five of the files referenced in the options, which file will the following code use for the resource bundle?

```
Locale.setDefault(new Locale("en", "US"));
var rb = ResourceBundle.getBundle("Colors",
    new Locale("ca","ES"));
System.out.print(rb.getString("red"));
```

   A. `Colors.properties`
   B. `Colors_en_US.properties`
   C. `Colors_US.properties`
   D. `Colors_ES.properties`
   E. `Colors_ca.properties`
   F. None of the above

19. What is the output of the following code snippet?

```
var d = LocalDate.parse("2022-04-01",
    DateTimeFormatter.ISO_LOCAL_DATE);
System.out.print(d.format(
    DateTimeFormatter.ISO_LOCAL_DATE_TIME));
```

   A. `2022 APRIL 1`
   B. `2022 MAY 0`
   C. `2022 MAY 1`
   D. `2022 APRIL 0`
   E. The code does not compile.
   F. An exception is thrown at runtime.

20. What is the output if the `launch()` method is applied to a `Properties` object loaded from `scifi.properties`?

scifi.properties
```
rocket=saturn5
moon=landing
```

```java
void launch(Properties props) {
    var a = props.getProperty("rocket", "?");
    var b = props.getProperty("earth");
    var c = props.getProperty("earth", "?");
    System.out.print(a + " " + b + " " + c);
}
```

- **A.** `saturn5 null ?`
- **B.** `saturn5 null null`
- **C.** `null null ?`
- **D.** `saturn5 ? ?`
- **E.** The code does not compile.
- **F.** An exception is thrown at runtime.

21. For what values of pattern will the following print `<02.1> <06.9> <10,00>`? (Choose two.)

```java
String pattern = "_____";
var message = DoubleStream.of(2.1, 6.923, 1000)
    .mapToObj(v -> new DecimalFormat(pattern).format(v))
    .collect(Collectors.joining("> <"));
System.out.print("<" + message + ">");
```

- **A.** `##,00.##`
- **B.** `##,00.#`
- **C.** `0,00.#`
- **D.** `#,00.#`
- **E.** `0,00.0`
- **F.** `#,##.#`

22. What is the result of the following?

```java
Map<String, String> map = new TreeMap<>();
map.put("tool", "hammer");
map.put("problem", "nail");

var props = new Property();             // p1
map.forEach((k,v) -> props.put(k, v));  // p2
```

```
String t = props.getProperty("tool");    // p3
String n = props.getProperty("nail");
System.out.print(t + " " + n);
```

A. `hammer nail`

B. The code does not compile due to line p1.

C. The code does not compile due to line p2.

D. The code does not compile due to line p3.

E. An exception is thrown at runtime.

F. None of the above.

23. Assuming the key `purple` is in all five of the files referenced in the options, which file will the following code use for the resource bundle?

```
Locale.setDefault(new Locale("en", "US"));
var rb = ResourceBundle.getBundle("Colors", new Locale("en"));
System.out.print(rb.getString("purple"));
```

A. `Colors_en_US.properties`

B. `Colors_en.properties`

C. `Colors_US.properties`

D. `Colors_fr.properties`

E. `Colors.properties`

F. None of the above

24. Which of the following are not valid `Locale` formats? (Choose two.)

A. `nl_BE`

B. `fr_CA`

C. `uk_ua`

D. `CR`

E. `no`

F. `ro_RO`

25. For currency, the US uses the $ symbol, the UK uses the £ symbol, and Germany uses the € symbol. Given this information, what is the expected output of the following code snippet?

```
Locale.setDefault(Locale.US);
Locale.setDefault(Category.FORMAT, Locale.GERMANY);
Locale.setDefault(Category.DISPLAY, Locale.UK);
System.out.print(NumberFormat.getCurrencyInstance()
    .format(6.95));
```

A. `$6.95`

B. `6,95 €`

    C. £6.95

    D. The code does not compile.

    E. An exception is thrown at runtime.

    F. The output cannot be determined without knowing the locale of the system where it will be run.

26. What is the output of the following code snippet?

```
var x = LocalDate.of(2022, 3, 1);
var y = LocalDateTime.of(2022, 1, 1, 2, 55);
var f = DateTimeFormatter.ofPattern("'yyyy-MM'");
System.out.print(f.format(x) + " " + f.format(y));
```

    A. 2022-03 2022-01

    B. 2022-01 2022-03

    C. 2022-02 2022-00

    D. yyyy-MM yyyy-MM

    E. The code does not compile.

    F. An exception is thrown at runtime.

27. Given the following two properties files, what does the following class output?

container.properties
```
name=generic
number=2
```

container_en.properties
```
name=Docker
type=container
```

```
void loadPod() {
   new Locale.Builder()
      .setLanguage("en")
      .setRegion("US").build();
   var rb = ResourceBundle.getBundle("container");
   String name = rb.getString("name");
   String type = rb.getString("type");
   System.out.print(name + " " + type);
}
```

    A. Docker container

    B. generic container

C. `generic null`

D. The output cannot be determined without knowing the locale of the system where it will be run.

E. An exception is thrown at runtime.

F. None of the above.

28. Given the two properties files from question 27, what does the following class output?

```
void loadContainer() {
    Locale.setDefault(new Locale("en"));
    var rb = ResourceBundle.getBundle("container");
    String name = rb.getString("name");
    String type = rb.getString("type");
    System.out.print(name + " " + type);
}
```

A. `Docker container`

B. `generic container`

C. `generic null`

D. The output cannot be determined without knowing the locale of the system where it will be run.

E. An exception is thrown at runtime.

F. None of the above.

29. Given the two properties files from question 27, what does the following class output?

```
void loadControlPlane() {
    Locale.setDefault(new Locale("en_US"));
    var rb = ResourceBundle.getBundle("container");
    String name = rb.getString("name");
    String type = rb.getString("type");
    System.out.print(name + " " + type);
}
```

A. `Docker container`

B. `generic container`

C. `generic null`

D. The output cannot be determined without knowing the locale of the system where it will be run.

E. An exception is thrown at runtime.

F. None of the above.

30. Assuming the `Forest.properties` file is the only resource file available, what is the output of calling the `hike()` method?

Forest.properties
```
trees=evergreen {0}
animals=squirrels
```

```
static void hike() {
    Locale.setDefault(new Locale.Builder()
        .setLanguage("en").build());
    var rb = ResourceBundle
        .getBundle("Forest", new Locale("fr"));
    System.out.print(MessageFormat.format("trees","pretty"));
}
```

- **A.** `trees`
- **B.** `trees pretty`
- **C.** `trees {0}`
- **D.** `trees null`
- **E.** The code does not compile.
- **F.** An exception is thrown at runtime.

Chapter

13

Annotations

THE OCP EXAM TOPICS COVERED IN THIS
PRACTICE TEST INCLUDE THE FOLLOWING:

✓ **Annotations**

- Create, apply, and process annotations

1. What modifier is used to mark an annotation element as optional?

   A. `optional`

   B. `default`

   C. `required`

   D. `value`

   E. `case`

   F. None of the above

2. Given a Broadway show, which information is best stored using annotations? (Choose two.)

   A. The number of people attending each day

   B. The maximum number of tickets a person can purchase

   C. The total number of people the theater can hold

   D. The price including discounts a person pays for a ticket

   E. A person's seat assignment

   F. The time a ticket is sold

3. Fill in the blank with the correct annotation usage that allows the code to compile.

   ```
   public interface CelestialBody {
       String name();
       double size() default 100;
       int lightYears = 2;
   }


   _____ class Planet {}
   ```

   A. `@CelestialBody(name="Venus")`

   B. `@CelestialBody(name="Pluto", size=2, lightYears=5)`

   C. `@CelestialBody(lightYears=10)`

   D. `@CelestialBody("Jupiter")`

   E. `@CelestialBody(size=3)`

   F. None of the above

4. Fill in the blank with the correct value for `@Target` that allows the code to compile.

   ```
   import java.lang.annotation.*;


   @Target({_____})
   public @interface LightSource {}


   @LightSource class Bulb {
       @LightSource void lightSwitch() {}
       @LightSource private Bulb() {}
   }
   ```

A. `ElementType.METHOD, ElementType.CONSTRUCTOR`

B. `ElementType.ANNOTATION_TYPE`

C. `ElementType.CONSTRUCTOR, ElementType.TYPE, ElementType.METHOD`

D. `ElementType.TYPE_USE`

E. `ElementType.LOCAL_VARIABLE, ElementType.FIELD`

F. None of the above

5. Which of the following are marker annotations? (Choose three.)

A. `@Target`

B. `@Inherited`

C. `@Override`

D. `@Retention`

E. `@Repeatable`

F. `@Documented`

6. Given the following declarations, which annotations can fill in the blank that would allow the code to compile? (Choose three.)

```
public @interface Music {
    String value() default "violin";
}

class Orchestra {
    _____ void play() {}
}
```

A. `@Music(super="piccolo")`

B. `@Music("viola")`

C. `@Music(value()="bass")`

D. `@Music`

E. `@Music(default="flute")`

F. `@Music(value="cello")`

7. How many lines of the following declaration contain a compiler error?

```
1: public @interface Thermometer {
2:     int minTemp();
3:     Integer maxTemp() default 1;
4:     double[] color();
5:     final String type;
6:     Boolean compact;
7: }
```

A. None

B. One

    C. Two

    D. Three

    E. Four

    F. Five

8. In what ways are annotations similar to interfaces? (Choose two.)

    A. They can both declare methods with bodies.

    B. They can both declare constructors.

    C. They can both declare constants.

    D. They can both be extended with the `extends` keyword.

    E. They can both be used in a class declaration.

    F. They both are declared with the `interface` type.

9. In how many of the marked places (`m1`, `m2`, `m3`) will adding the line `@SuppressWarnings()` independently allow the class to compile without any warnings?

```
import java.util.*;
// m1
public class Space {
    // m2
    final void frontier() {
        List<Object> stars = List.of(1,2,3);
        stars.add(4);

        // m3
        List planets = new ArrayList<>();
        planets.add(5);
    }
}
```

    A. None, the class does not compile as is.

    B. None, the class already compiles without warnings.

    C. One.

    D. Two.

    E. Three.

    F. None of the above.

10. An annotation cannot be applied to which of the following?

    A. Class declaration.

    B. Annotation declaration.

    C. Inner class declaration.

    D. Cast operation.

E. Local variable declaration using `var`.

F. An annotation can be applied to all of the above.

11. Which statements about the `@Override` annotation are correct? (Choose three.)

A. It can be optionally specified when a class implements an abstract interface method.

B. Adding it to a method may trigger a compiler error.

C. It is required whenever a class implements an abstract interface method.

D. It can be added to an interface declaration type.

E. It can be optionally specified when a method is overridden in a subclass.

F. It is required whenever a method is overridden in a subclass.

12. Given the following declarations, which annotation can be applied to a method declaration?

```
import java.lang.annotation.*;
@interface Bread {
    public int maker = 5;
    String baker();
}
@Inherited
@interface Toast {
    boolean buttered() default true;
    int freshness() default Bread.maker;
    static boolean wheat = false;
}
```

A. `@Toast(true)`

B. `@Toast`

C. `@Bread("null")`

D. `@Toast(wheat=true)`

E. `@Bread`

F. None of the above, as the annotation declarations do not compile

13. Which properties of the `Clean` annotation must be true for the following to compile? (Choose three.)

```
@Clean("Basement") public class House {}
```

A. The annotation must contain exactly one element.

B. The annotation must contain an element named `value`.

C. The element must not have a default value.

D. The element may have a default value.

E. The annotation may contain more than one element.

F. The annotation must contain an element named `values`.

14. Assume the following code compiles. Which annotation inserted in the line allows the code to print a non-null value at runtime?

```
// INSERT HERE
@interface Fast {
   int topSpeed() default 10;
}

@Fast class BigCat {}

public class Cheetah extends BigCat {
   public static void main(String... unused) {
      var a = Cheetah.class.getAnnotation(Fast.class);
      System.out.print(a);
   }
}
```

- **A.** @Inherited
- **B.** @Polymorphism
- **C.** @Inheritance
- **D.** @Retention
- **E.** @Subclass
- **F.** None of the above

15. How many lines of the following declaration contain a compiler error?

```
1: public @interface Student {
2:    final boolean likesPonies = true;
3:    int value default 100;
4:    int age();
5:    /** TODO **/
6:    String name() default "Olivia";
7: }
```

- **A.** None
- **B.** One
- **C.** Two
- **D.** Three
- **E.** Four
- **F.** Five

16. Which statement about the following declarations is correct?

```
import java.lang.annotation.*;
import java.util.List;

@Target(ElementType.TYPE_USE)
public @interface Friend {
   String value();
   String lastName() default null;
   int age = 10;
}
class MyFriends {
   void makeFriends() {
      var friends = List.of(new @Friend("Olivia") Object(),
            new @Friend("Adeline") String(),
            new @Friend("Henry") MyFriends());
   }
}
```

A. None of the declarations compile.

B. Only the declaration of `Friend` contains a compiler error.

C. Only the declaration of `MyFriends` contains a compiler error.

D. Both declarations contain compiler errors.

E. None of the above.

17. Which of the following are permitted to be used for annotation element type? (Choose three.)

A. `Object`

B. An annotation

C. `Class[]`

D. An enum

E. `Double`

F. `var`

18. Fill in the blanks with the lines of code that allow the program to compile. (Choose two.)

```
import java.lang.annotation.*;
@Repeatable(_____)  // t1
@interface Gift {
   String value();
}
@interface Presents {
   _____;            // t2
}
@Gift("Book") @Gift("Toy") public class Surprise {}
```

    A. `Presents` on line t1

    B. `@Presents` on line t1

    C. `Gift value()` on line t2

    D. `Presents.class` on line t1

    E. `Gift[] value()` on line t2

    F. `Gift[] gift()` on line t2

19. Which statements about annotations are correct? (Choose three.)

    A. Annotations contain data that changes throughout the program execution.

    B. Adding an annotation to a class that already compiles may trigger a compiler error and cause it to fail to compile.

    C. Annotations contain metadata about a Java type.

    D. Annotations cannot be applied to lambda expression variables.

    E. Annotations cannot be applied to other annotations.

    F. Removing all annotations from a class that already compiles will not introduce a compiler error.

20. Given the following declarations, which annotations can fill in the blank that would allow the code to compile? (Choose three.)

```
import java.util.*;
public @interface Vacuum {
    String[] value();
}

class Appliance {
    _____ void clean() {}
}
```

    A. `@Vacuum({})`

    B. `@Vacuum({"upright","new"})`

    C. `@Vacuum(List.of("portable"))`

    D. `@Vacuum`

    E. `@Vacuum("handheld")`

    F. `@Vacuum(default="shop")`

21. Which method declarations can `@SafeVarargs` be correctly applied to? (Choose two.)

    A. `protected void hum(double... tune)`

    B. `final int whistle(int length, float... measure)`

    C. `static void sing()`

    D. `private void listen(String... mp3)`

    E. `void dance(List<Integer>... beat)`

    F. `private static int play(int[] notes)`

22. Which annotation can be applied to an existing annotation X and ensures a class that uses X shows the annotation in its generated Javadoc?

   A. @Documented

   B. @Generated

   C. @JavaDoc

   D. @PreserveAnnotations

   E. @Retention

   F. None of the above

23. Fill in the blank with the value that allows the annotation to be accessible by the JVM in which it is executed?

```
import java.lang.annotation.*;
@Retention(_____)
public class Corn {}
```

   A. RetentionPolicy.CLASS

   B. RetentionPolicy.JRE

   C. RetentionPolicy.RUNTIME

   D. RetentionPolicy.SOURCE

   E. RetentionPolicy.LIVE

   F. None of the above

24. How many lines of the following declarations contain a compiler error?

```
1: @interface Sword {}
2: public @interface Zelda {
3:     private String game();
4:     Sword sword();
5:     java.util.List<Integer> gems;
6:     final boolean hasBossKey();
7:     public abstract int level() default 99;
8:     protected boolean continue();
9: }
```

   A. None

   B. One

   C. Two

   D. Three

   E. Four

   F. Five

25. Which of the following are permitted for an annotation element `default` value?
(Choose three.)

A. `""`

B. `(int)1_000.0`

C. `new String()`

D. `Integer.valueOf(3).intValue()`

E. `null`

F. `Integer.MAX_VALUE`

26. Assuming `@Weather` is a valid repeatable annotation that takes a `String`, with its associated containing type annotation `@Forecast`, which of the following can be applied to a type declaration? (Choose two.)

A. `@Forecast({"Storm", "Cloudy"})`

B. `@Forecast({@Weather("Storm"), @Weather("Cloudy")})`

C. `@Weather("Storm") @Weather("Cloudy")`

D. `@Weather({@Forecast("Storm"), @Forecast("Cloudy")})`

E. `@Forecast("Storm") @Forecast("Cloudy")`

F. `@Weather({"Storm", "Cloudy"})`

27. Which of the following interface declarations will still compile if `@FunctionalInterface` is applied to each? (Choose two.)

```
interface Dog {
   default void drink() {}
   void play();
}
interface Astra extends Dog {
   private static int eat() { return 1; }
   void fetch();
}
interface Webby extends Dog {
   abstract void play();
   default void rest() {}
   abstract String toString();
}
interface KC {}
interface Georgette extends Dog {
   int intelligence = 5;
   void jump();
}
```

A. Dog
B. KC
C. Georgette
D. Webby
E. Astra

28. How many lines of the following declarations contain a compiler error?

```java
import java.lang.annotation.*;

enum Colors { RED, BLUE, GREEN }
@Documented
public @interface Bouncy {
    int value();
    Colors color() default Colors.RED;
    double size();
}
@Bouncy(999, size=10.0) class Trampoline {}
```

A. None
B. One
C. Two
D. Three
E. Four
F. Five

29. Fill in the blanks: The _____ annotation allows annotations from a superclass to be applied to a subclass, while the _____ annotation determines whether annotations are present in generated Javadoc. (Choose two.)

A. @Retention in the first blank
B. @Inherited in the first blank
C. @Subclass in the first blank
D. @Javadoc in the second blank
E. @Retention in the second blank
F. @Documented in the second blank

30. Fill in the blank with the correct annotation usage that allows the code to compile without any warnings.

```
@Deprecated(since="5.0")
public class ProjectPlanner<T> {
    ProjectPlanner create(T t) { return this; }
}

@SuppressWarnings(_____)
class SystemPlanner {
    ProjectPlanner planner = new ProjectPlanner().create("TPS");
}
```

A. value=ignoreAll

B. value="deprecation","unchecked"

C. "unchecked","deprecation"

D. {"deprecation","unchecked"}

E. "deprecation"

F. None of the above

Chapter

14

Practice Exam 1

This chapter contains 50 questions and is designed to simulate a real 1Z0-819 exam. While previous chapters were focused on a specific set of objectives, this chapter covers all of the objectives on the exam. We recommend you take this exam only after you score well on the questions in the individual chapters.

For this chapter, you should try to simulate the real exam experience as much as possible. This means setting aside 90 minutes of uninterrupted time to complete the test, as well as not looking at any reference material while taking the exam. If you don't know an answer to a question, complete it as best you can and move on to the next question, just as you would on a real exam.

Remember, the exam permits writing material, such as a whiteboard. If you do not have a whiteboard handy, you can just use blank sheets of paper and a pencil. If you do well on this test, then you are hopefully ready to take the real exam. With that said, good luck!

1. What is the result of executing the following method?

```java
public static void main(String... args) {
    String name = "Desiree";
    int _number = 694;
    boolean profit$$$;
    System.out.println(name + " won. "
        + _number + " profit? " + profit$$$);
}
```

   A. The declaration of name does not compile.

   B. The declaration of _number does not compile.

   C. The declaration of profit$$$ does not compile.

   D. The println() statement does not compile.

   E. The code compiles and runs successfully.

   F. The code compiles and throws an exception at runtime.

2. Which statements about try-with-resources are true? (Choose two.)

   A. Any resource used must implement Closeable.

   B. If more than one resource is used, then the order in which they are closed is the reverse of the order in which they were created.

   C. If the try block and close() method both throw an exception, the one thrown by the try block is suppressed.

   D. Neither a catch nor a finally block is required.

   E. The close() method of the resources must throw a checked exception.

3. Bill wants to create a program that reads all of the lines of all of his books using NIO.2. Unfortunately, Bill may have made a few mistakes writing his program. How many lines of the following class contain compilation errors?

```java
1:  package bookworm;
2:  import java.io.*;
```

```
 3:  import java.nio.file.*;
 4:  public class ReadEverything {
 5:      public void readFile(Path p) {
 6:          try {
 7:              Files.readAllLines(p)
 8:                  .parallel()
 9:                  .forEach(System.out::println);
10:          } catch (Exception e) {}
11:      }
12:      public void read(Path directory) throws Exception {
13:          Files.walk(directory)
14:              .filter(p -> File.isRegularFile(p))
15:              .forEach(x -> readFile(x));
16:      }
17:      public static void main(String[] b) throws IOException {
18:          Path p = Path.get("collection");
19:          new ReadEverything().read(p);
20:      }
21: }
```

A. None. Bill's implementation is correct.

B. One.

C. Two.

D. Three.

E. Four.

F. Five.

4. Which of the following is a valid code comment in Java? (Choose three.)

A. `/** Insert */ in next method **/`

B. `/****** Find the kitty cat */`

C. `// Is this a bug?`

D. `$ Begin method - performStart() $`

E. `/*** TODO: Call grandma ***/`

F. `# Updated code by Patti`

5. What is the minimum number of `requires` directives that need to be removed to break the cyclic dependency?

```
module com.animal {
    exports com.animal;
    requires com.plant;
}
```

```
module com.plant {
   exports com.plant;
   requires com.animal;
}
module com.worm {
   exports com.worm;
   requires com.animal;
   requires com.plant;
}
module com.hedgehog {
   exports com.hedgehog;
   requires com.animal;
   requires com.plant;
}
```

A. None, there is no cyclic dependency

B. 1

C. 2

D. 3

E. 4

6. What is the result of the following?

```
package calendar;
public class Seasons {
   public static void seasons(String... names) {
      var v = names[1].length();        // s1
      System.out.println(names[v]);     // s2
   }
   public static void main(String[] args) {
      seasons("Summer", "Fall", "Winter", "Spring");
   }
}
```

A. Fall

B. Spring

C. The code does not compile.

D. The code throws an exception on line s1.

E. The code throws an exception on line s2.

7. What is the output of the following when run as `java EchoFirst.java seed flower plant`?

```java
import java.util.*;

public class EchoFirst {
    public static void main(String[] args) {
        var result = Arrays.binarySearch(args, args[0]);
        System.out.println(result);
    }
}
```

A. 0

B. 1

C. 2

D. The code does not compile.

E. The code compiles but throws an exception at runtime.

F. The output is not guaranteed.

8. Which method can fill in the blank that would cause the program to consistently print `Tie!` ten times?

```java
import java.util.concurrent.*;
import java.util.concurrent.locks.*;
public class TieShoes {
    private Lock shoes = new ReentrantLock();
    public void tie() {
        try {
            if (shoes._____) {
                System.out.println("Tie!");
                shoes.unlock();
            }
        } catch (Exception e) {}
    }
    public static void main(String... unused) {
        var gate = new TieShoes();
        for (int i = 0; i < 10; i++) {
            new Thread(() -> gate.tie()).start();
        }
    } }
```

A. `lock()`

B. `tryLock()`

C. `tryLock(10)`

D. The code does not compile regardless of what is placed in the blank.

E. None of the above.

9. Given the following three class declarations, which sets of access modifiers can be inserted, in order, into the following blank lines that would allow all of the classes to compile? (Choose three.)

```
// Alarm.java
package wake;
public class Alarm {
    _____ static int clock;
    _____ long getTime() {return clock;}
}
// Coffee.java
package wake;
public class Coffee {
    private boolean bringCoffee() {
        return new Alarm().clock<10;
    }
}
```

```
// Snooze.java
package sleep;
public class Snooze extends wake.Alarm {
    private boolean checkTime() { return getTime()>10;}
}
```

A. package-private (blank) and package-private (blank)

B. package-private (blank) and `protected`

C. `protected` and package-private (blank)

D. `protected` and `protected`

E. `private` and `public`

F. `public` and `public`

10. What is the result of the following?

```
var dice = new TreeSet<Integer>();
dice.add(6);
dice.add(6);
dice.add(4);
```

```
dice.stream()
   .filter(n -> n != 4)
   .forEach(System.out::println)
   .count();
```

A. It prints just one line.

B. It prints one line and then the number 3.

C. There is no output.

D. The code does not compile.

E. The code compiles but throws an exception at runtime.

11. Suppose the `pandas` table has one row with the name `Mei Xiang` and the location DC. What does the following code output?

```
var url = "jdbc:derby:pandas";
var sql = "SELECT name FROM pandas WHERE location = ?";
try (var conn = DriverManager.getConnection(url);
   var stmt = conn.prepareStatement(sql);          // s1
   stmt.setString(1, "DC");
   var rs = stmt.executeQuery()) {

   if (rs.next())
      System.out.println(rs.getString("name"));    // s2
   else
      System.out.println("No match");
}
```

A. `Mei Xiang`

B. `No match`

C. The code does not compile due to line s1.

D. The code does not compile due to line s2.

E. The code does not compile due to another line.

F. The code throws an exception at runtime.

12. Which of the following can fill in the blank to print out just the number 161?

```
import java.util.*;
import java.util.stream.*;
class Runner {
   private int numberMinutes;
   public Runner(int n) {
      numberMinutes = n;
   }
```

```
        public int getNumberMinutes() {
            return numberMinutes;
        } }
    public class Marathon {
        public static void main(String[] args) {
            var match = Optional.ofNullable(161);     // line z
            var runners = Stream.of(new Runner(183),
                new Runner(161), new Runner(201));
            var opt = runners_____;
        } }
```

A.

```
.map(Runner::getNumberMinutes)
.filter(m -> match.get().equals(m))
.peek(System.out::println)
.count()
```

B.

```
.map(Runner::getNumberMinutes)
.filter(m -> match.get().equals(m))
.peek(System.out::println)
.max()
```

C.

```
.map(Runner::getNumberMinutes)
.peek(System.out::println)
.filter(m -> match.get().equals(m))
.count()
```

D.

```
.map(Runner::getNumberMinutes)
.peek(System.out::println)
.filter(m -> match.get().equals(m))
.max()
```

E. The code does not compile due to line z.

F. None of the above.

13. Which of the following exceptions do not need to be handled or declared by the method in which they are thrown? (Choose three.)

    A. `FileNotFoundException`

    B. `ArithmeticException`

    C. `IOException`

    D. `BigProblem`

    E. `IllegalArgumentException`

    F. `RuntimeException`

14. What is the output of the following application?

```
package homework;
import java.util.*;
import java.util.stream.*;
public class QuickSolution {
   public static int findFast(Stream<Integer> s) {
      return s.findAny().get();
   }
   public static int findSlow(Stream<Integer> s) {
      return s.parallel().findFirst().get();
   }

   public static void main(String[] pencil) {
      var s1 = List.of(1,2,3,4,5).stream();
      var s2 = List.of(1,2,3,4,5).stream();
      int val1 = findFast(s1);
      int val2 = findSlow(s2);
      System.out.print(val1+" "+val2);
   }
}
```

- **A.** 1 1
- **B.** 3 1
- **C.** The answer cannot be determined until runtime.
- **D.** The code does not compile.
- **E.** The code compiles but throws an exception at runtime.
- **F.** None of the above.

15. What is the result of the following?

```
import java.time.*;
import java.time.format.*;
public class PiDay {
   public static void main(String[] args) {
      LocalDateTime pi = LocalDateTime.of(2017, 3, 14, 1, 59);
      DateTimeFormatter formatter = DateTimeFormatter
         .ofPattern("m.ddhh'MM'");
      System.out.print(formatter.format(pi));
   }
}
```

- **A.** 3.011459
- **B.** 3.1401MM
- **C.** 59.011459

D. 59.1401MM

E. The code does not compile.

F. The code compiles but throws an exception at runtime.

16. Which is part of the module service and has a `requires` directive?

A. Consumer

B. Service locator

C. Service provider

D. Service provider interface

E. None of the above

17. What option names are equivalent to –p and –cp on the `javac` command? (Choose two.)

A. `--module-path` and `–classpath`

B. `--module-path` and `–class-path`

C. `--module-path` and `--class-path`

D. `--path` and `–classpath`

E. `--path` and `–class-path`

F. `--path` and `--class-path`

18. What is the result of the following when called as `java Binary.java`?

```
import java.util.*;
public class Binary {
    public static void main(String[] args) {
        args = new String[] {"0", "1", "01", "10" };
        Arrays.sort(args);
        System.out.println(Arrays.toString(args));
    }
}
```

A. []

B. [0, 01, 1, 10]

C. [0, 01, 10, 1]

D. [0, 1, 01, 10]

E. The code does not compile.

F. The code compiles but throws an exception at runtime.

19. What is the output of the following application?

```
package music;
interface DoubleBass {
    void strum();
```

```
    default int getVolume() {return 5;}
}
interface BassGuitar {
    void strum();
    default int getVolume() {return 10;}
}
abstract class ElectricBass implements DoubleBass, BassGuitar {
    @Override public void strum() {System.out.print("X");}
}
public class RockBand {
    public static void main(String[] strings) {
        final class MyElectricBass extends ElectricBass {
            public int getVolume() {return 30;}
            public void strum() {System.out.print("Y");}
        }
    } }
```

A. X

B. Y

C. The application completes without printing anything.

D. ElectricBass is the first class to not compile.

E. RockBand is the first class to not compile.

F. None of the above.

20. What does the following do?

```
public class Shoot {
    interface Target {
        boolean needToAim(double angle);
    }
    static void prepare(double angle, Target t) {
        boolean ready = t.needToAim(angle);   // k1
        System.out.println(ready);
    }
    public static void main(String[] args) {
        prepare(45, d => d > 5 || d < -5);    // k2
    }
}
```

A. It prints true.

B. It prints false.

C. It doesn't compile due to line k1.

D. It doesn't compile due to line k2.

E. It doesn't compile due to another line.

21. Which of the following lambda expressions can be passed to a method that takes
`IntUnaryOperator` as an argument? (Choose three.)

A. `v -> {System.out.print("Hello!"); return 2%1;}`

B. `(Integer w) -> w.intValue()`

C. `(int j) -> (int) 30L`

D. `(int q) -> q / 3.1`

E. `(long x) -> (int) x`

F. `z -> z`

22. How many of these module declarations are valid?

```
module com.apple { exports com.apple; }
module com.4apple { requires com.apple;}
module com.apple4 { declares com.apple; }
module com.apple-four { }
module com.apple$ {}
```

A. None.

B. One.

C. Two.

D. Three.

E. Four.

F. Five.

23. What is the output of the following application?

```
package tax;
public class Accountant {
    public void doTaxes() throws Throwable {
        try {
            throw new NumberFormatException();
        } catch (ClassCastException
                | ArithmeticException e) { // p1
            System.out.println("Math");
        } catch (IllegalArgumentException | Exception f) { // p2
            System.out.println("Unknown");
        }
    }
    public static void main(String[] numbers) throws Throwable {
        try {
            new Accountant().doTaxes();
        } finally {
            System.out.println("Done!");
        }
    }
}
```

A. `Math`

B. `Unknown`

C. `Unknown` followed by `Done!`

D. The code does not compile due to line p1.

E. The code does not compile due to line p2.

F. None of the above.

24. What is the result of compiling and running the following application?

```java
package names;
import java.util.*;
import java.util.function.*;
interface ApplyFilter {
    void filter(List<String> input);
}
public class FilterBobs {
    static Function<String,String> first = s ->
        {System.out.println(s); return s;};
    static Predicate second = t -> "bob".equalsIgnoreCase(t);
    public void process(ApplyFilter a, List<String> list) {
        a.filter(list);
    }
    public static void main(String[] contestants) {
        final List<String> people = new ArrayList<>();
        people.add("Bob");
        people.add("bob");
        people.add("Jennifer");
        people.add("Samantha");
        final FilterBobs f = new FilterBobs();
        f.process(q -> {
            q.removeIf(second);
            q.forEach(first);
        }, people);
    }
}
```

A. It prints two lines.

B. It prints three lines.

C. One line of code does not compile.

D. Two lines of code do not compile.

E. Three lines of code do not compile.

F. The code compiles but prints an exception at runtime.

25. How many of these variables are `true`?

```
var lol = "lol";
var smiley = lol.toUpperCase() == lol;
var smirk = lol.toUpperCase() == lol.toUpperCase();
var blush = lol.toUpperCase().equals(lol);
var cool = lol.toUpperCase().equals(lol.toUpperCase());
var wink = lol.toUpperCase().equalsIgnoreCase(lol);
var yawn = lol.toUpperCase().equalsIgnoreCase(
    lol.toUpperCase());
```

A. One.

B. Two.

C. Three.

D. Four.

E. Five.

F. None. The code does not compile.

26. Let's say you are managing animals at a veterinary hospital using a new software application. Which metadata attributes would be best managed with an annotation? (Choose two.)

A. The number of animals that are checked at any given time

B. The maximum number of the animals the hospital can hold

C. The feeding schedule for each animal checked in

D. The name of every veterinarian in the building

E. Whether or not the hospital is capable of handling emergencies

F. The location of each animal within the hospital

27. What is the output of the following program?

```
public class Ghost {
    private final String name;
    public Ghost() {
        this(null);
        this.name = "Casper";
    }
    public Ghost(String n) {
        name = "Boo";
    }
    public static void main(String[] sound) {
        var d = new Ghost("Space");
        System.out.println(d.name);
    }
}
```

A. Casper

B. Boo

C. Space

D. The code does not compile.

E. The answer cannot be determined with the information given.

F. None of the above.

28. How many of the following variable declarations compile?

```
1:  import java.util.*;
2:  public class ListOfList {
3:      public void create() {
4:          List<?> n = new ArrayList<>();
5:          List<? extends RuntimeException> o
6:              = new ArrayList<Exception>();
7:          List<? super RuntimeException> p
8:              = new ArrayList<Exception>();
9:          List<T> q = new ArrayList<?>();
10:         List<T extends RuntimeException> r
11:             = new ArrayList<Exception>();
12:         List<T super RuntimeException> s
13:             = new ArrayList<Exception>();
14:     } }
```

A. None.

B. One.

C. Two.

D. Three.

E. Four.

F. Five.

29. What is the output of the following application?

```
package fly;
public class Helicopter {
    public int adjustPropellers(int length, String[] type) {
        length++;
        type[0] = "LONG";
        return length;
    }
    public static void main(String[] climb) {
        final var h = new Helicopter();
        var length = 5;
```

```
        var type = new String[1];
        length = h.adjustPropellers(length, type);
        System.out.print(length+","+type[0]);
    }
}
```

A. 5,LONG

B. 6,LONG

C. 5,null

D. 6,null

E. The code does not compile.

F. The code compiles but throws an exception at runtime.

30. Fill in the blank with code that belongs in a service provider.

```
String cheese = ServiceLoader.load(Mouse.class)
    .stream ()
    .map(_____)
    .map(Mouse::favoriteFood)
    .findFirst()
    .orElse("");
```

A. Mouse.get()

B. Mouse::get

C. Provider.get()

D. Provider::get

E. None of the above

31. Which lines can fill in the blank that would allow the code to compile? (Choose two.)

```
abstract public class Exam {
    boolean pass;
    protected abstract boolean passed();
    class JavaProgrammerCert extends Exam {
        private Exam part1;
        private Exam part2;

        _____

    }
}
```

A. boolean passed() { return part1.pass && part2.pass; }

B. boolean passed() { return part1.passed() && part2.passed(); }

C. private boolean passed() { return super.passed(); }

D. public boolean passed() { return part1.passed() && part2.passed(); }

   E. `public boolean passed() { return part1.pass && part2.pass; }`

   F. `public boolean passed() { return super.passed(); }`

32. Which of the following are valid lambda expressions? (Choose three.)

   A. `() -> {}`

   B. `(Double adder) -> {int y; System.out.print(adder); return adder;}`

   C. `(Long w) -> {Long w=5; return 5;}`

   D. `(int count, vote) -> count*vote`

   E. `dog -> dog`

   F. `name -> {name.toUpperCase()}`

33. How many lines of the following application contain compilation errors?

```
1:   package percussion;
2:
3:   interface MakesNoise {}
4:   abstract class Instrument implements MakesNoise {
5:      public Instrument(int beats) {}
6:      public void play() {}
7:   }
8:   public class Drum extends Instrument {
9:      public void play(int count) {}
10:     public void concert() {
11:        super.play(5);
12:     }
13:     public static void main(String[] beats) {
14:        MakesNoise mn = new Drum();
15:        mn.concert();
16:     }
17: }
```

   A. The code compiles and runs without issue.

   B. One.

   C. Two.

   D. Three.

   E. Four.

   F. None of the above.

34. Given the `Electricity` annotation, how many lines of the `Solar` class contain a compiler error?

```
1:   import java.lang.annotation.*;
2:   @Target(ElementType.METHOD)
3:   public @interface Electricity {
```

```
4:      int[] value() default 100;
5:      short type() default 1;
6:  }
7:  @Electricity() class Solar {
8:      @Electricity(2) @Electricity(0) void charge() {}
9:      @Electricity(value=9) void turnOn() {}
10:     @Electricity(6,5) void install() {}
11:     @Electricity(value=1,7) void turnOff() {}
12:     @Electricity(value=8) void storePower() {}
13: }
```

A. One.

B. Two.

C. Three.

D. Four.

E. Five.

F. Six.

G. None of the above.

35. What is the output of the following application?

```
1:  interface HasHue {String getHue();}
2:  enum COLORS implements HasHue {
3:      red {
4:          public String getHue() {return "FF0000";}
5:      }, green {
6:          public String getHue() {return "00FF00";}
7:      }, blue {
8:          public String getHue() {return "0000FF";}
9:      }
10:     private COLORS() {}
11: }
12: class Book {
13:     static void main(String[] pencils) {}
14: }
15: final public class ColoringBook extends Book {
16:     final void paint(COLORS c) {
17:         System.out.print("Painting: "+c.getHue());
18:     }
19:     final public static void main(String[] crayons) {
20:         new ColoringBook().paint(green);
```

```
21:    }
22: }
```

A. `Painting: 00FF00`
B. One line of code does not compile.
C. Two lines of code do not compile.
D. Three lines of code do not compile.
E. The code compiles but prints an exception at runtime.
F. None of the above.

36. What is the output of the following code snippet?

```
11: Path x = Paths.get(".","song","..","/note");
12: Path y = Paths.get("/dance/move.txt");
13: x.normalize();
14: System.out.println(x.resolve(y));
15: System.out.println(y.resolve(x));
```

A.

```
/./song/../note/dance/move.txt
/dance/move.txt
```

B.

```
/dance/move.txt
/dance/move.txt/note
```

C.

```
/dance/move.txt
/dance/move.txt/./song/../note
```

D.

```
/note/dance/move.txt
../dance/move.txt/song
```

E. The code does not compile.
F. The code compiles but an exception is thrown at runtime.

37. What is the result of running the following program?

```
1:  package fun;
2:  public class Sudoku {
3:      static int[][] game;
4:
5:      public static void main(String args[]) {
6:          game[3][3] = 6;
7:          Object[] obj = game;
```

```
8:          obj[3] = 'X';
9:          System.out.println(game[3][3]);
10:    }
11: }
```

A. 6

B. X

C. The code does not compile.

D. The code compiles but throws a `NullPointerException` at runtime.

E. The code compiles but throws a different exception at runtime.

F. The output is not guaranteed.

38. What is the output of the following?

```
var listing = new String[][] { { "Book", "34.99" },
   { "Game", "29.99" }, { "Pen", ".99" } };
System.out.println(listing.length + " " + listing[0].length);
```

A. 2 2

B. 2 3

C. 3 2

D. 3 3

E. The code does not compile.

F. The code compiles but throws an exception at runtime.

39. Which of the following are JDBC interfaces in the `java.sql` package?

A. Driver, Query

B. Driver, ResultSet

C. DriverManager, Query

D. DriverManager, ResultSet

E. Driver, DriverManager, Query

F. Driver, DriverManager, ResultSet

40. Given the following class, which statement is correct?

```
1:  import java.security.*;
2:  import java.util.*;
3:
4:  public class SecretFile {
5:      private String secret;
6:      // Constructors/Getters Omitted
7:
```

```
8:     private static class Folder {
9:         private final SecretFile value;
10:        private final Permission permission;
11:
12:        // Constructors/Getters Omitted
13:    }
14:
15:    public static Permission getPermission(String check) {
16:        // Implementation Omitted
17:    }
18:
19:    private static Map<String, Folder> c = new HashMap<>();
20:    public static SecretFile getSecret(String t) {
21:        var securityRecord = c.get(t);
22:        if (securityRecord != null) {
23:            return securityRecord.getValue();
24:        }
25:
26:        var p = getPermission(t);
27:        AccessController.checkPermission(p);
28:        var pc = p.newPermissionCollection();
29:        pc.add(p);
30:        var secret = AccessController.doPrivileged(
31:            new PrivilegedAction<SecretFile>() {
32:                public SecretFile run() {
33:                    return
34:                        new SecretFile(System.getProperty(t));
35:                }},
36:            new AccessControlContext(new ProtectionDomain[] {
37:                new ProtectionDomain(null, pc) }));
38:        c.put(t, new Folder(secret, p));
39:        return secret;
40:    } }
```

A. The class does not contain any security issues.

B. The class contains exactly one security issue.

C. The class contains exactly two security issues.

D. The class contains exactly three security issues.

E. None of the above.

41. How many objects are eligible for garbage collection immediately before the end of the `main()` method?

```
public class Tennis {
    public static void main(String[] game) {
        String[] balls = new String[1];
        int[] scores = new int[1];
        balls = null;
        scores = null;
    }
}
```

A. None.

B. One.

C. Two.

D. Three.

E. The code does not compile.

F. None of the above.

42. What is the output of the following application?

```
package rope;
import java.util.concurrent.*;
public class Jump {
    private static void await(CyclicBarrier b) {
        try { b.await(); } catch (Exception e) {}
    }
    public static void main(String[] chalk) {
        ExecutorService s = Executors.newFixedThreadPool(4);
        final var b = new CyclicBarrier(4,
            () -> System.out.print("Jump!"));
        for(int i=0; i<10; i++)
            s.execute(() ->await(b));
        s.shutdown();
    } }
```

A. `Jump!` is printed once, and the program exits.

B. `Jump!` is printed twice, and the program exits.

C. The code does not compile.

D. The output cannot be determined ahead of time.

E. A deadlock is produced at runtime.

F. None of the above.

43. Given the application shown here, which lines do not compile? (Choose three.)

```
package furryfriends;
interface Friend {
   protected String getName();                      // h1
}
class Cat implements Friend {
   String getName() {                                // h2
      return "Kitty";
   }
}
public class Dog implements Friend {
   String getName() throws RuntimeException {        // h3
      return "Doggy";
   }
   public static void main(String[] adoption) {
      Friend friend = new Dog();  // h4
      System.out.print(((Cat)friend).getName());  // h5
      System.out.print(((Dog)null).getName());    // h6
   }
}
```

- **A.** Line h1
- **B.** Line h2
- **C.** Line h3
- **D.** Line h4
- **E.** Line h5
- **F.** Line h6

44. Fill in the blanks: Using the _____ and _____ modifiers together allows a variable to be accessed from any class, without requiring an instance variable.

- **A.** class, static
- **B.** default, public
- **C.** final, package-private
- **D.** protected, instance
- **E.** public, static
- **F.** None of the above

45. Which statements when inserted independently will throw an exception at runtime? (Choose two.)

```
var x = new LinkedList<>();
x.offer(18);
// INSERT CODE HERE
```

   A. `x.peek(); x.peek();`

   B. `x.poll(); x.poll();`

   C. `x.pop(); x.pop();`

   D. `x.remove(); x.remove();`

46. Which of the following shows a valid `Locale` format? (Choose two.)

   A. `iw`

   B. `UA`

   C. `it_ch`

   D. `JA_JP`

   E. `th_TH`

   F. `ES_HN`

47. Which sets of lines can be removed without stopping the code from compiling and while printing the same output? (Choose three.)

```
14: String race = "";
15: outer:
16: do {
17: inner:
18:     do
19:     {
20:         race += "x";
21:     }
22:     while (race.length() <= 4);
23: } while (race.length() < 4);
24: System.out.println(race);
```

   A. Lines 15 and 17

   B. Lines 16 and 23

   C. Lines 17, 18, and 22

   D. Line 17

   E. Line 22

   F. Line 23

48. How many objects are eligible for garbage collection at the end of the main() method?

```
package store;
public class Shoes {
   static String shoe1 = new String("sandal");
   static String shoe2 = new String("flip flop");
   public void shopping() {
      String shoe3 = new String("croc");
      shoe2 = shoe1;
      shoe1 = shoe3;
   }
   public static void main(String... args) {
      new Shoes().shopping();
   }
}
```

A. None.

B. One.

C. Two.

D. Three.

E. The code does not compile.

F. None of the above.

49. Which of the following variable types can be used in a switch statement under some circumstances? (Choose three.)

A. An enumerated type

B. StringBuilder

C. Byte

D. Double

E. var

F. Exception

50. What is the output of the following?

```
1: import static java.util.stream.Collectors.*;
2: import java.util.*;
3:
4: public class Goat {
5:    private String food;
6:
7:    // constructor, getter and toString
```

```
8:
9:      public static void main(String[] args) {
10:        var goats = List.of(
11:            new Goat("can"),
12:            new Goat("hay"),
13:            new Goat("shorts"),
14:            new Goat("hay"));
15:
16:        goats.stream()
17:            .collect(groupingBy(Goat::getFood))
18:            .entrySet()
19:            .stream()
20:            .filter(e -> e.getValue().size() == 2)
21:            .map(e -> e.getKey())
22:            .collect(partitioningBy(e -> e.isEmpty()))
23:            .get(false)
24:            .stream()
25:            .sorted()
26:            .forEach(System.out::print);
27:    }
28: }
```

A. canshorts
B. hay
C. hayhay
D. shortscan
E. The code does not compile.
F. The code compiles but throws an exception at runtime.

Practice Exam 2

Like the previous chapter, this one contains 50 questions and is designed to simulate a real 1Z0-819 exam. Ready with your scratch paper and 90 minutes? Good luck!

1. What is the output of the following application?

```
1:  package fruit;
2:  enum Season {
3:      SPRING(1), SUMMER(2), FALL(3), WINTER(4);
4:      public Season(int orderId) {}
5:  }
6:  public class PickApples {
7:      public static void main(String... orchard) {
8:          final Season s = Season.FALL;
9:          switch(s) {
10:            case Season.FALL:
11:                System.out.println("Time to pick!");
12:            default:
13:                System.out.println("Not yet!");
14:         }
15:     }
16: }
```

A. `Time to pick!`

B. `Time to pick!` followed by `Not yet!`

C. One line of code does not compile.

D. Two lines of code do not compile.

E. Three lines of code do not compile.

F. The code compiles but prints an exception at runtime.

2. Which statements about the following class are correct? (Choose two.)

```
package knowledge;
class InformationException extends Exception {}
public class LackOfInformationException
        extends InformationException {
  public LackOfInformationException() {             // t1
      super("");
  }
  public LackOfInformationException(String s) {     // t2
      this(new Exception(s));
  }
  public LackOfInformationException(Exception c) {  // t3
      super();
  }
}
```

```
    @Override public String getMessage() {
        return "lackOf";
    }
}
```

A. `LackOfInformationException` compiles without issue.

B. The constructor declared at line t1 does not compile.

C. The constructor declared at line t2 does not compile.

D. The constructor declared at line t3 does not compile.

E. The `getMessage()` method does not compile because of the `@Override` annotation.

F. `LackOfInformationException` is a checked exception.

3. Assuming the following class is concurrently accessed by numerous threads, which statement about the `CountSheep` class is correct?

```
package fence;
import java.util.concurrent.atomic.*;
public class CountSheep {
    private static AtomicInteger counter = new AtomicInteger();
    private Object lock = new Object();
    public synchronized int increment1() {
        return counter.incrementAndGet();
    }
    public static synchronized int increment2() {
        return counter.getAndIncrement();
    }
    public int increment3() {
        synchronized(lock) {
            return counter.getAndIncrement();
    } } }
```

A. The class is thread-safe only if `increment1()` is removed.

B. The class is thread-safe only if `increment2()` is removed.

C. The class is thread-safe only if `increment3()` is removed.

D. The class is already thread-safe.

E. The class does not compile.

F. The class compiles but may throw an exception at runtime.

4. Which statements best describe the result of executing this code? (Choose two.)

```
package nyc;
public class TouristBus {
```

```
public static void main(String... args) {
   var nycTourLoops = new String[] {
      "Downtown", "Uptown", "Brooklyn" };
   var times = new String[] { "Day", "Night" };

      for (int i = 0, j = 0;
            i < nycTourLoops.length; i++, j++)

      System.out.println(
         nycTourLoops[i] + " " + times[j]);
   }
}
```

A. The println() causes one line of output.

B. The println() causes two lines of output.

C. The println() causes three lines of output.

D. The code terminates successfully.

E. The code throws an exception at runtime.

5. What is the output of the following application?

```
package woods;
interface Plant {
   default String grow() { return "Grow!"; }
}
interface Living {
   public default String grow() { return "Super Growing!"; }
}
public class Tree implements Plant, Living {  // m1
   public String grow() { return super.Plant.grow(); }
   public static void main(String[] leaves) {
      Plant p = new Tree();                    // m2
      System.out.print(((Living)p).grow());    // m3
   }
}
```

A. Grow!

B. Super Growing!

C. It does not compile because of line m1.

D. It does not compile because of line m2.

E. It does not compile because of line m3.

F. None of the above.

6. Which statements about the following application are true? (Choose two.)

```
package party;
import java.util.concurrent.*;
public class Plan {
    ExecutorService s = Executors.newScheduledThreadPool(10);
    public void planEvents() {
        Runnable r1 = () -> System.out.print("Check food");
        Runnable r2 = () -> System.out.print("Check drinks");
        Runnable r3 = () -> System.out.print("Take out trash");
        s.scheduleWithFixedDelay(r1,1,TimeUnit.HOURS);          // g1
        s.scheduleAtFixedRate(r2,1,1000,TimeUnit.SECONDS);   // g2
        s.execute(r3);                                            // g3
        s.shutdownNow();
    } }
```

   A. Line g1 does not compile.
   B. Line g2 does not compile.
   C. Line g3 does not compile.
   D. All of the lines of code compile.
   E. The code hangs indefinitely at runtime.
   F. The code throws an exception at runtime.

7. Which of the following is a valid method name in Java? (Choose two.)
   A. `_____`
   B. `%run`
   C. `check-Activity`
   D. `$Hum2`
   E. `sing\\3`
   F. `po#ut`

8. Which two options when inserted independently can fill in the blank to compile the code? (Choose two.)

   `javac _____ mods -d birds com-bird/*.java *.java`

   A. `-cp`
   B. `-m`
   C. `-p`
   D. `-classpath`
   E. `--classpath`
   F. `--module-path`

9. Which classes when inserted into the blank do not allow this code to compile? (Choose two.)

```
import java.io.*;
class Music {
    void make() throws IOException {
        throw new UnsupportedOperationException();
    }
}
public class Sing extends Music {
    public void make() throws _____ {
        System.out.println("do-re-mi-fa-so-la-ti-do");
    }
}
```

- **A.** FileNotFoundException
- **B.** NumberFormatException
- **C.** Exception
- **D.** Error
- **E.** Throwable
- **F.** RuntimeException

10. What is the result of compiling and executing the following application?

```
package reptile;
public class Alligator {
    static int teeth;
    double scaleToughness;
    public Alligator() {
        this.teeth++;
    }
    public void snap(int teeth) {
        System.out.print(teeth+" ");
        teeth--;
    }
    public static void main(String[] unused) {
        new Alligator().snap(teeth);
        new Alligator().snap(teeth);
    }
}
```

- **A.** 0 1
- **B.** 1 1
- **C.** 1 2
- **D.** 2 2

E. The code does not compile.

F. The code compiles but produces an exception at runtime.

11. Which are true statements about the majority of steps in migrating to a modular application? (Choose two.)

A. In a bottom-up migration, automatic modules turn into named modules.

B. In a bottom-up migration, named modules turn into automatic modules.

C. In a bottom-up migration, unnamed modules turn into named modules.

D. In a top-down migration, automatic modules turn into named modules.

E. In a top-down migration, named modules turn into automatic modules.

F. In a top-down migration, unnamed modules turn into named modules.

12. Which of the following are true about Java operators and statements? (Choose three.)

A. Both right-hand sides of the ternary expression are evaluated at runtime.

B. A `switch` statement may contain at most one `default` statement.

C. The post-increment operator (++) returns the value of the variable before the addition is applied.

D. The logical operators (|) and (||) are interchangeable, producing the same results at runtime.

E. The complement operator (!) operator may be applied to numeric expressions.

F. An assignment operator returns a value that is equal to the value of the expression being assigned.

13. Assume the file system is accessible, `/flower/rose.txt` exists, and the other two directories `/garden` and `/nursery` do not exist. What is the expected result after executing the following code snippet?

```
Files.createDirectories(Path.of("/garden"));
Files.createDirectory(Path.of("/nursery"));

Files.move(Path.of("/flower/rose.txt"),
    Paths.get("/garden"), StandardCopyOption.REPLACE_EXISTING);
Files.move(new File("/garden/rose.txt").toPath(),
    Paths.get("/nursery"), StandardCopyOption.ATOMIC_MOVE);
```

A. There is a file at `/nursery/rose.txt`

B. There is a file at `/flower/rose.txt`

C. The code does not compile.

D. The first `move()` statement throws an exception.

E. The second `move()` statement throws an exception.

F. None of the above.

14. Which of the following are valid functional interfaces? (Choose two.)

A.

```
interface CanClimb {
    default void climb() {}
    static void climb(int x) {}
}
```

B.

```
interface CanDance {
    int dance() { return 5; }
}
```

C.

```
interface CanFly {
    abstract void fly();
}
```

D.

```
interface CanRun {
    void run();
    static double runFaster() {return 2.0; }
}
```

E.

```
interface CanSwim {
    abstract Long swim();
    boolean test();
}
```

15. Suppose we have a peacocks table with two columns: name and rating. What does the following code output if the table is empty?

```
10: var url = "jdbc:derby:birds";
11: var sql = "SELECT name FROM peacocks WHERE name = ?";
12: try (var conn = DriverManager.getConnection(url);
13:     var stmt = conn.prepareStatement(sql)) {
14:
15:     stmt.setString(1, "Feathers");
16:
17:     try (var rs = stmt.execute()) {
18:         System.out.println(rs.next());
19:     }
20: }
```

A. false

B. true

C. The code does not compile due to lines 12–13.

D. The code does not compile due to lines 17–18.

E. The code does not compile due to another line.

F. The code throws an exception at runtime.

16. Which of the following are valid in a Java file, listed in the order in which they are declared? (Choose two.)

A. A package-private class declaration and a `public` interface declaration

B. Two `package` statements, an `import` statement, and a `public` interface declaration

C. A `package` statement, 128 `import` statements, and two `public` class declarations

D. 16 `import` statements, a `package` statement, and a `public` class declaration

E. 5 `import` statements and 7 package-private interface declarations

F. A `private` interface

17. Which of the following sequences can fill in the blanks so the code prints `-1 0 2`?

```
char[][] letters = new char[][] {
   new char[] { 'a', 'e', 'i', 'o', 'u'},
   new char[] { 'a', 'e', 'o', 'u'} };

var x = Arrays._____(letters[0], letters[0]);
var y = Arrays._____(letters[0], letters[0]);
var z = Arrays._____(letters[0], letters[1]);

System.out.print(x + " " + y + " " + z);
```

A. compare, mismatch, compare

B. compare, mismatch, mismatch

C. mismatch, compare, compare

D. mismatch, compare, mismatch

E. None of the above

18. What does the following output?

```
var dice = new LinkedList<Integer>();
dice.offer(3);
dice.offer(2);
dice.offer(4);
System.out.print(dice.stream().filter(n -> n != 4));
```

A. 2

B. 3

C. [3 2]

D. The code does not compile.

E. None of the above.

19. What is the output of executing the following code snippet?

```
var e = Executors.newSingleThreadExecutor();
Runnable r1 = () -> Stream.of(1,2,3).parallel();
Callable r2 = () -> Stream.of(4,5,6).parallel();

Future<Stream<Integer>> f1 = e.submit(r1);   // x1
Future<Stream<Integer>> f2 = e.submit(r2);   // x2

var r = Stream.of(f1.get(),f2.get())
    .flatMap(p -> p)                          // x3
    .parallelStream()                         // x4
    .collect(
        Collectors.groupingByConcurrent(i -> i%2==0));
System.out.print(r.get(false).size()
    +" "+r.get(true).size());
```

A. 3 3

B. 2 4

C. One of the marked lines (x1, x2, x3, x4) does not compile.

D. Two of the marked lines (x1, x2, x3, x4) do not compile.

E. Three of the marked lines (x1, x2, x3, x4) do not compile.

F. None of the above.

20. Which statements about the following class that loads a library on startup are correct? (Choose three.)

```
import java.io.FilePermission;
import java.security.*;
import java.util.List;

public class Startup {
    private static final List<String> files =
        List.of("my.secret","other.secrets");
    public void startup(String f) {
        var perm = new FilePermission(f,"write"); // j1
        AccessController.checkPermission(perm);    // j2
        AccessController.doPrivileged(
    new PrivilegedAction<Void>() {
            public Void run() {
                if(files.contains(f))
                    System.loadLibrary(f);         // j3
```

```
          return null;
        }
      });
   } }
```

A. Line j1 contains a security error or risk.

B. Line j2 contains a security error or risk.

C. Line j3 contains a security error or risk.

D. Line j1 does not contain a security error or risk.

E. Line j2 does not contain a security error or risk.

F. Line j3 does not contain a security error or risk.

21. How many times does this code print [2, 7, 8]?

```
1:   import java.util.*;
2:   import java.util.stream.*;
3:
4:   public class RemoveMe<T> {
5:       private List<T> values;
6:       public RemoveMe(T... values) {
7:           this.values = Arrays.stream(values)
8:               .collect(Collectors.toList());
9:       }
10:      public void remove(T value) {
11:          values.remove(value);
12:      }
13:      public static void main(String[] args) {
14:          var integer = new RemoveMe<Integer>(2, 7, 1, 8);
15:          var longs = new RemoveMe<Long>(2L, 7L, 1L, 8L);
16:          integer.remove(1);
17:          longs.remove(1L);
18:
19:          System.out.println(integer.values);
20:          System.out.println(longs.values);
21:
22:          var values = new ArrayList<Integer>();
23:          values.add(2);
24:          values.add(7);
25:          values.add(1);
26:          values.add(8);
27:          values.remove(1);
```

```
28:          System.out.println(values);
29:     }
30: }
```

A. Zero.

B. One.

C. Two.

D. Three.

E. The code does not compile.

F. The code compiles but throws an exception.

22. Fill in the blanks with the proper method names to deserialize an object. (Choose two.)

```
import java.io.*;
public class BoxOfSecrets {
    private void _____(ObjectInputStream in)
            throws IOException {
        // IMPLEMENTATION OMITTED
    }

    public Object _____() throws ObjectStreamException  {
        // IMPLEMENTATION OMITTED
    }
}
```

A. `writeObject` in the first blank

B. `writeResolve` in the first blank

C. `readObject` in the first blank

D. `writeReplace` in the second blank

E. `readResolve` in the second blank

F. `readReplace` in the second blank

23. How many lines of the following application do not compile?

```
1:  package castles;
2:  import java.io.*;
3:  public class Palace {
4:      public void openDrawbridge() throws Exception {
5:          try {
6:              throw new Exception("Problem");
7:          } catch (IOException e) {
8:              throw new IOException();
```

```
 9:          } catch (FileNotFoundException e) {
10:             try {
11:                 throw new IOException();
12:             } catch (Exception e) {
13:             } finally {
14:                 System.out.println("Almost done");
15:             }
16:         } finally {
17:             throw new RuntimeException("Unending problem");
18:         }
19:     }
20:
21:     public static void main(String[] moat)
22:             throws IllegalArgumentException {
23:         new Palace().openDrawbridge();
24:     }
25: }
```

A. None. The code compiles and produces a stack trace at runtime.

B. One.

C. Two.

D. Three.

E. Four.

F. Five.

24. Which of the following is true of the following module declaration?

```
1: module com.mammal {
2:     exports com.mammal.cat;
3:     exports com.mammal.mouse to com.mice;
4:     uses com.animal;
5: }
```

A. The first line that fails to compile is line 1.

B. The first line that fails to compile is line 2.

C. The first line that fails to compile is line 3.

D. The first line that fails to compile is line 4.

E. The code compiles.

25. What is the result of the following?

```
import java.util.*;
public class Museums {
```

```
    public static void main(String[] args) {
        String[] array = {"Natural History", "Science", "Art"};
        List<String> museums = Arrays.asList(array);
        museums.remove(2);
        System.out.println(museums);
    }
}
```

A. [Natural History, Science]

B. [Natural History, Science, Art]

C. The code does not compile.

D. The code compiles but throws an exception at runtime.

26. Which commands can include the following output? (Choose two.)

```
JDK Internal API    Suggested Replacement
sun.misc.Unsafe     See http://openjdk.java.net/jeps/260
```

A. jdeps sneaky.jar

B. jdeps -j sneaky.jar

C. jdeps -s sneaky.jar

D. jdeps --internals sneaky.jar

E. jdeps -jdkinternals sneaky.jar

F. jdeps --jdk-internals sneaky.jar

27. What is the output of the following?

```
public class Legos {
    public static void main(String[] args) {
        var ok = true;
        if (ok) {
            StringBuilder sb = new StringBuilder();
            sb.append("red");
            sb.deleteCharAt(0);
            sb.delete(1, 1);
        }
        System.out.println(sb);
    }
}
```

A. r

B. e

C. ed

D. red

E. The code does not compile.

F. The code compiles but throws an exception at runtime.

28. What is the output of the following when run as `java EchoFirst.java seed flower plant`?

```java
import java.util.*;

public class EchoFirst {
    public static void main(String[] args) {
        Arrays.sort(args);
        var result = Arrays.binarySearch(args, args[0]);
        System.out.println(result);
    }
}
```

A. 0

B. 1

C. 2

D. The code does not compile.

E. The code compiles but throws an exception at runtime.

F. The output is not guaranteed.

29. How many lines of the following declaration contain a compiler error?

```java
1: import java.lang.annotation.*;
2: @Inherited
3: public @interface Panic {
4:     public abstract alert() default 10;
5:     public final static int alarm_volume = 10;
6:     String[] type() default {"test"};
7:     Long range();
8:     abstract boolean silent();
9: }
```

A. None.

B. One.

C. Two.

D. Three.

E. Four.

F. Five.

30. What is the output of the method that `main()` calls?

```java
public class Hippo {
    private static void hippo(short num1, short num2) {
        System.out.println("shorts");
    }
    private static void hippo(int... nums) {
        System.out.println("varargs");
    }
    private void hippo(long num1, long num2) {
        System.out.println("longs");
    }
    private void hippo(int num1, int num2) {
        System.out.println("nums");
    }
    public static void main(String... args) {
        hippo(1, 5);
    }
}
```

A. `longs`

B. `nums`

C. `shorts`

D. `varargs`

E. The code does not compile.

31. Suppose you have a consumer that calls the `lion()` method within a `Lion` service. You have four distinct modules: consumer, service locator, service provider, and service provider interface. If you add a parameter to the `lion()` method, how many of the modules require recompilation?

A. Zero.

B. One.

C. Two.

D. Three.

E. Four.

32. Which annotations will trigger a compiler error if incorrectly applied to a method with no other annotations? (Choose three.)

A. `@Documented`

B. `@Deprecated`

C. `@SuppressWarnings("unchecked")`

D. `@Override`

E. `@SuppressWarnings("magic")`

F. `@SafeVarargs`

33. Which of the following cannot be instantiated directly by the caller using the constructor? (Choose two.)

   A. Locale

   B. ResourceBundle

   C. Locale.Builder

   D. Properties

   E. DateTimeFormatter

   F. HashMap

34. Which lines fail to compile?

```
package armory;
import java.util.function.*;

interface Shield {
    void protect();
}
class Dragon {
    int addDragon(Integer count) {
        return ++count;
    }
}

public class Sword {
    public static void main(String[] knight) {
        var dragon = new Dragon();
        Function<Shield, Sword> func = Shield::protect; // line x
        UnaryOperator<Integer> op = dragon::addDragon;  // line y
    }
}
```

   A. Only line x

   B. Only line y

   C. Both lines x and y

   D. The code compiles.

35. Fill in the blanks: The operators +=, _____, _____, _____, _____, and -- are listed in increasing or the same level of operator precedence. (Choose two.)

   A. ^, *, =, ++

   B. %, *, /, &&

   C. =, +, /, *

   D. ^, *, ==, ++

    E. `*, /, %, ++`

    F. `<=, >=, !=, !`

36. What is the result of the following?

```
1: import java.util.function.*;
2: public class Ready {
3:     private static double getNumber() {
4:         return .007;
5:     }
6:     public static void main(String[] args) {
7:         Supplier<double> s = Ready::getNumber;
8:         double d = s.get();
9:         System.out.println(d);
10:     }
11: }
```

    A. `0`

    B. `0.007`

    C. The code does not compile due to line 7.

    D. The code does not compile due to line 8.

    E. The code does not compile for another reason.

37. What is the result of the following?

```
import java.util.stream.*;

public class StreamOfStreams {

    public static void main(String[] args) {
      var result =
          Stream.of(getNums(9, 8), getNums(22, 33))  // c1
              .flatMap(x -> x)                        // c2
              .map((a, b) -> a - b)                   // c3
              .filter(x -> !x.isEmpty())              // c4
              .get();
      System.out.println(result);
    }
    private static Stream<Integer> getNums(int num1, int num2) {
        return Stream.of(num1, num2);
    }
}
```

A. The code compiles and outputs 1.

B. The code compiles and outputs 8.

C. The first compiler error is on line c1.

D. The first compiler error is on line c2.

E. The first compiler error is on line c3.

F. The first compiler error is on line c4.

38. Given that `FileNotFoundException` is a subclass of `IOException` and Long is a subclass of Number, what is the output of the following application?

```
package materials;

import java.io.*;

class CarbonStructure {
    protected long count;
    public abstract Number getCount() throws IOException; // q1
    public CarbonStructure(int count) { this.count = count; }
}
public class Diamond extends CarbonStructure {
    public Diamond() { super(15); }
    public Long getCount() throws FileNotFoundException { // q2
        return count;
    }
    public static void main(String[] cost) {
        try {
            final CarbonStructure ring = new Diamond(); // q3
            System.out.print(ring.getCount()); // q4
        } catch (IOException e) {
                e.printStackTrace();
        }
    }
}
```

A. 15

B. It does not compile because of line q1.

C. It does not compile because of line q2.

D. It does not compile because of line q3.

E. It does not compile because of line q4.

F. The class compiles but produces an exception at runtime.

39. Which of the following statements about `InputStream` and `Reader` are correct? (Choose two.)

    A. They are both `abstract` classes.

    B. They can both be used to read character data.

    C. One contains a `read()` method that returns a `byte` value, while the other contains a `read()` method that returns a `char` value.

    D. They are both interfaces.

    E. Only one of them contains a `flush()` method.

    F. Only one of them contains a `skip()` method.

40. Which are true statements about interfaces and abstract classes? (Choose three.)

    A. Abstract classes offer support for single inheritance, while interfaces offer support for multiple inheritance.

    B. All methods in abstract classes are `public`, while interfaces can use various access modifiers for their methods and variables, including `private` in some cases.

    C. Both abstract classes and interfaces can have `abstract` methods.

    D. Both abstract classes and interfaces can have `public` constructors.

    E. Interfaces can only extend other interfaces, while abstract classes can extend both abstract and concrete classes.

    F. Unlike abstract classes, interfaces can be marked `final`.

41. What is the output of the following?

```
var builder = new StringBuilder("Leaves growing");
do {
    builder.delete(0, 5);
} while (builder.length() > 5);
System.out.println(builder);
```

    A. `Leaves growing`

    B. `ing`

    C. `wing`

    D. The code does not compile.

    E. The code compiles but throws an exception at runtime.

42. Which of the following statements about nested classes are correct? (Choose three.)

    A. An anonymous class can declare that it implements multiple interfaces.

    B. All nested classes can contain constant variables.

    C. A local class can declare that it implements multiple interfaces.

    D. A member inner class can contain `static` methods.

    E. A `static` nested class can contain `static` methods.

    F. A local class can access all local variables prior to its declaration within a method.

43. Starting with `DoubleBinaryOperator` and going downward, fill in the values for the table.

Functional Interface	# Parameters in Method Signature
`DoubleBinaryOperator`	
`LongToIntFunction`	
`ToLongBiFunction`	
`IntSupplier`	
`ObjLongConsumer`	

  A. 1, 0, 0, 0, 2
  B. 1, 2, 1, 0, 1
  C. 2, 1, 0, 1, 2
  D. 2, 1, 1, 0, 1
  E. 2, 1, 2, 0, 2
  F. 3, 0, 2, 1, 1

44. Which of the following methods can run without error for at least one SQL query?

```
private static void choices(PreparedStatement ps,
    String sql) throws SQLException {

    try (var rs = ps.executeQuery()) {
        System.out.println(rs.getInt(1));
    }
}
private static void moreChoices(PreparedStatement ps,
    String sql) throws SQLException {

    try (var rs = ps.executeQuery()) {
        rs.next();
        System.out.println(rs.getInt(1));
    }
}
private static void stillMoreChoices(PreparedStatement ps,
    String sql) throws SQLException {

    try (var rs = ps.executeQuery()) {
        if (rs.next())
            System.out.println(rs.getInt(1));
```

```
        }
    }
}
```

A. moreChoices()

B. stillMoreChoices()

C. choices() and stillMoreChoices()

D. moreChoices() and stillMoreChoices()

E. All three methods

F. None of the above

45. What is true of the following method?

```
public void printColor() {
    System.out.println(color);
}
```

A. It is a correctly implemented accessor method.

B. It is a correctly implemented mutator method.

C. It is an incorrectly implemented accessor method.

D. It is an incorrectly implemented mutator method.

E. None of the above.

46. What can fill in the blank so the play() method can be called from all classes in the com.mammal.eland package, but not the com.mammal.gopher package?

```
package com.mammal;

public class Enrichment {
    _____ void play() {}
}
```

A. Leave it blank

B. private

C. protected

D. public

E. None of the above

47. Which of the following statements about performing a concurrent reduction are correct? (Choose two.)

A. If a collector is used, it must have the unordered characteristic.

B. The stream must operate on thread-safe collections.

   C. If the `reduce()` method is used with a lambda expression, then it should be stateful.

   D. The stream must inherit `ParallelStream<T>`.

   E. The stream must be parallel.

   F. If a collector is used, it must have the concurrent characteristic.

48. Which of the following statements about `java.lang.Error` are most accurate? (Choose two.)

   A. An `Error` should be thrown if a file system resource becomes temporarily unavailable.

   B. An application should never catch an `Error`.

   C. `Error` is a subclass of `Exception`, making it a checked exception.

   D. It is possible to catch and handle an `Error` thrown in an application.

   E. An `Error` should be thrown if a user enters invalid input.

   F. `Error` is a subclass of `RuntimeException`, making it an unchecked exception.

49. Given the following classes, what is the output of the `Watch` program?

```
1:  class SmartWatch extends Watch {
2:      private String getType() { return "smart watch"; }
3:      public String getName() {
4:          return getType() + ",";
5:      }
6:  }
7:  public class Watch {
8:      private String getType() { return "watch"; }
9:      public String getName(String suffix) {
10:         return getType() + suffix;
11:     }
12:     public static void main(String[] args) {
13:         Watch watch = new Watch();
14:         Watch smartWatch = new SmartWatch();
15:         System.out.print(watch.getName(","));
16:         System.out.print(smartWatch.getName(""));
17:     }
18: }
```

   A. `smart watch,smart watch`

   B. `smart watch,watch`

   C. `watch,smart watch`

   D. `watch,watch`

   E. The code does not compile.

   F. None of the above.

50. How many of the following lines contain a compiler error?

```
long min1= 123.0, max1 = 987L;
final long min2 = 1_2_3, max2 = 9__8__7;
long min3 = 123, int max3 = 987;
long min4 = 123L, max4 = 987;
long min5 = 123_, max5 = _987;
```

A. Zero
B. One
C. Two
D. Three
E. Four
F. Five

Chapter
16

Practice Exam 3

This is the third, and final practice exam chapter in the book. Make sure you have 90 minutes and scratch paper before you start. Good luck on both this chapter and the real exam!

1. What is the result of the following code?

```java
// Hopper.java
package com.animals;

public class Hopper {
    protected void hop() {
        System.out.println("hop");
    }
}
```

```java
// Grasshopper.java
package com.insect;
import com.animals.Hopper;

public class Grasshopper extends Hopper {
    public void move() {
        hop();   // p1
    }
}
```

```java
// HopCounter.java
package com.animals;

public class HopCounter {

    public static void main(String[] args) {
        var hopper = new Grasshopper();
        hopper.move();   // p2
        hopper.hop();    // p3
    }
}
```

A. The code prints hop once.
B. The code prints hop twice.
C. The first compiler error is on line p1.
D. The first compiler error is on line p2.
E. The first compiler error is on line p3.

2. Which of the following statements about `try/catch` blocks are correct? (Choose two.)

A. A `catch` block can never appear after a `finally` block.

B. A `try` block must be followed by a `catch` block.

C. A `finally` block can never appear after a `catch` block.

D. A `try` block must be followed by a `finally` block.

E. A `try` block can have zero or more `catch` blocks.

F. A `try` block can have zero or more `finally` blocks.

3. Which statements are correct? (Choose two.)

A. A `Comparable` implementation is often implemented by a lambda.

B. A `Comparable` object has a `compare()` method.

C. The `compare()` and `compareTo()` methods have the same contract for the return value.

D. It is possible to sort the same `List` using different `Comparator` implementations.

E. Two objects that return `true` for `equals()` will always return 0 when passed to `compareTo()`.

4. How many lines does this code output?

```
import java.util.*;
public class PrintNegative {
  public static void main(String[] args) {
    List<Integer> list = new ArrayList<>();
    list.add(-5);
    list.add(0);
    list.add(5);
    list.removeIf(e -> e < 0);
    list.forEach(x -> System.out.println(x));
  }
}
```

A. One.

B. Two.

C. Three.

D. None. It doesn't compile.

E. None. It throws an exception at runtime.

5. How many lines need to be changed to make this code compile?

```
1: public class Massage {
2:    var name = "Sherrin";
3:    public void massage(var num) {
4:        var zip = 10017;
```

```
5:        var underscores = 1_001_7;
6:        var _ = "";
7:    }
8: }
```

A. Zero

B. One

C. Two

D. Three

E. Four

6. Which two conditions best describe one or more threads that appear to be active but are perpetually stuck and never able to finish their task? (Choose two.)

A. Deadlock

B. Livelock

C. Loss of precision

D. Out of memory error

E. Race condition

F. Starvation

7. How many lines of the following interface do not compile?

```
15: public interface Piano {
16:     String type = "Grand";
17:     void play();
18:     public static int getNumberOfKeys() {
19:         return type.equals("Grand") ? 88 : 61;
20:     }
21:     private static void printPianoInfo() {
22:         play();
23:         System.out.println("Key Count: "+getNumberOfKeys());
24:     }
25:     default void tune() {
26:         play();
27:         printPianoInfo();
28:     } }
```

A. Zero

B. One

C. Two

D. Three

E. Four

F. None of the above

8. How many lines does the following code output?

```java
import java.util.*;
public class Exams {
    public static void main(String[] args) {
        List<String> exams = List.of("1Z0-817", "1Z0-819");
        for (var e : exams)
            for (int i=exams.size(); i>0 ; i-=2)
                System.out.print(e+" "+exams.get(i));
                System.out.println();
    }
}
```

A. One.

B. Two.

C. Four.

D. The code does not compile.

E. The code compiles but throws an exception at runtime.

F. The code compiles but enters an infinite loop at runtime.

9. How many lines of the main method fail to compile?

```java
10: public class Transport {
11:     static interface Vehicle {}
12:     static class Bus implements Vehicle {}
13:
14:     public static void main(String[] args) {
15:         Bus bus = new Bus();
16:
17:         System.out.println(null instanceof Bus);
18:         System.out.println(bus instanceof Vehicle);
19:         System.out.println(bus instanceof Bus);
20:         System.out.println(bus instanceof ArrayList);
21:         System.out.println(bus instanceof Collection);
22: } }
```

A. None

B. One

C. Two

D. Three

E. Four

F. Five

10. Which of the following are true? (Choose two.)

```
20: int[] crossword [] = new int[10][20];
21: for (int i = 0; i < crossword.length; i++)
22:    for (int j = 0; j < crossword.length; j++)
23:        crossword[i][j] = 'x';
24: System.out.println(crossword.size());
```

A. One line needs to be changed for this code to compile.

B. Two lines need to be changed for this code to compile.

C. Three lines need to be changed for this code to compile.

D. If the code is fixed to compile, none of the cells in the 2D array have a value of 0.

E. If the code is fixed to compile, half of the cells in the 2D array have a value of 0.

F. If the code is fixed to compile, all of the cells in the 2D array have a value of 0.

11. How many lines need to be changed to make this method compile?

```
1:  public void colors() {
2:      var yellow = "";
3:      yellow = null;
4:
5:      var red = null;
6:
7:      var blue = "";
8:      blue = 1;
9:
10:     var var = "";
11:     var = "";
12:
13:     var pink = 1;
14: }
```

A. Zero

B. One

C. Two

D. Three

E. Four

F. Five

12. What is the output of the following?

```
10: var result = 8;
11: monitor: while (result >= 7) {
12:     result++;
```

```
13:     do {
14:         result -= 2;
15:         continue monitor;
16:     } while (result > 5);
17: }
18: System.out.println(result);
```

A. 5

B. 6

C. 7

D. The code does not compile.

E. The code compiles but throws an exception at runtime.

F. The code compiles but enters an infinite loop at runtime.

13. Which of the following lambda expressions can be inserted into both blanks while still allowing the application to compile? (Choose three.)

```
package spooky;
import java.util.function.*;
abstract class Phantom {
    public void bustLater(DoubleConsumer buster, double value) {
        buster.accept(value);
    }
}
public class Ghost extends Phantom {
    public void bustNow(Consumer<Double> buster, double value) {
        buster.accept(value);
    }
    void call() {
        var value = 10.0;
        bustNow(_____, value);
        bustLater(_____, value);
    }
}
```

A. `System.out::print`

B. `a -> {System.out.println(a.intValue());}`

C. `g -> {System.out.println();}`

D. `u -> System.out.println((long)u)`

E. `v -> System.out.print(v)`

F. `w -> System.out::println`

14. Given the following class structure, what is the proper way to create an instance of `Spinner` inside the `bake()` method? (Choose three.)

```
public class Kitchen {
   class Mixer {
      class Spinner {}
   }
   public void bake() {
      // INSERT CODE HERE
   }
}
```

A. `var a = new Kitchen().new Mixer().new Spinner();`

B. `Mixer.Spinner b = Mixer.new Spinner();`

C. `var c = new Spinner();`

D. `var d = new Mixer().new Spinner();`

E. `Kitchen.Mixer.Spinner e = new Kitchen().new Mixer().new Spinner();`

F. `Spinner f = new Kitchen().new Mixer().new Spinner();`

15. Which line of code belongs in a service locator?

A. `ServiceLoader<Mouse> sl = ServiceLoader.load(Mouse.class);`

B. `ServiceLoader<Mouse> sl = ServiceLoader.loader(Mouse.class);`

C. `ServiceLoader<Mouse> sl = ServiceLoader.lookup(Mouse.class);`

D. `ServiceLocator<Mouse> sl = ServiceLoader.load(Mouse.class);`

E. `ServiceLocator<Mouse> sl = ServiceLoader.loader(Mouse.class);`

F. `ServiceLocator<Mouse> sl = ServiceLoader.lookup(Mouse.class);`

16. Fill in the blanks: The _____ annotation determines whether annotations are retained in generated Javadoc, while the _____ annotation determines the location an annotation can be applied. (Choose two.)

A. `@Documented` in the first blank

B. `@Javadoc` in the first blank

C. `@Preserve` in the first blank

D. `@Location` in the second blank

E. `@Retention` in the second blank

F. `@Target` in the second blank

17. Which of the following use generics and compile without warnings? (Choose two.)

A. `List<String> a = new ArrayList();`

B. `List<> b = new ArrayList();`

C. `List<String> c = new ArrayList<>();`

D. `List<> d = new ArrayList<>();`

E. `List<String> e = new ArrayList<String>();`

F. `List<> f = new ArrayList<String>();`

18. Which of the following changes, when applied independently, will print the same result as the original implementation? (Choose two.)

```
10: long sum = IntStream.of(4, 6, 8)
11:    .boxed()
12:    .parallel()
13:    .mapToInt(x -> x)
14:    .sum();
15: System.out.print(sum);
```

A. Change the type on line 10 to `double`

B. Change the type on line 10 to `int`

C. Change line 11 to `unboxed()`

D. Remove line 11

E. Remove line 12

F. Remove line 13

19. What does the following code print?

```
// Hare.java
package com.animal;

public class Hare {
   void init() {
      System.out.print("init-");
   }
   protected void race() {
      System.out.print("hare-");
   }
}
```

```
// Tortoise.java
package com.animal;

public class Tortoise {
   protected void race(Hare hare) {
      hare.init();    // x1
      hare.race();    // x2
      System.out.print("tortoise-");
   }
```

```
    public static void main(String[] args) {
        var tortoise = new Tortoise();
        var hare = new Hare();
        tortoise.race(hare);
    }
}
```

A. `init-hare-tortoise`

B. `init-hare`

C. The first line with a compiler error is `line x1`.

D. The first line with a compiler error is `line x2`.

E. The code does not compile due to a different line.

F. The code throws an exception.

20. Which statements are true about the `requires` directive? (Choose two.)

   A. Changing it to a `requires direct` directive is always allowed.

   B. Changing it to a `requires direct` directive is never allowed.

   C. Changing it to a `requires direct` directive is sometimes allowed.

   D. Including `requires java.base` is allowed, but redundant.

   E. Including `requires java.base` is never allowed.

   F. Including `requires java.base` is sometimes needed to change the meaning of a file.

21. What is the output of the following?

```
1:  package reader;
2:  import java.util.stream.*;
3:
4:  public class Books {
5:      public static void main(String[] args) {
6:          IntStream pages = IntStream.of(200, 300);
7:          long total = pages.sum();
8:          long count = pages.count();
9:          System.out.println(total + "-" + count);
10:     }
11: }
```

   A. `2-2`

   B. `200-1`

   C. `500-0`

   D. `500-2`

   E. The code does not compile.

   F. The code compiles but throws an exception at runtime.

22. What is the output of the following?

```java
public class InitOrder {
    { System.out.print("1"); }
    static { System.out.print("2"); }

    public InitOrder() {
        System.out.print("3");
    }
    public static void callMe() {
        System.out.print("4");
    }
    public static void main(String[] args) {
        callMe();
        callMe();
        System.out.print("5");
    }
}
```

- **A.** 1223445
- **B.** 2445
- **C.** 22445
- **D.** 223445
- **E.** 2233445
- **F.** None of the above

23. What is the output of the following application? Assume the file system is available and able to be written to and read from.

```java
package boat;
import java.io.*;
public class Cruise {
    private int numPassengers = 1;
    private transient String schedule = "NONE";
    { numPassengers = 2; }
    public Cruise() {
        this.numPassengers = 3;
        this.schedule = "Tropical Island";
    }

    public static void main(String... p) throws Exception {
        final String f = "ship.txt";
        try (var o = new ObjectOutputStream(
                new FileOutputStream(f))) {
```

```
        Cruise c = new Cruise();
        c.numPassengers = 4;
        c.schedule = "Casino";
        o.writeObject(c);
    }
    try (var i = new ObjectInputStream(
            new FileInputStream(f))) {
        Cruise c = i.readObject();
        System.out.print(c.numPassengers + "," + c.schedule);
    } } }
```

- **A.** `2,NONE`
- **B.** `3,null`
- **C.** `4,Casino`
- **D.** `4,null`
- **E.** One line would need to be fixed for this code to run without throwing an exception.
- **F.** Two lines would need to be fixed for this code to run without throwing an exception.

24. What does `ServiceLocator.load(ChocolateLab.class)` return?
    - **A.** `Collection`
    - **B.** `List`
    - **C.** `Stream`
    - **D.** None of the above

25. Fill in the blanks: Because of _____, it is possible to _____ a method, which allows Java to support _____.
    - **A.** abstract methods, override, inheritance
    - **B.** virtual methods, override, polymorphism
    - **C.** concrete methods, overload, inheritance
    - **D.** virtual methods, overload, interfaces
    - **E.** inheritance, abstract, polymorphism
    - **F.** abstract methods, inherit, multiple inheritance

26. What is true about the following?

```
import java.util.*;
public class Yellow {
    public static void main(String[] args) {
        List list = Arrays.asList("Sunny");
        method(list);                           // c1
    }
    private static void method(Collection<?> x) {   // c2
```

```
            x.forEach(a -> {});                              // c3
    }
}
```

A. The code doesn't compile due to line c1.

B. The code doesn't compile due to line c2.

C. The code doesn't compile due to line c3.

D. The code compiles and runs without output.

E. The code compiles but throws an exception at runtime.

27. What is the output of the following application?

```
abstract class TShirt {
    abstract int insulate();
    public TShirt() {
        System.out.print("Starting...");
    }
}
public class Wardrobe {
    abstract class Sweater extends TShirt {
        int insulate() {return 5;}
    }
    private void dress() {
        final class Jacket extends Sweater {  // v1
            int insulate() {return 10;}
        };
        final TShirt outfit = new Jacket() {  // v2
            int insulate() {return 20;}
        };
        System.out.println("Insulation:"+outfit.insulate());
    }

    public static void main(String... snow) {
        new Wardrobe().dress();
    }
}
```

A. `Starting...Insulation:20`

B. `Starting...Insulation:40`

C. The code does not compile because of line v1.

D. The code does not compile because of line v2.

E. The code does not compile for a different reason.

28. Suppose we have a `peacocks` table with two columns: `name` and `rating`. What does the following code output if the table is empty?

```
var url = "jdbc:derby:birds";
var sql = "SELECT name FROM peacocks WHERE name = ?";
try (var conn = DriverManager.getConnection(url);
    var stmt = conn.prepareStatement(sql)) {          // s1

    stmt.setString(1, "Feathers");

    try (var rs = stmt.executeQuery()) {              // s2
        while (rs.hasNext()) {
            System.out.println(rs.next());
        }
    }
}
```

   A. false
   B. true
   C. The code does not compile due to line s1.
   D. The code does not compile due to line s2.
   E. The code does not compile due to another line.
   F. The code throws an exception at runtime.

29. What is the output of the following application?

```
package ballroom;
public class Dance {
    public static void swing(int... beats)
            throws ClassCastException {
        try {
            System.out.print("1"+beats[2]);  // p1
        } catch (RuntimeException e) {
            System.out.print("2");
        } catch (Exception e) {
            System.out.print("3");
        } finally {
            System.out.print("4");
        }
    }
    public static void main(String... music) {
        new Dance().swing(0,0);             // p2
```

```
        System.out.print("5");
    }
}
```

A. 145

B. 1045

C. 24, followed by a stack trace

D. 245

E. The code does not compile because of line p1.

F. The code does not compile because of line p2.

30. What is the output of this code?

```
10: var m = new TreeMap<Integer, Integer>();
11: m.put(1, 4);
12: m.put(2, 8);
13:
14: m.putIfAbsent(2, 10);
15: m.putIfAbsent(3, 9);
16:
17: m.replaceAll((k, v) -> k + 1);
18:
19: m.entrySet().stream()
20:     .sorted(Comparator.comparing(Entry::getKey))
21:     .limit(1)
22:     .map(Entry::getValue)
23:     .forEach(System.out::println);
```

A. 1

B. 2

C. 3

D. 4

E. The code does not compile.

F. The code compiles but prints something else.

31. Which can fill in the blank so this code outputs `true`?

```
import java.util.function.*;
import java.util.stream.*;

public class HideAndSeek {
    public static void main(String[] args) {
```

```
        var hide = Stream.of(true, false, true);
        Predicate<Boolean> pred = b -> b;
        var found = hide.filter(pred)._____(pred);
        System.out.println(found);
    }
}
```

A. Only anyMatch

B. Only allMatch

C. Both anyMatch and allMatch

D. Only noneMatch

E. The code does not compile with any of these options.

32. _____ modules are on the classpath, while _____ modules never contain a module-info file.

A. Automatic, named

B. Automatic, unnamed

C. Named, automatic

D. Named, unnamed

E. Unnamed, automatic

F. Unnamed, named

33. Given the following class, how many lines contain compilation errors?

```
1:  import java.io.*;
2:  class StungException extends Exception {}
3:  class Suit implements Closeable {
4:      public void close() throws IOException {}
5:  }
6:  public class BeeCatcher {
7:      public static void main(String[] b) throws IOException {
8:          var s = new Suit();
9:          var t = new Suit();
10:         try (s; t) {
11:             throw new StungException();
12:         } catch (StungException | Exception e) {
13:             s = null;
14:         } finally {
15:         }
16:     }
17: }
```

A. One
B. Two
C. Three
D. Four
E. None. The code compiles as is.

34. What is the output of the Light program?

```
package physics;
class Wave {
    public int size = 7;
}
public class Light extends Wave {
    public int size = 5;
    public static void main(String... emc2) {
        Light v1 = new Light();
        var v2 = new Light();
        Wave v3 = new Light();
        System.out.println(v1.size +","+ v2.size +","+ v3.size);
    }
}
```

A. 5,5,5
B. 5,5,7
C. 5,7,7
D. 7,7,7
E. The code does not compile.
F. None of the above.

35. How many of the following could be valid JDBC URL formats for an imaginary driver named `magic` and a database named `box`?

```
String first = "jdbc;box;magic";
String second = "jdbc;magic;@127.0.0.1:1234";
String third = "jdbc;magic;127.0.0.1:1234/box";
```

A. Only `first`
B. Only `second`
C. Only `third`
D. `first` and `second`
E. `first` and `third`
F. None of these

36. Which of the following statements about interface methods are correct? (Choose three.)

   A. A `private static` interface method can call `default` methods.

   B. A `public static` interface method can call `abstract` methods.

   C. A `private static` interface method can call `static` methods.

   D. A `default` interface method can call `private static` methods.

   E. A `default` interface method can call `abstract` methods.

   F. A `public static` interface method can call `default` methods.

37. Which of the following are true right before the `main()` method ends? (Choose two.)

```
public static void main(String[] args) {
    String state1 = new String("ice");
    String state2 = new String("water");
    String state3 = new String("mist");

    state1 = state2;
    state2 = state3;
    state3 = state1;
}
```

   A. No objects are eligible for garbage collection.

   B. One object is eligible for garbage collection.

   C. Two objects are eligible for garbage collection.

   D. No objects are guaranteed to be garbage collected.

   E. One object is guaranteed to be garbage collected.

   F. Two objects are guaranteed to be garbage collected.

38. Which of the following can fill in the blank to output `sea lion, bald eagle`?

```
String names = Stream.of(
    "bald eagle", "pronghorn", "puma", "sea lion")


    _____


    .collect(Collectors.joining(", "));
System.out.println(names);
```

   A.

```
.filter(s -> s.contains(" "))
.collect(Collectors.toSet())
.stream()
.entrySet()
.stream()
```

```
.filter(e -> e.getKey())
.map(Entry::getValue)
.flatMap(List::stream)
.sorted(Comparator.reverseOrder())
```

B.

```
.filter(s -> s.contains(" "))
.collect(Collectors.toUnmodifiableSet())
.stream()
.entrySet()
.stream()
.filter(e -> e.getKey())
.map(Entry::getValue)
.flatMap(List::stream)
.sorted(Comparator.reverseOrder())
```

C.

```
.collect(Collectors.toUnmodifiableSet())
.stream()
.collect(Collectors.groupingBy(s -> s.contains(" ")))
.entrySet()
.stream()
.filter(e -> e.getKey())
.map(Entry::getValue)
.map(List::stream)
.sorted(Comparator.reverseOrder())
```

D.

```
.collect(Collectors.toSet())
.stream()
.collect(Collectors.groupingBy(s -> s.contains(" ")))
.entrySet()
.stream()
.filter(e -> e.getKey())
.map(Entry::getValue)
.flatMap(List::stream)
.sorted(Comparator.reverseOrder())
```

E.

```
.filter(s -> s.contains(" "))
.collect(Collectors.toUnmodifiableSet())
.stream()
.collect(Collectors.groupingBy(s -> s.contains(" ")))
```

```
.entrySet()
.stream()
.filter(e -> e.getKey())
.map(Entry::getValue)
.map(List::stream)
.sorted(Comparator.reverseOrder())
```

F.
```
.collect(Collectors.toUnmodifiableSet())
.stream()
.collect(Collectors.groupingBy(s -> s.contains(" ")))
.entrySet()
.stream()
.filter(e -> e.getKey())
.map(Entry::getValue)
.map(List::stream)
.sorted(Comparator.reverseOrder())
```

39. What is the minimum number of lines that need to be removed to make this code compile and be able to implemented as a lambda expression?

```
@FunctionalInterface
public interface Play {
    public static void baseball() {}
    private static void soccer() {}
    default void play() {}
    void fun();
    void game();
    void toy();
}
```

- **A.** 1
- **B.** 2
- **C.** 3
- **D.** 4
- **E.** The code compiles as is.

40. Which message does the following application print?

```
package ranch;
public class Cowboy {
    private int space = 5;
    private double ship = space < 2 ? 3L : 10.0f;   // g1
    public void printMessage() {
```

```
        if(ship>1) {
            System.out.print("Goodbye!");
        } if(ship<10 && space>=2)                    // g2
            System.out.print("Hello!");
        else System.out.print("See you again!");
    }
    public static final void main(String... stars) {
        new Cowboy().printMessage();
    }
}
```

A. Hello!

B. Goodbye!

C. See you again!

D. It does not compile because of line g1.

E. It does not compile because of line g2.

F. None of the above.

41. Which are included in the Java Platform Module System? (Choose three.)

A. A format for module JARs

B. A list of all possible modules for Java

C. A new file format called `jdeps`

D. Additional command-line options for Java tools

E. Decommissioning of the `jar` format

F. Partitioning of the JDK into modules

42. Given the following two classes in the same package, which constructors contain compiler errors? (Choose three.)

```
public class Big {
    public Big(boolean stillIn) {
        super();
    }
}
public class Trouble extends Big {
    public Trouble()  {}
    public Trouble(int deep) {
        super(false);
        this();
    }
    public Trouble(String now, int... deep) {
        this(3);
```

```
   }
   public Trouble(long deep) {
      this("check",deep);
   }
   public Trouble(double test) {
      super(test>5 ? true : false);
   }
}
```

A. public Big(boolean stillIn)

B. public Trouble()

C. public Trouble(int deep)

D. public Trouble(String now, int... deep)

E. public Trouble(long deep)

F. public Trouble(double test)

43. Fill in the blanks: The name of the abstract method in the Function interface is
_____, while the name of the abstract method in the Consumer interface is
_____.

A. accept(), apply()

B. accept(), get()

C. apply(), accept()

D. apply(), apply()

E. apply(), test()

44. How many lines fail to compile?

```
class Roller<E extends Wheel> {
   public void roll(E e) { }
}
class Wheel { }
class CartWheel extends Wheel { }

public class RollingContest {
   Roller<CartWheel> wheel1 = new Roller<CartWheel>();
   Roller<Wheel> wheel2 = new Roller<CartWheel>();
   Roller<? extends Wheel> wheel3 = new Roller<CartWheel>();
   Roller<? extends Wheel> wheel4 = new Roller<Wheel>();
   Roller<? super Wheel> wheel5 = new Roller<CartWheel>();
   Roller<? super Wheel> wheel6 = new Roller<Wheel>();
}
```

A. One

B. Two

C. Three

D. Four

E. Five

F. Six

45. What is the output of the following program?

```
var bed = List.of((short)2,(short)5);
var pillow = bed.parallelStream().reduce(0,
    (a,b) -> b.doubleValue() + a.doubleValue(),
    (c,d) -> d.doubleValue() + c.doubleValue());
System.out.println(pillow);
```

A. 0

B. 0.0

C. 7

D. 7.0

E. The code does not compile

F. None of the above

46. Given the following three property files, what does the following method output?

toothbrush.properties
```
color=purple
type=generic
```

toothbrush_es.properties
```
color=morado
type=lujoso
```

toothbrush_fr.properties
```
color=violette
```

```
void brush() {
    Locale.setDefault(new Locale.Builder()
        .setLanguage("es")
        .setRegion("MX").build());
    var rb = ResourceBundle.getBundle("toothbrush",
        new Locale("fr"));
    var a = rb.getString("color");
    var b = rb.getString("type");
    System.out.print(a + " " + b);
}
```

A. `morado null`

B. `violette generic`

C. `morado lujoso`

D. `violette null`

E. The code does not compile.

F. An exception is thrown at runtime.

47. Which of the following are valid functional interfaces in the `java.util.function` package? (Choose three.)

A. `BooleanSupplier`

B. `CharSupplier`

C. `DoubleUnaryOperator`

D. `ObjectIntConsumer`

E. `ToLongBiFunction`

F. `TriPredicate`

48. What change, if any, should be made to the following method to improve security?

```
10: public List<String> accessNetworkList(String fileName) {
11:     return AccessController.doPrivileged(
12:         new PrivilegedAction<List<String>>() {
13:         public List<String> run() {
14:             try {
15:                 return Collections.unmodifiableList(
16:                     Files.readAllLines(Path.of(fileName)));
17:             } catch (IOException e) {
18:                 throw new SecurityException("No access");
19:         } } });
20: }
```

A. On line 10, the method should be marked `private`.

B. On line 15, an `ArrayList` instance should be returned instead of an unmodifiable list.

C. Prior to line 16, the `fileName` should be validated against a list of constants.

D. The exception on line 18 should be removed and an empty `List` should be returned.

E. None of the above, as the code is safe as is.

49. What is the result of executing the `Clownfish` program?

```
package ocean;
class BubbleException extends Exception {}
abstract class Fish {
    Fish getFish() {
```

```
        throw new RuntimeException("fish!");
    }
}
public final class Clownfish extends Fish {
    public final Clownfish getFish() throws BubbleException {
        throw new RuntimeException("clown!");
    }
    public static void main(String[] bubbles) throws Exception {
        final var v = (Fish)new Clownfish();
        Clownfish f = v;
        f.getFish();
        System.out.println("swim!");
    }
}
```

A. The code compiles and prints swim!

B. The code compiles and prints fish!

C. The code compiles and prints a stack trace.

D. One line of the program does not compile.

E. Two lines of the program do not compile.

F. None of the above.

50. What statements about the following method are correct? (Choose three.)

```
public String findWaffles(String connectionStr, String search)
        throws SQLException {
    var query = "SELECT * FROM meal WHERE type = '"+search+"'";
    var con = DriverManager.getConnection(connectionStr);
    try (con;
            var ps = con.prepareStatement(query);
            var rs = ps.executeQuery()) {
        return rs.getString("name");
    } }
```

A. It protects against a denial of service attack.

B. It does not protect against denial of service attacks.

C. It protects against SQL injection because it uses a PreparedStatement.

D. It does not protect against SQL injection.

E. Assuming the database and related table exist and are available, this mode is expected to run without any exceptions being thrown.

F. This method will always produce an exception at runtime.

Appendix

Answers and Explanations

Chapter 1: Working with Java Data Types

1. **A,C.** An identifier name must begin with a letter, dollar sign ($), or underscore (_). Numbers are permitted only for subsequent characters. Therefore, option C is not a valid variable name. Additionally, an identifier may not be a single underscore, making option A an invalid variable name.

2. **A.** In a ternary expression, only one of the two right-most expressions is evaluated. Since `meal>6` is `false`, `tip--` is evaluated, and `tip++` is skipped. The result is that `tip` is changed from 2 to 1, making option A the correct answer. The value of `total` is 7, since the post-decrement operator was used on `tip`, although you did not need to know this to solve the question.

3. **A.** The `f` in `4.0f` means the type is a float, making option A correct. Local variable type inference chooses an exact match rather than using autoboxing to choose `Float`.

4. **D.** Trick question. There is no reverse method on the `String` class. There is one on the `StringBuilder` class. Therefore, the code does not compile, and option D is correct.

5. **D.** A `StringBuilder` is mutable, so the length is 2 after line 6 completes. The `StringBuilder` methods return a reference to the same object, so you can chain method calls. Therefore, `line` and `anotherLine` refer to the same object. This means that line 7 prints `true`. Then on line 9, both references point to the same object of length 2, and option D is correct.

6. **E.** The diagram represents all cases where `apples` or `oranges` is `true`, but `bananas` is `false`, making option E correct. Option A is close but is correct only if the top overlapping portion of `apples` and `oranges` was filled in. For fun, you should try to draw the diagrams that would represent the other answers.

7. **A.** A `String` is immutable, so a different object is returned on line 6. The object `anotherLine` points to is of length 2 after line 6 completes. However, the original `line` reference still points to an object of length 1. Therefore, option A is correct.

8. **B,E.** Options A and D are incorrect because `byte` and `short` do not store values with decimal points. Option C is tempting. However, `3.14` is automatically a `double`. It requires casting to `float` or writing `3.14f` to be assigned to a `float`. Therefore, option B is correct. Additionally, option E is correct because local variable type inference is able to automatically determine the type is `double`.

9. **A,B.** Option A is correct and lists the operators in the same or increasing level of operator precedence. In option B, the three operators actually have the same operator precedence, so it is correct. Option C is incorrect, as division (`/`) has a lower precedence than the decrement operator (`--`). Option D is incorrect because the logical complement operator (`!`) has a higher order of precedence than the other two operators. Option E lists the operators in the correct order, but they don't fit within not equals (`!=`) and the increment operator (`++`) as listed in the question. In particular, compound addition operator (`+=`) and short-circuit

logical operator (&&) have a lower precedence than the not equals operator (!=). Finally, option F is incorrect because the relational operator (<) does not fit between multiplication operator (*) and the division operator (/) in order of precedence.

10. D. Line 18 compiles because neither type is specified for the lambda parameters. Lines 19 and 22 compile because the lambda parameters use a type or `var` consistently. These are the three lines that compile, making option D correct. Lines 20 and 21 do not compile because `var` must be used for all parameters in a lambda if it is used for any.

11. B. The `charAt()` and `length()` methods are declared on both `String` and `StringBuilder`. However, the `insert()` method is declared only on a `StringBuilder` and not a `String`. Therefore, option B is correct.

12. B. Since `StringBuilder` is mutable, each call to append adds to the value. When calling `print`, `toString()` is automatically called, and `333 806 1601` is output. Therefore, option B is correct.

13. A. Option A does not compile because Java does not allow declaring different types as part of the same declaration. The other three options show various legal combinations of combining multiple variables in the same declarations with optional default values.

14. E. Local variable type inference requires a value, so that the type can be inferred. The statement `var color;` without a value is not allowed, making option E the answer.

15. A. The code starts by creating a list of three elements. On line 16, it removes two elements and then removes the final one on line 19. This prints an empty list, making option A the correct answer. Note that `num` is effectively final, so can be used in a lambda.

16. C. The `trim()` method returns a `String` with all leading and trailing white space removed. In this question, that's the seven-character `String`: `":) - (:"`. Options A and B are incorrect because they do not remove the first blank space in `happy`. Option D is incorrect because it does not remove the last character in `happy`. Therefore, option C is correct.

17. C. Underscores are allowed between any two digits in a numeric literal, causing `num4` to fail to compile. Additionally, underscores are not allowed adjacent to a decimal point, causing a compiler error in `num2`. Since two lines have errors, option C is the correct answer.

18. A. The code compiles, so option D is incorrect. The input to the constructor is ignored, making the assignment of end to be 4. Since `start` is 2, the subtraction of 4 by 2 results in the application printing 2, followed by 5, making option A the correct answer.

19. D. Line 4 creates a `String` of length 5. Since `String` is immutable, line 5 creates a new `String` with the value 1 and assigns it to `builder`. Remember that indexes in Java begin with zero, so the `substring()` method is taking the values from the fifth element through the end. Since the first element is the last element, there's only one character in there. Then line 6 tries to retrieve the second indexed element. Since there is only one element, this gives a `StringIndexOutOfBoundsException`, and option D is correct.

20. D. The code compiles and runs without issue, making option E incorrect. In this example, `partA` is the integer division of the two numbers. Since 3 does not divide 11

evenly, it is rounded down to 3. The variable `partB` is the remainder from the first expression, which is 2. The results are added together, resulting in the expression 3 * 5, or 15, and making option D correct.

21. C. Calling the constructor and then `insert()` is an example of method chaining. However, the `sb.length()` call is a problem. The `sb` reference doesn't exist until after the chained calls complete. Just because it happens to be on a separate line doesn't change when the reference is created. Since the code does not compile, option C is correct.

22. C. While parentheses are recommended for ternary operations, especially embedded ones, they are not required, so option D is incorrect. The first expression evaluates to 10 >= 10, so the first branch of the ternary operation is selected, and `"Leftovers"` can be eliminated. The expression in the second ternary operation evaluates to 3 <= 2, which is `false`, so `"Salad"` is selected, and option C is correct.

23. A. Since `String` is immutable, each call to `concat()` returns a new object with the new value. However, that return value is ignored, and the `teams` variable never changes in value. Therefore, it stays as 694, and option A is correct.

24. C. First, `bool` and `Bool` are not valid Java types. They should be `boolean` and `Boolean`, respectively. Next, objects are allowed to have a `null` reference while primitives cannot. Since `Integer` and `String` are objects, those lines compile. Finally, the line with `int` is a primitive, so assigning `null` to it does not compile. Therefore, option C is correct.

25. A. In the first expression, `height > 1` is `true`. Since it uses the logical operator (`|`), which evaluates both sides, the right side is still executed, resulting in `length` being assigned a value of 2 and `w` assigned a value of `true`. In the second expression, only the right-hand side of the expression is evaluated, so `x` is assigned a value of 2, and `length` is unchanged. The last expression evaluates to 2 % 2, which is 0, so `z` is assigned a value of 0.

26. A. Line 3 creates an empty `StringBuilder`. Line 4 adds three characters to it. Line 5 removes the first character, resulting in ed. Line 6 deletes the characters starting at position 1 and ending right before position 2, which removes the character at index 1, which is d. The only character left is e, so option A is correct.

27. D. Options A and B are not `true` if the `String` is `"deabc"`. Option C is not `true` if the `String` is `"abcde"`. Option D is `true` in all cases.

28. E. The code compiles, so option F is incorrect. The first expression evaluates to `true & false`, which sets `carrot` to `false`. The next expression resolves to `true ? true : false`, which results in `broccoli` being set to `true`. The last expression reduces to `false ^ false`, which sets `potato` to `false`. Therefore, option E is the correct output.

29. B. The code successfully defines a local variable inside the lambda. Each value is replaced with baby. Since we have a `List`, all three are output, and option B is the correct answer.

30. D. Line 4 creates a `StringBuilder` of length 5. Pay attention to the `substring()` method in `StringBuilder`. It returns a `String` with the value 321. It does not change the `StringBuilder` itself. Then line 6 retrieves the second indexed element from that unchanged value, which is 4. Therefore, option D is correct.

Chapter 2: Controlling Program Flow

1. B,F. A `switch` statement supports the primitive types `byte`, `short`, `char`, and `int` and the wrapper classes `Character`, `Byte`, `Short`, and `Integer`. It also supports `String` and enumerated types. Finally, it permits `var` if it can be resolved to one of the previous types. Floating-point types like `float` and `double` are not supported; therefore, option B is correct. `Object` is also not supported since it could include any class, making option F correct as well.

2. E. The code does not compile because parentheses, `()`, are used instead of braces, `{}`, making option E the correct answer. If the code was fixed to use braces, then option B would be the correct answer. The exclusive or (`^`) of two `true` values is `false`. Therefore, `gas` would be `true` at the end of the first loop and would exit since the loop condition `!gas` is `false`.

3. F. When getting this type of question, the best approach is to write down the values of the variables. Both start out as 0 on line 10. On the first iteration of the loop, n becomes 1, while m remains 0, so the clause in the `if` statement doesn't run. In the `switch` statement, the value of m remains 0, so it matches the first `case`. Since there is no `break`, the `default` block is also executed, and n is incremented twice and is now 3. Finally, m is incremented to 1.

On the second iteration of the loop, m goes from 1 to 2, and n goes from 3 to 6. On the third iteration, m goes from 2 to 3, and n goes from 6 to 8. On the fourth iteration m is 3, and the `continue` is executed with only n increasing in value by 1. This pattern continues with the loop never terminating, while n continues to increase by 1. Since the execution does not complete, option F is the correct answer.

4. B,D,E. A for-each loop accepts arrays and classes that implement `java.lang.Iterable`, such as `List`. For these reasons, options B, D, and E are correct. Option A is incorrect because it is a primitive value. Options C and F are incorrect because `StringBuilder` and `String` do not implement `Iterable`.

5. C,D. A `default` statement inside a `switch` statement is optional and can be placed in any order within the `switch`'s `case` statements, making options A and B incorrect and option C correct. Option D is also correct because a `default` statement does not take a parameter value. Options E and F are incorrect rules about `switch` statements.

6. A. A `while` loop requires a `boolean` condition. While `singer` is a variable, it is not a `boolean`. Therefore, the code does not compile, and option A is correct.

7. A,F. A traditional `for` loop gives you full control over the order of iteration. This means you can iterate through the array backward or forward. By contrast, with a for-each loop, the iteration order is determined for you. With an array, this means starting with index 0. Options A and F match this scenario.

8. D. This code does not compile because it has two `else` statements as part of a single `if` statement. Notice that the second `if` statement is not connected to the last `else` statement. For this reason, option D is the correct answer.

9.   A,E. The code compiles as is. Due to the `break` statement on line 27, the loop executes only once. It prints a single `x`, which means option A is the first correct answer. While the label on line 24 is present with lines 25 and 28 removed, it no longer points to a loop. This causes the code to not compile, and option E is the other correct answer.

10. A,D. The method prints the elements of the array in the reverse order in which they are defined. Option A correctly accomplishes this using a different starting value for the loop. Options B and F do not compile, as they do not use the correct syntax in a for-each loop. Option C compiles and runs without issue, but prints the items in their natural ordering, as opposed to the reverse ordering. Option D is correct, as it increments in positive order but reverses the output within the body of the `for` loop. Finally, option E is incorrect. The first element read is `circus[circus.length+1]`, which results in an `ArrayIndexOutOfBoundsException`.

11. C. The first time through the loop, `type` is 1, and `plastic-` is output. The `break` statement then terminates the loop, with end bring printed. If the `break` keyword was removed, then this would be an infinite loop because `type` is not incremented between loop executions.

12. F. The code does not compile because the `switch` statement is missing the `case` keyword for each value. Also, two case values cannot be combined as in `4,5`.

13. A. First, determine whether the `if` statement's expression is executed. The expression `8 % 3` evaluates to 2. The right-hand side of the expression is evaluated next since `+` has a higher precedence than `>`. Since `2 > 2` is `false`, the expression `triceratops++` is not called. Notice there are no braces, `{}`, in the `if` statement. Despite the `triceratops--` line being indented, it is not part of the `if` statement. Therefore, `triceratops--` is always executed, resulting in a value of 2 for `triceratops`, and making option A the correct answer.

14. F. The value of a `case` statement must be a constant, a literal value, or a `final` variable. Since `red` is missing the `final` attribute, no variable type allows the code to compile, making option F the correct answer. If the `final` modifier was added to the declaration of `red`, then `int` or `var` would be correct. The other options use types that are incompatible with `switch` statements or with `colorOfRainbow`.

15. D. Line 15 does not compile because the post-decrement operator can be applied only to variables, not values. Line 16 also does not compile because the label `LOOP` is out of scope after line 15. Finally, line 18 does not compile because `trick` is declared within the do/while loop and out of scope after line 17. For these reasons, option D is the correct answer.

16. C. If the code follows the arrow, then it prints each letter once, breaking out of the inner loop on every iteration. Since a `break` without a label applies to the innermost structure, `break` and `break numbers` are equivalent, and both of these are correct answers. Likewise, `continue` and `continue numbers` are both equivalent although both wrong in this case since they resume operation of the inner loop. That leaves `break letters` and `continue letters`. In this case, `break letters` stops the outer loop after printing just one letter, so it is incorrect. On the other hand, `continue letters` exits the inner loop and returns control to the outer loop, which is the desired behavior. Since three statements are correct, option C is correct.

17. B. The code compiles without issue, so options D and E are incorrect. A var can be used in a switch statement, provided the underlying type resolves to a supported switch type. Next, notice there are no break statements. Once the matching case statement, 30, is reached, all remaining case statements will be executed. The variable eaten is increased by 1, then 2, then reduced by 1, resulting in a final value of 2, making option B the correct answer.

18. A,D,F. A while loop and do/while loop both require a boolean expression, making options A and D correct and options B and E incorrect. Option C is incorrect because a for-each statement requires an assignment type and an object to iterate on. Option F is correct and shows a traditional for loop with no arguments.

19. C. Option A goes through five indexes on the iterations: 0, 1, 2, 3, and 4. Option B also goes through five indexes: 1, 2, 3, 4, and 5. Option D goes through five iterations as well, from 0 to 4. However, option C goes through six iterations since the loop condition is at the end of the loop. Therefore, it is not like the others, and option C is the correct answer.

20. B. On the first iteration of the loop, stops[++count] evaluates to stops[1], while also setting count to 1. Since stops[1] is Monroe and it has six characters, the break is reached, and the loop stops. For this reason, 1 is printed, making option B correct.

21. C. The statement if(jumps) evaluates to if(0), and since 0 is not a boolean value, the code does not compile. Java requires boolean expressions in if statements.

22. B. The initializer, which is alpha, runs first. Then Java checks the condition, which is beta, to see whether loop execution should start. Since beta returns false, the loop is never entered, and option B is correct.

23. B. On the first iteration of the loop, the if statement executes and prints inflate-. Then the loop condition is checked. The variable balloonInflated is true, so the loop condition is false, and the loop completes and done is printed.

24. B. Options A and C print one line if numChipmunks is 1, 2, or 3. Option B does not behave the same way if numChipmunks is 1 or 2. There is no break statement, so the case statements fall through, and more than one statement will be printed.

25. A,C,D. A do/while loop requires a body, making option A correct. Options B and E are incorrect, as both types of while loops can be exited early with a return statement. Both also require a conditional expression, making option C correct. What distinguishes a do/while loop from a while loop is that it executes its body at least once, making option D correct and option F incorrect.

26. F. Option A is incorrect because the enum type Season is not used within a case statement. If it were just case WINTER:, then it would compile. Options B and C do not compile because switch statements do not support multiple values within a case statement. Option D is incorrect because -> is used instead of :. Option E is incorrect because FALL is not defined in the list of values for the enum Season. Since none of the lines of code is correct, option F is correct.

27. B. In a traditional for loop, only one initialization type is allowed to be specified. If more than one variable is supplied, then they are separated by a comma. Therefore, options A, C, and D do not compile. Options B and E both compile, although only option B prints a single line at runtime. Option E instead prints two lines since `nycTour` is of size 3 and `times` is of size 2.

28. C. The braces on lines 12/27 are required because they comprise the method body. The braces on lines 24/26 are required because a `switch` statement needs braces regardless of how many `case` statements are inside. Finally, the braces on lines 18/21 are required because the `else` has two statements inside.

The braces on lines 14/23, 15/22, and 16/18 are all optional because there is only one statement inside. Since there are three pairs, option C is correct.

29. B. The method prints the elements of the list in the order in which they are defined. Option A is incorrect and prints the first element repeatedly. Option B is correct and prints the elements using a for-each loop. Options C and E are incorrect because the first element read results in an `ArrayIndexOutOfBoundsException`. Finally, option D is incorrect because the entire list is printed each time.

30. D. The code snippet compiles, making options A, B, and C incorrect. Notice that the inner for-each loop does not use braces, `{}`, so the `break` statement applies to the outer loop only. On the first iteration of the outer loop, the inner loop prints 9_1Z0-811 and 9_1Z0-819. Then, the `break` statement is encountered, and the outer loop is terminated, making option D correct. If braces were added around lines 7 and 8, then the code would instead print 9_1Z0-811, 10_1Z0-811, and 11_1Z0-811, and option E would be correct.

Chapter 3: Java Object-Oriented Approach

1. F. The program does not compile because `Story` is marked `final`, which means it cannot be extended by `Adventure`. If the `final` modifier were removed, the rest of the code would compile and print 93 at runtime.

2. C,F. A class can start with a comment, an optional `package` statement, or an `import` statement if there is no `package` statement. It cannot start with a variable definition or method declaration, since those cannot be declared outside a type. Therefore, options C and F are correct.

3. C,E. An abstract method cannot include the `final` or `private` modifier. If a method contained either of these modifiers, then no concrete subclass would ever be able to override it with an implementation. For these reasons, options A and B are incorrect. Option D is also incorrect because the `default` keyword applies to concrete interface methods, not abstract methods. Option F is incorrect because there is no concrete modifier. That leaves options C and E as the correct answer. The `protected`, package-private, and `public` access modifiers can each be applied to abstract methods.

4.   C. The code does not compile because of line 5, making option C the correct answer. For this question, it helps to understand variable scope. The `main()` method is `static` and does not have access to any class instance variables. The `birds` variable is not `static` and requires a class instance variable to access. Therefore, the code does not compile when the `static` method attempts to access a non-`static` variable without an instance of the class.

5.   E. The `public` access modifier allows access to members in the same class, package, subclass, or even classes in other packages, while the `private` modifier allows access only to members in the same class. Therefore, the `public` access modifier allows access to everything the `private` access modifier does, and more, making option E the correct answer. Options A, B, C, and D are incorrect because the first term is a more restrictive access modifier than the second term.

6.   F. There is no modifier that can prevent a `default` method from being overridden in a class implementing an interface, making option F correct.

7.   B. Notice in this question that `main()` is not a `static` method; therefore, it can access both class and instance variables. Since there are two class variables and two instance variables defined, option B is the correct answer.

8.   B,D. Option A is incorrect because `new` cannot be used to declare a type. Option C is incorrect because `null` is a literal and cannot be used as the name of a class. Options E and F are incorrect because a `void` method cannot return a value. That leaves options B and D as the correct answers. Note that `10` can be returned as an `int` or implicitly promoted to a `long`, without issue.

9.   C,E. Options A and B are `static` methods rather than constructors. Option D is a method that happens to have the same name as the class. It is not a constructor because constructors don't have return types. Option C is a valid constructor.

As for the output, the key is that Java uses "pass by value" to send object references to methods. Since the `Phone` reference `p` was reassigned in the first line of the `sendHome()` method, any changes to the `p` reference were made to a new object. In other words, no changes in the `sendHome()` method affected the object that was passed in. Therefore, the value of `size` was the same before and after the method call, making the output `3` and option E the correct answer.

10.   C,F. Options A and E are incorrect because the `new` keyword before `Pterodactyl` is required to create an instance of the member inner class `Pterodactyl` using a member of the outer class `Dinosaur`. Option B is incorrect, as this is not a valid way to instantiate a member inner class. Option C is correct and relies on the `dino` instance variable for the outer class instance. Option D would be correct if Dino was changed to the correct class name, `Dinosaur`. Finally, option F is correct and relies on the fact that `roar()` is an instance method, which means there's an implicit instance of the outer class `Dinosaur` available. The `Dinosaur.` prefix is optional, though.

11.   C. Both objects are instances of the class `Laptop`. This means the overridden `startup()` method in the `Laptop` class gets called both times thanks to polymorphism, making option C correct.

12. E. In Java, the lack of an access modifier indicates that the member is package-private; therefore, option E is correct. Note that the `default` keyword is used for interfaces, annotations, and `switch` statements, and is not an access modifier.

13. E. A `static` initializer is not allowed inside a method. It should go on the class level rather than the method level. Therefore, the code does not compile, and option E is correct.

14. B,D,F. Option A is incorrect as methods cannot be marked `final` within an interface. Interfaces support `static` methods that are marked `public` or `private`, making options B and D correct and option E incorrect. Option F is correct and lack of access modifier makes the method implicitly `public`, not package-private, making option C incorrect.

15. B. A static nested class cannot access instance members of the enclosing class, making option B correct. The rest of the options form true statements.

16. E. The first `woof()` method does not compile because `bark` is a primitive, not an object, and does not have a `toString()` method. The `main()` method also does not compile because it is `static` and all of the `woof()` methods require an instance of `Canine`. Since these two lines do not compile, option E is the correct answer. If the `toString()` was removed from the first method and all of the methods were marked `static`, then the program would print 15 at runtime.

17. C. A local variable is effectively final when its primitive value or object reference does not change after it is initialized, making option C the correct answer. Note that option D is incorrect because any change to the variable after it is initialized disqualifies it for being considered effectively final.

18. C. The `sell()` method is declared `final` in the `Vegetable` class. The `Turnip` class then attempts to override this method, resulting in a compilation error, making option C the correct answer.

19. D. The `case` statements incorrectly use the enum name as well as the value, such as `DaysOff.ValentinesDay`. Since the type of the enum is determined by the value of the variable in the `switch` statement, the enum name is not allowed and causes a compilation error when used. For this reason, option D is correct. If the enum name `DaysOff` was removed, the application would output 12, since the lack of any `break` statements causes multiple blocks to be reached, and option C would have been the correct answer.

20. B,E. There is no `that` keyword, so options A and D are incorrect. Option B is correct, as `this` can access all members declared within the class. Option C is incorrect, as only inherited members can be accessed. For example, `private` members declared in a parent class cannot be accessed using `super`. Option E is correct, as `this` allows access to members declared in the class and those inherited from a parent. Finally, option F is incorrect, as `static` methods do not have access to `this` or `super` references.

21. D. A class can implement an interface, not extend it, ruling out options A, B, and C. Classes do extend an `abstract` class, ruling out option F. Finally, an interface can only extend another interface, making option D the correct answer.

22. B. Three instances of `Chicken` are created on lines 8–10. On line 11, the value of `eggs` in the first two instances is set to 2, while the third instance has a value of 3. On line 12, the original instance that was pointed to by `c1` (with an `eggs` value of 2) is dereferenced and eligible for garbage collection. The `c1` and `c2` variables now both point to the same instance with an `egg` value of 2. Finally, on line 13, the `eggs` value for `c3` is changed from 3 to `null`.

23. C. Java does not allow multiple inheritance, so having one class implement two interfaces that both define the same `default` method signature leads to a compiler error, unless the class overrides the method. In this case, the `talk(String...)` method defined in the `Performance` class is an overloaded method, not an overridden one, because the signatures do not match. Therefore, the `Performance` class does not compile, making option C correct.

24. C. A functional interface must contain exactly one `abstract` method. The `Bend` interface contains two `abstract` methods, `pump()` and `bend()`, since it extends `Pump` and inherits `pump()`. For this reason, the `Bend` interface is not a valid functional interface and therefore cannot be used as a lambda expression, making option C the correct answer. The rest of the code compiles without issue. Note that the usage of an instance variable to call a `static` method, `r.apply()` in the `main()` method, is permitted but discouraged.

25. B. If the variables are `public`, the class is not encapsulated because callers have direct access to them. This rules out options C and D. Having `private` methods doesn't allow the callers to use the data, making option A an undesirable answer. Option B is correct and the classic definition of encapsulation where the data is not exposed directly.

26. A. Package-private allows access by code within the same package, while the `private` modifier allows access only to members in the same class. This makes option A the correct answer. Options B, C, and D are incorrect because the first term is a more restrictive access modifier than the second term.

27. C. The `stroke()` method is `static`, which means it cannot access the instance method `breath()` on line k2, making option C correct.

28. D. The `Hammer` class is a subclass of the `Tool` class. The `repair()` method can be declared in the `Hammer` subclass with a different return type because the parent method is not inherited. For these reasons, options A and C are incorrect. On the other hand, the `use()` method is package-private in `Tool`, with the overridden version in `Hammer` reducing the visibility to `private`. This is an invalid override, making option D correct. The rest of the lines compile without issue.

29. E. Methods cannot be both `abstract` and `final`, making option A incorrect. Abstract interface methods are always `public`, making option C incorrect. Finally, `interface` and `void` are not modifiers on a method, making options B and D incorrect. Therefore, option E is the answer.

30. A. While both objects are instances of `Bush`, we are not calling methods in this example. Virtual method invocation works only for methods, not instance variables. For instance variables, Java looks at the type of the reference and calls the appropriate variable based on the reference. Based on the reference types of the three variables (`Plant`, `Bush`, `Plant`), option A is correct.

31. A,F. An instance variable can be referenced only from instance methods in the class, making option A correct. A `static` variable can be referenced from any method. Therefore, option F is correct.

32. D. Java classes are defined in this order: `package` statement, `import` statements, class declaration. That makes option D the only correct answer. Note that not all of these statements are required. For example, a class may not have a `package` statement, but if it does, it must come first in the file.

33. A, C, E. The code does compile as is, making option A correct. Removing line 2 would cause a compiler error in the `main()` method since the `enum` inside `Chick` is not referenced. This makes option C the next answer. Finally, option E is the final answer because an `enum` cannot be defined in a non-static inner class. Only top-level types and `static` nested classes can define `static` members other than `static` constants, and enums are implicitly `static`.

34. B,F. A `static` method can access `static` variables, but not instance variables. The `getNumRakes()` method does not compile, so option B is correct.

The `main()` method calls the constructor, which outputs a. Then the main method calls the `run()` method. The `run()` method calls the constructor again, which outputs a again. Then the `run()` method calls the `Sand()` method, which happens to have the same name as the constructor. This outputs b. Therefore, option F is correct.

35. C. While an anonymous class can extend another class or implement an interface, it cannot be declared `final` or `abstract` since it has no class definition. For this reason, option C is correct. The other classes may be declared `final` or `abstract` since they have a class definition.

36. C,E,F. The `public` access modifier is the broadest, making options E and F correct. Package-private access limits references to those in the same package. The `protected` access modifier adds on subclass access, making option C correct.

37. B. Java does not allow multiple variables to be declared in the same statement using local variable type inference. Lines `x2` and `x3` both have compiler errors. Since the question asks about the first line with a compiler error, option B is the answer.

38. E. All four members of the `Telephone` interface are implicitly `public`, making option E correct. Only `private` and `private static` interface methods are not `public`, and they must be explicitly marked `private`.

39. C. The `new` keyword is used to call the constructor for a class and instantiate an instance of the class, making option C correct. A primitive cannot be created using the `new` keyword, so option B is incorrect. Dealing with references happens after the object created by `new` is returned. The other options are invalid.

40. B. From within a method, an array or varargs parameter is treated the same. However, there is a difference from the caller's point of view. A varargs parameter can receive either an array or individual values, making line 19 and 20 compile. However, an array parameter can take only an array, which permits line 23 but prevents line 22 from compiling. Both lines 21 and

24 compile because `null` can be passed to a method taking an array or a varargs. Since there is only one line that doesn't compile, option B is the answer.

41. A,C,F. Both abstract classes and interfaces can include `static` methods, so options A and C are correct. Of all the nested class types, only `static` nested classes can include `static` methods, making option F correct, and options B, D, and E incorrect.

42. E. This code is already a functional interface and compiles without any changes. The `Play` interface has a single `abstract` method: `fun()`. The other methods have a method body, which shows they are not `abstract`.

43. F. Both of these descriptions refer to variable and `static` method hiding, respectively, making option F correct. Only instance methods can be overridden, making options A and B incorrect. Options C, D, and E are also incorrect because replacing and masking are not real terms in this context.

44. F. This class is a good example of encapsulation. It has a `private` instance variable and is accessed by a public method. No changes are needed to encapsulate it, and option F is correct.

45. B,D. Option A is incorrect because `static` methods cannot call instance methods directly. Options B and D are correct and are the primary reasons to create a `static` interface method. Options C and E are incorrect and describe attributes of a `default` method. Option F applies only to `private static` interface methods, not `public` ones.

46. C. The `Bottle` class includes a `static` nested class `Ship` that must be instantiated in a `static` manner. Line w2 uses an instance of `Bottle` to instantiate the `Ship`. Therefore, line w2 does not compile, and option C is the correct answer. Note that if `Ship` were changed to be a member inner class, the code would still not compile since a member inner class cannot include `static` members and enums are inherently `static`.

47. E. The instance variables, constructor, instance and `static` initializers, and method declarations can appear in any order within a class declaration.

48. A. First, all of the lines compile, but they produce various different results. Remember that the default initialization of a `boolean` instance variable is `false`, so `outside` is `false` at line p1. Therefore, `this(4)` will cause `rope` to be set to 5, while `this(5)` will cause `rope` to be set to 6. Since 5 is the number we are looking for, option A is correct, and option C is incorrect. Option B is incorrect. While the statement does create a new instance of `Jump`, with `rope` having a value of 5, that instance is nested, and the value of `rope` does not affect the surrounding `instance` of `Jump` that the constructor was called in. Option D is also incorrect. The value assigned to `rope` is 4, not the target 5. Options E and F do not compile because the superclass is `Object`, which does not have a constructor taking an `int`.

49. B,E. Option A is true because encapsulation improves security because instance variables cannot be accessed directly. Implementing encapsulation prevents internal attributes of a class from being modified directly, so option D is a true statement. By preventing access to internal attributes, we can also maintain class data integrity between elements, making option C a true statement. Option F is also a true statement about encapsulation, since well-encapsulated classes are often easier to use. Option B is an incorrect statement. Encapsulation makes no guarantees about performance and concurrency. Option E is also an incorrect statement because it describes immutability.

50. B,D. Line u2 does not compile because getPartner() is overridden with a return type that is not covariant, as Follower is not the same type nor a subtype of the Leader class. Line u4 also does not compile because SwingDancer is marked abstract and cannot be instantiated directly. For these reasons, options B and D are the correct answers. The rest of the code compiles without issue.

51. C. Option A is allowed because the turnOn() method is public and can be called from anywhere. Options B and D are allowed since the method is in the same class, which is always allowed! Option C is not allowed because wash() is a package-private method in another package. Option C is the correct answer.

52. C. The display() method has protected access. This means it can be accessed by instance methods in the same package and any subclasses. There are no subclasses in this example, so we only need to count the classes in the same package. Option C is correct because Flashlight and Phone are in the package.

53. B,D. While Java does not allow a class to extend more than one class, it does allow a class to implement any number of interfaces. Multiple inheritance is, therefore, only allowed via interfaces, making option B correct. Interfaces can extend other interfaces, making option D the other answer.

54. B. The Dress type is declared as a class, not an interface. For this reason, it cannot contain the default method getSize(), making option B correct. The rest of the methods compile within the class declaration without issue.

55. E. The main() method attempts to define an anonymous class instance but fails to provide the class or interface name, or use the new keyword. The right-hand side of the assignment to the seaTurtle variable should start with new CanSwim(). For this reason, option E is the correct answer. If the code was corrected with the proper declaration, then the program would output 7 at runtime.

56. E. The Puppy class does not declare a constructor, so the default no-argument constructor is automatically inserted by the compiler. What looks like a constructor in the class is actually a method that has a return type of void. Therefore, the line in the main() method to create the new Puppy(2) object does not compile, since there is no constructor capable of taking an int value, making option E the correct answer.

57. B. The method signature has package-private, or default, access; therefore, it is accessible to classes in the same package, making option B the correct answer.

58. D. First, both CanBurrow and HasHardShell compile as functional interfaces since they contain exactly one abstract method, although only the latter uses the optional @FunctionalInterface annotation. The declarations of these two interfaces, along with the abstract class Tortoise, compile without issue, making options A, B, and C incorrect. The class DesertTortoise inherits two abstract methods, one from the interface CanBurrow and the other from the abstract parent class Tortoise. Since the class implements only one of them and the class is concrete, the class declaration of DesertTortoise fails to compile, making option D the correct answer.

59. C. The interface declarations compile without issue. When inheriting two `default` methods with the same signature, the `Tower` class is required to override both methods even if the class is marked `abstract`. For this reason, line `m3` is the first line that does not compile, and option C is correct. Note that there is no possible overridden method that can fulfill both inherited `default` methods since the return types are not covariant.

60. D. The `height` variable is declared within the `if-then` statement block. Therefore, it cannot be referenced outside the `if` statement, and the code does not compile.

61. A,E,F. Java supports three types of comments: single-line (`//`), multiline (`/* */`), and Javadoc (`/** **/`), making options A, E, and F correct. The other options may be comments in other languages, but not in Java.

62. A,C,F. An `abstract` method is one that will be implemented by a subclass. For this reason, it cannot be combined with `final` or `private`, as both prevent a method from being over-ridden, making options B and D incorrect. An `abstract` method can also not be marked `static`, since `static` members belong to the class level, not an instance, making option E incorrect. Options A, C, and F are the correct answers. Note that marking a `private` method `final` has no practical implication, although it is allowed.

63. E. The class data, `stuff`, is declared `public`, allowing any class to modify the `stuff` variable and making the implementation inherently unsafe for encapsulation. Therefore, there are no values that can be placed in the two blanks to ensure the class properly encapsulates its data, making option E correct. Note that if `stuff` were declared `private`, options A, B, C, and D would all be correct. Encapsulation does not require any specific method names, just that the internal attributes are protected from outside access, which all of these sets of values do achieve.

64. C. The second row is incorrect, as `private` methods belong to an instance, not the class. The fourth row is also incorrect, as `default` methods require a method body. The rest of the rows are correct, making option C correct.

65. D. The `super()` statement is used to call a constructor in the parent class, while `super` is used to reference a member of the parent class. The `this()` statement is used to call a con-structor in the current class, while `this` is used to reference a member of the current class. For these reasons, option D is the correct answer.

66. B. Line 15 calls the method on line 9 since it is a `Watch` object. That returns `watch`, making option A incorrect. Line 16 calls the method on line 3 since it is a `SmartWatch` object and the method is properly overridden. That returns `smart watch`, so option B is the answer, and option C is incorrect.

67. F. The `Cinema` class defines a constructor that takes a `String` value, which means the com-piler does not insert the default no-argument constructor. Therefore, it is not available in the `Movie` constructor, and an explicit constructor must be called with `super()`. Since this is not done, the `Movie` constructor does not compile, making option F the correct answer. The rest of the code compiles without issue.

68. A,D,E. A `final` instance must be assigned a value (exactly once) on the line it is declared, in an instance initializer, or in a constructor. This makes options A, D, and E correct.

69. C. This example deals with method signatures rather than polymorphism. Since the hop() methods are static, the precise method called depends on the reference type rather than the actual type of the object. Since the first reference is Rabbit, the first value printed is hop. The second reference actually is FlemishRabbit, so HOP is printed, and option C is the answer.

70. A. If the program is called with a single input south, then south would be printed at runtime. If the program is called with no input, then the compass array would be of size zero and an ArrayIndexOutOfBoundsException would be thrown at runtime. Finally, if the program is called with a string that does not match one of the values in Direction, then an IllegalArgumentException would be thrown at runtime. The only result not possible is WEST, since the enum value is in lowercase, making option A the correct answer.

71. C. Encapsulation doesn't allow callers access to the instance variables, which makes it easier to change the code. The instance variables can be any type, which means they can be mutable or immutable. There are not constraints on the implementation of methods. The purpose of encapsulation is to lessen how tightly tied or coupled the classes are. Option C is the opposite of this, making it the answer.

72. C. A class cannot contain two methods with the same method signature, even if one is static and the other is not. Therefore, the code does not compile because the two declarations of playMusic() conflict with one another, making option C the correct answer.

73. A,E,F. First, the return types of an overridden method must be covariant, making option A correct. They can be the same, but it is not required, making option C incorrect. Next, the access modifier must be the same or broader in the child method, making option B incorrect and option F correct. Option D is incorrect as an overridden method is not required to throw a checked exception declared in the parent version of the method. If it does declare a checked exception, it cannot be new or broader than the ones declared in the superclass, making option E correct.

74. D. A private non-static interface method may only be accessed from other private or default methods declared within the interface. Lines 15 and 21 do not compile because the private method is called within static methods. Line 26 does not compile because a private interface method cannot be called in a method outside the interface declaration. Since these three lines do not compile, option D is correct.

75. B. Interface variables are implicitly public, static, and final. Variables cannot be declared as abstract in interfaces, nor in classes. Therefore, option B is the answer.

76. B. Integer is the name of a class in Java. While it is bad practice to use the name of a class as your local variable name, this is legal. Therefore, k1 does compile. It is not legal to use a reserved word as a variable name. All of the primitives including int are reserved words. Therefore, k2 does not compile, and option B is the answer. Lines k4 and k5 don't compile either, but the question asks about the first line to not compile.

77. C. The code compiles and runs without issue, so options A and B are incorrect. The question relies on your ability to understand variable scope. The variable today has local scope to the method in which it is executed. The variable tomorrow is re-declared in the method, but the reference used on line y is to the instance variable with a value of 10. Finally, the variable yesterday is `static`. While using an instance reference to access a `static` variable is not recommended, it does not prevent the variable from being read. The result is line y evaluates and prints 31 (20 + 10 + 1), making option C the correct answer.

78. E. If an enum contains anything other than a list of values, then a semicolon (`;`) must follow the list of values. The `Snow` enum includes a method, so there must be a semicolon after the last value, `FLURRY`. For this reason, the code does not compile, and option E is correct. If the semicolon was added, then the code would compile and print 0 Sunny at runtime, with the overridden `toString()` replacing the default value of `FLURRY`.

79. A. Option A is the correct answer because the first line of a constructor could be `this()` or `super()`, making it an untrue statement. Option B is a true statement because the compiler will insert the default no-argument constructor if one is not defined. Option C is also a true statement, since zero or more arguments may be passed to the parent constructor, if the parent class defines such constructors. Option D is also true. The value of a `final` instance variable must be set when it is declared, in an initialization block, or in a constructor.

80. E. If only the `com.mammal` class needed access, option A would be correct. Access modifiers cannot be used to grant access to a list of packages. The Java Platform Module Framework can do this, but it is not an option in this question. Therefore, option E is correct.

81. E. The code does not compile because `super.height` is not visible in the `Rocket` class, making option E the correct answer. Even though the `Rocket` class defines a `height` value, the `super` keyword looks for an inherited version. Since there are none, the code does not compile. Note that `super.getWeight()` returns 3 from the variable in the parent class, as polymorphism and overriding do not apply to instance variables.

82. B,E. The key here is understanding which of these features of Java allow one developer to build their application around another developer's code, even if that code is not ready yet. For this problem, an interface is the best choice. If the two teams agree on a common interface, one developer can write code that uses the interface, while another developer writes code that implements the interface. Assuming neither team changes the interface, the code can be easily integrated once both teams are done. For these reasons, option B is correct. Interfaces expose methods using the `public` keyword, making option E the other answer.

83. F. The code compiles, even if the blank is replaced with a constant value, making option E incorrect. Note that the class correctly overrides both inherited `default` methods. While it is possible to call a specific inherited `default` method, even when it has been overridden, it requires calling `super`, which is not accessible from a `static` method. For these reasons, options A, B, C, and D do not work, making option F correct.

84. B. An enum declaration itself cannot be marked `abstract`, nor can any of its values, but its methods can be marked `abstract`, making option B the correct answer. Note that if an enum contains an abstract method, then every enum value must include an override of this `abstract` method.

85. C. The `static` initializer is run only once. The `static` method is run twice since it is called twice. Therefore, three lines are printed, and option C is correct. The instance initializer block is never run because the `Cars` class is never constructed.

86. C. Dot notation is used for both reading and writing instance variables, assuming they are in scope. It cannot be used for referencing local variables, making option C the correct answer. It is possible that bar is a `static` variable, although accessing it in this manner is not recommended.

87. A,D,E. The reference type of unknownBunny must be Bunny or a supertype of Bunny, including any abstract classes, concrete classes, or interfaces that Bunny inherits. For this reason, options A and E are correct, and option C is incorrect. Option B is incorrect. Since it already points to an instance of Bunny, casting it to a Bunny reference is allowed. Option D is trivially true. If the reference types of both are the same, then they can call the same instance members. Option F is incorrect, as casting is required to access members declared in Bunny that are not defined in `Object`.

88. C,E. Methods marked `private` or `static` are never inherited, so options A, B, and D are incorrect. Interface methods cannot be `final`, so option F is incorrect. That leaves `default` and `abstract` methods, which are both inherited by classes implementing the interface.

89. C. The code does compile, so option E is incorrect. A functional interface is required to have exactly one `abstract` method. In both interfaces, that is roar(). The toString() and hashCode() method signatures match those from `Object`. Since they are provided to all subclasses, they are not considered `abstract`. Since roar() is the only `abstract` method, both are functional interfaces, making option C the answer.

90. C,E. To call a constructor, you must use the new keyword, making option E correct. It cannot be called as if it was a normal method. This rules out options A and B. Further, option D is incorrect because the parentheses are required. Option C is also correct, as var may be used as a variable name.

91. C. To a call an instance method, you can use the `this` prefix. The class name is not included, ruling out the last three methods. A method may contain at most one varargs parameter, and it must appear as the last argument in the list. For this reason, the sing_do() method is the only method using varargs that compiles. The sing() method also compiles without using varargs. Therefore, option C is the answer.

92. B. The code compiles without issue. The first print() statement refers to level declared in the Deeper class, so 5 is printed. The second and third print() statements actually refer to the same value in the Deep class, so 2 is printed twice. The prefix Matrix. is unnecessary in the first of the two print() statements and does not change the result. For these reasons, option B is the correct answer.

93. A. The play() method is overridden in Violin for both MusicCreator and StringInstrument, so the return type must be covariant with both. Long is a subclass of Number, and therefore, it is covariant with the version in MusicCreator. Since it matches the type in StringInstrument, it can be inserted into the blank, and the code would compile.

While Integer is a subclass of Number, meaning the override for MusicCreator is valid, it is not a subclass of Long used in StringInstrument. Therefore, using Integer would cause the code to not compile.

Finally, Number is compatible with the version of the method in MusicCreator but not with the version in StringInstrument, because Number is a superclass of Long, not a subclass. For these reasons, Long is the only class that allows the code to compile, making option A the correct answer.

94. E. The `IsoRightTriangle` class is `abstract`; therefore, it cannot be instantiated on line g3. If the `abstract` modifier was removed from the `IsoRightTraingle` declaration, then the rest of the code would compile and print `irt` at runtime.

95. F. The `private static` method `wagTail()` attempts to access an instance-based `default` method `chaseTail()`, which results in a compiler error, making option F correct. While `buryBone()` is not used, it does not result in a compiler error, making option D incorrect. Overridden methods are permitted to declare new unchecked exceptions, and since `IllegalArgumentException` is unchecked, the override is allowed, making option E incorrect.

96. B,C,D. Enumerated types support creating a set of reusable values whose values are fixed and consistent across the entire application. For these reasons, options B and D are correct, and option F is incorrect. Option C is also correct, as it provides callers of a method with a list of acceptable values. Finally, options A and E are incorrect. Using an enum does not, by itself, improve performance or support concurrency.

97. E. While you can suggest to the JVM that it might want to run a garbage collection cycle, the JVM is free to ignore your suggestion. Option B is how to make this suggestion. Since garbage collection is not guaranteed to run, option E is correct.

98. D. The access modifier of `strength` is `protected`, meaning subclasses and classes within the same package can modify it. Changing the value to `private` would improve encapsulation by making the `Protect` class the only one capable of directly modifying it. For these reasons, option D is correct.

99. A,D. A lambda can reference any instance variable, `static` variable, or lambda parameter that is in scope, making option A correct. Lambdas require local variables and method parameters to be effectively final in order to use them, making option D the other correct answer.

100. E. A `static` import is used to import `static` members of another class. In this case, the `withdrawal()` and `deposit()` methods in the `Bank` class are not marked `static`. They require an instance of `Bank` to be used and cannot be imported as `static` methods. Therefore, option E is correct. If the two methods in the `Bank` class were marked `static`, then option A would be the correct answer since wildcards can be used with `static` imports to import more than one method. Options C and D reverse the keywords `static` and `import`, while option B incorrectly imports a class, which cannot be imported via a `static` import.

101. A,C,E. Option A returns `true` since `Coral` inherits `Friendly` from its superclass `Animal`. Option B is `false`, as using `null` with the `instanceof` operator always returns `false`. Options C and E both return `true` because all classes inherit `Object`, even those that don't explicitly extend it. Option D is `false` because `Fish` does not inherit the `Friendly` interface. Finally, option F does not compile as `Dolphin` is abstract and cannot be instantiated directly. If it was not marked `abstract`, then it would return `true`.

102. B. While it is not recommended to change the value of an enum after it is created, it is legal. Each enum value has its own copy of `numDays`. This means the setter changes it for `CHICKEN`, but not for `PENGUIN`. Therefore, option B is correct. Both calls on `CHICKEN` print the updated value of 20, while `PENGUIN` retains the original 75.

103. B. Line 3 does not compile, as a method with a body within an interface must be explicitly marked `static`, `default`, or `private`, making option B correct. The rest of the lines compile without issue. For this question, it helps to remember which implicit modifiers the compiler will insert, and which it will not. On line 2, the compiler will insert `public static final` automatically, and on lines 4 and 6, the compiler will insert `public` automatically. The compiler will also insert `abstract` on line 4 since the method does not declare a body.

104. E. The type of the variable in the `switch` statement is the enum `Currency`, but the `case` statements use `int` values. While the enum class hierarchy does support an `ordinal()` method, which returns an `int` value, the enum values cannot be compared directly with int values. For this reason, the `Bank` class does not compile, making option E the correct answer.

105. D. Lines 3 and 4 do not compile because the returned values of `double` and `long` are not compatible with `int`. Lines 6 through 8 compile without issue, since each method takes a different set of input arguments. The first line of the `main()` method does not compile either, making option D correct. The no-argument version of the `nested()` method does not return a value, and trying to output a `void` return type in the `print()` method doesn't compile.

106. B. A class can trivially be assigned to a superclass reference variable but requires an explicit cast to be assigned to a subclass reference variable. For these reasons, option B is correct.

107. D. A functional interface may have any number of `static`, `default`, `private static`, or `private` methods. It can have only one qualified `abstract` method, though, making option D correct.

108. D. This class has poor encapsulation since the `age` variable is `public`. This means that a developer could modify the body of `main()` to change the value of `mandrill.age` to any integer value, and option D is correct.

109. C. All three references point to the `String` object `"lion"`. This makes the other two `String` objects eligible for garbage collection and makes option C correct.

110. B,F. A functional interface has exactly one `abstract` method. This includes inherited methods. If `Panther` has a single `abstract` method, `Cub` is a functional interface if it does not add any more `abstract` methods. This matches option B. However, if `Panther` has two `abstract` methods, there is no code in `Cub` that can make it a functional interface, and option F is the other answer.

111. A,C. A local class can access `final` or effectively final local variables, making options A and C the correct answer. Local variables cannot be marked `private` or `static`, making options B and D incorrect. Options E and F are also incorrect, as those are not valid variable modifiers.

112. B. When the `main()` method instantiates the object, line 2 first runs and sets the variable using the declaration. Then the instance initializer on line 6 runs. Finally, the constructor runs. Since the constructor is the last to run of the three, that is the value that is set when we print the result, so option B is correct.

113. C. An `abstract` method cannot define a body, meaning the declaration of `getNumberOfRings()` is invalid and option C is correct. The rest of the code compiles without issue. While the compiler will prevent cycles within overloaded constructors, it does not do so for methods, meaning option F is incorrect.

114. B,F. The type is determined based on the value at initialization. It cannot be `null` at that point, but the variable can be assigned as `null` later, making option B correct. Both primitives and objects can be used with `var`, making option F correct.

115. A. The `protected` modifier allows access by any subclass or class that is in the same package; therefore, option A is the correct answer.

116. C. The `main()` method defines a local class `Oak` that correctly extends `Tree`, a `static` nested class. The method `getWater()` is not permitted to read the local variable `water`, though, since it is not `final` or effectively final, making option C correct. If the last line of the method was removed, though, then the program would compile and print 8.

117. B,D. A class can implement multiple interfaces, making option B correct. An interface can extend multiple interfaces, making option D correct as well.

118. D. The method looks like a setter or mutator method. However, it is incorrectly implemented since the method is missing a `this` reference and doesn't actually change the value. Therefore, option D is correct.

119. A,C,F. Option A is correct and option B is incorrect because `this()` calls another constructor in the same class. Option C is correct because `this()` without parameters is the default constructor and is not inserted automatically by the compiler if another constructor is present. Options D and E are both incorrect because only one of `super()` or `this()` can be used from the same constructor. Finally, option F is correct as `super()` or `this()` must come first.

120. E. The code compiles and runs without issue, so option A is incorrect. The question involves understanding the value and scope of each variable at the `print()` statement. The variables `feet` and `tracks` are locally scoped and set to 4 and 15, respectively, ignoring the value of `tracks` of 5 in the instance of the class. Finally, the `static` variable `s.wheels` has a value of 1. The result is that the combined value is 20, making option E the correct answer.

121. C,F. Line m3 does not compile because `isDanger()` is an invalid method override. An overridden method may not throw a broader checked exception than it inherits. Since `Exception` is a superclass of `Problem`, the code does not compile, and option C is correct. Line m6 does not compile because the return type of `isDanger()` is `void`, which cannot be assigned to a variable, making option F also correct.

122. C,E,F. Top-level classes can be set only with `public` and package-private access, making option A incorrect. On the other hand, member inner classes can be set with any of the four access levels, making option D incorrect. Both types of classes can be declared with `final` or `abstract` modifier, making option B incorrect and option F correct. Both can also include constructors, making option C correct. Finally, option E is correct and one of the primary features of inner classes.

123. A. Option A is the only correct answer as a `class` declaration is the only required component in a Java class file. Note that we said a Java class file here; Java also allows interfaces, annotations, modules, and enums to be defined in a file. A class file may have a single `package` statement or any number of `import` statements. Neither is required.

124. B. On line 9, all three objects have references. The `elena` and `zoe` objects have a direct reference. The `janeice` object is referenced through the `elena` object. On line 10, the reference to the `janeice` object is replaced by a reference to the `zoe` object. Therefore, the `janeice` object is eligible to be garbage collected, and option B is correct.

125. D. Both the `Drive` and `Hover` interfaces define a `default` method `getSpeed()` with the same signature. The class `Car` implements both interfaces, which means it inherits both `default` methods. Since the compiler does not know which one to choose, the `Car` class must override the `default` method. Since it does not, the code does not compile, and option D is correct. Note that the `RaceCar` class does properly override the `default` method, the problem is with the `Car` class.

126. C,D. On line 10, we are passing a `float`. Since there is no exact match, Java attempts promotion of the primitive type to `double`, before trying to wrap it as a `Float`, making option D correct. On line 11, the value 2 is first cast to a `byte`. It is then increased by one using the addition + operator. The addition + operator automatically promotes all `byte` and `short` values to `int`. Therefore, the value passed to `choose()` in the `main()` method is an `int`. The `choose(int)` method is called, returning 5 and making option C the correct answer. Note that without the addition operation in the `main()` method, `byte` would have been used as the parameter to the `choose()` method, causing the `choose(short)` to be selected as the next closest type and outputting 2, making option A the correct answer.

127. C,F. An interface can be extended by another interface and a class can be extended by another class. This makes the second part of options A, D, and E incorrect. Among nested classes, all types can be extended except an anonymous class since it does not declare a class name, making option F correct and both parts of option B incorrect. Option C is correct because an enum cannot be extended.

128. D. Line 3 does not compile because `printColor()` is marked `final` and cannot be overridden. Line 5 does not compile because the method `toSpectrum()` is marked `abstract` and must be overridden by each enum value. Finally, line 6 does not compile because enum constructors are implicitly `private`. For these three reasons, option D is correct.

129. E. The override of `getEqualSides()` in `Square` is invalid. A `static` method cannot override a non-`static` method and vice versa. For this reason, option E is the correct answer. The rest of the lines compile without issue. If the `static` modifier were added to the method declaration on line x2, then the code would print 4 at runtime.

130. A. Since only one package needs access and it is the same package the class is in, option A is correct.

131. D. A concrete class is not allowed to have `abstract` methods, but the other two types are. This makes the second row in the first column incorrect. All three types are allowed to have `static final` constants, making the whole second column correct. In the last column, there are two errors. An `abstract` class can have a constructor, but an interface cannot. Note that an `abstract` class cannot be instantiated. Instead, it requires a subclass. This gives us a total of three incorrect cells, making option D the answer.

132. B,C,E. A functional interface must have exactly one `abstract` method, which is option B. There are no restrictions on the number of `private` or `static` methods, which make options C and E also correct.

133. D. Only local variables have such a small scope, making option D the correct answer.

134. C. The code contains a compilation error in regard to the `contents` instance variable. The `contents` instance variable is marked `final`, but there is a `setContents()` instance method that can change the value of the variable. Since these two are incompatible, the code does not compile, and option C is correct. If the `final` modifier were removed from the `contents` variable declaration, then the expected output would be of the form shown in option A.

135. B,E. One of the motivations for adding `default` interface methods to Java was for backward compatibility. These methods allow developers to update older classes with a newer version of an interface without breaking functionality in the existing classes, making option B correct. Option E is also correct, as classes implementing the interface can share common methods. Option A is incorrect, as interface methods can already be overloaded. Option C is incorrect because methods in interfaces cannot be marked `final`. Option D sounds plausible, but could be accomplished with `static` interface methods alone. Option F is incorrect as that statement only applies to `private` interface methods.

136. D. The method `fly()` defined in `CanFly` defines an implementation, an empty `{}`, meaning it cannot be assumed to be `abstract`; therefore, the code does not compile.

Next, the implementation of `fly(int speed)` in the `Bird` class also does not compile, but not because of the signature. The method body fails to return an `int` value.

Finally, the `Eagle` class does not compile because it extends the `Bird` class, which is marked `final` and, therefore, cannot be extended. For these three reasons, option D is the correct answer.

137. B. Options A, C, and D are true statements. Option A is correct because `public` allows any class to access it. Option C is true because `protected` access also provides package-private access. Option D allows us to write the `equals()` methods between two objects that compare `private` attributes of the class. Option B is false. Package-private attributes are visible only if the two classes are in the same package, regardless of whether one extends the other.

138. D. This example deals with polymorphism since the methods are being called on the object instance. Since both objects are of type `FlemishRabbit`, HOP is printed twice, and option D is the correct answer.

139. B,D,E. Class names follow the same requirements as other identifiers. Underscores (`_`) and dollar signs (`$`) are allowed, but no other symbols are allowed, making option C incorrect. Since Java 9, a single underscore is not permitted as an identifier, making option A incorrect. Numbers are allowed, but not as the first character. Therefore, option F is incorrect. The rest of the options are valid class names, making the answer options B, D, and E correct. Note that class names begin with an uppercase letter by convention, but this is not a requirement.

140. A. The code compiles without issue. Java allows methods to be overridden, but not variables. Therefore, marking them `final` does not prevent them from being reimplemented in a subclass. Furthermore, polymorphism does not apply in the same way it would to methods as it does to variables. In particular, the reference type determines the version of the `secret` variable that is selected, making the output `2.0` and option A the correct answer.

141. C. To solve this problem, it helps to remember that Java is a pass-by-value language in which copies of primitives and object references are sent to methods. This also means that an object's data can be modified within a method and shared with the caller, but not the reference to the object. Any changes to the object's reference within the method are not carried over to the caller. In the `slalom()` method, the `Ski` object is updated with an `age` value of 18. Although the last line of the `slalom()` method changes the variable value to `null`, it does not affect the `mySkier` object or reference in the `main()` method. Therefore, the `mySkier` object is not `null`, and the `age` variable is set to 18, making options A and D incorrect.

Next, the `name` variable is reassigned to the `Wendy` object, but this does not change the reference in the `main()` method, so `myName` remains `Rosie`. Finally, the `speed` array is assigned a new object and updated. Since the array is updated after the reference is reassigned, it does not affect the `mySpeed` array in the `main()` method. The result is that `mySpeed` continues to have a single element with the default int value of 0. For these reasons, option B is incorrect, and option C is correct.

142. C. The `Penguin` class includes a member inner class `Chick`. Member inner classes can only include `static` variables if they are marked `final`. Since the variable `volume` is not marked `final`, the `Chick` does not compile, making option C correct. Note that the variable `volume` referenced in the `chick()` method is one defined in the `Penguin` outer class. If the `final` modifier was added to the `volume` variable in the `Chick` class, then the rest of the code would compile, printing `Honk(1)!` at runtime.

143. F. An anonymous class can implement a single interface, and a top-level class can implement any number of interfaces. Since a functional interface is an interface with additional rules, both anonymous class and top-level class are correct. Additionally, a lambda expression can also implement a functional interface. Since all three are correct, the answer is option F.

144. B. The code compiles, even if the blank is replaced with a constant `char` value, making option E incorrect. Note that the class correctly overrides both inherited `default` methods. It is possible to access a `default` method, even if it is overridden in the class, but requires using the `super` keyword properly. Option B demonstrates the correct syntax. Note that option D would not be correct even if there was only one inherited `default` method.

145. C. Option A is incorrect because the keywords `static` and `import` are reversed. The `Closet` class uses the method `getClothes()` without a reference to the class name `Store`; therefore, a `static` import is required. For this reason, option B is incorrect since it is missing the `static` keyword. Option D is also incorrect since `static` imports are used with members of the class, not a class name. Finally, option C is the correct answer since it properly imports the method into the class using a `static` import.

146. B. The `drive()` method in the `Car` class does not override the `private` version in the `Automobile` class since the method is not visible to the `Car` class. Therefore, the `final` attribute in the `Automobile` class does not prevent the `Car` class from implementing a method with the same signature. The `drive()` method in the `ElectricCar` class is a valid override of the method in the `Car` class, with the `public` access modifier expanding access in the subclass. In the `main()` method, the object created is an `ElectricCar`, even if it is assigned to a `Car` or `Automobile` reference. Due to polymorphism, the method from the `ElectricCar` will be invoked, making option B the correct answer.

147. A. The code compiles, so option F is incorrect. The `Music` class is loaded, and the `static` initializers are executed in order, with `re-fa-` being printed first. Next, the first line of the `main()` method is executed, printing `ti-`. The second line of the `main()` method creates a `Music` object, with the instance initializers being called first, printing `do-mi-`. Finally, the no-argument constructor is executed, and `so-` is printed last.

148. D. All of the options attempt to create an instance using an anonymous class that extends `Sky`. Option A is incorrect because when you create an anonymous class, you do not specify a name. Even if there was a `Sunset` class, the declaration of an anonymous class can only extend or implement one type directly. Since it would already extend `Sunset`, it cannot specify `Sky` at the same time. Option B is incorrect because `Sky` is `abstract` and cannot be instantiated directly. Option C is incorrect because it is missing a semicolon (`;`) at the end. Option D is the correct answer. Remember that all nested classes can have `static` variables if they are marked `final`.

149. E. The code may look complicated, but it does not compile for a simple reason. The `abstract read()` method defined in `Book` cannot have a method body. Since it does, the code does not compile, and option E is correct.

150. C. While using `null` with `instanceof` compiles, it always returns `false`. The other two `instanceof` calls show that `instanceof` can be used with both classes and interfaces. They both return `true` since `Bus` implements `Vehicle`, making option C correct.

151. D. The first row is incorrect as the `private` modifier is required for `private` interface methods. The second row is correct. The third row is also incorrect because the `static` modifier is required, not optional, for `static` interface methods. The `public` modifier is optional, though, as the `static` method is implicitly `public` without it. The last row is incorrect as the `abstract` modifier can be implied if the method does not declare a body. Since three rows contain an error, option D is correct.

152. D. A `final` instance variable must be assigned a value when it is declared, in an instance initializer, or by a constructor. The `Dwarf(String)` constructor does not assign a value since it contains a local variable called `name` already. For this reason, this constructor does not compile, and option D is correct. If the assignment in the constructor was changed to `this.name`, then the program would compile and print `Sleepy`.

153. A. The `AddNumbers` interface is a valid functional interface. While it includes both `static` and `default` methods, it includes only one `abstract` method, the precise requirement for it to be considered a functional interface, making option B incorrect. The class compiles and prints 8 at runtime, making option A correct.

154. B. There is no such thing as package variables, so option A is incorrect. Option C is incorrect as the variable is only in scope within a specific instance of the class. Option D is also incorrect as the variable is only in scope for a single method that it is defined in. Option B is the only correct answer as class variables are in scope within the program.

155. D. The super() statement is used to call a constructor in a parent class, while the this() statement is used to call a constructor in the same class, making option D correct and option C incorrect. Options A, B, and E are incorrect because they are not built-in functionality in Java.

156. C,D. The default no-argument instructor is inserted by the compiler whenever a class, abstract or concrete, does not declare any constructors. For this reason, option A is incorrect, and option D is correct. Even if a parent class does not declare a no-argument constructor, the child class can still declare one, making option B incorrect. If the parent class does not declare a no-argument constructor (and none is inserted by the compiler), then the child class must declare at least one constructor, making option C correct. Without a constructor call, inserting the default no-argument constructor into the child class would lead to a compiler error on the implicit super() call. Finally, options E and F are incorrect, as a child class of a parent with a no-argument constructor is free to declare or not declare any constructors.

157. C. Interfaces allow Java to support multiple inheritance because a class may implement any number of interfaces. On the other hand, an anonymous class may implement or extend at most one interface or class, respectively, since it does not have a class definition. For these reasons, option C is the correct answer.

158. B. The hop() method has protected access, which allows subclasses to call it. Both the move() method and main() method are allowed to call hop() since Grasshopper is a subclass. The code runs without error and prints hop twice, making option B the answer.

159. A. This code is not a functional interface because it has three abstract methods: fun(), game(), and toy(). Removing two of these three methods would cause the code to compile. However, there is no requirement that the code be a functional interface. Since it only needs to compile, removing the @FunctionalInterface annotation would also cause the code to compile. Option A is correct since only the annotation needs to be removed.

160. C,E. Options A and B are incorrect and describe properties of default interface methods. Option C is correct and one of the primary reasons to add a private interface method. Option D is not a property of private interface methods. Option E is also correct, as private interface methods are not exposed to classes implementing the interface. Option F is a nonsensical statement.

161. C. The speak() method has private access, which does not allow code outside the class to call it. Therefore, option C is the answer.

162. D. The sell() method does not compile because it does not return a value if both of the if-then statements' conditional expressions evaluate to false. While logically it is true that price is either less than 10 or greater than or equal to 10, the compiler does not know that. It just knows that if both if-then statements evaluate to false, then it does not have a return value; therefore, it does not compile.

163. E. Options A and C do not compile, as they are invalid ways of accessing a member variable. Options B and D both compile but print 100 at runtime, since they reference the speed variable defined in the Engine class. Option E is the correct answer, accessing the speed variable in the Racecar class and printing 88 at runtime.

164. B,C,F. A `static` initializer can create instances of any class it has access to, so option A is incorrect. It can assign values to `static final` variables, specifically ones that have not been assigned a value already, so option B is correct. A `static` initializer is executed when the class is first loaded, not when an object is created or loaded, making option C correct, and options D and E incorrect. If the class is never loaded, then they will not be executed, making option F correct.

165. D. The class is loaded first, with the `static` initialization block called and 1 is printed. When the `BlueCar` is created in the `main()` method, the superclass initialization happens first. The instance initialization blocks are executed before the constructor, so 32 is out-putted next. Finally, the object is created with the instance initialization blocks again being called before the constructor, outputting 45. The result is that 13245 is printed, making option D the correct answer.

166. B. Recall that `this` refers to an instance of the current class. Therefore, any superclass of `Canine` can be used as a return type of the method, including `Canine` itself, making option A an incorrect answer. Option D is also incorrect because `Canine` implements the `Pet` interface. An instance of a class can be assigned to any interface reference that it inherits. Option C is incorrect because `Object` is the superclass of all instances in Java. Finally, option B is the correct answer. `Canine` cannot be returned as an instance of `List` because `Canine` does not inherit `List`.

167. D. The `static` method `getDrink()` attempts to access an instance-based `private` method `buyPopcorn()` that results in a compiler error, making option D correct. The rest of the code compiles without issue.

168. C. An instance method can access both instance variables and `static` variables. Both methods compile, and option C is correct.

169. A. As ugly as the class looks, it does compile, making option A correct. Lines 2–4 each define an instance method since they each have a name and return type. There is no rule saying you cannot define a method with the same name as the class, although it is considered bad style. The `main()` method calls the default no-argument constructor on line 6, inserted by the compiler. Finally, line 7 calls the method declared on line 2.

170. C. This method has package-private access, which means only classes in the same package can access it. In our case, this is the `Red` and `Blue` classes, making option C correct.

171. D. This variable has `protected` access, which means code in the same package can access it in addition to subclasses. There are two classes in the `com.color` package and one class that subclasses it, making option D the answer.

172. A. The `protected` modifier allows access to the same package and subclasses, which are options B, C, and D. Therefore, the correct answer is option A.

173. F. The declarations of the local classes `Robot` and `Transformer` compile without issue. The only compilation problem in this program is the last line of the `main()` method. The variable `name` is defined inside the local class and not accessible outside class declaration without a reference to the local class. Due to scope, this last line of the `main()` method does not compile, making option F the correct answer. Note that the first part of the `print()` statement in the `main()` method, if the code compiled, would print `GiantRobot`.

174. D. When overriding a method, a new or broader checked exception cannot be declared. The `getNumStudents()` method in `HighSchool` is an invalid override since it declares `FileNotFoundException`, which is not declared in the parent method. Since this is the only line that does not compile, option D is correct. Note that an `abstract` method can be overridden with a `final` method, as shown with `getNumTeachers()`.

175. C. Having one class implement two interfaces that both define the same `default` method signature leads to a compiler error unless the class overrides the `default` method. In this case, the `Sprint` class overrides both `walk()` methods correctly; therefore, the code compiles without issue, and option C is correct. Note that the return types of the two `default` methods are different, but the overridden method uses a return type that is covariant with both.

176. A. Interface methods are implicitly `public`, giving both the same signature. This means a class implementing them must implement a single `wriggle()` method, and option A is correct.

177. D. The code does compile, so option E is incorrect. A functional interface is required to have exactly one `abstract` method. Both interfaces have two. In both interfaces, `roar()` is `abstract`. The `equals(Lion)` method is similar to the `equals(Object)` in `Object` but is not an override of that method. Similarly, the `toString()` method in `Tiger` is also an `abstract` method. While there is a `toString()` method in `Object`, it does not take any parameters. Since each method has two `abstract` methods, neither is a functional interface, making option D the answer.

178. B. The `gold` variable is marked `final`, which means it must be set either when it is declared or in a `static` initializer, as shown on line 17. It cannot be modified by a method, though, so line 15 does not compile. Since this is the only line that does not compile, option B is correct. Line 8 compiles because the `static` method is modifying the local variable `scaly`, not the instance variable of the same name. Line 12 also compiles. While accessing a `static` variable via an instance is not recommended, it is allowed.

179. A. The method is a correct getter or accessor, making option A is correct.

180. A. From within a method, an array parameter and a varargs parameter are treated the same. From the caller, an array parameter is more restrictive. Both types can receive an array. However, only a varargs parameter is allowed to automatically turn individual parameters into an array. Therefore, the answer is option A.

181. A,C. Marking a class `final` tends to improve security by guaranteeing the behavior of a class is not replaced by overridden methods at runtime. For this reason, options A and C are correct. Option B is incorrect and is the opposite of what marking a class `final` does. Options D and E are incorrect and have nothing to do with marking a class `final`. Option F is incorrect as the contents of the class can still be changed, even if the class is marked `final`.

182. E. The code does not compile because the constant variable `circumference` does not declare a value, making option E correct. Remember that all variables within interfaces are implicitly `static` and `final`. The rest of the lines of code compile without issue. Note that while the `static` method `leaveOrbit()` cannot access the instance-based `default` method `getCircumference()` directly, it can through the reference variable `earth`.

183. F. Trick question! Overloaded methods is correct in the first part of the sentence, but none of the answers is correct in the second part of the sentence. Remember, overridden methods can have covariant return types. They do not need to be the same. For this reason, option F is the correct answer.

184. D. This class creates a `final` instance `toy` variable, but it is assigned a value twice. First, it is assigned a value in an instance initializer and then in a constructor. For this reason, the second line of the constructor does not compile, and option D is correct. The first line of the constructor, in which a `static` variable is referenced from an instance variable, is permitted but discouraged. Also, initializers may reference variables defined later in the class declaration.

185. C. Lines 15–17 create the three objects. Lines 18–19 change the references, so `orange` and `banana` point to each other. Lines 20–21 wipe out two of the original references. This means the object with `name` as `x` is inaccessible. Option C matches this scenario.

186. C. Option A is incorrect because Java inserts a no-argument constructor only if there are no other constructors in the class. Option B is incorrect because the parent can have a default no-argument constructor, which is inserted by the compiler and accessible in the child class. Option D is incorrect. A class that contains two no-argument constructors will not compile because they would have the same signature. Finally, option C is correct. If a class extends a parent class that does not include a no-argument constructor, the default no-argument constructor cannot be automatically inserted into the child class by the compiler. Instead, the developer must explicitly declare at least one constructor and explicitly define how the call to the parent constructor is made.

187. B. `Building` and `House` are both properly declared inner classes. Any `House` object can be stored in a `Building` reference, making the declarations for b3 and b4 compile. The declaration for h3 is also correct. It so happens that b2 is a `House` object, so the cast works. The declaration of h2 is a problem, though. While the cast itself is fine, a `Building` cannot be stored in a `House` reference, which means the assignment fails to compile. Option B is correct and is the only line with a compiler error in this code. Note that if the declaration of h2 was removed, the declaration of b3 would produce a `ClassCastException` at runtime.

188. E. This `main()` method declares an anonymous class that implements the `Tasty` interface. Interface methods are `public`, whereas the override in the anonymous class uses package-private access. Since this reduces the visibility of the method, the declaration of `eat()` on line 9 does not compile. Next, the declaration of the `apple` object must end with a semicolon (`;`) on line 12, and it does not. For these two reasons, the code does not compile, and option E is the correct answer. Note that if these two issues were corrected, with the `public` modifier and missing semicolon (`;`), then the correct answer would be option C because the code does not actually call the `eat()` method; it just declares it.

189. B. Java supports only a single return data type or `void`. Therefore, it is not possible to define a functional interface that returns two data types, making option A incorrect. Although Java does not include built-in support for primitive functional interfaces that include `float`, `char`, or `short`, there is nothing to prevent a developer from creating them in their own project, making option B the true statement and the correct answer.

Option C is incorrect because a functional interface that takes no values and returns `void` is possible. In fact, `Runnable` is one such example. Option D is also incorrect, since `IntFunction<R>` takes a primitive argument as input and a generic argument for the return type.

190. C. The `init()` method is accessible only from the same package. Since `Tortoise` is in a different package, the method is not available, and option C is correct. Line x2 does not compile either since `Tortoise` is in a different package and not a subclass. However, the question asks about the first line.

191. A. The code does not contain any compilation errors. While an `abstract` class cannot be marked `final`, a concrete class extending it can be. Likewise, a concrete method overriding an `abstract` one can also be marked `final`. In the `ParkVisit` class, the `getValue()` method accesses the effectively final variables `width` and `fun`. Finally, a class can override a method that it inherits from both an interface and an abstract class, provided the method signatures are compatible.

192. D. The `Sheep` class does not compile because there is no `default` access modifier keyword. If the `default` keyword were omitted, the code would use package-private access. Since `Sounds` is in a different package, option C would then be the answer. However, since both classes have problems, Option D the correct answer.

193. B. Marking an interface method `private` improves the encapsulation of the class, making option B correct. Options A and D are incorrect as `static` methods cannot be overridden, regardless if they are marked `private`. Option C is incorrect, as adding `private` to a method reduces the visibility of the method. Options E and F are flat out wrong.

194. D. Since a constructor call is not the first line of the `RainForest()` constructor, the compiler inserts the no-argument `super()` call. Since the parent class, `Forest`, does not define a no-argument `super()` constructor, the `RainForest()` constructor does not compile, and option D is correct.

195. B. First, the `color` variable defined in the instance and set to `red` is ignored in the method `printColor()`. Since local scope overrides instance scope, option A is incorrect. The value of `color` passed to the `printColor()` method is `blue`, but that is lost by the assignment to `purple`, making option B the correct answer and option C incorrect. Option D is incorrect as the code compiles and runs without issue.

196. E. The `play()` method is overridden in `Saxophone` for both `Horn` and `Woodwind`, so the return type must be covariant with both. `Object` and `Number` do not work, because neither is a subclass of `Integer` or `Short`. As stated in the question text, both `Integer` and `Short` extend `Number` directly, so neither can be a subclass of the other. Therefore, nothing can fill in the blank that would allow this code to compile, and option E is correct.

197. A,B,C. Options A, B, and C are correct statements about abstract classes. Option D is incorrect as Java allows a class to extend only one class directly, abstract or otherwise. Option E is incorrect, as a class can implement or inherit an interface. Option F is also incorrect as classes can only extend classes, and interfaces can only extend interfaces.

198. C. The code does not compile. First, the enum list is not terminated with a semicolon (`;`), which is required when an enum includes anything beyond just the list of values. Second, the access modifier of TRUE's implementation of `getNickName()` is package-private, but the `abstract` method signature has a `protected` modifier. Since package-private is a more restrictive access than `protected`, the override is invalid, and the code does not compile. For these two reasons, option C is the correct answer. Note that the `value` variable is not `final` nor properly encapsulated and can therefore be modified by callers outside the enum. This is permitted but considered a poor practice.

199. B,C,D. A Java class file may have at most one `package` statement and any number of `import` statements and comments. For this reason, option A is incorrect, and options B and C are correct. When declaring a class, the name comes first, before instance declarations, making option D correct and option E incorrect. Finally, Java does not support fragments of code outside of a top-level type, such as a class or interface, making option F incorrect.

200. E. The `hop()` method has `protected` access, which allows subclasses to call it, making line p1 correct. The HopCounter class is allowed to call the `move()` method because it is `public`. However, it is not allowed to call the `hop()` method since it is referencing a subclass, but not in one. Therefore, option E is the answer.

201. C. Interfaces cannot contain `protected` methods, making option C the answer.

202. B. Options A and D would not allow the class to compile because two methods in the class cannot have the same name and arguments, but a different return value. Option C would allow the class to compile, but it is not a valid overloaded form of our `findAverage()` method since it uses a different method name. Option B is a valid overloaded version of the `findAverage()` method, since the name is the same but the argument list differs.

203. A,E. Options A and E are correct since method names may include the underscore (`_`) character as well as the dollar (`$`) symbol. Note that there is no rule that requires a method start with a lowercase character; it is just a practice adopted by the community. Options B and F are incorrect because the hyphen (`-`) and pound (`#`) characters may not be part of a method name. Option C is incorrect since `new` is a reserved word in Java. Finally, option D is incorrect. A method name must start with a letter, the dollar (`$`) symbol, or an underscore (`_`) character.

204. C. A functional interface must include exactly one `abstract` method, either by inheritance or declared directly. It may also have any number, including zero, of `default` or `static` methods. For this reason, both parts of option D are incorrect. The first part of option A is incorrect because more than one `abstract` method disqualifies it as a functional interface. The first part of option B is incorrect because the method must be `abstract`; that is to say, any method will not suffice. Finally, option C is the correct answer. The first part of the sentence defines what it means to be a functional interface. The second part refers to the optional `@FunctionalInterface` annotation. It is considered a good practice to add this annotation to any functional interfaces you define because the compiler will report a problem if you define an invalid interface that does not have exactly one `abstract` method.

205. F. The code compiles, even if the blank is replaced with a constant `int` value, making option E incorrect. The `private` method `play()` declared in the `Sport` interface is not accessible in the `Game` class. For this reason, option F is correct.

206. E. The code does not compile because two of the constructors contain a cyclic reference to each other. The `MoreMusic(int)` constructor calls `this(null)`, which only matches the `MoreMusic(String)` constructor. Then, the `MoreMusic(String)` constructor calls `this(9)`, which only matches the `MoreMusic(int)` constructor. The compiler notices this circular dependency and does not allow the code to compile.

207. A. Both classes compile without issue, and the `Hug` program prints `kitty - 5.0`, making option A the answer. In the `Kitten` class, all of the variables have package-private access as the access modifiers are commented out. Also, there is no `age` variable since the entire line is commented out. If the comment syntax was removed around `private`, then the `Hug` class would not compile on the line that accesses the `cuteness` variable.

208. A,B. A `switch` statement that uses an enum must include `case` statements that reference the value of the enum, without the enum type. For this reason, option A is correct and option C is incorrect. The `ordinal()` value or position cannot be used in `case` statements when the `switch` statement takes an enum value, making option B correct and option E incorrect. Finally, not every value in enum must be present in the `case` statement, regardless of whether a `default` branch is present, making options D and F incorrect.

209. A. The code compiles without issue. The `main()` method creates an instance of an anonymous class of `Ready`. Calling `r.first` retrieves the `static` variable within `Ready`, printing 2 on line n3. On line n2, there is no reference so the `static` variable of `GetSet` is called, printing `10`. For these reasons, option A is correct.

210. D. The `init()` method is accessible from any code. However, the `race()` method is available only within the `Hare` class. Since `Tortoise` is a different class, the method is not available, and option D is correct.

211. D. The `Sheep` class does not compile since a `static` method cannot call an instance method. The `Sounds` class does not compile because it does not have access to the `speak()` method. Since neither class compiles, option D is correct.

212. C. The `Rotorcraft` class includes an `abstract` method, but the class itself is not marked `abstract`. Only interfaces and abstract classes can include abstract methods. Since the code does not compile, option C is the correct answer.

213. A,C,E. All of the interface methods without a `private` modifier are implicitly `public`. In a class, though, a method without a modifier is package-private by default. For this reason, the `write()` and `think()` methods do not compile because they are missing the `public` modifier, making options A and C correct. These are the only compiler errors, making option B incorrect. Option D is incorrect because the `process()` method is not accessible with `Twins` because it is `private`. Option E is correct, as all methods are accessible. Even the overridden `default` method can be accessed in the `Twins` class by calling `Michael.super.write()`. Finally, option F is incorrect as the class still compiles if it is marked `abstract`.

214. D. The Super class is marked `final`, which mean its cannot be used as the supertype of an anonymous class. For this reason, line 6 does not compile, and option D is correct. Line 7 also does not compile as a local class can only contain `static` variables that are marked `final`.

215. D. The `final` variable DEFAULT_VALUE is not a `static` variable; therefore, the `static` nested class GetSet cannot access it without a reference to the class. For this reason, the declaration of the `static` nested class GetSet does not compile, and option D is the correct answer. The rest of the code compiles without issue. If the DEFAULT_VALUE variable was modified to be `static`, then the code would compile and print 5, 10 at runtime.

216. B,C. The `static` class variables cannot be used with `var` since they are not local variables. Therefore, options E and F are incorrect. Options B and C are correct because numeric addition is used here instead of concatenation.

217. F. The code does not compile, as the constructor calls on the first four lines of the `main()` method are missing the `new` keyword. If the missing `new` keywords were added to each line, then the code would compile, and three Gems objects would be available for garbage collection.

218. B. The code does not compile, so option A is incorrect. The class contains two methods and one constructor. The first method, Stars(), looks a lot like a no-argument constructor, but since it has a return value of void, it is a method, not a constructor. Since only constructors can call `super()`, the code does not compile due to this line. The only constructor in this class, which takes an `int` value as input, performs a pointless assignment, assigning a variable to itself. While this assignment has no effect, it does not prevent the code from compiling. Finally, the `main()` method compiles without issue since we just inserted the full package name into the class constructor call. This is how a class that does not use an `import` statement could call the constructor. Since the method is in the same class, and therefore the same package, it is redundant to include the package name but not disallowed. Because only one line causes the class to fail to compile, option B is correct.

219. A. Although the casting is a bit much, the object in question is a SoccerBall. Since SoccerBall extends Ball and implements Equipment, it can be explicitly cast to any of those types, so no compilation error occurs. At runtime, the object is passed around and, due to polymorphism, can be read using any of those references since the underlying object is a SoccerBall. In other words, casting it to a different reference variable does not modify the object or cause it to lose its underlying SoccerBall information. Therefore, the code compiles without issue, and option A is correct.

220. F. The question may appear to be about method overriding, but it is in fact about member inner classes. In fact, all of the method overrides are valid in this class. The code does not compile because the `charge()` method is `static` (even though it is called on an instance), which means it requires an instance to instantiate a member of the member inner class MyTrunk. For this reason, the call to `new MyTrunk()` does not compile, and option F is correct.

Chapter 4: Exception Handling

1. **B.** The `throws` keyword is used in method declarations, while the `throw` keyword is used to send an exception to the surrounding process, making option B the correct answer. The `catch` keyword is used to handle exceptions. There is no `throwing` keyword in Java.

2. **E.** To throw an exception with the `throw` keyword, an existing or new exception must be provided. In this case, the `new` keyword is missing in front of `Exception()` in the `think()` method. It is treated as a method call that does not exist, and this line does not compile, making option E correct. If the `new` keyword were added, though, the line would still not compile as the checked exception is not handled or declared within the `think()` method.

3. **A,C.** The correct order of blocks is `try`, `catch`, and `finally`. For a traditional `try/catch` block at least one `catch` or `finally` must be used. In addition, multiple `catch` blocks are allowed, although at most one `finally` block is allowed. For these reasons, options A and C are correct, and the rest are incorrect.

4. **C.** Unlike a try-with-resources statement, in which the `catch` and `finally` blocks are optional, a traditional `try` statement requires a `catch` or `finally` block to be used, or both. For this reason, option C is correct.

5. **E.** The code does not compile because the `throw` keyword is incorrectly used in the `toss()` method declaration. The keyword `throws` should have been used instead. For this reason, option E is the correct answer. If the correct keyword was used, then the code would compile and `Caught!` at runtime.

6. **E.** The code does not compile because `s` is defined within the try-with-resources block. It is out of scope by the time it reaches the `catch` and `finally` blocks, making option E correct.

7. **D.** The `Exception` class contains multiple constructors, including one that takes `Throwable`, one that takes `String`, and a no-argument constructor. The first `WhaleSharkException` constructor compiles, using the `Exception` constructor that takes a `String`. The second `WhaleSharkException` constructor also compiles. The two statements, `super()` and `new Exception()`, actually call the same constructor in the `Exception` class, one after another. The last `WhaleSharkException` compiles with the compiler inserting the default no-argument constructor `super()`, because it exists in the `Exception` class. For these reasons, all of the constructors compile, and option D is the correct answer.

8. **D.** The application first enters the `try` block and prints A. It then throws an `ArrayIndexOutOfBoundsException`, which is caught by the first `catch` block since `ArrayIndexOutOfBoundsException` is a subclass of `RuntimeException`, printing B. The exception is then rethrown, but since there isn't a separate `try/catch` block around it, it does not get caught by the second `catch` block. Before printing the stack trace, the `finally` block is called, and D is printed. For these reasons, option D is correct.

9. **C,F.** While `Exception` and `RuntimeException` are commonly caught in Java applications, it is not recommended that `Error` and `Throwable` (which includes `Error`) be caught. An `Error` often indicates a failure of the JVM, which cannot be recovered from. For these reasons, options C and F are correct, and options A and D are incorrect. Options B and E are class names that are not part of the standard Java API.

10. E. A variable declared before the start of a try-with-resources statement may be used if it is `final` or effectively final. Since `g` is modified after it is set, it is neither; therefore, the class does not compile, and option E is correct. If the last line of the `main()` method were removed, then the code would compile and print `2459` at runtime.

11. C. The class does not compile because in line `r2`, curly braces, `{}`, are used instead of parentheses, `()`, in the try-with-resources statement, making option C the correct answer. If this line was fixed to use parentheses, `()`, then the rest of the class would compile without issue and print `This just in!` at runtime.

12. C. Since `IOException` and `Exception` are checked exceptions, `ColoringException` and `WritingException` are checked exceptions. Further, `CursiveException` is also checked since it extends a checked exception. By contrast, `IllegalStateException` is an unchecked exception. This means that `DrawingException` and `SketchingException` are also unchecked, and option C is the answer.

13. C. The code does not compile because the variable `v` is used twice in the `main()` method, both in the method declaration and in the `catch` block, making option C the correct answer. If a different variable name were used in one of the locations, the program would print one line, `complete`, making option A the correct answer. Note that while an exception is created inside the `turnOn()` method, it is not thrown.

14. A,E. When more than one resource is used in a try-with-resources statement, they are closed in the reverse order in which they are declared, making option A the first false statement. In addition, resources are separated by semicolons, not commas, making option E the other false statement. The rest of the statements are true. Note that ability to declare resources before they are used in a try-with-resources statement is new since Java 9.

15. A. The program compiles without issue, so option D is incorrect. The narrower `SpellingException` and `NullPointerException`, which inherit from `Exception`, are correctly presented in the first `catch` block, with the broader `Exception` being in the second `catch` block. The if-then statement evaluates to `true`, and a new `SpellingException` instance is created, but it is not thrown because it is missing the `throw` keyword. For this reason, the `try` block ends without any of the `catch` blocks being executed. The `finally` block is then called, making it the only section of code in the program that prints a line of text. For this reason, option A is the correct answer.

16. A,D,F. Any class that inherits `Exception` but not `RuntimeException` is a checked exception and must be handled or declared. For this reason, option F is trivially correct. Options A and D are also checked exceptions. Options B and E are incorrect since they inherit `RuntimeException`. Finally, option C is incorrect as `Error` inherits `Throwable` but not `Exception`.

17. C. The `finally` block of the `snore()` method throws a new checked exception on line `x1`, but there is no try-catch block around it to handle it, nor does the `snore()` method declare any checked exceptions. For these reasons, line `x1` does not compile, and option C is the correct answer. The rest of the lines of code compile without issue. Note that the code inside the `try` block, if it ran, would produce an `ArrayIndexOutOfBoundsException`, which would be caught by the `RuntimeException catch` block, printing `Awake!`.

18. E. The `ProblemException` class compiles without error. However, the `MajorProblemException` class has, well, a major problem. The constructor attempts to call a superclass constructor with a `String` parameter, but the `ProblemException` class only has a constructor with an `Exception` parameter. This causes a compiler error, which is option E.

19. B,D. First, option A is an incorrect statement, because the `AutoCloseable` interface does not define a `default` implementation of `close()`. Next, the `close()` method should be idempotent, which means it is able to be run multiple times without triggering any side effects. For this reason, option B is correct. After being run once, future calls to `close()` should not change any data. Option D is correct, and option C is incorrect because the `close()` method is fully capable of throwing exceptions if there is a problem. In fact, the signature of the method in `AutoCloseable` throws a checked `Exception`. Option E is incorrect because the return type of `close()` is `void`, which means no return value can be returned.

20. D. Option D is the correct model. The class `RuntimeException` extends `Exception`, and both `Exception` and `Error` extend `Throwable`. Finally, like all Java classes, they all inherit from `Object`. Notice that `Error` does not extend `Exception`, even though we often refer to these generally as exceptions.

21. F. The classes `MissingMoneyException` and `MissingFoodException` do not extend any exception classes; therefore, they cannot be used in a method declaration. The code does not compile regardless of what is placed in the blank, making option F correct.

22. B,D. `Closeable` extends `AutoCloseable`, making option B correct and option A incorrect. The `close()` method in `AutoCloseable` throws `Exception`, while the `close()` method in `Closeable` throws `IOException`, making option E incorrect. Since `IOException` is a subclass of `Exception`, both `close()` methods can throw an `IOException`, making option C incorrect. On the other hand, `Exception` is not a subclass of `IOException`. For this reason, the `close()` method in a class that implements `Closeable` cannot throw an instance of the `Exception` class, because it is an invalid override using a broader exception type, making option D the correct answer. Finally, the return type for both is `void`, making option F incorrect.

23. B,F. Option A does not compile because a multi-catch expression uses a single variable, not two variables. Since the `TideException` is handled and neither exception class is a subtype of the other, option B is correct. Option C does not compile because the compiler notices that it is not possible to throw a checked `IOException` in this `try` block. Option D does not compile because multi-catch blocks cannot contain two exceptions in which one is a subclass of the other. If it did, one of the two exceptions would be redundant. Option E does not compile because the checked `TideException` is not handled or declared by the `surf()` method. Remember, `Error` and `Exception` are not subclasses of each other, although they both inherit `Throwable`. Option F is correct because `TideException` is a subclass of `Exception`, so both are handled by `Exception`.

24. B,C. Option A is incorrect. You should probably seek help if the computer is on fire! Options B and C are correct answers, as invalid or missing data/resources should be expected of most programs. Option D is incorrect because code that does not compile cannot run and therefore cannot throw any exceptions. Option E is incorrect; finishing sooner is rarely considered a problem. Option F is incorrect because an `Error` is thrown in this situation, and it should not be caught, as the JVM cannot usually recover from this scenario.

25. A. The program compiles, making options D and E incorrect. At runtime, line 12 is executed, calling the `play()` method. Line 5 then throws an exception that is immediately caught on line 6. Line 7 throws a new unchecked exception that is not caught by the program, with this exception being thrown to the caller, and making option A correct. In this case, line 13 is never executed. Even though the stack trace for the exception may include information about the cause, only one exception is actually thrown to the caller.

26. D. The code does not compile due to an invalid override of the `operate()` method. An overridden method must not throw any new or broader checked exceptions than the method it inherits. While both `IOException` and `Exception` are checked exceptions, `Exception` is broader than `IOException`. For this reason, the declaration of `operate()` in `Heart` does not compile, and option D is correct.

27. C,F. Option A is a true statement and one of the primary motivations for using a try-with-resources statement. Option B is also true, although it is recommended you let the try-with-resources statement automatically close the resource. The `catch` blocks are run after the declared resources have been closed, making option C the first answer. Options D and E are both true, since `Closeable` extends `AutoCloseable` and the requirement for try-with-resources is that they must be of type `AutoCloseable`. A try-with-resources statement can be used with a `finally` block, making option F the other answer.

28. D. The code compiles without issue. It first prints `Tracking` from the `try` block. Upon the completion of the `try` block, the `close()` method is called, and `Thunder` is printed. No exception is thrown so the `catch` block is skipped. In the `finally` block, `Storm gone` is printed, followed by `Thunder`. Since four lines were printed, option D is correct. While it is not recommended to close a resource twice, it is allowed.

29. C. `Error` is a terrible name for an exception since it is a built-in class. However, it is legal. Next, `_X` is also a bad choice, but it is valid exception as Java identifiers can begin with underscores. By contrast, `2BeOrNot2Be` does not compile because identifiers are not allowed to begin with a number. `NumberException` is not a valid exception, because it uses generics, and the parent class does not. Finally, `Worry` is not an exception, because it is an interface. Since only two are valid exceptions, option C is the answer.

30. C. `ClassCastException` is a subclass of `RuntimeException`, so it must appear first in any related `catch` blocks. For this reason, option C is correct.

31. D. The `openDrawbridge()` method declares a checked exception that is not handled or declared in the `main()` method where it is called. For this reason, line p3 does not compile, and option D is correct. The rest of the lines do not contain any compiler errors. If the `main()` method were changed to declare `Exception`, then the class would compile and print `Opening!Walls` at runtime.

32. B. The code compiles and runs without issues. The `try` block throws a `ClassCastException`. Since `ClassCastException` is not a subclass of `ArrayIndexOutOfBoundsException`, the first `catch` block is skipped. For the second `catch` block, `ClassCastException` is a subclass of `Throwable` so that block is executed. Afterward, the `finally` block is executed, and then control returns to the `main()` method with no exception being thrown. The result is that `1345` is printed, making option B the correct answer.

33. C,E. A `finally` block requires curly braces, making option C correct. A `finally` block can throw an exception in which case not every line of the `finally` block will be executed. For this reason, option E is correct, and options A and D are incorrect. Option B is incorrect because a `finally` block is called regardless of whether the related `catch` block is executed. A `finally` block can throw both checked and unchecked exceptions, making option F incorrect. If the exception is checked, then it must be handled or declared in the method in which the `finally` block is used.

34. A. The application compiles without issue and prints `Hello`, making option A the correct answer. The `ReadSign` and `MakeSign` classes are both correctly implemented, with both overridden versions of `close()` dropping the checked exceptions. The try-with-resources statement is also correctly implemented for two resources and does not cause any compilation errors or runtime exceptions. Note that the semicolon (`;`) after the second resource declaration is optional.

35. E. The `try` block is entered and 2 is printed, followed by an exception. Upon completion of the `try` block, the resources are closed in the reverse order in which they are declared, printing 8 followed by 1. Next, the `catch` block executes, printing 3, followed by the `finally` block printing 4. For these reasons, option E is correct.

36. D. A multi-catch block cannot contain two exception types in which one inherits from the other. Since `RuntimeException` inherits `Exception`, `RuntimeException` is redundant. For this reason, the code does not compile, and option D is correct.

37. D. In the `try` block, the code prints 1 and throws an exception. The `catch` block successfully handles it by printing 2 and throwing another exception. Both the inner and outer `finally` blocks run printing 3 and 4, respectively. Then the stack trace for the exception thrown by the inner `try` block is printed.

38. C. The code compiles without issue. Line 8 calls the `compute()` method, which throws a `NullPointerException` on line 4. This is caught in the `main()` method on line 9, since `NullPointerException` is a subclass of `RuntimeException`, printing `zero` followed by a stack trace to the caller and making option C correct.

39. F. The `UnsupportedOperationException` class is an unchecked exception that is a direct child of `RuntimeException`. For this reason, we can eliminate any answer that does not inherit from `RuntimeException` including options A and E. Options C and D are close, but `UnsupportedOperationException` is a direct subclass of `RuntimeException`. Option B is incorrect because `RuntimeException` is a subclass, not a superclass, of `Exception`. The correct diagram would be to reverse option B and put `RuntimeException` at position 1, and `Exception` at position 2. Since this is not available, option F is correct.

40. E. The `close()` method in each of the resources throws an `Exception`, which must be handled or declared in the `main()` method. The `catch` block supports `TimeException`, but it is too narrow to catch `Exception`. Since there are no other `catch` blocks present and the `main()` method does not declare `Exception`, the try-with-resources statement does not compile, and option E is the correct answer. If the `catch` block were modified to handle `Exception` instead of `TimeException`, the code would compile without issue and print 3215 at runtime, closing the resources in the reverse order in which they were declared.

41. B,D,E. Checked exceptions are commonly used to notify or force a caller to deal with an expected type of problem, such as the inability to write a file to the file system, and give them the opportunity to recover without terminating the program. For these reasons, options B, D, and E are correct. Option A is incorrect as a corrupted JVM is likely an `Error` that cannot be recovered from. Option C is also incorrect, as some problems should result in the application terminating. Finally, option F is incorrect and is ideally never the motivation for adding a checked exception to a method signature!

42. C. A multi-catch block cannot contain two exceptions in which one is a subtype of the other, since it is a redundant expression. Since `CarCrash` is a subclass of `RuntimeException` and `RuntimeException` is a subclass of `Exception`, line w3 contains a compilation error, making option C the correct answer. The rest of the lines of code do not contain any compilation errors.

43. A,B,F. Since `IOException` and `SQLException` are checked exceptions, Happy and Grumpy are checked exceptions, respectively, making options A and F correct. Since Dopey inherits Grumpy, option B is also a checked exception. Options C and D are unchecked exceptions because those classes inherit `RuntimeException`. Option E is also an unchecked exception because all `Error` classes are unchecked.

44. E. The code compiles without issue, so option D is incorrect. The key here is noticing that count, an instance variable, is initialized with a value of 0. The `getDuckies()` method ends up computing 5/0, which leads to an unchecked `ArithmeticException` at runtime, making option E the correct answer.

45. B,D,F. An `IllegalArgumentException` is an unchecked exception. It can be handled or declared in the method in which it is defined, although it is optional and not required. For this reason, options B, D, and F are correct, and options A and C are incorrect. Option E is incorrect, as there is no requirement where in a method this exception can be thrown.

46. D. While a `catch` block is permitted to include an embedded try-catch block, the issue here is that the variable name e is already used by the first `catch` block. In the second `catch` block, it is equivalent to declaring a variable e twice. For this reason, line z2 does not compile, and option D is the correct answer. If a different variable name was used for either `catch` block, then the code would compile without issue, printing Failed at runtime.

47. D. The declaration of `IncidentReportException` does not provide any constructors, which means only the default constructor is available. Since the code attempts to pass an `IOException` as a parameter, the `main()` method does not compile, so the correct answer is option D.

48. A. The try-catch block already catches `Exception`, so the correct answer would be the one that is not a subtype of `Exception`. In this case, `Error` extends `Throwable` and is the only choice that allows the code to compile, making option A correct.

49. F. The application does not compile because the `roar()` method in the `BigCat` class uses `throw` instead of `throws`, making option F correct. Note that if the correct keyword was used, then the code would compile and print `Meow` at runtime.

50. D. The `MissedCallException` is a checked exception since it extends `Exception` and does not inherit `RuntimeException`. For this reason, the first `catch` block fails to compile, since the compiler detects that it is not possible to throw this checked exception inside the `try` block, making option D the correct answer. Note that if `MissedCallException` was changed to extend the unchecked `RuntimeException` class, then the code would compile and the `RuntimeException` from the `finally` block would replace the `ArrayIndexOutOfBoundsException` from the `try` block and `Text` would be in the message to the caller.

51. A. Both `IllegalArgumentException` and `NullPointerException` inherit `RuntimeException`, but neither inherits from each other. For this reason, they can be listed in `catch` blocks in either order, making option A the correct statement.

52. C. While `RuntimeException` is broader than `IllegalArgumentException`, the restriction on overriding methods applies only to checked exceptions, not unchecked exceptions. In other words, the code would not compile if both of the exceptions were checked. Since they are unchecked, though, the method override is valid. The program compiles and prints `thud?` at runtime, making option C correct.

53. C. The `Closeable` interface defines a `close()` method that throws `IOException`. The overridden implementation of `MyDatabase`, which implements `Closeable`, declares a `SQLException`. This is a new checked exception not found in the inherited method signature. Therefore, the method override is invalid, and the `close()` method in `MyDatabase` does not compile, making option C the correct answer.

54. C. Custom exception classes may simply use the default constructor. It is also common to override the constructors that take a single `Exception` or a single `String`, making option C correct.

55. A. While this code looks a bit strange, it does compile. An exception can be passed to a method or set as the return type of a method. In this case, the exception passed to the `order()` method is thrown and caught on line h4. The output is just the name of the class, making option A correct.

56. C,F. A Java application tends to only throw an `Error` when the application has encountered an unrecoverable error. Failure of a user to sign in or register are common occurrences, making options A, B, and E incorrect. On the other hand, calling a method infinitely can lead to an unrecoverable `StackOverflowError`, making option C correct. Option D uses the word temporarily, meaning the network connection could come back up allowing the application to recover. Option F is the other correct answer. Over time, failing to release database connections could result in the application running out of available database connections or worse, out of memory, and being unable to recover.

57. E. The code does not compile because `john` is declared in the try-with-resources statement and not accessible in the `finally` block.

58. B. The code does compile, making options C and D incorrect. The `catch` block successfully catches the `IncidentReportException` and prints the `IOException` passed to its constructor, making option B the correct answer.

59. B. The code compiles without issue, making option C incorrect. In the `climb()` method, two exceptions are thrown. The `RuntimeException` thrown in the `try` block is considered the primary exception, while the `FallenException` thrown by the `close()` method is suppressed. For this reason, `java.lang.RuntimeException` is reported to the caller in the `main()` method, and option B is the correct answer.

60. D. For this question, notice that all the exceptions thrown or caught are unchecked exceptions. First, the `ClassCastException` is thrown in the `try` block and caught by the second `catch` block, since it inherits from `RuntimeException`, not `IllegalArgumentException`. Next, a `NullPointerException` is thrown, but before it can be returned the `finally` block is executed and a `RuntimeException` replaces it. The application exits, and the caller sees the `RuntimeException` in the stack trace, making option D the correct answer. If the `finally` block did not throw any exceptions, then `NullPointerException` would be printed at runtime.

Chapter 5: Working with Arrays and Collections

1. A. While the `ArrayList` is declared with an initial capacity of one element, it is free to expand as more elements are added. Each of the three calls to the `add()` method adds an element to the end of the `ArrayList`. The `remove()` method call deletes the element at index 2, which is `Art`. Therefore, option A is correct.

2. B. The array brackets, `[]`, are not allowed to appear before the type, making the `lions` declaration incorrect. When using an array initializer with braces, `{}`, you are not allowed to specify the size separately. The size is inferred from the number of elements listed. Therefore, `tigers` and `ohMy` are incorrect. When you're not using an array initializer, the size is required. An empty array initializer is allowed. Option B is correct because only `bears` is legal.

3. E. When declaring a class that uses generics, you must specify a name for the formal type parameter. Java uses the standard rules for naming a variable or class. A question mark is not allowed in a variable name, making options A and C incorrect. While it is common practice to use a single uppercase letter for the type parameter, this is not required. It certainly isn't a good idea to use existing class names like the `News` class being declared here or the `Object` class built into Java. However, both are allowed, making option E the answer.

4. B,E. Option B is one answer because line 26 does not compile. The ? wildcard cannot be used when instantiating a type on the right side of the assignment operator. The other lines do compile. Additionally, option E is correct because lines 28 and 29 use autoboxing. They convert a primitive to a wrapper object, in this case `Double` and `Integer`, respectively. Line 30 is correct and does not use autoboxing. It places a `null` reference as the `Integer` object.

5. C. A two-dimensional array is declared by listing both sizes in separate pairs of brackets, `[]`. Option C correctly shows this syntax.

6. D. The `offer()` method inserts an element at the end of the queue. This means the queue contains `[snowball, minnie, sugar]`. The `peek()` method returns the element at the front of the queue without removing it. Therefore, `snowball` is printed twice, but the queue remains with three elements. This matches option D.

7. E. Notice how there is unnecessary information in this description. The fact that patrons select books by name is irrelevant. The checkout line is a perfect example of a `Queue`. We need easy access to one end of the `Queue` for patrons to add themselves to the queue. We also need easy access for patrons to get off the queue when it is their turn. Since a `LinkedList` is a `Queue`, this narrows down the answer to options D, E, and F.

The book lookup by ISBN is a lookup by key. We need a map for this. A `HashMap` is probably better here, but it isn't a choice. So the answer is option E, which does include both a `Queue` and a `Map`.

8. B. Line 8 attempts to store a `String` in an array meant for an `int`. Line 8 does not compile, and option B is correct.

9. B. Options C and D are incorrect because the method signature is incorrect. Unlike the `equals()` method, the method in `Comparator<String>` takes the type being compared as the parameters when using generics. Option A is a valid `Comparator<String>`. However, it sorts in ascending order by length. Option B is correct. If `s1` is three characters and `s2` is one character, it returns `-2`. The negative value says that `s1` should sort first, which is correct, because we want the longest `String` first.

10. B. In Java, arrays are indexed starting with `0`. While it is unusual for the loop to start with `1`, this does not cause an error. It does cause the code to output six lines instead of seven, since the loop doesn't cover the first array element. Therefore, option B is correct.

11. C. Java talks about the collections framework, but the `Map` interface does not actually implement the `Collection` interface. `TreeMap` has different methods than the other options. It cannot fill in the blank, so option C is correct.

12. B,F. In Java, `Arrays.binarySearch()` returns a positive `int`, representing the index of a match if one is found. An `int` cannot be stored in a `String` variable, making option F one of the answers. When using the correct data type and searching for `seed`, we find it at index 1. Therefore, option B is the other correct answer.

13. C. As with a one-dimensional array, the brackets, `[]`, must be after the type, making `alpha` and `beta` illegal declarations. For a multidimensional array, the brackets may be before and/or after the variable name. They do not need to be in the same place. Therefore, `gamma`, delta, and epsilon are correct. Finally, var can be used as a local variable, but not with array brackets after it. The code would compile if it said var zeta. Since three options are correct, the answer is option C.

14. **A.** First the code creates an ArrayList of three elements. Then the list is transformed into a TreeSet. Since sets are not allowed to have duplicates, the set only has two elements. Remember that a TreeSet is sorted, which means that the first element in the TreeSet is 3. Therefore, option A is correct.

15. **D,E.** Three dots in a row is a varargs parameter. While varargs is used like an array from within the method, it can only be used as a method parameter. This syntax is not allowed for a variable, causing a compiler error on line 5. Line 6 does not compile because linearSort() should be sort(). On line 7, the method name is also incorrect. The search() should be binarySearch(). Finally, line 9 uses size() instead of length. Since there are four errors, option D is correct. If all these errors were corrected, original[0] would cause an exception because the array is empty. Therefore, option E is also correct.

16. **A,D,F.** Line 20 does not compile for a Map because it requires two generic types. Line 23 does not compile for a Set because the elements are unordered and do not have an index. This makes options D and F correct. Additionally, option A is correct because line 23 replaces the second element with a new value, making chars contain [a, c]. Then line 24 removes the first element, making it just [c]. There is only one element, but it is not the value b.

17. **E.** The Magazine class doesn't implement Comparable<Magazine>. It happens to implement the compareTo() method properly, but it is missing actually writing implements Comparable. Since TreeSet doesn't look to see if the object can be compared until runtime, this code throws a ClassCastException when TreeSet calls add(), so option E is correct.

18. **B.** Arrays begin with an index of 0. This array is a 3x3 array, making only indexes 0, 1, and 2 valid. Line r2 throws an ArrayIndexOutOfBoundsException. Therefore, option B is correct.

19. **D.** The generic declaration on line R is valid. It sets a constraint on the generic type used when declaring a Fur object. Lines S and T compile as they meet this constraint. However, line U has a problem since Sat does not extend Mammal. Since this line does not compile, option D is the answer.

20. **C.** Line 18 puts 3 in nums since it is the smaller value. Since a Set must have unique elements, line 19 does not add another value to nums. Line 20 adds the final value of 16. The set has a total of two elements, 3 and 16. A HashSet does not commit to an output order, making option C correct.

21. **B.** Note that LinkedList is a Deque, or double-ended queue. This lets us add elements at both ends. The offer() method adds an element to the back of the queue. After line 7 completes, the queue contains 18 and 5 in that order. The push() method adds an element to the front of the queue. How rude! The element 13 pushes past everyone on the line. After line 8 completes, the queue now contains 13, 18, and 5, in that order. Then we get the first two elements from the front, which are 13 and 18, making option B correct.

22. E,F. TreeMap and TreeSet keep track of sort order when you insert elements. TreeMap sorts the keys and TreeSet sorts the objects in the set. This makes options E and F correct. Note that you have the option of having JellyBean implement Comparable, or you can pass a Comparator to the constructor of TreeMap or TreeSet. Option D is trying to trick you as SortedArray is not a class or interface in the collections framework.

23. B. Array indices start with 0, making options C and D incorrect. The length attribute refers to the number of elements in an array. It is one past the last valid array index. Therefore, option B is correct.

24. B. Since the method does not have any declared exceptions, it can only throw unchecked exceptions. Option B is the only one that requires the elements of coll to be RuntimeException or any subclasses.

25. D. Options A and B show that the brackets, [], can be before or after the variable name and produce the same array. Option C specifies the same array the long way with two arrays of length 1. Option D is the answer because it is different than the others. It instead specifies an array of length 1 where that element is of length 2.

26. D. Java requires having a sorted array before calling the binarySearch() method. You do not have to call Arrays.sort to perform the sort, though. This array happens to already be sorted, so it meets the precondition. The target string of "Linux" is the first element in the array. Since Java uses zero-based indexing, search is 0. The Arrays.mismatch() method returns −1 if the arrays are the same and returns the index of the first difference if they are not. In our cases, mismatch1 is 0 because the first element differs, and mismatch2 is −1 because the arrays are the same. This makes option D the correct answer.

27. D. The Comic<C> interface declares a formal type parameter. This means that a class implementing it needs to specify this type. The code on line 21 compiles because the lambda reference supplies the necessary context making option A incorrect. Option B declares a generic class. While this doesn't tell us the type is Snoopy, it punts the problem to the caller of the class. The declaration of c2 on line 22 compiles because it supplies the type, making option B incorrect. The code on line 23 compiles because the SnoopyClass itself supplies the type, making option C incorrect.

Option D has a problem. SnoopyClass and SnoopyComic appear similar. However, SnoopyComic refers to C. This type parameter exists in the interface. It isn't available in the class because the class has said it is using Snoopy as the type. Since the SnoopyComic class itself doesn't compile, the line with c4 can't instantiate it, and option D is the answer.

28. C. When implementing Comparable<Truck>, you implement the compareTo() method. Since this is an instance method, it already has a reference to itself and only needs the item it is comparing. Only one parameter is specified, and option C is correct. By contrast, the Comparator<Truck> interface uses the compare() method, and the method takes two parameters.

29. B. There is nothing wrong or tricky about this code. It correctly creates a seven-element array. The loop starts with index 0 and ends with index 6. Each line is correctly output. Therefore, option B is correct.

30. A,B. Options E and F are incorrect because they do not compile. `List` is an interface and does not have a constructor. `ArrayList` has a constructor but not one that takes individual elements as parameters. Options C and D are incorrect because `List.of()` creates an immutable list. Trying to change one of its values causes an exception at runtime.

Options A and B are correct. Since we are creating the list from an array, it is a fixed size. We are allowed to change elements. When successfully completing this code, `museums` is [`Art`, `Science`] for both solutions.

31. F. The `Wash` class takes a formal type parameter named T. Options A and E show the best ways to call it. These option declare a generic reference type that specifies the type is `String`. Option A uses local variable type inference, whereas option E uses the diamond syntax to avoid redundantly specifying the type of the assignment.

Options B, C, and D show that you can omit the generic type in the reference and still have the code compile. You do get a compiler warning scolding you for having a raw type. But compiler warnings do not prevent compilation. With the raw type, the compiler treats T as if it is of type `Object`. That is OK in this example, because the only method we call is `toString()` implicitly when printing the value. Since `toString()` is defined on the `Object` class, we are safe, and options B, C, and D work. Since all can fill in the blank, option F is the answer.

32. B. Options A, C, and D represent 3×3 2D arrays. Option B best represents the array in the code. It shows there are three different arrays of different lengths.

33. B,E. The goal is to write code that sorts in descending order. Option A sorts ascendingly and option B sorts descendingly. Similarly, option C sorts ascendingly and option E sorts descendingly. Option D attempts to call the `reverse()` method, which is not defined.

34. B. When creating an array object, a set of elements or size is required. Therefore, `lion` and `bear` are incorrect. The brackets containing the size are required to be after the type, making `ohMy` incorrect. The only one that is correct is `tiger`, making the correct answer option B.

35. C. This code creates a two-dimensional array of size 1×2. Lines `m1` and `m2` assign values to both elements in the outer array. Line `m3` attempts to reference the second element of the outer array. Since there is no such position, it throws an exception, and option C is correct.

36. C. All four of these return immutable collections. Options B and D take a varargs rather than a `List`. Option A returns a `List`, not a `Set`. Option C meets both our requirements.

37. C,E. The code sorts before calling the `binarySearch()` method, so it meets the precondition for that method. The target string of `"RedHat"` is not found in the sorted array. If it were found, it would be between the second and third elements. The rule is to take the negative index of where it would be inserted and subtract 1. It would need to be inserted as the third element. Since indexes are zero-based, this is index 2. We take the negative, which is -2, and subtract 1, giving −3.

The target string of `"Mac"` is the second element in the sorted array. Since array indices begin with zero, the second position is index 1. This makes the answer options C and E.

38. D. Line x1 returns a Set of map entries. Set does not have a getKey() method, so line x2 does not compile, and option D is the answer.

39. A,C,D. The offerLast() and offer() methods insert an element at the back of the queue, while the offerFirst() method inserts the element at the front of the queue. This means the queue initially contains [snowball, sugar, minnie]. The poll() method returns the element at the front of the queue and removes it. In this case, it prints snowball, and the queue is reduced from three elements to [sugar, minnie]. Then, the removeFirst() method removes sugar, leaving the queue as only containing [minnie]. Further, the queue becomes one smaller, and 1 is printed. These are options A, C, and D.

40. B. All of the variables except nums2b point to a 4D array. Don't create a 4D array in practice; it's confusing. The options show that the brackets, [], can be before or after the variable in any combination. Option B is the answer because nums2b points to a 3D array. It has only three pairs of brackets before the variable and none after. By comparison, nums2a has three pairs of brackets before the variable and the fourth pair of brackets after.

41. C. Option E is the longest way to specify this code. Options A and D shorten it by using the diamond operator (<>). Options A and B shorten it using var. Option C does not compile because the diamond operator cannot be used on the left side of the assignment.

42. C. The Arrays.compare() method looks at each element in turn. Since the first elements are different, we get the result of comparing them. In this case, we get a positive number because 3 is larger than 2, and option C is correct.

43. E. List.of() makes an immutable list. Attempting to sort throws an exception so option E is the answer. If we were calling, Arrays.asList() instead, option C would be the answer because it is the only option to sort ascendingly by length.

44. C. Line 20 creates a List<Character>. Line 21 does not compile because it is the wrong type. Char should be Character. Line 22 uses unboxing to get a primitive. Line 23 also compiles because Character can be unboxed and widened to int automatically. However, line 24 does not compile as Integer and Character are not in the same class hierarchy. The Character value cannot be unboxed, widened to int, and then autoboxed as Integer. Finally, line 25 is correct as Character is a subclass of Object. Since two lines of code fail to compile, option C is the answer.

45. B. This one is tricky since the array brackets, [], are split up. This means that bools is a 3D array reference. The brackets both before and after the variable name count. For moreBools, it is only a 2D array reference because there are only two pairs of brackets next to the type. In other words, boolean[][] applies to both variables. Then bools gets another dimension from the brackets right after the variable name. However, moreBools stays at 2D, making option B correct.

46. E. A custom sort order is specified using a Comparator to sort in descending order. However, this Comparator is not passed when searching. When a different sort order is used for searching and sorting, the result is undefined. Therefore, option E is correct.

47. C. The `binarySearch()` method requires a sorted array in order to return a correct result. If the array is not sorted, the results of a binary search are undefined.

48. B,F. The `<>` is known as the diamond operator. Here, it works as a shortcut to avoid repeating the generic type twice for the same declaration. On the right side of the expression, this is a handy shortcut. Java still needs the type on the left side, so there is something to infer. Positions Q and S are on the right side, making option B correct. In this question, the generic type is never specified, so it is `Object`. Since it is not `String`, option F is correct.

49. B,D. Since no arguments are passed from the command line, this creates an empty array. Sorting an empty array is valid and results in an empty array printed on line 6. Then line 7 attempts to access an element of the empty array and throws an `ArrayIndexOutOfBoundsException`. Therefore, options B and D are correct.

50. A. The generic declaration on line R is not valid due to the question mark (`?`) wildcard. While a question mark is allowed on the left side of a declaration, it is not allowed when specifying a constraint on a class. Since line R does not compile, option A is the answer.

51. E. Line 6 assigns an `int` to a cell in a 2D array. This is fine. Line 7 casts to a general `Object[]`. This is dangerous, but legal. Why is it dangerous, you ask? That brings us to line 8. The compiler can't protect us from assigning a `String` to the `int[]` because the reference is more generic. Therefore, line 8 throws an `ArrayStoreException` because the type is incorrect, and option E is correct. You couldn't have assigned an `int` on line 8 either because `obj[3]` is really an `int[]` behind the scenes and not an `int`.

52. D. `TreeSet` does not allow `null` values because it needs to compare the values. While `HashSet` does call `hashCode()`, it knows to skip that call if the value is `null`. `ArrayList` and `LinkedList` do not make method calls on their contents. Three of the four allow inserting `null` values, making option D the answer.

53. B. Unfortunately, you do have to memorize two facts about sort order. First, numbers sort before letters. Second, uppercase sorts before lowercase. Since, the first value is 3 and the last is `three`, option B is correct.

54. C. Since the brackets in the declaration are before the variable names, the variable type `boolean[][][]` applies to both variables. Therefore, both `bools` and `moreBools` can reference a 3D array.

55. D. Line 25 does not compile, making option D the answer. On an `ArrayList`, the method to get the number of elements is `size()`. The `length()` method is used for a `String` or `StringBuilder`. If this were fixed, the answer would be option E. Line 23 empties the `ArrayList`. Then line 24 attempts to access an index that is not present.

56. C. The `?` is an unbounded wildcard. It is used in variable references but is not allowed in declarations. In a `static` method, the type parameter specified inside the `<>` is used in the rest of the method declaration. Since it needs an actual name, options A and B are incorrect. We need to specify a type constraint so we can call the `add()` method. Regardless of whether the type is a class or interface, Java uses the `extends` keyword for generics. Therefore, option D is incorrect, and option C is the answer.

57. D. Java requires having a sorted array before calling the `binarySearch()` method. Since the array is not sorted, the result is undefined, and option D is correct. It may happen that you get 1 as the result, but this behavior is not guaranteed. You need to know for the exam that this is undefined even if you happen to get the "right" answer.

58. A. A multidimensional array is created with multiple sets of size parameters. The first line should be `char[] ticTacToe = new char[3][3];`. Therefore, option A is the answer.

59. B. On a stream, the `filter()` method only keeps values matching the lambda. The `removeIf()` does the reverse on a `Collection` and keeps the elements that do not match. In this case, that is `Austin` and `Boston`, so option B is correct.

60. D. The `names.length` value is the number of elements in the array. The last valid index in the array is one less than `names.length`. In Java, arrays do not resize automatically. Therefore, the code throws an `ArrayIndexOutOfBoundsException`, and option D is correct.

61. A. An `ArrayList` expands automatically when it is full. An array does not, making option A the answer. The other three statements are true of both an array and an `ArrayList`.

62. C. The `forEach()` method that takes one parameter is defined on the `Collection` interface allowing options A and B to fill in the blank. Option C requires you to notice that only one generic parameter is passed. A `Map` needs two parameters, so option C is the answer.

63. D. Option A is incorrect because `coll` could be any type, which doesn't necessarily allow exceptions to be added. Option B is incorrect because neither `add()` method compiles. We could have `Collection<IllegalStateException>` as a parameter. That would not allow either type to be added. Finally, option C is incorrect as the second `add()` method does not compile because broader types than the generic allows are a problem when adding to `coll`. Therefore, option D is the answer.

64. A,D. Lines 35–38 create a `Map` with three key/value pairs. Lines 40–43 sort just the values ascendingly by year. Lines 45 and 48 show you can assign the `Integer` values to an `int` via unboxing or an `Integer` directly. Line 46 shows the values are properly sorted, making option A correct. Finally, line 48 throws an exception because `sorted.size()` returns 3 and the maximum index in the `List` is 2. This makes option D correct as well.

65. C. Arrays are indexed using numbers, not strings, making options A and B incorrect. Since array indexes are zero-based, option C is the answer.

66. B. This code shows a proper implementation of `Comparable`. It has the correct method signature. It compares the magazine names in alphabetical order. Remember that uppercase letters sort before lowercase letters. Since `Newsweek` starts with uppercase, option B is correct.

67. B. Options A and C are incorrect because a generic type cannot be assigned to another direct type unless you are using upper or lower bounds in that statement. Now, we just have to decide whether a lower or upper bound is correct for the `T` formal type parameter in `Wash`. The clue is that the method calls `size()`. This method is available on `Collection`, and all classes that extend/implement it. Therefore, option B is correct.

68. D. In Java, arrays are indexed starting with 0. While it is unusual for the loop to start with 1, this does not cause an error. What does cause an error is the loop ending at `data.length`, because the `<=` operator is used instead of the `<` operator. The last loop index is 6, not 7. On the last iteration of the loop, the code throws an `ArrayIndexOutOfBoundsException`. Therefore, option D is correct.

69. B. This array has two elements, making `listing.length` output 2. While each array element does not have the same size, this does not matter because we are only looking at the first element. The first element has one. This makes the answer option B.

70. E. The `addFirst()` and `addLast()` methods are on the `Deque` interface. While `ArrayDeque` does implement this interface, it also implements `Queue`. Since the q variable is of type `Queue`, these methods do not compile, and option E is the answer. If the correct interface were used, `minnie minnie 3` would be printed.

71. D. The code does compile, making option A incorrect. Line 13 creates a fixed-size list. While we are using `var`, the type is `List<Integer>`. Line 14 successfully changes the contents of the list to `[3, null, 4]`. Line 15 automatically unboxes to the primitive 3. Line 16 has a problem. The list has a `null` value at index 1. This cannot be unboxed to a primitive and throws a `NullPointerException`. Therefore, option D is the answer. If line 16 were commented out, line 17 would have thrown an exception because Java uses zero based indexes, and there is no element at index 3.

72. F. We need to first sort descendingly and then ascendingly by first character. Options A, B, and C are missing the logic to sort descendingly. Options D and E call the `andCompare()` and `thenCompare()` methods, which do not exist. Option F is correct.

73. B,C. Array indexes begin with zero. `FirstName` is the name of the class, not an argument. The first argument is `Wolfie`, making option B correct. There is not a second argument, and the array is of size 1, so option C is also correct.

74. C. This one is tricky. Line 11 creates an `ArrayList` with a generic type `Object` rather than `Integer`. This is allowed since we aren't trying to assign any of the values to an `int` or `Integer` after getting them from `pennies`. This gives us the list `[1, 2, 3, 4]`.

The next trick is that there are two `remove()` methods available on `ArrayList`. One removes an element by index and takes an `int` parameter. The other removes an element by value and takes an `Object`. On line 16, the `int` primitive is a better match, and the element with index 2 is removed, which is the value of 3. At this point, we have `[1, 2, 4]`.

Then on line 17, the other `remove()` method is called because we are explicitly using the wrapper object. This deletes the object that is equal to 1, and now we have `[2, 4]`. This brings us to option C as the answer.

75. C,D. The code will output 0 when the array is sorted in ascending order since `flower` will be first. Option C is the most straightforward way of doing this, making it one of the answers. Reversing the order of the variables or adding a negative sign sorts in descending order makes options A, B, E, F, and G incorrect. Doing both is a complicated way of sorting in ascending order, making option D the other correct answer.

76. B. The elements of the array are of type `String` rather than `int`. Therefore, we use alphabetical order when sorting. The character 1 sorts before the character 9, alphabetically making option A incorrect. Shorter strings sort before longer strings when all the other characters are the same, making option B the answer.

77. D. This code is correct. Line `r1` correctly creates a 2D array. The next three lines correctly assign a value to an array element. Line `r3` correctly outputs `3 in a row!`

78. A,D,F. Line 40 does not compile since `getOrDefault()` requires two parameters. This makes option A the first answer. The rest of the code does compile. Option D is the next answer because `getOrDefault()` returns the value from the map when the key is present. Finally, option F is correct because `getOrDefault()` returns the second parameter when the key is not present.

79. E. Lines 18 and 19 create a list with five elements. Line 20 makes a set with the same five elements. Line 21 does not change the contents of the set since sets must have unique elements. The loop on line 22 tries to delete elements but instead throws a `ConcurrentModificationException`, making option E the answer.

80. C. Option C is correct because all the types being added are of type `Exception` or direct subclasses.

Chapter 6: Working with Streams and Lambda Expressions

1. F. The source is the first operation, and the terminal operation comes last, making option F the answer. You need to know this terminology.

2. B. The lambda expression `s -> true` is valid, making options A, C, and D incorrect. Parentheses, `()`, are not required on the left-hand side if there is only one variable. Braces, `{}`, are not required if the right-hand side is a single expression. Parameter data types are only required if the data type for at least one parameter is specified; otherwise, none are required. The remaining choice, the arrow operator, `->`, is required for all lambda expressions, making option B the correct answer.

3. C. The `Supplier` functional interface does not take any inputs, while the `Consumer` functional interface does not return any data. This behavior extends to the primitive versions of the functional interfaces, making option C the correct answer. Option A is incorrect because `IntConsumer` takes a value, while `LongSupplier` returns a value. Options B and D are incorrect because `Function` and `UnaryOperator` both take an input and produce a value.

4. F. A `List` instance, which inherits the `Collection` interface, does not have a `parallel()` method. Instead, `parallelStream()` must be used, making option F correct. If the code was corrected to use `parallelStream()`, then the first and third streams would be consistently printed in the same order. Remember that the `forEachOrdered()` method forces parallel streams to run in sequential order. The order of the second operation would be unknown ahead of time, since it uses a parallel stream.

5. A,E. The `UnaryOperator` and `BiFunction` return a generic argument, such as `Double`, making options A and E correct. Option B is incorrect because all predicate functions return `boolean`. Option C is incorrect because `BiOperator` does not exist in the `java.util.function` package. The correct name is `BinaryOperator`. Option D is incorrect because all consumer functions return `void`. Finally, option F is incorrect because `BiSupplier` does not exist in the `java.util.function` package. Supplier functions return values, and Java does not support methods with more than one return type.

6. B. The stream pipeline is correct and filters all values out that are 10 characters or smaller. Only `San Francisco` is long enough, so c is 1. The `stream()` call creates a new object, so stream operations do not affect the original list. Since the original list is still 3 elements, option B is correct.

7. B,C,E. Interface X is tricky. If it returned a `boolean` primitive, option A would be correct as `Predicate` returns a `boolean`. However, it returns a wrapper object, so it has to be a `Supplier`, making option B the answer instead.

Interface Y and Z are more straightforward as a `Comparator` and `Consumer`, respectively. This makes options C and E the final two answers.

8. C. Option A is incorrect because a pipeline still runs if the source doesn't generate any items and the rest of the pipeline is correct. Granted, some of the operations have nothing to do, but control still passes to the terminal operation. Option B is incorrect because intermediate operations are optional. Option C is the answer. The terminal operation triggers the pipeline to run. Option D is incorrect because the code would not compile at all if the version of Java were too old.

9. A. The `LongSupplier` interface does not take any input, making option D incorrect. It also uses the method name `getAsLong()`. The rest of the functional interfaces all take a `long` value but vary on the name of the `abstract` method they use. `LongFunction` contains `apply()` and `LongPredicate` contains `test()`, making options B and C, respectively, incorrect. That leaves us with `LongConsumer`, which contains `accept()`, making option A the correct answer.

10. F. The correct method to obtain an equivalent sequential stream of an existing stream is `sequential()`, which is inherited by any class that implements `BaseStream<T>`. Since this isn't an option, option F is correct. Note that `unordered()` creates a stream that can be evaluated in any order, but it can still be processed in a sequential or parallel stream.

11. B. Option A is incorrect because the lambda expression is missing a semicolon (`;`) at the end of the `return` statement. Option C is incorrect because the local variable `test` is used without being initialized. Option D is also incorrect. The parentheses are required on the left-hand side of the lambda expression when there is more than one value or a data type is specified. Option B is the correct answer and the only valid lambda expression.

12. **B,D.** The second line throws a `NullPointerException` when you pass a `null` reference to the `of()` method. The others compile and run successfully, making option B correct. The first and third lines return `false` because they represent an empty `Optional`. This makes option D the other answer.

13. **D.** Both are functional interfaces in the `java.util.function` package, making option A true. Additionally, both lack parameters, making option B true. The major difference between the two is that `Supplier<Double>` takes the generic type `Double`, while the other does not take any generic type and instead uses the primitive `double`. For this reason, options C and E are true statements. For `Supplier<Double>` in option C, remember that the returned `double` value can be implicitly autoboxed to `Double`. Option D is the correct answer. Lambdas for `Supplier<Double>` can return a `null` value since `Double` is an object type, while lambdas for `DoubleSupplier` cannot; they can only return primitive `double` values.

14. **A.** Even though a parallel stream is used, the `forEachOrdered()` method forces the stream to operate in the order of its data source. The code compiles and runs without issue printing 12345 every time, and making option A correct. If `forEach()` was used instead, then the output would vary at runtime.

15. **C.** The first line that contains the lambda expression will actually compile with any of the functional interfaces listed in the options. The stream operation, though, will compile only if `ToIntFunction<Integer>` is used. It requires this functional interface, which takes a generic argument and returns `int`. For this reason, option C is correct. Option F is incorrect because `sum()` on an `IntStream` returns an `int`, not an `OptionalInt`. Note that the `peek()` operations in this stream have no effect.

16. **E.** Option A is incorrect because `anyMatch()` returns a `boolean`. Option B is incorrect because `findAny()` might not return 1. The result could be any of the three numbers. Option C is incorrect because there is no `first()` method available as a terminal operation. Option D is tempting because there is a `min()` method. However, since we are working with a `Stream` (not a primitive stream like `IntStream`), this method requires a `Comparator` as a parameter. Therefore, option E is the answer.

17. **D.** Line 8 does not compile. `String::new` is a constructor reference. This constructor reference is equivalent to writing the lambda `() -> new String()`. It participates in deferred execution. When it is executed later, it will return a `String`. It does not return a `String` on line 8, though. The method reference is a `Supplier<String>`, which cannot be stored in `list`. Since the code does not compile, option D is correct.

18. **C.** The lambda `(s,p) -> s+p` takes two arguments and returns a value. For this reason, options A and B are incorrect because `BiConsumer` does not return any values. Option E is also incorrect, since `Function` takes only one argument and returns a value. This leaves us with options C and D, which both use `BiFunction`, which takes two generic arguments and returns a generic value. Option D is incorrect because the datatype of the unboxed sum `s+q` is `int`, and `int` cannot be both autoboxed and implicitly cast to `Double`. Option C is correct. The sum `s+p` is of type `double`, and `double` can be autoboxed to `Double`.

19. D. The word *reduction* is used with streams for a terminal operation, so options A, B, and C are incorrect. Option E describes a valid terminal operation like `anyMatch()`, but is not a reduction. Option D is correct because a reduction has to look at each element in the stream to determine the result.

20. C,D. The class compiles and runs without throwing an exception, making option C correct and options A, B, and F incorrect. The class defines two values that are incremented by multiple threads in parallel. The first `IntStream` statement uses an atomic class to update a variable. Since updating an atomic numeric instance is thread-safe by design, the first number printed is always `100`, making option D correct. The second `IntStream` statement uses an `int` with the pre-increment operator (`++`), which is not thread-safe. It is possible two threads could update and set the same value at the same time, a form of race condition, resulting in a value less than `500` and making option E incorrect.

21. A. The `filter()` method either passes along a given element or doesn't, making options D, E, and F incorrect. The `flatMap()` method doesn't pass along any elements for empty streams. For nonempty streams, it flattens the elements, allowing it to return zero or more elements. This makes option B incorrect. Finally, the `map()` method applies a one-to-one function for each element. It has to return exactly one element, so option A is the correct answer.

22. A,B,D. To begin with, `ToDoubleBiFunction<T,U>` takes two generic inputs and returns a `double` value. Option A is correct because it takes an `Integer` and `Double` and returns a `Double` value that can be implicitly unboxed to `double`. Option B is correct because `long` can be implicitly cast to `double`. While we don't know the data types for the input arguments, we know that some values, such as using `Integer` for both, will work. Option C cannot be assigned and does not compile because the variable v is of type `Object` and `Object` does not have a `length()` method. Option D is correct. The variable y could be declared `Double` in the generic argument to the functional interface, making y/z a `double` return value. Option E is not correct because the lambda only has one parameter. Finally, option F is incorrect because the interface uses the class `Double` rather than primitive `double`.

23. C. The correct method to obtain an equivalent parallel stream of an existing stream is `parallel()`, which is inherited by any class that implements `BaseStream<T>`. For this reason, option C is correct.

24. A. The lambda is a `Function<Integer, ArrayList>`. We need a constructor reference that uses the `new` keyword where a method name would normally go in a method reference. It can implicitly take zero or one parameters just like a method reference. In this case, we have one parameter, which gets passed to the constructor. Option A is correct. Options B, C, and D use syntax that is not supported with method references.

25. C. The `average()` method returns an `OptionalDouble`. This reflects that it doesn't make sense to calculate an average when you don't have any numbers. Similarly, `max()` returns an `OptionalDouble` because there isn't a maximum of no number. By contrast, counting without any numbers gives the `long` number `0` and summing gives the `double` number `0.0`. Since only two methods matches the desired return type, option C is correct.

26. D,E. The `BiPredicate` interface takes two generic arguments and returns a `boolean` value. Next, `DoubleUnaryOperator` and `IntUnaryOperator` exist and transform values of type `double` and `int`, respectively. Last, `ToLongFunction` takes a generic argument and returns a `long` value. That leaves options D and E, which is the answer. While there are `ObjDoubleConsumer` and `ObjIntConsumer` functional interfaces, there is no such thing as `ObjectDoubleConsumer` or `ObjectIntConsumer`. Remember that `Object` is abbreviated to `Obj` in all functional interfaces in `java.util.function`.

27. A. The `findAny()` method can return the first, last, or any element of the stream, regardless of whether the stream is serial or parallel. While on serial streams this is likely to be the first element in the stream, on parallel streams the result is less certain. For this reason, option A is the correct answer. The `anyMatch()` and `count()` methods produce the same result, regardless of whether the stream is serial or parallel. The rest of the operations force the stream to behave in a sequential manner when applied to an ordered stream, even if it is parallel. Note that the behavior is not the same on an unordered stream. For example, `findFirst()` can return any element when applied to an unordered stream.

28. C. The result of the source and any intermediate operations are chained and eventually passed to the terminal operation. The terminal operation is where a nonstream result is generated, making option C correct.

29. C. The `groupingBy()` collector always returns a `Map` (or a specific implementation class of `Map`), so options D, E, and F are incorrect. The other two are definitely possible. To get one, you can group using a `Function` that returns an `Integer` such as `s.collect(groupingBy(String::length))`. To get the other, you need to group using a `Function` that returns a `Boolean` and specify the type, such as `s.collect(groupingBy(String::isEmpty, toCollection(HashSet::new)))`. Therefore, option C is correct.

30. F. The `flatMap()` method works with streams rather than collections. Line 18 is problematic because the return value is not a stream. Since the code does not compile, option F is correct. If the lambda was changed to `x -> x.stream()`, option B would be the answer.

31. E. Since no generic type is specified, `list` is a `LinkedList<Object>`. Line w compiles because no generic type is specified. However, Java only allows you to operate on a stream once. The final line of code throws an `IllegalStateException` because the stream has already been used up, making option D correct.

32. D. The code does not compile, so options A, B, and E are incorrect. The `IntUnaryOperator` functional interface is not generic, so the argument `IntUnaryOperator<Integer>` in the `takeTicket()` does not compile, making option D the correct answer. The lambda expression compiles without issue, making option C incorrect. If the generic argument `<Integer>` was dropped from the argument declaration, the class would compile without issue and output 51 at runtime, making option B the correct answer.

33. A,C,E. Options A, C, and E are the precise requirements for Java to perform a concurrent reduction using the `collect()` method, which takes a `Collector` argument. Recall from your studies that a `Collector` is considered concurrent and unordered if it has the `Collector.Characteristics` enum values CONCURRENT and UNORDERED, respectively. The rest of the options are not required for a parallel reduction.

34. C,E. While it is common for a `Predicate` to have a generic type, it is not required. However, it is treated like a `Predicate` of type `Object` if the generic type is missing. Since `startsWith()` does not exist on `Object`, line 28 does not compile.

Line 34 would be a correct lambda declaration in isolation. However, it uses the variable `s`, which is already taken from the `main()` method parameter. This causes a compiler error on line 34. These are the only two compiler errors, making option C correct. If `Predicate` were changed to `Predicate<String>` and lambda variable were changed to `x`, the `Consumer` would in fact print `pink`, making option E the other answer.

35. A. Option A is the correct answer because `BiPredicate` takes two generic types and returns a primitive `boolean` value. Option B is incorrect, since `CharSupplier` does not exist in `java.util.function`. Option C is also incorrect, since `LongFunction` takes a primitive `long` value and returns a generic type. Remember, Java only includes primitive functional interfaces that operate on `double`, `int`, or `long`. Option D is incorrect because `UnaryOperator` takes a generic type and returns a generic value. Finally, option E is incorrect because `TriDoublePredicate` is not a built-in functional interface.

36. B,E. An accumulator in a serial or parallel reduction should be associative and stateless. In a parallel reduction, problematic accumulators tend to produce more visible errors. Option A is not associative, since `(a-b)-c` is not the same as `a-(b-c)` for all values a, b, and c. Options C and D are incorrect because they represent stateful lambda expressions, which should be avoided especially on parallel streams. Option F doesn't even compile, since the return type is a `boolean`, not an `Integer`. That leaves us with the correct answers, options B and E. While these accumulators may not seem useful, they are both stateless and associative, which meets the qualifications for performing a reduction.

37. D. The `Optional` class has an `isPresent()` method that doesn't take any parameters. It returns a `boolean` and is commonly used in `if` statements. There is also an `ifPresent()` method that takes a `Consumer` parameter and runs it only if the `Optional` is nonempty. The methods `isNotNull()` and `forEach()` are not declared in `Optional`. Therefore, option D is correct.

38. B. The lambda is a `Supplier<Double>`. Since the `random()` method is `static`, we need a `static` method reference. It uses `::` to separate the class name and method name. Option B is correct. Options A, C, and D use syntax that is not supported with method references.

39. D. Options A and B are incorrect because they are not operations in a stream pipeline. A source and the terminal operation are required parts of a stream pipeline and must occur exactly once. The intermediate operation is optional. It can appear zero or more times. Since more than once falls within zero or more, option D is correct.

40. D. All of the code compiles. The first stream source has three elements. The intermediate operations both sort the elements of this stream and then we request one from `findAny()`. The `findAny()` method is not guaranteed to return a specific element. Since we are not using parallelization, it is highly likely that the code will print `a`. However, you need to know this is not guaranteed. Additionally, the stream on line 28 prints `Optional[a]`, `Optional[b]`, or `Optional[c]`. Since only lines 23–26 print a single character, option D is the answer.

41. E. First, the `forEach()` method requires a `Consumer` instance. Option D can be immediately discarded because `Supplier<Double>` does not inherit `Consumer`. For this same reason, option C is also incorrect. `DoubleConsumer` does not inherit from `Consumer`. In this manner, primitive functional interfaces cannot be used in the `forEach()` method. Option A seems correct, since `forEach()` does take a `Consumer` instance, but it is missing a generic argument. Without the generic argument, the lambda expression does not compile because the expression p<5 cannot be applied to an `Object`. Option B is also close, however, a `Double` cannot be passed to an `Integer`. The correct functional interface is `Consumer<Double>`, and since that is not available, option E is the correct answer.

42. A. Option A is the invalid lambda expression because the type is specified for the variable j, but not the variable k. The rest of the options are valid lambda expressions. To be a valid lambda expression, the type must be specified for all of the variables, as in option C, or none of them, as in options B and D.

43. B. The code compiles and runs without issue. The three-argument `reduce()` method returns a generic type, while the one-argument `reduce()` method returns an `Optional`. The `concat1()` method is passed an identity "a", which it applies to each element, resulting in the reduction to aCataHat. The lambda expression in the `concat2()` method reverses the order of its inputs, leading to a value of HatCat. For these reasons, option B is the correct answer.

44. C. `BiFunction<Double,Double,Double>` and `BinaryOperator<Double>` both take two `Double` input arguments and return a `Double` value, making them equivalent to one another. On the other hand, `DoubleFunction<Double>` takes a single `double` value and returns a `Double` value. For this reason, it is different from the other two, making option C correct and option D incorrect.

45. B,E. For a concurrent reduction, the underlying type should be a thread-safe collection. For this reason, option A is incorrect and option E is correct. The streams must all be parallel, making option B correct and option F incorrect. Options C and D are incorrect, as there is no two-argument version of `collect()` within the `Stream` interface.

46. E. Option A is the only one of the three options to compile. However, it results in no lines being output since none of the three strings is empty. Options B and C do not even compile because a method reference cannot have an operator next to it. Option D does not compile because String does not have an `isNotEmpty()` method. Therefore, option E is correct.

47. C. The source of this stream is infinite. Sorting something infinite never finishes, so the stream pipeline never completes. This corresponds to option C.

48. D. The code compiles and does not throw any exception at runtime, so options A and B are incorrect. The code snippet is serial, by default, so the order is predictable, making option F incorrect. The `peek()` method executes on each member of the pipeline, printing five numbers as the elements are then collected into a `List`, which gives us 345. They are then printed again, making the final output 345345 and option D correct.

49. C. The program does not compile, so option A is incorrect. The `Supplier` functional interface normally takes a generic argument, although generic types are not strictly required, since they are removed by the compiler. Therefore, line d1 compiles while triggering a compiler warning, and options B and D are incorrect. On the other hand, line d2 does cause a compiler error, because the lambda expression does not return a value. Therefore, it is not compatible with Supplier, making option C the correct answer.

50. B. First, the class uses a synchronized list, which is thread-safe and allows modification from multiple threads, making option E incorrect. The process generates a stream of numbers from 1 to 5 and sends them into a parallel stream where the map() is applied, possibly out of order. This results in elements being written to db in a random order. The stream then applies the forEachOrdered() method to its elements, which will force the parallel stream into a single-threaded state. At runtime, line p1 will print the results in order every time as 12345. On the other hand, since the elements were added to db in a random order, the output of line p2 is random and cannot be predicted ahead of time. Since the results may sometimes be the same, option B is the correct answer. Part of the reason that the results are indeterminate is that the question uses a stateful lambda expression, which, based on your studies, should be avoided!

51. B,F. Primitive streams, like LongStream, declare an average() method that returns an OptionalDouble object. This object declares a getAsDouble() method rather than a get() method. Therefore, option A is incorrect, and option B is correct.

    By contrast, the summary statistics classes provide getters in order to access the data. The getAverage() method returns a double and not an OptionalDouble, which makes option F correct. The other options do not compile.

52. D. Remember that all Supplier interfaces take zero parameters. For this reason, the third value in the table is 0, making options A, C, and E incorrect. Next, DoubleConsumer and IntFunction each take one value, double and int, respectively. On the other hand, ObjDoubleConsumer takes two values, a generic value and a double, and returns void. For this reason, option D is correct, and option B is incorrect.

53. F. All Consumer functional interfaces have a void return type. For this reason, the first and last values in the table are both void, making options A, B and C incorrect. IntFunction takes an int and returns a generic value, ruling out option D. Finally, LongSupplier does not take any values and returns a long value. For this reason, option E is incorrect, and option F is correct.

54. A. The code compiles and runs without issue. The JVM will fall back to a single-threaded process if all of the conditions for performing the parallel reduction are not met. The stream used in the main() method is not parallel, but the groupingByConcurrent() method can still be applied without throwing an exception at runtime. Although performance will suffer from not using a parallel stream, the application will still process the results correctly. Since the process groups the data by year, option A is the correct answer.

55. C. This code is almost correct. Calling two different streams is allowed. The code attempts to use a method reference when calling the forEach() method. However, it does not use the right syntax for a method reference. A double colon needs to be used. The code would need to be changed to System.out::println to work and print two lines for each call. Since it does not compile, option C is correct.

56. C. First, option A does not compile, since the variables p and q are reversed, making the return type of the method and usage of operators invalid. The first argument p is a `String` and q is an `int`, but the lambda expression reverses them, and the code does not compile. Option B also does not compile. The variable d is declared twice, first in the lambda argument list and then in the body of the lambda expression. The second declaration in the body of the lambda expression causes the compiler to generate a duplicate local variable message. Note that other than it being used twice, the expression is valid; the ternary operator is functionally equivalent to the `learn()` method in the `BiologyMaterial` class. Option C is the correct answer since it compiles and handles the input in the same way as the `learn()` method in the `BiologyMaterial` class. Option D compiles but does not return the same result.

57. A,F. This code does compile. Remember that imports are implied, including the `static` import for `Collectors`. The collector tries to use the number of characters in each stream element as the key in a map. This works fine for the first two elements, `speak` and `bark`, because they are of length 5 and 4, respectively. When it gets to `meow`, it sees another key of 4. The merge function says to use the first one, so it chooses `bark` for the value. Similarly, `growl` is 5 characters, but the first value of `speak` is used. There are only two distinct lengths, so option A is correct.

If the stream had a `null` instead of `"meow"`, the code would throw a `NullPointerException`, since we need to check the length of the `String` to determine which part of the `Map` it goes in. Since you cannot call a method on `null`, option F is correct.

58. A. Option A is correct as the source and terminal operation are mandatory parts of a stream pipeline. Option B is incorrect because a `Stream` must return objects. Specialized interfaces like `IntStream` are needed to return primitives. Option C is incorrect because `Stream` has methods such as `of()` and `iterate()` that return a `Stream`. Option D is incorrect because infinite streams are possible.

59. F. Trick question! The correct method to obtain an equivalent parallel stream of an existing `IntStream` is `parallel()`, but for an `IntStream` this returns another `IntStream`, not a generic `Stream<T>`. For this reason, option F is correct.

60. A. This code generates an infinite stream of integers: 1, 2, 3, 4, 5, 6, 7, etc. The `Predicate` checks if the element is greater than 5. With `anyMatch()`, the stream pipeline ends once element 6 is hit, and the code prints `true`. For the `allMatch()` operator, it sees that the first element in the stream does not match, and the code prints `false`. Similarly, the `noneMatch()` operator gets to the point where i is 6 and returns `false` because there is a match. Therefore, option A is correct.

61. D. Option A is incorrect because it doesn't print out one line. The `peek()` method is an intermediate operation. Since there is no terminal operation, the stream pipeline is not executed, so the `peek()` method is never executed, and nothing is printed. Options B and C are incorrect because they correctly output one line using a method reference and lambda, respectively, and don't use any bad practices. Option D is the correct answer. It does output one line. However, it is bad practice to have a `peek()` method that has side effects like modifying a variable.

62. C. The code does not compile, so option A, D, and E are incorrect. The lambda expression compiles without issue, making option B incorrect. The task variable is of type `UnaryOperator<Doll>`, with the abstract method `apply()`. There is no `accept()` method defined on that interface, therefore the code does not compile, and option C is the correct answer. If the code was corrected to use the `apply()` method, the rest of it would compile without issue. At runtime, it would then produce an infinite loop. On each iteration of the loop, a new `Doll` instance would be created with 5, since the post-decrement (`--`) operator returns the original value of the variable, and that would be option D.

63. D. The code compiles and does not throw any exception at runtime, so options A and B are incorrect. As an element goes through the pipeline, it is printed once by the `peek()` method, then once by the `forEach()` method. For example, `0.1 0.1 0.54 0.54 0.6 0.6 0.3 0.3` is a possible output from this code. For this reason, option D is correct.

64. B,D,F. The `findAny()` method is capable to return any element of the stream regardless of whether it is serial, parallel, ordered, or unordered. For this reason, options B, D, and F are correct. Option C is actually invalid, as an unordered stream does not have a first element.

65. C. To begin with, `Consumer` uses `accept()`, making option A incorrect. Next, `Function` and `UnaryOperator` use `apply()`, making options B and D, respectively, incorrect. Finally, `Supplier` uses `get()`, making option C the correct answer.

66. C. Option D is incorrect as the syntax is fine. Option E is incorrect because there is a `charAt()` instance method. While option B is correct that the method takes in an `int` parameter, autoboxing would take care of conversion for us if there were no other problems. So, option B is not the answer either. Option A is not true because there are constructor and instance method references. This method reference could be assigned to `BiFunction<String,Integer, Character>`. However, it cannot be assigned to a `Function`. This makes option C the correct answer.

67. B,C,D. While the second and third stream operations compile, the first does not. The `parallel()` method should be applied to a stream, while the `parallelStream()` method should be applied to a `Collection<E>`. For this reason, option A is incorrect, and options B and C are correct. Neither the second or third stream operation are expected to produce an exception at runtime, making option D correct and option E incorrect. Note that calling `parallel()` on an already parallel stream is unnecessary but allowed. Finally, the output of the second and third stream operations will vary at runtime since the streams are parallel, making option F incorrect.

68. D. Since the code uses a `BiPredicate`, it takes two parameters in the `test()` call. The first is the instance of `String` and the second is the substring value to check. Since both parameters are passed in, we use the type of `String` in the method reference, making option D the correct answer.

69. C. This code compiles. It creates a stream of `Ballot` objects. Then it creates a map with the contestant's name as the key and the sum of the scores as the value. For `Mario`, this is 10 + 9, or 19, so option C is correct.

70. D. The map() method can fill in the blank. The lambda converts a String to an int, and Java uses autoboxing to turn that into an Integer. The mapToInt() method can also fill in the blank, and Java doesn't even need to autobox. There isn't a mapToObject() in the stream API. Note there is a similarly named mapToObj() method on IntStream. Since both map() and mapToInt() work here, option D is correct.

71. A,C. This is a correct example of code that uses a lambda. The interface has a single abstract method. The lambda correctly takes one double parameter and returns a boolean. This matches the interface. The lambda syntax is correct. Since it compiles, option C is correct. Finally, option A is correct because 45 is greater than 5.

72. C. The reduction is parallel, but since the accumulator and combiner are well-behaved (stateless and associative), the result is consistent, making option D incorrect. The identity is 1, which is applied to every element meaning the operation sums the values (1+1), (1+2), and (1+3). For this reason, 9 is consistently printed at runtime, making option C correct.

73. E. The average() method returns an OptionalDouble. This interface has a getAsDouble() method rather than a get() method, so the code does compile. However, the stream is empty, so the optional is also empty. When trying to get the value on line 12, the code throws a NoSuchElementException, making option E correct.

74. B,E. Options A and D are incorrect since they are missing the arrow (->), which makes them lambdas. Options C and F are incorrect as they try to mix lambdas and method references. This leaves options B and E as the answers.

75. F. Both Collectors.groupingBy() and Collectors.partitioningBy() are useful for turning a stream into a Map. The other two methods do not exist. The partitioningBy() method automatically groups using a Boolean key. However, we can also have a Boolean key with groupingBy(). For example, we could write s -> s.length() > 3. Therefore, option F is correct.

76. B. Option A is incorrect because "3" is a String, which is not compatible with the return type int required for IntSupplier. Option B is the correct answer. Although this will result in a divide-by-zero issue at runtime, the lambda is valid and compatible with IntSupplier. Option C is incorrect because the lambda expression is invalid. The return statement is allowed only inside a set of braces ({}). Finally, option D is incorrect. The method reference is used for Consumer, not Supplier, since it takes a value and does not return anything.

77. A. The code compiles without issue, so options C and D are incorrect. The value for distance is 2, which based on the lambda for the Predicate will result in a true expression, and Saved will be printed, making option A correct.

78. E. The correct method to obtain a parallel stream from a Collection<E> is parallelStream(), making option E correct.

79. C. The filter() method takes a Predicate, which requires a boolean return type from the lambda or method reference. The getColor() method returns a String and is not compatible. This causes the code to not compile and option C to be the answer.

80. B,E. The generate() and iterate() sources return an infinite stream. Further, the of() source returns a finite stream, which shows option B is one of the answers.

The limit() intermediate operation returns a finite stream. When given an infinite stream, the map() intermediate operations keeps the infinite stream, which means option E is the other correct answer.

81. E. Like a lambda, method references use type inference. When assigned to a local variable, var cannot be used because there is not enough information to infer the type. Due to this, lines 17, 18, and 19 do not compile.

Consumer<Object> takes a single Object argument and does not return any data. The classes ArrayList and String do not contain constructors that take an Object, so lines 14 and 15 do not compile either. Line 16 does support an Object variable, since the System.out.println(Object) method exists. For these reasons, option E is the correct answer.

82. E. Based on the reduction operation, the data types of w, y, and z are Integer, while the data type of x is StringBuilder. Since Integer does not define a length() method, both the accumulator and combiner lambda expressions are invalid, making option E correct.

83. C,F. The first intermediate operation, limit(1), gets rid of the null. The partitioningBy() method returns a map with two keys, true and false, regardless of whether any elements actually match. If there are no matches, the value is an empty list, making option C correct. If line k is removed, the code throws a NullPointerException, since null is neither true nor false. Therefore, option F is the other answer.

84. D. The code does not compile because flatMapToInt() requires a Function with a return value of IntStream, not Stream, making option D correct.

85. D. A lambda expression can match multiple functional interfaces. It matches DoubleUnaryOperator, which takes a double value and returns a double value. Note that the data type of s+1 is double because one of the operands, in this case s, is double. It also matches Function<String,String> since the addition (+) operator can be used for String concatenation. Finally, it matches IntToLongFunction, since the int value s+1 can be implicitly cast to long. On the other hand, the lambda expression is not compatible with UnaryOperator without a generic type. When UnaryOperator is used without a generic argument, the type is assumed to be Object. Since the addition operator is not defined on Object, the code does not compile due to the lambda expression body, making option D the correct answer. Note that if the lambda expression did not rely on the addition operator, such as s -> s, then UnaryOperator would be allowed by the compiler, even without a generic type.

86. B,D. Applying forEachOrdered() to a parallel stream forces the terminal operation to be performed in a single-threaded, rather than parallel, manner. For this reason, it is likely that it will be slower, making option B correct. Intermediate operations can still take advantage of parallel processing, since forEachOrdered() is only applied at the end of the pipeline. For this reason, option D is correct.

87. C,F. The code does not compile because the class should be `IntSummaryStatistics`, not `IntegerSummaryStatistics`. This makes option C correct. The purpose of using the summary statistics class is to avoid multiple trips through the stream pipeline, making option F the other answer.

88. C. Both lambda and method references can be passed to another method as a parameter and executed later ruling out options A and D. One big difference is with a lambda like: `() -> s.charAt(3)`. The `s` variable must be `final` or effectively final variable in both lambdas and method references, making option B incorrect. However, there isn't a way to use the hard-coded number in a method reference. Therefore, option C is a difference and the answer.

89. E. A stream pipeline is allowed to have zero or more intermediate operations. This means both `filter()` and `sorted()` can be removed. The source and terminal operations are required, so cannot be removed. Therefore, `generate()` and `findFirst()` must stay. The `ifPresent()` call is not part of the stream pipeline. It is a method on `Optional`.

90. B,C,E. The `orElseThrow()` method throws a `NoSuchElementException` when the `Optional` is empty. Since this exception is not caught, a stack trace is printed. This matches option B. The overloaded method that takes a parameter throws the specified exception. Since we do catch an `IllegalArgumentException`, the code prints the message, which is option C. Finally, the `orElse()` method returns the specified string, and option E is correct.

91. C. Predicate is an interface with one method. The method signature is `boolean test(T t)`. Option C is the answer because the method accepts one parameter rather than two.

92. B,C. The `BiFunction` interface takes two different generic values and returns a generic value, taking a total of three generic arguments. Next, `ToDoubleFunction` takes exactly one generic value and returns a `double` value, requiring one generic argument. The `ToIntBiFunction` interface takes two generic values and returns an `int` value, for a total of two generic arguments. For these reasons, Options A, D, and E have the correct number of generics.

`BinaryOperator<T>` takes two parameters of a generic type and returns the same type. Therefore, only one generic is needed when declaring the type. `DoubleFunction<R>` takes a `double` value and returns a generic result, taking exactly one generic argument, not two. This makes the answer options B and C.

93. C. To execute a parallel reduction with the `collect()` method, the stream or `Collector` must be unordered, the `Collector` must be concurrent, and the stream must be parallel. Since an unordered `Set` is used as the data source, the first property is fulfilled. To be a parallel reduction, though, `Collectors.groupByConcurrent()` should be used instead of `Collectors.groupingBy()`. In addition, `parallelStream()` should be called on the `Set`, instead of `stream()`. For these two reasons, option C is correct.

94. D. This is a correct stream pipeline. The source creates a stream of three elements. The first operation makes a stream of one element, `one`. Then that single element is made uppercase and sorted to complete the intermediate operations. Finally, the terminal operation prints `ONE`, which corresponds to option D.

95. B. `BinaryOperator<Long>` takes two `Long` arguments and returns a `Long` value. For this reason, option A, which takes one argument, and option D, which takes two `Integer` values that do not inherit from `Long`, are both incorrect. Option C is incorrect because the local variable `c` is re-declared inside the lambda expression, causing the expression to fail to compile. The correct answer is option B because `intValue()` can be called on a `Long` object. The result is then be cast to `long`, which is autoboxed to `Long`.

96. A. `BooleanSupplier` is the only functional interface that does not involve `double`, `int`, or `long`, making option A the correct answer. The rest of the functional interfaces are not found in `java.util.function`. Java does not have built-in support for primitive functional interfaces that include `char`, `float`, or `short`.

97. D,F. Certain stream operations, such as `limit()` or `skip()`, force a parallel stream to behave in a serial manner, so option A is incorrect, and option F is correct. Option B is also incorrect. The stream must be explicitly set to be parallel in order for the JVM to apply a parallel operation. Option C is incorrect because parallel stream operations are not synchronized. It is up to the developer to provide synchronization or use a concurrent collection if required. Option D is also correct. The `BaseStream` interface, which all streams inherit, includes a `parallel()` method. Of course, the results of an operation may change in the presence of a parallel stream, such as using a problematic (non-associative) accumulator. For this reason, option E is incorrect.

98. D. The `sorted()` method allows an optional `Comparator` to be passed as a reference. However, `Comparator.reverseOrder()` does not implement the `Comparator` interface. It takes zero parameters instead of the required two. Since it cannot be used as a method reference, the code does not compile, and option D is correct.

99. F. The `mapToDouble()` method compiles. However, it converts `9` into `9.0` rather than the single digit `9`. The `mapToInt()` method does not compile because a `long` cannot be converted into an `int` without casting. The `mapToLong()` method is not available on `LongStream` so it does not compile. It is available on `DoubleStream`, `IntStream`, and `Stream` implementations. Since none of the options outputs the single digit `9`, option F is correct.

100. E. The code does not compile because the lambda expression `p -> p*100` is not compatible with the `DoubleToIntFunction` functional interface. The input to the functional interface is `double`, meaning `p*100` is also `double`. The functional interface requires a return value of `int`, and since `double` cannot be implicitly cast to `int`, the code does not compile, making option E the correct answer. If the correct cast was applied to make `(p*100)` an `int`, then the rest of the class would compile and `250` would be printed at runtime, making option C correct.

101. A,E. Stateful lambda expressions should be avoided with both serial and parallel streams because they can lead to unintended side effects, making option A correct. A common way to remove a stateful lambda expression that modifies a `List` is to have the stream operation output a new `List`. For this reason, option E is correct. Options D and F are incorrect because while a concurrent or synchronized list may make the stream operation thread-safe, they are still stateful lambda expressions.

102. E. The code does not compile, making option E the answer. In particular, the call to `test()` should have one parameter instead of two.

103. B. Lazy evaluation delays execution until it is needed. Option B is the only one that matches this requirement. While option A is true, this can be done without lazy evaluation. Option C requires parallelization rather than deferred execution. Option D is incorrect as data loss is bad. Finally, pipelines are run by the computer, which does not get tired.

104. F. The `distinct()` and `filter()` methods can reduce the number of elements in a stream but do not change the generic type, making options A and E incorrect. The `iterate()` method creates a new stream and cannot be applied to an existing stream, making option B incorrect. The `peek()` and `sorted()` methods do not alter the generic type of the stream, making options C and D incorrect. For these reasons, option F is correct.

105. B,F. Option B fills in the first blank because `BiFunction` includes the `apply()` method. `DoubleUnaryOperator` contains the `applyAsDouble()` method, making option F correct. For the exam, pay attention to methods that have a different name for primitives.

106. D. The `forEachOrdered()` method is available on streams, not collections. For this reason, line q1 does not compile. and option D is correct. If the `forEach()` method was used instead, then the code would compile with the values printed on line q1 varying at runtime and the values printed on line q2 being consistent.

107. A. The `sorted()` method takes an optional `Comparator` as the parameter, which takes two `String` parameters and returns an `int`. Option A is correct because the lambda implements this interface. Option B is incorrect because the method reference doesn't take any parameters, nor does it return an `int`. While `generate()` starts with an infinite stream, the `limit()` intermediate operation immediately makes it finite. Finally, the `distinct()` intermediate operation gives us one star instead of three.

108. D. Options A, B, and C are true statements about functional interfaces. A lambda may be compatible with multiple functional interfaces, but it must be assigned to a functional interface when it is declared or passed as a method argument. Also, a method can be created with the return type that matches a functional interface, allowing a lambda expression to be returned. Option D is the correct answer. Deferred execution means the lambda expression is not evaluated until runtime, but it is compiled. Compiler errors in the lambda expression will still prevent the code from compiling.

109. D. This code generates an infinite stream of the number 1. The `Predicate` checks if the element is greater than 5. This will never be `true`. With `allMatch()`, the stream pipeline ends after checking the first element. It doesn't match, so the code prints `false`. Both `anyMatch()` and `noneMatch()` keep checking and don't find any matches. However, they don't know if a future stream element will be different, so the code executes infinitely until the process is terminated. Therefore, option D is correct.

110. D. To start with, line 5 does not compile because `Function` takes two generic arguments, not one. Second, the assignment statement on line 7 does not end with a semicolon (`;`), so it also does not compile. Finally, the `forEach()` method on line 10 requires a `Consumer`, not a `Function`, so this line does not compile. For these three reasons, option D is the correct answer.

111. A,D,E. The findFirst() method always returns the first element on an ordered stream, regardless if it is serial or parallel, making options A and E correct. Option D is also correct, as it is free to return any element if the stream is unordered. Option C is actually invalid, as an unordered stream does not have a first element.

112. E. The only one of these references to compile is option D. However, the original code prints Carrying 1. The version with a method reference would just print 1. Option E is the answer because this is not the same output.

113. F. A stream cannot be used again once it is executed. Line 21 creates a stream. Line 22 creates a second stream; however, the reference is lost on line 23. Lines 23 and 24 add intermediate operations to the stream that was created on line 21. Due to lazy evaluation, they do not run it. Line 25 does execute the stream pipeline and prints 0. However, line 26 attempts to execute the same stream and throws an IllegalStateException. This matches option F.

114. A,B,F. Options A and B are correct because the type may be var or omitted in a lambda. If there are multiple parameters, all must be handled the same way. Option C is tricky but incorrect. While a lambda can have zero parameters, a Predicate cannot. A Predicate is defined as a type mapping to a boolean.

Option D is clearly incorrect as -> separates the parts of a lambda. Options E and F are similar. Option E is incorrect because return is allowed only when the braces are present. Option F is correct.

115. E. The newValue variable is locally scoped to the lambda. It is not available outside the lambda, so the println() does not compile, and option E is the answer.

116. D. The DoubleToLongFunction interface takes a double argument and returns a long value. Option A is compatible since the int value 1 can be implicitly cast to long, and 2L is already a long. Option B is also compatible, since the double value 10.0*e is explicitly cast to int then implicitly cast to long. Next, option C is compatible because an explicit cast of the double to a long value is used. Option D cannot be assigned and is the correct answer. Although the Double class does have a longValue() method, the left-hand side of the lambda expression must use the primitive double, not the wrapper Double. This lambda expression violates the signature of the functional interface, since it allows Double values to be sent to the interface, including those that could be null.

117. B,D. Option A is incorrect because sets are unordered. Options C and F are incorrect because the correct method call is parallelStream(). Option E is incorrect because the accumulator and combiner in the divide() method are not well-behaved. In particular, they are not associative and in a parallel stream, could produce various results at runtime. On a serial ordered stream, though, the results will be processed sequentially and in a predictable order, making option B correct. Option D is correct because the stream has only one element, so the identity is the only thing that will be applied.

118. C. Four of the five examples print miny. Option C does not compile. The difference is that partitioningBy() requires a Predicate that returns a boolean. When getting a question like this on the exam, focus on the differences between the provided options.

119. D. The correct method to obtain an equivalent parallel stream of an existing stream is `parallel()`, which is inherited by any class that implements `BaseStream<T>` including the primitive streams. For this reason, option D is correct.

120. C. Method references are a shorter way of writing lambdas, and all method references can be expanded to lambdas. However, this does not apply in reverse. Consider the lambda: `() -> s.charAt(n)`. The n variable can only be an effectively final variable in lambdas, but not in method references. Since only method references can always be converted, option C is correct.

121. D. First, options A and B are incorrect because the second functions for both return a `double` or `Double` value, respectively. Neither of these values can be sent to a `UnaryOperator<Integer>` without an explicit cast. Next, option C is incorrect. The first functional interface `Function<Double,Integer>` takes only one input, but the diagram shows two inputs for the first functional interface.

That leaves us with option D. The first functional interface `BiFunction<Integer,Double,Integer>` takes an `int`, which can be implicitly auto-boxed to `Integer`, and a `Double` and returns an `Integer`. The next functional interface, `BinaryOperator<Integer>`, takes two `Integer` values and returns an `Integer` value. Finally, this `Integer` value can be implicitly unboxed and sent to `IntUnaryOperator`, returning an `int`. Since these behaviors match our diagram, option D is the correct answer.

122. C,E. The `DoublePredicate` interface takes a `double` value and returns a `boolean` value. `LongUnaryOperator` takes a `long` value and returns a `long` value. `ToIntBiFunction` takes two generic values and returns an `int` value. `ShortSupplier` and `ToStringOperator` are not built-in functional interfaces. Recall that Java only includes primitive functional interfaces that operate on `double`, `int`, or `long`. For this reason, Options C and E are correct.

123. D. The lambda expression is invalid because the input argument is of type `Boss`, and `Boss` does not define an `equalsIgnoreCase()` method, making option D the correct answer. If the lambda was corrected to use `s.getName()` instead of `s`, the code would compile and run without issue, printing `[JENNY, GRACE]` at runtime and making option A the correct answer.

124. E. `Serval` is not a valid interface let alone a functional interface. The `cat()` method specifies an implementation, but does not have one of the modifiers that allows a body: `default`, `private`, or `static`. For this reason, option E is correct. If `cat()` was made an abstract method, then `Serval` would be a valid functional interface with `n -> true` being a valid lambda that matches it.

125. A. Let's use the process of elimination here. `Comparator` returns an `int`, causing lines 17 and 18 to not compile. `Supplier` does not take any parameters further, ruling out lines 21 and 22.

`Predicate` at least has the right number of parameters and the correct `boolean` return type. However, line 19 is not correct because the parentheses are missing around the type and variable. The parentheses can be omitted only if no type declaration is present, making line 20 correct. Since only one of these lines of code compiles, option A is the answer.

126. A. Option A is the answer because there is a getCount() method that returns a long rather than a method named getCountAsLong(). Option B is incorrect because there is in fact a getMax() method. Option C is incorrect because toString() is declared on Object, which means it is inherited by all classes.

127. A. The method reference System.out::println takes a single input and does not return any data. Consumer<Sheep> is compatible with this behavior, making option A the correct answer. Note that option B does not even compile because void cannot be used as a generic argument. Similarly, option C does not take a parameter. Option D is also incorrect, since System.out::println() does not return any data, and UnaryOperator requires a return value.

128. C,E,F. The correct method to obtain a parallel stream of an arbitrary stream is parallel(), while the correct method to obtain a parallel stream that operates on a Collection is parallelStream(). For this reason, options C, E, and F are correct. Note that option E retrieves a parallel stream of an already parallel stream, which is allowed.

129. A,F. The code, as written, prints rabbit, since it starts with the letter r. This is option A. The prefix variable is effectively final and, therefore safe to use in a lambda. Uncommenting line 7 changes the prefix variable, and it is no longer effectively final. Since this causes a compiler error, option F is the other answer.

130. B. The code compiles, so options E and F are incorrect. The stream operations on lines 12–13 reduce the stream to the values [2, 3, 4]. Line 14 then converts the Stream<Integer> to an IntStream. On line 15, the first element of the IntStream is skipped, so the stream has only two elements [3, 4]. On line 16–17, the IntStream is converted to a Stream<Integer>, then a DoubleStream. Finally, on lines 18–19 the sum of the remaining elements is calculated and printed. Since 7.0 is printed, option B is correct.

131. B. Since the first two rows are already finite streams, boxes M and N do not require an intermediate operation to complete, so options D, E, and F are incorrect. Box P does not need an intermediate operation either, since findFirst() will cause the stream to terminate, making options A and C incorrect. Box O does need to be filled in with code such as limit(1). This allows the code to terminate, and option B is the answer.

132. C. Since the first two rows are already finite streams, boxes M and N meet this criteria. The last two rows can be filled in with code such as sorted(), which does not terminate for an infinite stream. Therefore, neither allows the code to terminate, and option C is the answer.

133. C. A Comparator takes two parameters, so options A and B are incorrect. Option D doesn't compile. When returning a value using braces, a return keyword and semicolon are required. Option C is a correct implementation.

134. E. The methods anyMatch(), allMatch(), and noneMatch() take a Predicate as a parameter. This code does not compile because the parameter is missing, making option E correct.

135. B. Since the lambda references an effectively final variable, the method reference needs to as well. Option B is a correct method reference that meets this criteria. Options A and C use syntax that is not supported with method references. Option D is incorrect because the

Predicate passes only one value at runtime, so one of the instance variable or method parameter would need to be supplied.

136. E. Both pred4 and pred5 are valid as they use a type or var without final. Both pred1 and pred3 are valid because the final modifier can only be used if a type or var is specified. Since pred2 is missing a data type and is the only line that does not compile, option E is the answer.

137. A. This code does compile, making options D and E incorrect. It correctly uses a Predicate<String> and removes all the elements from names and prints out 0. Therefore, option A is the answer.

138. B. Since it's not a primitive stream, the underlying type is Stream<Integer>, which means the data type of x is Integer. On the other hand, the data type of w, y, and z is Float. Because Integer and Float both define a floatValue() method, all of the lines compile. The code snippet prints 9.0 at runtime, making option B correct.

139. B. The flatMap() method is used to turn a stream of collections into a one-dimensional stream. This means it gets rid of the empty list and flattens the other two. Option A is incorrect because this is the output you'd get using the regular map() method. Option B is correct because it flattens the elements. Notice how it doesn't matter that all three elements are different types of Collection implementations.

140. D. Pay attention to the data types. The forEach() method is looping through a list of objects. This is a good example of using a lambda with list. By contrast, the Predicate passed to removeIf() uses an Integer. Since Integer is not compatible with String, line 9 does not compile.

141. C. To start with, IntFunction<Integer> takes an int value and returns an Integer. Line 8 takes an Integer instead of int as the input argument, and is therefore not compatible. Line 9 is compatible, since the return type null can be used as an Integer return type. Line 10 is also valid. An int can be autoboxed to Integer. Lines 11 and 12 do not compile because they do not take a parameter. Since only two statements compile, option C is the correct answer.

142. C,D,F. Using a parallel stream does not guarantee concurrent execution or a specific number of threads, making option A incorrect. Option B is also incorrect, as stateful lambda expressions should be avoided with all streams, serial or parallel. In fact, if a stateful lambda expression is used, the result of the stream may change, making option F correct and option E incorrect. Option C is correct, as a parallel stream may improve performance. Option D is also correct, though, as a parallel stream may add extra overhead to a stream that is forced into a serial operation, such as when the findFirst() method is called.

143. A. The code compiles, so options D and E are incorrect. The code first splits the stream into a Map<Boolean, List<String> based on whether the landmark contains a space. Using the flatMap() method, it then takes the List<String> values of the Map and reforms them as a Stream<String>. This new stream is similar to the original stream, although with elements in a possibly different order. Finally, the groupingBy() collector splits the stream based on whether it does not start with an "S". Since Set and Map were used, the order may vary, but option A is one possible output.

144. E. Option A doesn't compile because the `get()` method on `Optional` doesn't take any parameters. Options B, C, and D do compile, but print `Cupcake` since the `Optional` is not empty. Therefore, option E is correct.

145. F. There is no source in this attempt at a stream pipeline. While a `Collection` does have some of the same methods as a stream, such as `forEach()`, the `limit()` method is not one of them, so the code as written causes a compile error. Since this error is not on line x, option F is the answer. If `stream()` were inserted before `limit()`, then `ONE` would be printed.

146. E. The `num` variable is not effectively final because the value changes. This means it cannot be used in a lambda and the code does not compile, which is option E.

147. C. There is not a stream pipeline method called `sort()`. There is one called `sorted()`. Since the code does not compile, option C is correct. If this was fixed, option A would be correct since the `Comparator` sorts in ascending order.

148. A. A lambda can only implement an interface with a single abstract method ruling out option B. Developers can write their own functional interfaces, making option A correct.

149. C. The primitive `Supplier` functional interfaces, such as `BooleanSupplier` and `LongSupplier`, do not have a `get()` method. Instead, they have methods such as `getAsBoolean()` and `getAsLong()`, respectively. For this reason, the first line of the `checkInventory()` method does not compile, making option C the correct answer. If the method call was changed to `getAsBoolean()`, then the rest of the code would compile without issue, print `Plenty!` at runtime, and option A would be the correct answer.

150. E. The code does not compile because the collector returns a `ConcurrentMap`, which requires a `BiConsumer` in the `forEach()` method. For this reason, option E is correct.

Chapter 7: Java Platform Module System

1. F. The `module-info.java` file is used to declare a module. You must memorize the name of this file.

2. E. The service locator contains a `load()` method, not an `exports()` method, making option E the answer.

3. B,D. A service is comprised of the interface, any classes the interface references, and a way to look up implementations of the interface. Option B covers the lookup, and option D covers the interface itself.

4. B. A named module must be on the module path and contain a `module-info` file. Only `dog.bark` meets this criterion, making option B the answer.

5. C. An automatic module must be on the module path but does not contain a module-info file. Option C is correct because dog.hair matches this description.

6. E. You need to know about three types of modules for the exam: automatic, named, and unnamed. There is no such thing as a default module. The question was trying to trick you, and option E is correct.

7. C. An unnamed module must be on the classpath. It is rare to have a module-info file in an unnamed module, but it is allowed. Therefore, both dog.fluffy and dog.husky meet this criterion, making option C correct.

8. B,F. It is recommended to specify all exports directives in the module-info file. While it is legal to use the --add-exports option, it is not recommended, making option B correct. You do not need to know how to use it for the exam, just that it is not a good idea. There is no equivalent option for requires, making option F correct.

9. B. Since Java does not allow dashes in identifier names, the second and fourth declarations are invalid. Additionally, access modifiers are not permitted in module declarations, making the third and fourth declarations invalid. The only one that is legal is the first declaration, so option B is correct.

10. D. The consumer is generally separate ruling out options A, B, and C. The service provider is decoupled from the service provider interface ruling out option F. It is most logical to combine the service locator and service provider interface because neither has a direct reference to the service provider. Therefore, option D is correct.

11. C. The java command has an option to list all the modules that come with the JDK. Option C is correct since that option is called --list-modules. The other options are not supported by the java command. Options B and E are similar to options that exist: --describe-module and --show-module-resolution. But neither gives a list of all the modules that come with the JDK.

12. C. The rules for determining the name include removing the extension, removing numbers, and changing special characters to periods (.). This leaves us with dog.arthur, which is option C.

13. C. All parts of a modules service must point to the service provider interface. This tells us the service provider interface must be X, ruling out options A, B, and E. Now, we have to decide if Y or Z are the service provider interface. We can tell because nothing has a direct dependency on the service provider. Since this makes the service provider Y, the answer is option C.

14. B. The consumer depends on the service provider interface and service locator, but not the service provider. Only W has two arrows starting from it so, it must be the consumer. This rules out options C, D, and E. The service locator references the service provider interface directly and the service provider indirectly, making the service locator Z and option B the answer.

15. C. A cyclic dependency is when two things directly or indirectly depend on each other. If chicken.jar depends on egg.jar, and egg.jar depends on chicken.jar, we have a cyclic dependency. Since only two JAR files are needed to create this situation, option C is the answer.

16. E. The `ServiceLoader` class has a `load()` method that returns a `Collection` of `Provider`, not a stream. Since the call to `stream()` is missing, option E is the answer. If the call to `stream()` were added, option D would be the answer.

17. C. Each module is required to have its own `module-info.java` file in the root directory of the module. For module `com.ny`, that is location W, and for module `com.sf`, that is location Y. Therefore, option B is correct.

18. E. Options A, C, and D are incorrect because `export` and `require` are not keywords in modules. Option B is incorrect because that directive goes in the `com.ny` module, not the `com.sf` one. Option E is correct rather than option F because the `requires` directive references a module name rather than a package.

19. D. Options A and B are incorrect because `export` is not a keyword in modules. Option E belongs in the `com.sf` module, not the `com.ny` one. Option F is incorrect because the `requires` directive references a module name rather than a package. Finally, option D is the answer rather than option C because the `exports` directive references a package name rather than a module.

20. E. The `Maple` class is intended to be an implementation of the `Tree` interface. However, this interface needs to be accessible. This module is missing a `requires nature.sapling;` statement, making option E the correct answer.

21. B. The `-d` option specifies the directory. The `-p` option specifies the module path. The `-m` option is not available on the `javac` command.

22. A,C,E. The `java.base` module is automatically available to any module without specifying it, making option A correct. Options C and E are also correct because `java.desktop` and `java.sql` are modules supplied with the JDK. You do need to be able to identify built-in modules for the exam.

23. A,C. Option A is correct because a top-down migration starts by moving all the modules to the module path as automatic modules. Then, the migration changes each module from an automatic module to a named module, making option C the other correct answer.

24. A. Option A is correct because a consumer has two dependencies. It `requires` both the service provider interface and the service locator.

25. A,C. Option A is correct, and option B is incorrect as we want to create named modules when possible. We also need to be on the lookout for cyclic dependencies. While option D would work, it is better to be more granular and create a third module as in option C. Option E is incorrect because dots are used as separators in names.

26. B. The `jdeps` command lists information about dependencies within a module. The `-s` option provides a summary of output rather than verbose output, making option B the correct answer. There is no `-d` option. The `jmod` command is for working with JMOD files.

27. C. Option C is correct because a service provider `requires` the interface. It also `provides` the implementation.

28. E. When running a module, the module name is listed before the slash, and the fully qualified class name is after the slash. Option E is the only one that meets this criterion.

29. B. An unnamed module is on the classpath. While it is permitted to have a `module-info` file, the file is ignored if present. An automatic module is on the module path and does not have a `module-info` file. A named module is required to have a `module-info` file, making option B the correct answer.

30. B. Option B is correct because a service locator `uses` the interface. It also `requires` the service provider interface module and `exports` the package with the locator.

31. A,B. Option A is correct because modules provide a mechanism to export specific packages. This creates module-level access since some packages can be used only in a module. Option B is correct because `jlink` allows creating a distribution with just the parts of the JDK that are needed. Option C is not correct because modules are usually distributed as a JAR file. Option D is incorrect because modules actually require one extra file: `module-info.java`. Option E is incorrect because `var` can be used with or without modules. Finally, option F is incorrect because "write once, run anywhere" is a core benefit of Java independent of modules.

32. E. A consumer `requires` both the service locator and service provider interface. A service locator and service provider interface need to have an `exports` statement. A service provider needs a `provides` directive. Since none of them matches, option E is the correct answer.

33. F. An unnamed module is permitted to have a `module-info` file, but the file is ignored if present. An automatic module does not have a `module-info` file. A named module is required to have a `module-info` file. Therefore, option F is correct.

34. A. A `module-info` file is required to start with `module` rather than `class`. Therefore, the first line doesn't compile, and option A is correct.

35. B. You need to know these keywords: `exports`, `requires`, `requires transitive`, `provides`, `opens`, and `uses`. Of these, only `uses` is in the list of candidates in the question. Note that `export` and `require` are invalid because they should be `exports` and `requires`, respectively.

36. D. Option D is correct because a service provider interface exposes the interface without depending on any of the other options.

37. D,E,F. The `java.base` module is automatically available to any module without specifying it. However, this question tries to trick you with option A by specifying `jdk.base` instead. Similarly, `java.desktop` exists, but not `jdk.deskop`, making option C wrong. Options D, E, and F are correct because `jdk.javadoc` , `jdk.jdeps`, and `jdk.net` are modules supplied with the JDK. You do need to be able to recognize the names of built-in modules.

38. B,C,F. A top-down migration starts by moving all the modules to the module path as automatic modules, making options B and F correct. A bottom-up migration moves each module after all modules it depends on have been migrated, making option C correct.

39. B. The service locator contains a `load()` method, making option B correct.

40. E. Module names are permitted to be any valid variable name with the addition of dot separators (`.`). The only one that is problematic is `com-leaf` because dashes are not allowed, making option E correct. As a reminder, numbers are permitted as long as they are not the first character in a segment. Capital letters are discouraged but allowed.

41. A. Option A is correct because `ServiceLoader` allows you to make your application extensible. A service can be added without recompiling the entire application. It is a class, but the service provider implementation does not reference it, making options C and D incorrect. Option B is not a feature of Java.

42. A,F. Code on the classpath has not yet been migrated to modules and can reference any code in the application. This is true whether that code is in automatic, named, or unnamed modules, matching option A. Code on the module path operates in a stricter world and cannot reference code on the classpath. Since unnamed modules cannot be accessed in this situation, option F is the second answer.

43. C. Option A is incorrect because it exports the package to all modules. Option C is correct because it limits package sharing to the `com.park` module. Option E is incorrect because a package must be exported from the module that contains it. Options B and D are incorrect because `from` is not valid syntax.

44. F. It is not possible to provide access outside the module while also limiting access within the `com.duck` module. Options A and C are tempting because they do provide access in `com.park`. However, they do not prevent the `Egg` class in the `com.egg` package from accessing the `com.duckling` package. Remember that the `com.egg` package is in the `com.duck` module, so the access cannot be restricted. Therefore, option F is correct.

45. E. The correct way to specify this is `requires com.duck; requires com.bread;`. There is no way to combine two module `requires` statements into one. Additionally, note that the `requires` statement works with a module name, not a package name.

46. E. Only the service provider has a `provides` directive. Since it is not part of the service, option E is the correct answer.

47. D. Both options A and B note that the JAR depends on the `jdk.unsupported` module. However, they do not list suggested replacements. Options C and E are invalid because flags of this format need two dashes. Option D is correct and option F is incorrect because the desired flag is `--jdkinternals`. Note that `--jdk-internals` is also acceptable.

48. C. Option C is correct because only unnamed modules are on the classpath.

49. D. The service locator contains a `ServiceLoader` call to look up the service loader. It takes the type of class it looked up as a parameter and returns a generic, making option D the correct answer.

50. B,D. Option B is correct because it depends on the change. If a method is added to the service provider interface or a `public` method is changed, the service providers must be recompiled. However, if a change is made that does not affect the service provider, such as a new `static` method, recompilation is not needed. Option D is also correct because return types and parameter types are considered part of the service.

51. D. Unnamed modules are on the classpath. Option D is correct because automatic and named modules are on the module path.

52. F. The consumer needs to depend on the shared module, making it X. The shared module then has to be Z, and the service provider has to be Y. However, the service provider should not know about the consumer, and the dotted line in the diagram does not make sense. This means none of the options can create a valid scenario, and option F is the correct answer.

53. B. Without any command line flags, jdeps lists packages and module dependencies. The −s flag provides a summary omitting the package name, which means option B is the correct answer.

54. B,C,F. Options A, D, and E are incorrect because they are benefits of Java even without modules. Option B is correct because the module-info file clarifies dependencies. Option C is correct because a smaller deployment package can be faster. Finally, option F is correct because the module system prevents the same package from being used from multiple JAR files.

55. F. The first clue is that the −m and −p options are on the java command. Beyond that, you need to memorize the name of the --show-module-resolution option.

56. B. This module is a service provider interface. The only requirement is that the module needs to export the package containing the interface. In this case, that is the animal.insect.api.bugs package, which matches option B.

57. A,E. This module is a service provider. It needs a requires directive for the service provider interface, which is option A. It also needs a provides directive, which specifies both the interface and implementation. Option E has both in the correct order.

58. C,F. This module is a service locator. It needs three directives: exports, requires, and uses. The requires directive specifies the module it depends on, which is option C. The uses directive specifies the service provider interface it references, which is option F.

59. A,B. This module is a consumer. It needs two requires directives. Option A represents the service provider interface, and option B represents the service locator. The uses directive should be in the service locator, not the consumer.

60. A. Without any command line flags, jdeps lists packages and module dependencies, making option A correct. Option D will also list the packages; however, it is longer than option A.

61. C. The com.light module does not have any dependencies, so it is fine. However, com.animal and com.plant depend on each other giving us a cyclic dependency. Finally, com.worm depends on all the modules but does not introduce any more problems. It will not compile until com.animal or com.plant are fixed, but is not part of the cycle itself. Option C is correct, since only two modules are part of the cycle.

62. C. The −d option is a shorthand for --describe-module on both the jar and java commands. Therefore, option C is correct.

63. C. The javac command takes −p for the module path rather than −m. Since there is no −m on the javac command, option C is the correct answer.

64. A. Option B is tempting because the java.lang package is available to all classes. However, the question asks about modules. Option A is the correct answer because the java.base module is available to all modules. The other options are incorrect because those modules do not exist.

65. A,B,C. The jmod command has five possible modes: create, extract, describe, list, and hash.

66. A. There is no such thing as a side-to-side migration, ruling out option B. In a top-down migration, all modules are moved to the module path first, making option C incorrect. In a bottom-up migration, modules are moved, starting with those without dependencies. Therefore, option A is correct.

67. C,E. In a bottom-up migration, the lowest-level modules are migrated to named modules on the module path first. This makes option E one of the answers. The modules that remain on the classpath are unnamed modules, making option C the other answer.

68. D. The `com.magic` module exports only one package. This makes the `com.magic.unicorn` package accessible, but not the `com.magic.dragon` package. Both packages in `com.science` are accessible because it is an automatic module. When a module on the module path does not contain a `module-info` file, all packages are exported. This gives us three packages that are accessible and a correct answer of option D.

69. A. Modules on the module path cannot access anything from the classpath, making option A the correct answer.

70. E. Option E is correct as this code does compile. While it is uncommon, a module is not required to have any directives in the body. Similarly, module names are lowercase and have more than one component by convention. None of these problems prevents the file from compiling, though.

71. E. One of the benefits of services is not having to recompile existing code when adding a new implementation. This makes option E the correct answer.

72. C. The `java` command uses `-m` and `--module` to supply the module name. The `jdeps` command uses `-s` and `--summary` to specify the output should be limited. Option C matches both of these.

73. B. A service is comprised of the interface, any classes the interface references, and a way to look up implementations of the interface. It does not include the implementation. This makes option A the correct answer.

74. E. Option E is correct because both `java` and `jdeps` meet the criteria. The `jar` command does as well although the options mean different things than working with modules.

75. A,E. This question is tricky because the service provider code is shown, but the question asks about the service locator, and you need to infer information about the service provider interface. The `requires` directive is option A due to process of elimination. Option B is incorrect because the `requires` directive references a module name rather than an interface. Option C is incorrect because we need the service provider interface module, and it refers to the service provider module. Option E is easier, since the `uses` directive works with an interface name.

76. A,F. A bottom-up migration leaves unnamed modules on the classpath until they are migrated to the module path, making option A correct and option D incorrect. A top-down migration immediately moves all modules to the module path as automatic modules making options B and E incorrect. Therefore, option F is the other correct answer.

77. D. The `ServiceLoader` class has a `load()` method that returns a `Collection` of `Provider`. Option D is correct because we need to convert the `Provider` into a `Mouse`.

78. B,C,E. The `mammal` module depends on two other modules. Since `requires` references module names, options C and E are correct. The module also has one package, which is referenced in the `exports` directive. This makes option B correct as well.

79. C. The `transitive` keyword goes after `requires`, ruling out all but options C and D. Just like `requires`, `requires transitive` references a module name, narrowing it down to option C.

80. D. Any requires directives must reference unique modules. Using the `transitive` keyword does not change this requirement, making option D the correct answer.

81. D. There can be multiple service providers for a single service provider interface, making option D the correct answer.

82. A,D,E. The `java.logging`, `java.management`, and `java.naming` modules exist, making options A, D, and E correct. Option B is tempting. However, `jdk.javadoc` exists, not `java.javadoc`. Options C and F are completely made up.

83. B,E. Option E is correct because all modules on the classpath are unnamed modules. On the module path, we can have automatic or named modules. In this case, it is an automatic module because there is no `module-info.class` at the root of the JAR. Having that file in another directory is ignored. This makes option B the other answer.

84. A. The consumer needs to depend on the shared module, making it X. The shared module then has to be Z, and the service provider has to be Y. This makes option A correct.

85. B,D. The method call of `ServiceLoader.load(Poodle.class)`, takes a parameter making option B correct and option A incorrect. When using a `Stream`, you call `Provider::get`, making option D the other answer. Option C is incorrect because you don't need to call the `get()` method when using a loop.

86. B. The rules for determining the name include removing the extension, removing numbers and changing special characters to periods (`.`). Additionally, we remove the version information from the end, which is `1.0.0-SNAPSHOT`. Finally, we normalize the duplicate dots, which gives us option B: `lizard.cricket`.

87. D. The `jar` file format is most common. The JMOD `jmod` format is used as well. Therefore, option D is correct.

88. B. Option B is correct because a service provider should not contain an `exports` directive. The service locator is used to reference any implementation exposed by `provides`.

89. A. The `com.light` module is a dependency for all the other modules but does not depend on them. Similarly, the `com.animal` module is a dependency for the two higher-level modules but does not depend on them. Finally, the `com.plant` module is a dependency for the `com.worm` module but does not depend on it. While the modules are not defined in this order, the question is about cyclic dependencies rather than order of compilation. There is no cyclic dependency, making option A correct.

90. C,E. The `jdeps` command outputs `requires mandated java.base` except when run in summary mode, making option C correct. Since this module is an implicit dependency in all modules, option E is also correct.

Chapter 8: Concurrency

1. C. The code does not compile because `Callable` must define a `call()` method, not a `run()` method, so option C is the correct answer. If the code was fixed to use the correct method name, then it would complete without issue, printing XXXXXXXXXXDone! at runtime. The `f.get()` call will block and wait for the results before moving on to the next iteration of the `for` loop.

2. A,D. Option A is correct, as `ExecutorService` does not define nor inherit an overloaded method `execute()` that takes a `Callable` parameter. `ExecutorService` defines two shutdown methods, `shutdown()` and `shutdownNow()`, one of which is shown in option B. Option D is correct, as `exit()` does not exist and is not one of shutdown methods. The `ExecutorService` interface defines the two `submit()` methods shown in options C and E. Because `ExecutorService` extends `Executor`, it also inherits the `execute(Runnable)` method presented in option F.

3. F. The code compiles and runs without issue. Even though the thread-safe `AtomicBoolean` is used, it is not used in a thread-safe manner. The `flip()` method first retrieves the value and then sets a new value. These two calls are not executed together in an atomic or synchronized manner. For this reason, the output could be `true` or `false`, with one or more of the flips possibly being lost, and making option F correct.

4. C. Option A is incorrect, although it would be correct if `Executor` were replaced with `ExecutorService`. Option B is also incorrect, but it would be correct if `start()` were replaced with `run()`. Option C is correct and is a common way to define an asynchronous task using a lambda expression. Option D is incorrect, as `Runnable` does not inherit a `begin()` method.

5. A. If the `tryLock()` method returns `true`, then a lock is acquired that must be released. That means the `lockUp()` method actually contains two calls to lock the object and only one call to unlock it. For this reason, the first thread to reach `tryLock()` obtains a lock that is never released. For this reason, `Locked!` is printed only once, and option A is correct. If the call to `lock()` inside the `if` statement was removed, then the expected output would be to print the statement five times.

6. C. `CopyOnWriteArrayList` makes a copy of the array every time it is modified, preserving the original list of values the iterator is using, even as the array is modified. For this reason, the `for` loop using copy1 does not throw an exception at runtime. On the other hand, the `for` loops using copy2 and copy3 both throw `ConcurrentModificationException` at runtime since neither allows modification while they are being iterated upon. Finally, the `ConcurrentLinkedQueue` used in copy4 completes without throwing an exception at runtime. For the exam, remember that the

Concurrent classes order read/write access such that access to the class is consistent across all threads and processes, while the synchronized classes do not. Because exactly two of the for statements produce exceptions at runtime, option C is the correct answer.

7. C. Resource starvation is when a single active thread is perpetually unable to gain access to a shared resource. Livelock is a special case of resource starvation, in which two or more active threads are unable to gain access to shared resources, repeating the process over and over again. For these reasons, option C is the correct answer. Deadlock and livelock are similar, although in a deadlock situation the threads are stuck waiting, rather than being active or performing any work. Finally, a race condition is an undesirable result when two tasks that should be completed sequentially are completed at the same time.

8. E. The class does not compile because the Future.get() on line 8 throws a checked InterruptedException and a checked ExecutionException, neither of which is handled nor declared by the submitReports() method. If the submitReports() and accompanying main() methods were both updated to declare these exceptions, then the application would print 1null at runtime. For the exam, remember that Future can be used with Runnable lambda expressions that do not have a return value but that the return value is always null when completed.

9. A,B. Options C, D, E, and F are all proper ways to obtain instances of ExecutorService. Remember that newSingleThreadExecutor() is equivalent to calling newFixedThreadPool(int) with a value of 1. The correct answers are options A and B, as neither of these methods exist.

10. A. The code compiles without issue but hangs indefinitely at runtime. The application defines a thread executor with a single thread and 12 submitted tasks. Because only one thread is available to work at a time, the first thread will wait endlessly on the call to await(). Since the CyclicBarrier requires four threads to release it, the application waits endlessly in a frozen condition. Since the barrier is never reached and the code hangs, the application will never output Ready, making option A the correct answer. If newCachedThreadPool() had been used instead of newSingleThreadExecutor(), then the barrier would be reached three times, and option C would be the correct answer.

11. E. Trick question! ExecutorService does not contain any of these methods. To obtain an instance of a thread executor, you need to use the Executors factory class. For this reason, option E is the correct answer. If the question had instead asked which Executors method to use, then the correct answer would be option C. Options A, B, and D do not create enough threads for a CyclicBarrier expecting to reach a limit of five concurrent threads. Option C, on the other hand, will create threads as needed and is appropriate for use with a CyclicBarrier.

12. C. Part of synchronizing access to a variable is ensuring that read/write operations are atomic or happen without interruption. For example, an increment operation requires reading a value and then immediately writing it. If any thread interrupts this process, then data could be lost. In this regard, option C shows proper synchronized access. Thread 2 reads a value and then writes it without interruption. Thread 1 then reads the new value and writes it. The rest of the answers are incorrect because one thread writes data to the variable

in-between another thread reading and writing to the same variable. Because a thread is writing data to a variable that has already been written to by another thread, it may set invalid data. For example, two increment operations running at the same time could result in one of the increment operations being lost.

13. F. The code compiles and runs without issue. The two methods `hare()` and `tortoise()` are nearly identical, with one calling `invokeAll()` and the other calling `invokeAny()`. Calling the `invokeAll()` method causes the current thread to wait until all tasks are finished, while calling the `invokeAny()` method will cause the current thread to wait until at least one task is complete. Both `ExecutorService` methods operate synchronously, waiting for a result from one or more tasks, but each method call has been submitted to the thread executor as an asynchronous task. For this reason, both methods will take about one second to complete, and since either can finish first, the output will vary at runtime, making option F correct. Note that this program does not terminate, since the `ExecutorService` is not shut down.

14. B,D. `ConcurrentSkipList` does not exist as a concurrent collection, making option A incorrect. `ConcurrentSkipListSet` implements the `SortedSet` interface, in which the elements are kept sorted, making option B correct. `ConcurrentSkipListMap` implements the `SortedMap` interface, in which the keys are kept sorted, making option D correct. The other options define structures that are ordered, but not sorted. Remember, if you see `SkipList` as part of a concurrent class name, it means it is sorted in some way.

15. C. The code compiles without issue, so options D and E are incorrect. The `f1` declaration uses the version of `submit()` in `ExecutorService`, which takes a `Runnable` and returns a `Future<?>`, while the `f2` declaration uses an overloaded version of `submit()`, which takes a `Callable` expression and returns a generic `Future` object. The call `f1.get()` waits until the task is finished and always returns `null`, since `Runnable` expressions have a `void` return type, so `[Filing]null` is printed first. The call to `f2.get()` returns then prints `3.14159`. For these reasons, option C is the correct answer.

16. C,D. The code compiles and runs without issue. While an `AtomicLong` is used, there are two calls on this variable, the first to retrieve the value and the second to set the new value. These two calls are not executed together in an atomic or synchronized manner. For this reason, the `incrementBy10()` method is not thread-safe, and option C is correct. That said, the code performs in single-threaded manner at runtime because the call to `get()` in the `main()` method waits for each thread to finish. For this reason, the output is consistently `1000`, making option D correct.

17. D. The `synchronized` block used in the `getQuestion()` method requires an object to synchronize on. Without it, the code does not compile, and option D is the correct answer. What if the command was fixed to synchronize on the current object, such as using `synchronized(this)`? Each task would obtain a lock for its respective object and then wait a couple of seconds before requesting the lock for the other object. Since the locks are already held, both wait indefinitely, likely resulting in a deadlock. We say most likely because even with corrected code, a deadlock is not guaranteed. It is possible, albeit very unlikely, for the JVM to wait five seconds before starting the second task, allowing enough time for the first task to finish and avoiding the deadlock completely.

18. B. Options A, D, and E include method names that do not exist in `ScheduledExecutorService`. The `scheduleAtFixedRate()` method creates a new task for the associated action at a set time interval, even if previous tasks for the same action are still active. In this manner, it is possible multiple threads working on the same action could be executing at the same time, making option B the correct answer. On the other hand, `scheduleWithFixedDelay()` waits until each task is completed before scheduling the next task, guaranteeing at most one thread working on the action is active in the thread pool.

19. F. The application compiles, so option D is incorrect. The `stroke` variable is thread-safe in the sense that no write is lost, since all writes are wrapped in a `synchronized` method, making option E incorrect. The issue here is that the `main()` method reads the value of `getStroke()` while tasks may still be executing within the `ExecutorService`. The `shutdown()` method stops new tasks from being submitted but does not wait for previously submitted tasks to complete. Therefore, the result may output 0, 1000, or anything in between, making option F the correct answer. If the `ExecutorService` method `awaitTermination()` is called before the value of `stroke` is printed and enough time elapses, then the result would be `1000` every time.

20. C. A race condition is an undesirable result when two tasks that should be completed sequentially are completed at the same time. The result is often corruption of data in some way. If two threads are both modifying the same `int` variable and there is no synchronization, then a race condition can occur with one of the writes being lost. For this reason, option C is the correct answer. Option A is the description of resource starvation. Options D and E are describing livelock and deadlock, respectively, while option B is the potential result of either of those events occurring.

21. B. The class compiles without issue. The class attempts to create a synchronized version of a `List<Integer>`. The `size()` and `addValue()` help synchronize the read/write operations. Unfortunately, the `getValue()` method is not synchronized so the class is not thread-safe, and option B is the correct answer. It is possible that one thread could add to the `data` object while another thread is reading from the object, leading to an unexpected result.

22. D. The post-decrement operator (`--`) decrements a value but returns the original value. It is equivalent to the atomic `getAndDecrement()` method. The pre-increment operator (`++`) increments a value and then returns the new value. It is equivalent to the `incrementAndGet()` atomic operation. For these reasons, option D is the correct answer.

23. C. Line 13 does not compile because the `execute()` method has a return type of `void`, not `Future`. Line 15 does not compile because `scheduleAtFixedRate()` requires four arguments that include an initial delay and period value. For these two reasons, option C is the correct answer.

24. B. When a `CyclicBarrier` goes over its limit, the barrier count is reset to zero. The application defines a `CyclicBarrier` with a barrier limit of 5 threads. The application then submits 12 tasks to a cached executor service. In this scenario, a cached thread executor will use between 5 and 12 threads, reusing existing threads as they become available. In this manner, there is no worry about running out of available threads. The barrier will then trigger twice, printing five values for each of the sets of threads, for a total of ten W characters. For this reason, option B is the correct answer.

25. D. The application does not terminate successfully nor produce an exception at runtime, making options A and B incorrect. It hangs at runtime because the CyclicBarrier limit is 5, while the number of tasks submitted and awaiting activation is 12. This means that two of the tasks will be left over, stuck in a deadlocked state, waiting for the barrier limit to be reached but with no more tasks available to trigger it. For this reason, option D is the correct answer. If the number of tasks was a multiple of the barrier limit, such as 15 instead of 12, then the application will still hang because the ExecutorService is never shut down, and option C would be correct. The isShutdown() call in the application finally block does not trigger a shutdown. Instead, shutdown() should have been used.

26. C. The Lock interface does not include an overloaded version of lock() that takes a time-out value and returns a boolean. For this reason, the code does not compile, and option C is correct. If tryLock(long,TimeUnit) had been used instead of lock(), then the program would have been expected to print TV Time three times at runtime.

27. B. The for loops using copy1 and copy4 both throw a ConcurrentModificationException at runtime, since neither allows modification while they are being iterated upon. Next, CopyOnWriteArrayList makes a copy of the collection every time it is modified, preserving the original list of values the iterator is using. For this reason, the for loop using copy2 completes without throwing an exception or creating an infinite loop. On the other hand, the loop with copy3 enters an infinite loop at runtime. Each time a new value is inserted, the iterator is updated, and the process repeats. Since this is the only statement that produces an infinite loop, option B is correct.

28. E. The shutdown() method prevents new tasks from being added but allows existing tasks to finish. In addition to preventing new tasks from being added, the shutdownNow() method also attempts to stop all running tasks. Neither of these methods guarantees any task will be stopped, making option E the correct answer. Options C and D are incorrect because they name methods that do not exist in ExecutorService.

29. E. The program compiles and does not throw an exception at runtime. The class attempts to add and remove values from a single cookie variable in a thread-safe manner but fails to do so because the methods deposit() and withdrawal() synchronize on different objects. The instance method deposit() synchronizes on the bank object, while the static method withdrawal() synchronizes on the static Bank.class object. Since the compound assignment operators (+=) and (-=) are not thread-safe, it is possible for one call to modify the value of cookies while the other is already operating on it, resulting in a loss of information. For this reason, the output cannot be predicted, and option E is the correct answer. If the two methods were synchronized on the same object, then the cookies variable would be protected from concurrent modifications, printing 0 at runtime.

30. A. The code attempts to search for a matching element in an array using multiple threads. While it does not contain any compilation problems, it does contain an error. Despite creating Thread instances, it is not a multithreaded program. Calling run() on a Thread runs

the process as part of the current thread. To be a multithreaded execution, it would need to instead call the `start()` method. For this reason, the code completes synchronously, waiting for each method call to return before moving on to the next and printing `true` at the end of the execution, making option A the correct answer. On the other hand, if `start()` had been used, then the application would be multithreaded but not thread-safe. The calls to update `foundMatch` are not synchronized, and even if they were, the result might not be available by the time `print()` in the `main()` method was called. For this reason, the result would not be known until runtime.

Chapter 9: Java I/O API

1. D. The code does not compile because `Path.get()` is not a valid NIO.2 method, making option D correct. Either `Paths.get()` or `Path.of()` should be used instead. If the correct method was used, then `DirectoryNotEmptyException` would be the correct answer. The `AtomicMoveNotSupportedException` in option A is possible only when the `ATOMIC_MOVE` option is passed to the `move()` method. Similarly, the `FileAlreadyExistsException` in option C is possible only when the `REPLACE_EXISTING` option is not passed to the `move()` method.

2. A. The constructor for `Console` is `private`. Therefore, attempting to call `new Console()` outside the class results in a compilation error, making option A the correct answer. The correct way to obtain a `Console` instance is to call `System.console()`. Even if the correct way of obtaining a `Console` had been used, and the `Console` was available at runtime, `stuff` is `null` in the `printItinerary()` method. Referencing `stuff.activities` results in a `NullPointerException`.

3. D,F. `BufferedWriter` is a wrapper class that requires an instance of `Writer` to operate on. Since `FileOutputStream` does not inherit `Writer`, the code does not compile, and option D is correct. If `FileWriter` was used instead of `FileOutputStream`, then the code would compile without issue and print 1. The try-with-resources statement closes `System.out` before the `catch` or `finally` blocks are called. When the `finally` block is executed, the output has nowhere to go, which means the last value of 3 is not printed, making option F correct.

4. F. The code does not compile. There are no `createDirectory()`, `createDirectories()`, and `delete()` methods defined on the `Path` interface. Instead, the NIO.2 `Files` class should be used. Since four lines of code do not compile, option F is the correct answer. If the lines were corrected to use the `Files` class, then the application would print an exception at line k1, as the directory already exists.

5. A,C. Generally speaking, classes should be marked with the `Serializable` interface if they contain data that we might want to save and retrieve later. Options B, D, E, and F describe the type of data that we would want to store over a long period of time. Options A and C, though, define classes that manage transient or short-lived data. Application processes change quite frequently, and trying to reconstruct a process is often considered a bad idea.

6. D. First, p2 is an absolute path, which means that p1.resolve(p2) just returns p2. For this reason, options B and C are incorrect. Since p1 is a relative path, it is appended onto p2, making option D correct and option A incorrect. Option A would be correct if normalize() was applied.

7. B. Writer is an abstract class, so options A, D, and E are incorrect. Classes extend abstract classes; they do not implement them, making option B correct. Note that InputStream, OutputStream, and Reader are also abstract classes.

8. D. After calling createDirectories(), the directory /home is guaranteed to exist if it does not already. The second argument of the copy() command should be the location of the new file, not the folder the new file is placed in. Therefore, the program attempts to write the file to the path /home. Since there is already a directory at that location, a FileAlreadyExistsException is thrown at runtime, making option D correct.

9. E. The code does not compile because readAllLines() returns a List<String>, not a stream, making option E the answer. If the correct method lines() was used instead, then five lines would be printed at runtime.

10. E. The size variable is properly serialized with a value of 4. Upon deserialization, none of the class elements that assign a value to an instance variable are run, leading to size being deserialized as 4. Since the name variable is marked transient, this value is deserialized as null. For these reasons, option E is correct.

11. B. The readPassword() returns a char array for security reasons. If the data was stored as a String, it would enter the shared JVM string pool, potentially allowing a malicious user to access it, especially if there is a memory dump. By using a char array, the data can be immediately cleared after it is written and removed from memory. For this reason, option B is the correct answer.

12. A. While you might not be familiar with FilterOutputStream, the diagram shows that the two classes must inherit from OutputStream. Options B, C, and E can be eliminated as choices since PrintOutputStream and Stream are not the name of any java.io classes. Option D can also be eliminated because OutputStream is already in the diagram, and you cannot have a circular class dependency. That leaves us with the correct answer, option A, with BufferedOutputStream and PrintStream both extend FilterOutputStream. Note that ByteArrayOutputStream and FileOutputStream referenced in Options C and D, respectively, do not extend FilterOutputStream, although knowing this fact was not required to solve the problem.

13. D. Line 15 is the first line to not compile, as relativize() is an instance method, not a static method. Line 16 also does not compile, as size(), not length(), should be used to retrieve a file size. Finally, line 17 does not compile because view is an attribute class, not an attribute view. For line 17 to compile, line 13–14 would have to use Files.getFileAttributeView() with BasicFileAttributeView.class as the class. The rest of the lines do not contain any compiler errors, making option D correct.

14. C. The code compiles and runs without issue. The first two values of the ByteArrayInputStream are read. Next, the markSupported() value is tested. Since -1 is not one of the possible options, we assume that ByteArrayInputStream does support

marks. Two values are read and three are skipped, but then `reset()` is called, putting the stream back in the state before `mark()` was called. In other words, everything between `mark()` and `reset()` can be ignored. The last value read is 3, making option C the correct answer.

15. B. The class compiles and runs without issue, so option F is incorrect. The class defines three variables, only one of which is serializable. The first variable, `chambers`, is serializable, with the value 2 being written to disk and then read from disk. Note that constructors and instance initializers are not executed when a class is deserialized. The next variable, `size`, is `transient`. It is discarded when it is written to disk, so it has the default object value of `null` when read from disk. Finally, the variable `color` is `static`, which means it is shared by all instances of the class. Even though the value was RED when the instance was serialized, this value was not written to disk, since it was not part of the instance. The constructor call `new Valve()` between the two try-with-resources blocks sets this value to BLUE, which is the value printed later in the application. For these reasons, the class prints `2,null,BLUE`, making option B the correct answer.

16. A,D. Simplifying the path symbols, options B, C, and F become `/objC/forward/Sort.java`, which applying the symbol link becomes `/java/Sort.java`. Option E just becomes `/java/Sort.java`, without any path symbols involved. Option A is correct, as the `resolve()` method concatenates the path to be `/objC/bin/objC/forward/Sort.java`. Option D is also correct, as the simplified path is `/objC/java/forward/Sort.java`. In both of these cases, the symbolic link `/objC/forward` cannot be applied.

17. D. The `skip(1)` method just reads a single byte and discards the value. The `read()` method can be used for a similar purpose, making option D the correct answer. Option A is incorrect because there is no `jump()` method defined in `Reader`. Options B, C, and E are incorrect because they cannot be used to skip data, only to mark a location and return to it later.

18. F. Trick question! The code does not compile; therefore, option F is correct. The `toRealPath()` interacts with the file system, and therefore throws a checked `IOException`. Since this checked exception is not handled inside the lambda expression, the class does not compile. If the lambda expression was fixed to handle the `IOException`, then the expected number of `Path` values printed would be six, and option C would be the correct answer. A `maxDepth` value of 1 causes the `walk()` method to visit two total levels, the original `/flower`, and the files it contains.

19. D. The statements in options A, B, and C are each correct, making option D correct. If `System.console()` is available, then the program will ask the user a question and then print the response to the error stream. On the other hand, if `System.console()` is not available, then the program will exit with a `NullPointerException`. It is strongly recommended to always check whether `System.console()` is `null` after requesting it. Finally, the user may choose not to respond to the program's request for input, resulting in the program hanging indefinitely.

20. E. The code compiles, so option C is incorrect. Not all `InputStream` classes support the `mark()` operation. If `mark()` is supported, then 7 is printed at runtime. Alternatively, if `mark()` is not supported, then an `IOException` will be printed at runtime. For this reason, option E is correct. Always remember to call `markSupported()` before using a `mark()` operation on an `InputStream`.

21. A. The `Files.find()` method requires a `maxDepth` value as the second parameter. Since this parameter is missing, the method does not compile, and option A is correct. If a `maxDepth` parameter was added, then the method would compile but not print anything at runtime since the stream does not include a terminal operation.

22. F. `Serializable` is a marker interface, which means it does not contain any abstract methods that require implementation, making option F correct. The interface is only meant to indicate the object is capable of serialization.

23. B. First, the class compiles without issue. It is not without problems, though. The `Files.isSameFile()` method call on line j1 first checks if the `Path` values are equivalent in terms of `equals()`. One is absolute, and the other is relative, so this test will fail. The `isSameFile()` method then moves on to verify that the two `Path` values reference the same file system object. Since we know the directory does not exist, the call to `isSameFile()` on line j1 will produce a `NoSuchFileException` at runtime, making option B the correct answer.

24. D. Both stream statements compile without issue, making options A, B, and C incorrect. The two statements are equivalent to one another and print the same values at runtime. For this reason, option D is correct. There are some subtle differences between the two methods calls. The `walk()` call does not include a depth limit, but since `Integer.MAX_VALUE` is the default value, the two calls are equivalent. Furthermore, the `walk()` statement prints a stream of absolute paths stored as `String` values, while the `find()` statement prints a stream of `Path` values. If the input p was a relative path, then these two calls would have very different results, but since we are told p is an absolute path, the application of `toAbsolutePath()` does not change the results.

25. A,E. An attribute view has the advantage of reading all of the file information on a single trip, rather than multiple trips to the file system making option A correct. Option B is incorrect because nothing guarantees it will perform faster, especially if the `Files` method is only being used to read a single attribute. Option C is also incorrect because both sets of methods have built-in support for symbolic links. Options D and F are incorrect because memory and resource leaks are not related to reading file attribute views. Finally, option E is correct, as NIO.2 supports file-system dependent attribute view classes.

26. A,C,F. Since you need to read primitives and `String` values, the `InputStream` classes are appropriate. Therefore, you can eliminate options B and D since they use `Reader` classes. Option E is incorrect, as this is not a `java.io` class. The data should be read from the file using an `FileInputStream` class, buffered with a `BufferedInputStream` class for performance, and deserialized into Java-accessible data types with an `ObjectInputStream` class, making options A, C, and F correct.

27. B. The method compiles, so option A is incorrect. The method reads all of the elements of a directory tree, keeping only directories. The `forEach()` method does not print anything, though, making option B correct. If the lambda in the `forEach()` method was modified to print something, such as `s -> System.out.println(Files.isDirectory(s))`, then it would print `true` at least once for the coffee directory. It would then print `true` for each directory within the directory tree.

28. D,F. The code compiles and runs without issue, so options A and B are incorrect. The problem with the implementation is that checking if `ios.readObject()` is `null` is not the recommended way of iterating over an entire file. For example, the file could have been written with `writeObject(null)` in between two non-`null` records. In this case, the reading of the file would stop on this `null` value, before the end of the file has been reached. For this reason, option D is the correct answer. Note that the valid way to iterate over all elements of a file using `ObjectInputStream` is to continue to call `readObject()` until an `EOFException` is thrown. Finally, `score` is marked `transient`, which means the default `int` value of 0 will be set when the class is deserialized, making option F correct.

29. A,C. The `Console` class contains `readLine()` and `readPassword()` methods, but not a `read()` method, making option A one of the correct answers, and options D and E incorrect. It also contains a `reader()` method that returns a `Reader` object. The `Reader` class defines a `read()` method, but not a `readLine()` method. For this reason, option C is the other correct answer, and option B is incorrect. Recall that a `BufferedReader` is required to call the `readLine()` method.

30. F. The `relativize()` method requires that both path values be absolute or relative. Based on the details provided, `p1` is a relative path, while `p2` is an absolute path. For this reason, the code snippet produces an exception at runtime, making option F the correct answer. If the first path was modified to be absolute by dropping the leading dot (`.`) in the path expression, then the output would match the values in option A.

31. E. The code compiles without issue. Even though `tricks` would be dropped in the normalized path `/bag/of/disappear.txt`, there is no `normalize()` call, so `path.subpath(2,3)` returns `tricks` on line 5. On line 6, the call to `getName()` throws an `IllegalArgumentException` at runtime. Since `getName()` is zero-indexed and contains only one element, the call on line 6 throws an `IllegalArgumentException`, making option E the correct answer. If `getName(0)` had been used instead of `getName(1)`, then the program would run without issue and print `/home/tricks`.

32. A,F. The `lines()` method returns `Stream<String>`, while the `readAllLines()` method returns `List<String>`, making option A correct and option D incorrect. Neither method is guaranteed to be faster or slower than the other, making options B and E incorrect. The `lines()` method lazily reads the file as the stream is processed, while the `readAllLines()` method reads the entire file into memory at once. For this reason, the `readAllLines()` method may require more memory to hold a large file, making option F correct and option C incorrect.

33. A. First, the code compiles. The format of the `String` on line v1 is valid, making option D incorrect. While `System.console()` throws a `NullPointerException` if it is not available, `System.in` does not, making option E incorrect.

The first part of the code runs without issue, printing a message such as `bone fetched in 1.8 seconds`. The I/O stream `System.in` is closed at the end of the try-with-resources block. That means calling `readLine()` again results in an operation on a closed stream, which would print an exception at runtime and make option C correct, except `System.err` is already closed due to the try-with-resources block! Therefore, only one message is printed, and option A is correct.

34. D. The `Files.delete()` and `Files.list()` declare a checked `IOException` that must be handled or declared. For this reason, the code does not compile, and option D is correct.

35. B,F. All of the options compile except option E, since `FileInputStream` does not have a `readLine()` method. A `BufferedReader` should be used instead. Options A and C suffer from the same problem. If the file is not exactly a multiple of 123 bytes, then extra information will be written to the file from the end of the `data` array. Option D is incorrect because the second argument should be an offset, and the third argument should be the number of bytes to read from the `data` array.

Option B is correct and uses an array to read a fixed number of bytes and then writes that exact number of bytes to the output file. Option F is also correct, although it does not use an array. Instead, a single byte is read and written on each iteration of the loop.

36. F. The `Bowl` class does not implement the `Serializable` interface; therefore, attempting to write the instance to disk, or calling `readObject()` using `ObjectInputStream`, will result in a `NotSerializableException` at runtime. Remember, all instance members of a class must be serializable or marked `transient` for the class to properly implement the `Serializable` interface and be used with Java serialization. For this reason, option F is the correct answer. If the `Bowl` class did implement `Serializable`, then the value of `name` and `sugar` would be `CornLoops` and `0`, respectively, since none of the constructors, initializers, or setters methods are used on deserialization, making option B the correct answer.

37. B. The program compiles and runs without issue, making options C and D incorrect. The first variable, `halleysComet`, is created with `subpath(1,5)` and `normalize()` being applied right away, leading to `halleysComet` being assigned a value of `m1.meteor`. The second variable, `lexellsComet` is assigned a value on line 14, but lines 15–16 do not include an assignment operation. Since `Path` instances are immutable, the changes are lost. For this reason, the two objects are not equivalent on lines 18–19, and option B is correct. If `lexellsComet` was assigned the value created on line 15–16, though, then the path value of `lexellsComet` would be `m1.meteor` and option A would be correct.

38. F. When data is deserialized, none of variable initializers, instance initializers, or constructors is called. The class can have `static` initializers, but they are not called as part of deserialization. Finally, there is no `restoreObject()` method that is used in standard deserialization. For these reasons, option F is correct.

39. A,B,E. The code moves a file from `/nursery/sapling.seed` to the new location of `/forest`, not `/forest/sapling.seed`. For this reason, options C and D are both incorrect. If there is no file or directory at `/forest`, then the program completes successfully. If a file already exists at that location, then an exception is thrown since the `REPLACE_EXISTING` flag is not set. For these reasons, options A and B are both correct. Since the `ATOMIC_MOVE` flag is set, option E is correct, and option F is incorrect.

40. C. The program compiles and runs without issue, making options A, D, and E incorrect. The program uses `Files.list()` to iterate over all files within a single directory. For each file, it then iterates over the lines of the file and sums them. For this reason, option C is the correct answer. If the `count()` method had used `Files.walk()` instead of `Files.lines()`, then the class would still compile and run, and option B would be the correct answer. Note that we had to wrap `Files.lines()` in a `try/catch` block, because using this method directly within a lambda expression without one leads to a compilation error.

Chapter 10: Secure Coding in Java SE Application

1. B. This class does not implement `Serializable`, so option A is incorrect. This code is well encapsulated because the instance variables are `private`. While the instance variable references do not change after the object is created, the contents `fauna` can be modified, so it is not immutable. For these reasons, option B is correct.

2. C,E. Options B, D, and F are not supported options in Java. The `serialVersionUID` class variable can be used in serialization, but it relates to the version of the class stored, not the choice in fields serialized, making option A incorrect. That leaves options C and E as the correct answers. The `serialPersistentFields` class variable defines a whitelist of fields to serialize, while the `transient` modifier constructs a blacklist of fields to skip.

3. B. The method compiles, so option E is incorrect. It is recommended to use a `PreparedStatement` with bind variables, over a `Statement`, to avoid SQL injection. Since the data type of the variable is `String`, it needs to be escaped making this method at risk for SQL injection.

   Further, there is no risk of a resource leak that could be exploited in a denial of service attack. The `Connection` object is declared immediately before the try-with-resources block and closed by it, so it cannot be left open. For these reasons, option B is correct.

4. B. Option B is correct because mutability means the state can change, and immutability means it cannot. The other options are invalid. In option C, rigidity is not a common programming term.

5. C,D,E. A denial of service attack is about overloading the system with too much data or too many requests to process legitimate incoming requests. Option A is incorrect, and option C is correct because a try-with-resources or `finally` block should be used to close resources to prevent a resource leak. Option B is incorrect because SQL injection is a form of injection attack, not one based on volume or resources.

   Option D is correct because a malicious attack could send a lot of bad requests with huge files. Option E is also correct as numeric overflow can be used to overwhelm a system. Option F is incorrect because immutability does not usually play a part in DoS attacks.

6. A,D. The policy compiles and uses correct syntax, making option A correct. However, it gives permissions that are too broad. The user needs to be able to read a recipe, so `write` permissions should not be granted, making option D also correct.

7. C,F. Inclusion attacks occur when multiple files or components are embedded within a single entity, such as a zip bomb or the billion laughs attack. Both can be thwarted with depth limits, making option C and F correct. The rest of the options are not related to inclusion attacks.

8. B,D,E. Immutable objects are ones that are not modified after they are created. Immutable objects can have `public` constructors. There is no need to change the access modifier to

`private`, making option A incorrect. All instance variables should be `private` in an immutable class to prevent subclasses and classes within the package from modifying them outside the class, making option B correct and option C incorrect. They should not have any setter methods, making option D correct. The class should also either be marked `final` or contain `final` methods to prevent subclasses from altering the behavior of the class, making option E correct. Finally, option F is incorrect as `String` is immutable, so a defensive copy is not required. Note that if `species` were a mutable type, like `List`, a defensive copy would be required.

9.   A,C,F. The best way to protect a sensitive class is to prevent the class from being extended or prevent any of its methods from being overridden. Options A and C accomplish this. Option F also is appropriate. By marking all constructors `private`, only `static` methods that the class controls can be used to obtain instances of the object. Options B and D are incorrect because they do not prevent methods from being overridden that could change the behavior of the class. Option E is incorrect because constructors cannot be marked `final`.

10. C. The class compiles, so option E is incorrect. It is recommended to use a `PreparedStatement` over a `Statement` to avoid SQL injection although it is not strictly necessary. In this case, because the data type of the variable is `int`, Java already prevents a malicious `String` from being entered into the query. Therefore, this method is not at risk for SQL injection, making option B incorrect.

On the other hand, the code is a risk of a resource leak that could be exploited in a denial of service attack. While the `Connection` object doesn't need to be declared in the try-with-resources block, it should be declared right before it. In this case, there's a line in between, `con.createStatement()`, that could throw an exception, thereby preventing the `Connection` from ever being closed. For these reasons, option C is correct.

11. B,G. Line `p1` only partially validates the input from the user, since it performs a case insensitive match. Therefore, the code executed on line `p2` could be any variant of the magic word such as `Abracadabra`, `aBraCadAbra`, `abracaDABRA`, etc. In this manner, the user has access to many system properties to read from on line `p2`, making option B correct. The code also does not protect its input because `trick` is returned to the user, who is free to modify the `List`. Instead, an immutable collection should be returned on line `p3`, making option G correct.

12. E. By definition, you cannot change the value of an instance variable in an immutable class. There are no setter methods, making option A incorrect. While option B would allow you to set the value, the class would no longer be immutable. Option C is incorrect because that would not modify the original instance. Option E is correct. If you are an advanced developer, you might know that you can use reflection to change the value. Don't read into questions like this on the exam. Reflection isn't on the exam, so you can pretend it doesn't exist.

13. F. The class is not marked `Serializable`, meaning none of the changes will work and making option F correct. If it was corrected to implement `Serializable`, then it would serialize all of the fields, not just `flour` as written. This is because `serialPersistentFields` is declared without the `static` modifier. Alternatively, all of the other fields besides `flour` could be marked `transient` to achieve the desired result.

14. B,D. Ensuring resources are released helps prevent a denial of service attack. Stream methods, such as `Files.lines()`, do not automatically close the file. Option B is correct since the programmer needs to do it. Without this, the system could run out of file resource handles as part of a denial of service attack.

When a resource is locked using an instance of the concurrent `Lock` interface, it should be unlocked in a `finally` block to ensure this step is not missed. Therefore, option D is the other correct answer. Without this, it's possible an acquired lock is kept indefinitely, and a deadlock ensues as part of a denial of service attack.

15. C. A distributed denial of service attack is a denial of service attack that comes from multiple sources, making option C correct. There is no such thing as a million frowns attack. The rest of the answers are real attacks but can be executed from a single source.

16. B. The method only grants someone access if they appear in either the `approved` or `rejected` list. The combined data set forms a conceptual whitelist, making option B correct. The variable names chosen were meant to be tricky. If the code was checked to block people from the rejected list as well, then it would be both a whitelist and blacklist implementation.

17. B,F. The `clone()` method is inherited from the `Object` class. For this reason, it can be called on any `Object` without resulting in a compiler error, making options A and C incorrect. Option B is correct and defines the default behavior of `clone()` if the class does not implement `Cloneable`. On the other hand, if a class implements `Cloneable` but does not override `clone()`, then Java will perform a shallow copy by default, making option D incorrect. Finally, if the class implements `Cloneable` and overrides `clone()`, then the behavior of the `clone()` method is entirely dependent on the implementation. For this reason, option F is correct, and option E is incorrect.

18. A,D,F. Sensitive information should not be written to `System.out`, `System.err`, or a stack trace. For this reason, option A is correct, and option C is incorrect. It is preferable to use `char[]` instead of `String` for sensitive data so that it does not enter the `String` pool and become available as part of a memory dump. For this reason, option D is correct, and option B is incorrect. Note that `Console` does have a `readPassword()` method that returns `char[]`. Finally, the correct Java policy permission to prevent write access is to only grant read access, making option F correct and option E incorrect.

19. E,F. Encrypting or customizing the handling of certain sensitive fields are good reasons to customize the serialization process via methods, making options E and F correct. Options A, B, and D are invalid and are not reasons to customize the process. Option C is incorrect as the `transient` modifier or `serialPersistentFields` can be used to exclude fields from serialization without the need to add any serialization methods.

20. D. A good solution when input validation fails is to stop processing a request and throw an `Exception` to the calling method to deal with the problem, making option D correct. Options A and B are incorrect because throwing `Error` should be avoided for situations where the application can recover. Also, assertions are often disabled at runtime. Option C is incorrect as the user should not be allowed to continue if they have provided invalid input. Finally, option E is incorrect for obvious reasons.

21. C,E. When invoking `doPrivileged()`, make sure there is no chance for a user to pass their own, unprotected values into the request. Since a constant `SCORES` is used to read the system property on line m2, rather than user provided input, the code is safe from tainted inputs from the user. The code validates its inputs enough that an injection attack is not possible, making option E correct.

22. E. The `GetField` class is used with the `readObject()` method, making option E correct. There is also a `PutField` class used with the `writeObject()` method that you should be familiar with for the exam.

23. A. An immutable class must not allow the state to change. The `Flower` class does this correctly. While the class isn't `final`, the getters are, so subclasses can't change the value returned. The `Plant` class lacks this protection, which makes it mutable. Option A is correct.

24. B,F. Option A is incorrect because access control restricts who can do something rather than preventing an injection attack. Option B is correct because unsanitized input from the command line can do something undesirable like delete a file. Option C is incorrect because the programmer typed those constants rather than a hostile party.

Option D is incorrect because changing the values of an object is not an injection attack. Option E is incorrect because serialization is writing data to disk rather than executing. Option F is correct because XML parsing can load hostile values into your program.

25. A,B. The code is well encapsulated because all instance variables are `private`, making option A correct. It is susceptible to a denial of service attack since there is no input validation. For example, if the maximum integer value of 2,147,483,647 is passed, then it will make a huge number of calls to the database, potentially tying up the system and blocking valid requests. For this reason, option B is correct. To fix this code, a limit on the inputted value should be used. Option E is incorrect because the class is thread-safe since the instance methods are all `synchronized`. The rest of the options do not apply to this class.

26. F. Confidential information includes things like credit card numbers and passwords. Options A, B, and C are incorrect because they expose confidential information to the environment in which the application is running. Option D is incorrect because it allows the data to enter the `String` pool, where it can get printed if a memory dump occurs. Option E is incorrect, as passwords should not be sent over email. For these reasons, option F is correct.

27. B,C,F. While it is permitted to declare a resource outside a try-with-resources statement and still have it be protected, declaring two is not recommended. In particular, if `con.createStatement()` fails, then the `Connection` is not closed. For this reason, the code is susceptible to denial of service attacks, making option B correct.

While it does not use a `PreparedStatement`, the code is safe from SQL injection because the query does not take any parameters, making option C correct. Finally, if the method completes without throwing an exception, then that means the try-with-resources block was successfully entered. In this case, all resources would have been closed properly making option F correct.

28. D. This class does not implement `Serializable`, so option A is incorrect. This code is well encapsulated because the instance variables are `private`. The algae and wave variables are immutable because they are marked `final`, and there are no methods that can change them. The getAlgae() method creates a defensive copy, preventing direct access to the algae object. Finally, the sun variable is initialized to 0 and is not able to be changed after its creation. The setSun() method is missing a `this` reference, so the assignment sun = sun assigns the method parameter sun to itself. For these reasons, the class is immutable, and option D is correct.

29. A,D,F. This class implements `Serializable` and contains serializable instance variables making option A correct. This code is not well encapsulated because the instance variables are `public`, which matches option D. While a defensive copy of fauna is made in the getter, the instance variable is `public`, and elements can be added or removed directly. Therefore, the object is not immutable, and option F is correct.

30. A,E,F. A malicious attacker could extend this class and override the security check() method, so marking it `final` is a good idea, making option A correct. Next, the Console class offers a readPassword() method that does not echo what the user types and uses char[] instead of String to avoid a password entering the String pool. For these reasons, option E is correct. Finally, line 10 prints the user's password to the System.out log file, which is a terrible security idea. It should be changed or removed, making option F correct. The rest of the options are incorrect and do not improve the security of this class.

31. B,D. The read methods are used as part of deserialization, not serialization, making options A and E incorrect. Option B and D are correct because they use the correct method parameters and return types for writeReplace() and writeObject().

32. B. An inclusion attack is one in which multiple components are embedded within a single file, such as zip bomb or XML exploit (billion laughs attack). Since the maximum file size is given to be small, this would be the most likely type of attack used, making option B correct. Note that if the file size was not limited, then this could be a regular denial of service attack in which a large file is sent repeatedly to overwhelm the system.

33. B,C,F. Caching permissions for a user is allowed, so option F is correct. That said, the security on using the cached data must be checked. The class is missing calls to AccessController.checkPermission() before lines h1 and h2. On line h1, this can result in a user reading a cached permission they do not have access to, making option B correct. On line h2, security permissions could be elevated since access is not checked, making option C correct.

34. F. The query uses a `PreparedStatement` so that the name is properly escaped. For this reason, SQL injection is not possible, and option F is correct. For the exam, you don't need to know how to write a query to cause SQL injection, just how to prevent it.

35. B,D,E. An immutable class can have `public` constructors, so option A is incorrect. Options B, D, and E make up the requirements for an immutable class. Option D can be fulfilled by making the class `final` or marking the methods `final`. Option C is incorrect because instance variables can still be declared with a value or set by an instance initializer. Option F is also incorrect. While it is common to mark instance variables `final`, as long as there is no way for them to be changed after the constructor is executed, the class can still be considered immutable.

36. A,C. A denial of service attack is one in which one or more requests attempt to overwhelm the system and disrupt legitimate requests. Option A is an access or confidentiality problem. Option C is about gaining access or changing data that the user should not be permitted to. Options B, D, E, and F are all denial of service attacks because they increase load in an attempt to bring a system down. Remember, a zip bomb is when a small file is expanded to become a much larger file.

37. B,D,E. The `Fruit` class must implement `Cloneable`; otherwise, an exception would be thrown at runtime, making option E correct. The `Fruit` class must also override the `clone()` method. If it did not, then a shallow copy would be performed on the `sweet` object, resulting in the code printing `true` at runtime. Since this is not the case, option D is correct. Finally, we've already ruled out a shallow copy, so by process of elimination it must perform a deep copy. For this reason, option B is correct.

38. C,E. The primary way SQL injection occurs is from concatenating SQL queries without properly escaping the values. Avoiding concatenation and using a `PreparedStatement` with bind variables are the commonly accepted ways to prevent this. For these reasons, options C and E are correct.

Option A is incorrect because a database that takes no query parameters of any kind would be pretty limited in its capabilities. For example, it would be challenging to log a user in if you couldn't search for that user. Option B is also incorrect, as you can't prevent a SQL injection after it is already successful. Option D is incorrect, as a resource leak is more susceptible to a denial of service attack in which resources are exploited, rather than SQL injection in which data is manipulated. Finally, option F is incorrect, as avoiding using a relational database is not a commonly accepted practice for avoiding SQL injection.

39. C. Option C is the correct answer. A hacker could override the `setSecret()` method to first steal the inputted secret value and email it herself and then pass the data along to the parent by calling `super.setSecret()` without anyone noticing any difference. One fix would be to mark this method `final` in the `Secret` class or make the `Secret` class `final`.

Option B is incorrect because variables can only be hidden, not overridden, so declaring a new `mySecret` variable would not grant access to the parent variable. Option D is incorrect as overriding this method won't allow the attacker to access the `mySecret` variable directly. Option E is trivially incorrect, as `private` methods cannot be overridden. Finally, option F is incorrect as adding a constructor does not grant access to `private` members in the parent class.

40. B. An immutable class must not allow the state to change. In the `Faucet` class, the caller has a reference to the `List` being passed in and can change the size or elements in it. Similarly, any class with a reference to the object can get the `List` by calling `get()` and make these changes. The `Faucet` class is not immutable. The `Spout` class shows how to fix these problems and is immutable, making option B correct.

Chapter 11: Database Applications with JDBC

1. E. Connection is a JDK interface for communicating with the database. PreparedStatement and ResultSet are typically used to write queries and are also in the JDK. Driver is tricky because you don't write code that references it directly. However, you are still required to know it is a JDBC interface. DriverManager is used in JDBC code to get a Connection. However, it is a concrete class rather than an interface. Since only four out of the five are JDBC interfaces, option E is correct.

2. F. Database-specific implementation classes are not in the java.sql package. The implementation classes are in database drivers and have package names that are specific to the database. Therefore, option F is correct. The Driver interface is in the java.sql package. Note that these classes may or may not exist. You are not required to know the names of any database-specific classes, so the creators of the exam are free to make up names.

3. D. All JDBC URLs begin with the protocol jdbc followed by a colon as a delimiter. Option D is the only one that does both of these, making it the correct answer.

4. A. The Driver interface is responsible for getting a connection to the database, making option A the answer. The Connection interface is responsible for communication with the database but not making the initial connection. The Statement interface knows how to run the SQL query, and the ResultSet interface knows what was returned by a SELECT query.

5. C. Connection is an interface. Since interfaces do not have constructors, option D is incorrect. The Connection class doesn't have a static method to get a Connection either, making option A incorrect. The Driver class is also an interface without static methods, making option B incorrect. Option C is the answer because DriverManager is the class used in JDBC to get a Connection.

6. F. The DriverManager.getConnection() method can be called with just a URL. It is also overloaded to take the URL, username, and password. Since this is not one of the options, the answer is option F.

7. D. This code is missing a call to rs.next(). As a result, rs.getInt(1) throws a SQLException with the message Invalid cursor state - no current row. Therefore, option D is the answer.

8. E. The execute() method is allowed to run any type of SQL statements. The executeUpdate() method is allowed to run any type of the SQL statement that returns a row count rather than a ResultSet. Both DELETE and UPDATE SQL statements are allowed to be run with either execute() or executeUpdate(). They are not allowed to be run with executeQuery() because they do not return a ResultSet. Therefore, option E is the answer.

9. A. This code uses a PreparedStatement without bind variables (?). While it would be better to use bind variables, this code does run. The ResultSet has one value and does print Mei Xiang successfully. Therefore, option A is the answer.

10. F. While the table has two columns, the SQL query has only one bind variable (?). Therefore, the code throws an exception when attempting to set the second bind variable, and option F is correct.

11. B. This code is correct. It executes the first update to add the first row and then sets the parameters for the second. When it updates the second time, it adds the second row. Therefore, option B is the answer.

12. E. `CallableStatement` and `PreparedStatement` are interfaces that extend the `Statement` interface. You don't need to know that for the exam. You do need to know that a database driver is required to provide the concrete implementation class of `Statement` rather than the JDK. This makes option E correct.

13. B. Unlike arrays, JDBC uses one-based indexes. Since `num_pages` is in the second column, the parameter needs to be 2, ruling out options A and C. Further, there is not a method named `getInteger()` on the `ResultSet` interface, ruling out option D. Since the proper method is `getInt()`, option B is the answer.

14. B,D. Since JDBC does not begin indexes with zero, option A is incorrect, and option B is correct. Similarly, the second parameter is at index 2, so option C is incorrect, and option D is the other answer. Note that `setObject()` can be called instead of a more specific type.

15. D. Option A does not compile because you have to pass a column index or column name to the method. Options B and C compile. However, there are not columns named 0 or 1. Since these column names don't exist, the code would throw a `SQLException` at runtime. Option D is correct as it uses the proper column name.

16. D. A JDBC URL has three components separated by colons. All three of these URLs meet those criteria. For the data after the component, the database driver specifies the format. Depending on the driver, this might include an IP address and port. Regardless, it needs to include the database name or alias. The `first` and `second` URLs could both be valid formats because they mention the database `box`. However, `third` is incorrect because it has `jdbc@` instead of `jdbc:`. Therefore, option D correct.

17. C,D. JDBC uses Java and SQL, so it is not language independent, making option A incorrect. It is used with relational databases, ruling out option B. A `CallableStatement` supports stored procedures, not a `PreparedStatement`, making option E incorrect.

Options C and D are correct. Using bind variables with a `PreparedStatement` produces code that is easier to read than one with a lot of `String` concatenation. Further, when used properly, a `PreparedStatement` prevents SQL injection.

18. B. `Connection` is an interface rather than a concrete class. Therefore, it does not have a constructor and line `s1` does not compile. As a result, option B is the answer. Option A would be the answer if the code `new Connection()` was changed to `DriverManager .getConnection()`.

19. E. When manually closing database resources, they should be closed in the reverse order from which they were opened. This means the `ResultSet` object is closed before the `Statement` object and the `Statement` object is closed before the `Connection` object. This makes option E the answer.

20. A. This code correctly obtains a `Connection` and `PreparedStatement`. It then runs a query, getting back a `ResultSet` without any rows. The `rs.next()` call returns `false`, so nothing is printed, making option A correct.

21. F. The SQL query has two bind variables, but the code sets only one. This causes a `SQLException` when `executeQuery()` is called, making option F the answer.

22. A. This code uses a `PreparedStatement` and properly sets a bind variable (`?`). The `ResultSet` has one value and does print `Mei Xiang` successfully. Therefore, option A is the answer.

23. C. Option A is incorrect because `Driver` is an interface, while `DriverManager` is a concrete class. The inverse isn't true either; `DriverManager` doesn't implement `Driver`. Option B is incorrect because the `Connection` implementation comes from a specific database driver JAR. Option C is correct as bind variables (`?`) are used.

24. A. The `count(*)` function in SQL always returns a number. In this case, it is the number zero. This means line `r1` executes successfully because it positions the cursor at that row. Line `r2` also executes successfully and prints `0`, which is the value in the row. Since the code runs successfully, option A is the answer.

25. B. This code is correct. It executes the first update to add the first row and then sets the parameters for the second. For the second update, only one parameter is set. The other is reused since it was set earlier. Therefore, option B is the answer.

26. A,D. The `PreparedStatement` interface extends the `Statement` interface, which matches option D. One of the benefits of a `PreparedStatement` is performance. While a `PreparedStatement` may not be faster if run only once, it will quickly become so. Therefore, option A is the other correct answer.

27. E. In JDBC, the bind variable is always a question mark (`?`), making option A incorrect. A `PreparedStatatement` is not limited to specific types of SQL, making options B and C incorrect as well. This makes option E the correct answer.

28. F. While this code compiles, it isn't right. Since we have a `SELECT` statement, we should be calling `execute()` or `executeQuery()`. Option F is the answer because the code throws an exception when attempting to call `executeUpdate()`.

29. D. When running a query on a `PreparedStatement`, Java closes any already open `ResultSet` objects associated with the statement. This means that `rs1` is closed on line 8. Therefore, it throws a `SQLException` on line 9 because we are trying to call `next()` on a closed `ResultSet`, and option D is correct.

30. C. This question is trickier if you know more JDBC than is on the exam. If you know only what is on the exam, you would assume the `createStatement()` method doesn't exist. However, it does, and `stmt` is a `Statement` object. Since `setString()` does not exist on `Statement`, the code does not compile. This means the answer is option C regardless of your level of knowledge of JDBC.

Chapter 12: Localization

1. **A,E,F.** Oracle defines a locale as a geographical, political, or cultural region, making options A, E, and F correct. A local address and city are too granular for a locale. Also, time zones often span multiple locales.

2. **E.** Java starts out by looking for a properties file with the requested locale, which in this case is the `fr` language. It doesn't find it, so it moves onto the default locale `en_US`, which it does find, making option E correct.

3. **C.** Currencies vary in presentation by locale. For example, `9,000` and `9.000` both represent nine thousand, depending on the locale. Similarly, for dates, `01-02-2022` and `02-01-2022` represent January 2, 2022, or February 1, 2020, depending on the locale. This makes option C the answer.

4. **E.** The `Locale` object provides `getDefault()` and `setDefault()` methods for working with the default locale, so option E is correct. The rest of the methods do not exist in the `Locale` class.

5. **B.** Calling `Locale.setDefault()` changes the default locale within the program. It does not change any settings on the computer. The next time you run a Java program, it will have the original default locale rather than the one you changed it to.

6. **C.** The code compiles and runs without issue. The data is in a valid date format, so the text is parsed as January 21, 2022. Date values are indexed from `1`, not `0`, making option C the correct output. Note that a date formatter is able to format a date/time value, as the time element can be discarded.

7. **E.** The first line of the method is correct, as `Properties` inherits `Map` and has a `get()` method. The `get()` method does not have an overloaded version that takes a default value, though. For this reason, the second and third `get()` calls do not compile, and option E is correct. If `getProperty()` were instead used on the second and third call, then the output would be `bag null trick`.

8. **F.** Options A and B are incorrect because `formatDate()` is not a valid method name in `DateTimeFormatter`. Option E is incorrect because the code compiles if either option C or D is used. Both options C and D will produce an exception at runtime, though, as the date pattern is invalid. In particular, the apostrophe in `o'clock` should be escaped. Option C is also incorrect because there is no hour value `h` for a `LocalDate`. If the pattern string was corrected with `o''clock`, then option D would be correct and print `March at 5 o'clock` at runtime.

9. **A,B.** In Java, a locale can be represented by a language code in lowercase, or a language and country code, with language in lowercase and country in uppercase. For these reasons, options A and B are correct. Options C, D, and E are incorrect because the lowercase language must be before the uppercase country. Option F is incorrect because the language is missing. Remember, the exam won't expect you to know which language and country codes exist, but it will expect you to know how to use them.

10. F. Java starts out by looking for a properties file with the requested locale, which in this case is the `fr_CH` language and country. It doesn't find `Colors_fr_CH.properties`, so it moves onto the locale with just a language code `fr`. It also does not find `Colors_fr.properties`. It then moves on to the default locale `it_CH` checking `Colors_it_CH.properties`, but there is still no match. It drops the country code and checks `it` for `Colors_it.properties`, but still doesn't find a match. Lastly, it checks for a `Colors.properties` file but since that's not an option, it fails. The result is a `MissingResourceException` is thrown at runtime, making option F correct.

11. C. The code compiles, so option D is incorrect. In this sample, the default locale is set to US, while the default locale format is set to GERMANY. Neither is used for formatting the value, as `getCurrencyInstance()` is called with UK as the locale. For this reason, the £ symbol is used, making option C correct.

12. D. The getBundle() does not find `Cars_de_DE.properties` or `Cars_de.properties`, so it moves on to the default locale. Since `Cars_en.properties` is available, it will use this file, falling back to `Cars.properties` if any values are not available. Therefore, it selects `engine` and `horses` from the first file, and `country` from the second file, printing `engine 241 earth` and making option D correct.

13. F. The getBundle() method matches `Cars_fr_FR.properties`. It will then fall back to `Cars_fr.properties` (which does not exist) and `Cars.properties` if the value is not available. For this reason, the first and third values would be `France` and `moteur`. While the second value `horses` is in the default locale, it is not available if the requested locale has been found. As a result, the code throws a `MissingResourceException`, making option F the answer.

14. A. The getBundle() method matches `Cars_fr_FR.properties`. It will then fall back to `Cars_fr.properties` (which does not exist) and `Cars.properties` if the value is not available. For this reason, the first value printed is `moteur` from `Cars.properties`, while the next two values printed are `autoroute` and `France` from `Cars_fr_FR.properties`, making option A correct.

15. F. There are no get() or of() methods in Locale. You need to use a constructor or a predefined Locale constant to obtain a Locale reference. Therefore, option F is the correct answer. Options B and C are close in that `Locale.ITALIAN` does reference a Locale object. However, it should not be passed to the nonexistent get() method.

16. A. Java starts out by looking for a properties file with the requested locale, which in this case is the `zh_CN` language and country. It doesn't find it, so it moves onto the locale with just a language code `zh`, which it also does not find. It then moves on to the default locale `en_US`, but there is still no match. It drops the country code and does find a match with `en`, making option A correct.

17. D. This code compiles and runs without exception, making option D the correct answer. Line 3 uses a predefined Locale constant. Line 5 passes a language and country code for English in Australia. Line 7 incorrectly passes capital letters as a language code. However, Java automatically converts it to lowercase without throwing an exception. The three lines printed by the code are ko, en_AU, and en.

18. E. Java starts out by looking for a properties file with the requested locale, which in this case is the `ca_ES` language and country. It doesn't find it, so it moves onto the locale with just a language code `ca`, which it does find, making option E correct.

19. F. The `parse()` method properly reads the date as April 1, 2022. The `format()` tries to use a date/time formatter on a date, which produces an exception at runtime since the time element is missing. For this reason, option F is correct.

20. A. The first line of the method retrieves the value for the property with key `rocket`, which is `saturn5`. The next line retrieves the value for `earth`, but since it's not found, `null` is returned. The last functions similarly to the previous line but uses ? as the default value since `earth` is not set. The code then prints `saturn5 null ?`, making option A the correct answer.

21. B,D. Options B and D correctly print the same string value in the specified format. Option A is incorrect because `<06.92>` is printed instead of `<06.9>`. Options C and E are incorrect, because (among other things) commas are printed as part of both of the first two values. Option F is incorrect because `<2.1> <6.9>` is printed instead of `<02.1> <06.9>`.

22. B. The class on line p1 should be `Properties` rather than `Property`. As written, it is incorrect and does not compile, making option B the correct answer.

23. B. Java starts out by looking for a properties file with the requested locale, which in this case is the `en` language. It finds it right away, making option B correct.

24. C,D. In Java, a locale can be represented by a language code in lowercase, or a language and country code, with *language* in lowercase and *country* in uppercase. Option C is invalid because both values are lowercase. Option D is invalid because the value is in uppercase. The rest of the options are valid locale formats. Remember, the exam won't expect you to know which language and country codes exist, but it will expect you to know how to use them.

25. B. The code compiles, so option D is incorrect. While three distinct locale values are set, the one that is used for formatting text is `Category.FORMAT`. For this reason, the GERMANY locale is used to formatting the data with the € symbol, making option B correct.

26. D. The date/time pattern uses single quotes to escape the date/time values, meaning the output is `yyyy-MM` for all valid inputs. For this reason, option D is correct. If the single quotes were removed, then `2022-03 2022-01` would be the correct output.

27. D. The method creates a resource bundle using a builder but never sets it. Since we don't know the default locale of the code, the answer depends on where it is executed, making option D correct.

28. A. This code sets the default locale to English and then tries to get a resource bundle for `container`. It finds the resource bundle `container_en.properties` as the most specific match. Both keys are found in this file, so option A is the answer.

29. E. The `Locale` constructor that takes a single argument expects a language code, not a concatenation of language and region codes. Therefore, the language is set as `en_us`, not `en`, with no region code set. Since no properties files match the language `en_us`, the default `container.properties` is used. Since `type` is not found in this properties file, a `MissingResourceException` is thrown at runtime.

30. A. The code compiles, so option E is incorrect. Java starts out by looking for a properties file with the requested locale, which in this case is the `fr` language. It doesn't find `Forest_fr.properties`, so it moves onto the default locale `en`. It also doesn't find `Forest_en.properties`. It settles on `Forest.properties` without throwing an exception, so option F is incorrect. The first argument to `MessageFormat.format()` should be a pattern `String` value. Since `trees` is sent, the output of the formatting string is `trees`, making option A correct. If `rb.getString("trees")` was passed instead of just `trees`, then the output would be `evergreen pretty`.

Chapter 13: Annotations

1. B. The `default` modifier along with a value is used to mark an annotation element as optional, as opposed to required.

2. B,C. Annotations are about storing metadata, or data about data. The maximum number of tickets per person and total number of people the theater can hold define rules that are unlikely to change frequently, so they are best stored with annotations. The number of people attending, price, and time the ticket is sold are likely to change frequently and should be part of the transactional information for the ticket. The seat assignment also changes for every ticket sold.

3. F. `CelestialBody` is not an annotation definition because it is not declared with the `@interface` type, making option F correct. If the correct declaration was used, then option A would be the correct answer. Options B and C are incorrect, because `lightYears` is a constant and cannot be set as part of the annotation. Options C and E are also incorrect because they are missing a `name` element. Option D is incorrect because there is no `value()` element.

4. C. Option C uses the correct values and allows all three annotations to compile. Option A is incorrect because the class declaration usage does not compile. Using option B or E does not allow any of the annotations to compile. Option D allows the class and constructor annotations to compile, but not the method usage.

5. B,C,F. Options B, C, and F are each marker annotations because they do not contain any elements. Option A is incorrect because `@Target` requires an `ElementType[]` value. Option D is incorrect because `@Retention` requires a `RetentionPolicy` value. Option E is incorrect because `@Repeatable` requires a `Class` value.

6. B,D,F. Option B is correct and relies on the fact that the single element `value()` can be used without an element name. Option D is correct because the annotation has a default value; therefore, `value` is optional. Option F is correct and uses the correct name for `value`. Options A, C, and E are incorrect because they use the wrong name for the element.

7. D. Lines 3 and 6 do not compile because wrapper classes are not permitted as annotation element types. Line 5 does not compile because a constant must be declared with a value. For these reasons, option D is correct. The rest of the lines compile without issue.

8. C,E. Options A and D are incorrect. An interface can define a method and be extended, but an annotation cannot. Neither type can declare constructors, making option B incorrect. Annotations and interfaces can both declare constants and be applied to a class declaration, making options C and E correct. Interfaces use the `interface` type, while annotations use the `@interface` type, making option F incorrect.

9. F. The class compiles as is but generates warnings for unchecked/unsafe operations with the `planets.add(5)` operation, so options A and B are incorrect. Inserting `@SuppressWarnings()`, though, will cause a compiler error as it requires at least one value. For this reason, option F is correct. If `@SuppressWarnings("unchecked")` was used instead, then inserting it on lines `m1` and `m2` would allow the code to compile without any warnings.

10. F. An annotation can be applied to all of these Java declarations, making option F correct.

11. A,B,E. The `@Override` annotation is always optional for methods and never required. For this reason, options A and E are correct, and options C and F are incorrect. Option B is correct because adding it to a method that is not actually overriding an inherited method will cause a compiler error. Option D is incorrect because it can be applied only to method declarations.

12. B. The declaration compiles, so option F is incorrect. The `Bread` annotation is declared with one required element, while `Toast` is declared with no required elements. For these reasons, option B is correct, and option E is incorrect. Options A and C are incorrect because neither annotation contains a `value()` element. Option D is incorrect because `wheat` is a constant, not an element.

13. B,D,E. An annotation may omit the element name if it contains an element named `value`, declared as `value()`, making option B correct and option F incorrect. Additionally, it may contain any number of additional elements, provided none of them is required, making option E correct. Finally, the element may optionally have a default value, making option D correct. The other options are incorrect statements that contradict the correct answers.

14. F. Trick question! By default, annotations are not present at runtime. To print a non-null value, both `@Retention(RetentionPolicy.RUNTIME)` and `@Inherited` would be required, making option F correct. The `@Retention` annotation would preserve the annotation for runtime, while the `@Inherited` annotation would apply it to the subclass `Cheetah`.

15. B. Only line 3 contains a compiler error, as an element declared in an annotation must use parentheses after its name, making option B correct. If `value()` was used instead of `value`, then the code would compile.

16. B. A default annotation element value must be a non-null constant expression. Since `lastName()` provides a `null` value by default, the declaration of `Friend` contains a compiler error. The declaration of `MyFriends` does not contain any compiler errors, so option B is correct.

17. B,C,D. An annotation element type must be a primitive type, a `String`, a `Class`, an enum, another annotation, or an array of any of these types. For this reason, options B, C, and D are correct. Option A is incorrect because `Object` is not supported. While primitives are supported, wrappers are not, making option E incorrect. Option F is also incorrect as local variable type inference with `var` is not permitted, even if a `default` value is provided.

18. D,E. `Gift` is a repeatable annotation. It requires specifying a container type annotation using the `Class` object, making option D correct. The containing type annotation referenced must declare a `value()` element that is an array of the repeatable annotation, making option E correct.

19. B,C,F. Option A is incorrect, as annotations generally contain information that is constant throughout the program execution. Option B is correct. For example, adding an `@Override` annotation to a method that is not a valid override will trigger a compiler error. Option C is also correct and is the primary purpose of annotations. Options D and E are incorrect, as annotations can be applied to a variety of types including lambda expression variables and other annotations. Finally, option F is correct. Annotations are optional metadata, and removing all of them from a class does not cause a compiler error.

20. A,B,E. Options A, B, and E are correct and rely on the fact that the element name is optional for an annotation with a single element named `value()`. Option E also relies on annotations supporting a single element for an array. Note that the array provided is not required to have any elements. Option C is incorrect because Java does not automatically convert from a `List` to an array. Option D is incorrect because the annotation contains a required element. Finally, option F is incorrect because `default` is the wrong element name.

21. B,D. The `@SafeVarargs` annotation requires the method to which it is applied contain a varargs parameter and be unable to be overridden, aka marked `static`, `final`, or `private`. Options B and D fulfill this requirement. Options A and E are missing a modifier that prevents them from being overridden. Options C and F are missing a vararg parameter. While a primitive array `int[]` can be passed to a method containing a varargs parameter, to apply the `@SafeVarargs` annotation, the method must be declared with a varargs annotation.

22. A. The correct annotation that preserves information about annotations in generated Javadoc files is `@Documented`. The rest are incorrect.

23. F. The `@Retention` annotation can be applied only to an annotation declaration, not a class declaration, making option F the correct answer. Applying it to a class will result in a compiler error. If `Corn` were an annotation, though, then `RetentionPolicy.RUNTIME` would be correct.

24. E. Lines 3 and 8 do not compile because annotation elements must be `public`, implicitly or explicitly. Line 8 also does not compile because `continue` is a keyword in Java. Line 5 does not compile. While arrays are permitted as element types, collections like `List` are not.

Line 6 does not compile because annotation elements cannot be marked `final`, as they are implicitly `abstract`. For these reasons, option E is correct. Line 4 compiles because an annotation can declare another annotation as the element type. Line 7 also compiles. While the `public` and `abstract` modifiers aren't required for an annotation element, they can be specified.

25. A,B,F. An annotation element can include a `default` value if it is a non-null constant expression. Options A, B, and F fulfill this criteria. Option C is incorrect because it creates a new object. Option D is incorrect because it uses method calls. Option E is incorrect because `null` is not permitted.

26. B,C. `@Weather` is the repeatable annotation, so it can be used twice on the same type declaration, making option C correct. A containing type annotation `@Forecast` takes an array of the repeatable annotation `@Weather`, making option B also correct. Options A and F are incorrect, as those represent an annotation that takes an array of `String` values. Option D and E are incorrect because the repeatable and containing type annotations are reversed.

27. A,D. To correctly apply the `@FunctionalInterface` annotation, the interface must pass the single abstract method test. Also, note that none of the `default` or `static` methods contributes to the abstract method count.

    `Dog` contains a single abstract method `play()`, so it will compile, making option A correct. `Webby` extends `Dog` with the same abstract method as `Dog`. It also declares `toString()`, but since this is inherited from `java.lang.Object`, it does not count as an abstract method. Therefore, `Webby` passes the single abstract method test for functional interfaces, making option D correct. `Astra` is incorrect because it contains two abstract methods, `play()` and `fetch()`. KC is incorrect because it does not extend `Dog` and does not contain any abstract methods. Finally, `Georgette` is incorrect because it contains two abstract methods, `play()` and `jump()`.

28. B. The declaration of `Colors` and `Bouncy` compile without issue. The declaration of `Trampoline` does not compile, though. The `Bouncy` annotation has two required elements, `value()` and `size()`, so the name of the element `value` cannot be dropped. For this reason, option B is correct.

29. B,F. The `@Inherited` annotation determines whether annotations applied to a supertype are applied to its subtypes, while the `@Documented` annotation allows annotations to be included in generated Javadoc. For these reasons, options B and F are correct.

30. D. The `SystemPlanner` class compiles although it contains two warnings. First, the `ProjectPlanner` class is used, which is deprecated. Second, the `create()` method uses an unchecked/unsafe operation taking a `String` for the generic type. For this reason, both `unchecked` and `deprecation` options are required for the code to compile without any warnings. Option D uses the correct format for passing an array to an annotation. Note that `ignoreAll` is not a known parameter that the JVM accepts.

Chapter 14: Practice Exam 1

1. D. Variables are allowed to start with an underscore and are allowed to contain a $. Therefore, all the variable declarations compile, making options A, B, and C incorrect. However, the `println()` refers to the uninitialized local `boolean`. Since local variables are not automatically initialized, the code does not compile, and option D is correct.

2. B,D. The try-with-resources statement requires resources that implement `AutoCloseable`. While `Closeable` extends `AutoCloseable`, it is certainly possible to have a class that implements `AutoCloseable` and works with try-with-resources but does not implement `Closeable`, making option A incorrect. Option B is correct and a valid statement about how resources are closed in try-with-resources statements. Option C is incorrect because the exception in the `try` block is reported to the caller, while the exception in the `close()` method is suppressed. Option D is the other correct answer because neither `catch` nor `finally` is required when try-with-resources is used. Lastly, option E is incorrect. While the `AutoCloseable` interface does define a `close()` method that throws a checked exception, classes that implement this method are free to drop the checked exception, per the rules of overriding methods.

3. E. The code does contain compilation errors, so option A is incorrect. The first is on line 8. The `readAllLines()` method returns a `List<String>`, not a `Stream<String>`. While `parallelStream()` is allowed on a `Collection`, `parallel()` is not. Next, line 14 does not compile because of an invalid method call. The correct NIO.2 method call is `Files.isRegularFile()`, not `File.isRegularFile()`, since the legacy `File` class does not have such a method. Line 18 contains a similar error. `Path` is an interface, not a class, with the correct call being `Paths.get()`. Lastly, line 19 does not compile because the `read()` method throws `Exception`, which is not caught or handled by the `main()` method. For these four reasons, option E is the correct answer.

4. B,C,E. Java supports three types of comments: single-line (`//`), multi-line (`/* */`), and Java-doc (`/** **/`), making options B, C, and E correct. Option A contains a `*/` in the middle of the expected comment, making the part after the comment `Insert */` invalid. Option D is incorrect because a dollar sign (`$`) is not a valid comment in Java. Finally, the hash (`#`) is not a comment character in Java, so option F is incorrect.

5. B. Modules have a cyclic dependency when they depend on each other. In this example, `com.animal` and `com.plant` depend on each other. The other two modules depend on `com.animal` and `com.plant` but do not participate in the cycle. If the `requires` directive in either `com.animal` or `com.plant` were removed, we would no longer have a cyclic dependency. Since only one directive needs to be removed, option B is correct.

6. E. The code does compile. Line s1 is a bit tricky because `length` is used for an array and `length()` is used for a `String`. Line s1 stores the length of `Fall` in a variable, which is 4. Line s2 throws an `ArrayIndexOutOfBoundsException` because 4 is not a valid index for an array with four elements. Remember that indices start counting with zero. Therefore, option E is correct.

7. F. The array is not sorted. It does not meet the pre-condition for a binary search. Therefore, the output is not guaranteed and the answer is option F.

8. E. Option A is incorrect because the `lock()` method does not return a `boolean` value. Option B allows the class to compile (making option D incorrect), but is not guaranteed to print `Tie!` ten times. Depending on the thread ordering, it may print the value 1 to 10 times. Option C is incorrect because `tryLock()` with a time value also requires a `TimeUnit` parameter. For these reasons, option E is the correct answer.

9. B,D,F. The `clock` variable is accessed by a class in the same package; therefore, it requires package-private or less restrictive access (`protected` and `public`). The `getTime()` method is accessed by a subclass in a different package; therefore, it requires `protected` or less restrictive access (`public`). Options B, D, and F conform to these rules, making them the correct answer. Options A and C cause the `Snooze` class to fail to compile because the `getTime()` method is not accessible outside the package, even though `Snooze` is a subclass of `Alarm`. Option E causes the `Coffee` class to fail to compile because the `clock` variable is only visible within the `Alarm` class.

10. D. This code attempts to use two terminal operations, `forEach()` and `count()`. Only one terminal operation is allowed, so the code does not compile, and option D is correct. The author of this code probably intended to use `peek()` instead of `forEach()`. With this change, the answer would be option A.

11. E. All code in a try-with-resources declaration must implement `Closeable` or `AutoCloseable`. The call to `stmt.setString()` does not meet that criteria. Since it doesn't compile, option E is the answer.

12. A. Option E is incorrect since the `ofNullable()` method creates an `Optional` whether or not the parameter is `null`. Options B and D are incorrect because `max()` takes a parameter to specify the logic for determining the order. Both options A and C compile. The order of the pipeline methods matter here. Option C prints all three numbers since the `filter()` operation happens after the `peek()`. Option A is correct as the methods are in the correct order.

13. B,E,F. Unchecked exceptions inherit the `RuntimeException` class and are not required to be caught in the methods where they are declared. Since `ArithmeticException` and `IllegalArgumentException` extend `RuntimeException`, they are included as unchecked exceptions, making options B, E, and F correct. `FileNotFoundException` and `IOException` are checked exceptions, which must be handled or declared, making options A and C incorrect. Option D is also incorrect, as it is not the name of an exception class in Java.

14. C. The class compiles and runs without issue, so options D and E are incorrect. The result of `findSlow()` is deterministic and always 1. The `findFirst()` method returns the first element in an ordered stream, whether it be serial or parallel. This makes it a costly operation for a parallel stream, since the stream has to be accessed in a serial manner. On the other hand, the result of `findFast()` is unknown until runtime. The `findAny()` method may return the first element or any element in the stream, even on serial streams. Since both 1 1 and 3 1 are possible outputs of this program, the answer cannot be determined until runtime, and option C is the correct answer.

15. D. The code compiles and runs without issue. The m symbol represents minute, so 59 is the first value printed, followed by a period. The next symbols ddhh represent day and hour in 2-digit formats, so 1401 is printed. Finally, 'MM' represents an escaped string using single quotes, so it is printed just as MM. For these reasons, option D is correct.

16. B. Only the service locator and service provider interface are part of the service. The service locator has a requires directive, and the service provider interface has an exports directive, which matches option B.

17. A,C. The javac command uses -p and --module-path to supply the module path. There are two valid long forms of the classpath option: -classpath and --class-path. Options A and C match these.

18. B. While no arguments are passed from the command line, this doesn't matter because the main() method redefines the args array. Remember that String values sort alphabetically rather than by number. Therefore, 01 sorts before 1, and option B is correct.

19. D. The application does not compile, so options A, B, and C are incorrect. The ElectricBass class does not compile, since it inherits two default methods with the same signature. Even though the class is marked abstract, it still must override this default method. Since ElectricBass fails to do so, option D is correct. If the ElectricBass class did correctly override the getVolume() method, then the rest of the code would compile without issue. In this case, there would be nothing printed at runtime. The main() method just declares a local inner class but does not actually use it.

20. D. The lambda syntax is incorrect. It should be ->, not =>. Therefore, option D is correct. If this was fixed, option A would be correct.

21. A,C,F. The IntUnaryOperator takes an int value and returns an int value. Options B and E are incorrect because the parameter types, Integer and long, respectively, are not int. Option B is incorrect because unboxing can be used for expressions, but it cannot be used for parameter matching. Option D is incorrect because dividing an int by a double value 3.1 results in q/3.1 being a double value, which cannot be converted to int without an explicit cast. Option E is incorrect because the parameter type must match, and long is not the same as int. The rest of the lambda expressions are valid, since they correctly take an int value and return an int value.

22. C. This question is tricky because it mixes testing valid identifier names with module concepts. The com.apple module is valid and demonstrates a simple module. Additionally, the com.apple$ module is valid since $ characters are permitted in identifier names. The com.4apple and com.apple-four modules are invalid because identifier or identifier segments may not start with a digit nor contain a dash. The com.apple4 module is invalid because declares is not a valid module directive. Since only two are valid, option C is the answer.

23. E. The second catch block on line p2 does not compile. Since IllegalArgumentException is a subclass of Exception, they cannot be used in the same multi-catch block, since it is redundant. For this reason, option E is correct. If the redundant exception class was removed from line p2, then the rest of the program would compile and print Unknown followed by Done! at runtime.

24. D. The code does not compile, so options A, B, and F are incorrect. The first compilation error is in the declaration of the lambda expression for `second`. It does not use a generic type, which means t is of type `Object`. Since `equalsIgnoreCase()` expects a `String` as a parameter, the lambda expression does not compile. The second compilation issue is in the lambda expression in the `main()` method. Notice that `process()` takes an `ApplyFilter` instance, and `ApplyFilter` is a functional interface that takes a `List<String>` object. For this reason, q in this lambda expression is treated as an instance of `List<String>`. The `forEach()` method defined in `Collections` requires a `Consumer` instance, not a `Function`, so the call `q.forEach(first)` does not compile. For these two reasons, option D is the correct answer, since the rest of the code compiles without issue.

25. C. The variables `smiley` and `smirk` are both `false`, since a `String` should be compared with a method rather than ==, especially when not comparing two values from the string pool. The variable `blush` is also `false` because one value is uppercase and the other is lowercase. The variable `cool` is `true` because both values are uppercase. Finally, the variables `wink` and `yawn` print `true` because they don't look at the case. This makes option C the answer.

26. B,E. Annotations define metadata that generally do not change. Options B and E define metadata that would not likely change without major changes to the hospital. Options A, C, D, and F define attributes that would likely change numerous times throughout the day and would be better stored in a database or some other data structure.

27. D. The `name` instance variable is marked `final` and must be assigned a value at most once when it is declared, by an instance initializer, or by a constructor. The no-argument constructor calls the `Ghost(String)` constructor, which assigns a value of `"Boo"` to name. The process returns and the constructor assigns a value of `"Casper"` to name. Since name is `final`, it cannot be assigned a value twice. The compiler detects this error, making option D the correct answer.

28. C. Lines 9–13 do not compile because neither the class nor method defines a generic type T. The declaration on lines 5–6 does not compile because `? extends RuntimeException` cannot have a broader type. This leaves us with two declarations that do compile, making option C the correct answer. Line 4 compiles, since any type of generic list can go in `List<?>`. The declaration on lines 7–8 also compiles because `? super RuntimeException` does allow a broader exception type.

29. B. The application compiles and runs without issue, so options E and F are incorrect. Java uses pass-by-value, so even though the change to `length` in the first line of the `adjustPropellers()` method does not change the value in the `main()` method, the value is later returned by the method and used to reassign the `length` value. The result is that `length` is assigned a value of 6, due to it being returned by the method. For the second parameter, while the `String[]` reference cannot be modified to impact the reference in the calling method, the data in it can be. Therefore, the value of the first element is set to LONG, resulting in an output of `6,LONG`, making option B the correct answer.

30. E. The service provider does not have code to look up the service, making option E correct.

31. D,E. Each option presents a potential override of the `passed()` method, since the method signature is the same. Options A, B, and C are incorrect because the method reduces the visibility of the `protected` method version declared in the parent class. Option F is incorrect, as the parent version of `passed()` is `abstract` and cannot be invoked. That leaves options D and E as valid overrides of this method.

32. A,B,E. First, option A is a valid functional interface that matches the `Runnable` functional interface. Option B is also a valid lambda expression that matches `Function<Double,Double>`, among other functional interfaces. Option C is incorrect because the local variable w cannot be declared again in the lambda expression body, since it is already declared as a lambda parameter. Option D is also incorrect. If the data type is specified for one variable in a lambda expression, it must be specified for all variables within the expression. Next, option E is correct because this lambda expression matches the `UnaryOperator` functional interface. Lastly, option F is incorrect. The statement `name.toUpperCase()` is missing a semicolon (`;`) that is required to terminate the statement.

33. D. The code definitely does not compile. The first problem with this code is that the `Drum` class is missing a constructor causing the class declaration on line 8 to fail to compile. The default no-argument constructor cannot be inserted if the superclass, `Instrument`, defines only constructors that take arguments. The second problem with the code is that line 11 does not compile, since it calls `super.play(5)`, but the version of `play()` in the parent class does not take any arguments. Finally, line 15 does not compile. While mn may be a reference variable that points to a `Drum()` object, the `concert()` method cannot be called unless it is explicitly cast back to a `Drum` reference. For these three reasons, the code does not compile, and option D is the correct answer.

34. D. Line 7 does not compile because the `@Target` annotation with the `METHOD` value prohibits usage on a class. Line 8 does not compile because `Electricity` is not marked as a repeatable annotation. Lines 10 and 11 do not compile because the braces, `{}`, are required around the list of elements. The rest of the lines compile. Note that the `value` name is optional since there are no required elements beyond the `value()` element.

35. C. Line 10 does not compile because line 9 is missing a semicolon(`;`) at the end of it. A semicolon is required after a list of enum values if the enum contains anything besides the list of values. Line 20 does not compile because the enum name is missing before the enum value `green`. For these two reasons, option C is correct.

36. C. Line 13 does not modify the value of x because `Path` is immutable and x is not reassigned to the new value. On line 14, the `resolve()` method is called using y as the input argument. If the parameter passed to the `resolve()` method is absolute, then that value is returned, leading the first `println()` method call to output `/dance/move.txt`. On line 15, the absolute path is concatenated with the relative path, printing `/dance/move.txt/./song/../note` at runtime. For these reasons, option C is correct.

37. D. This question appears to ask you about involved array logic. Instead, it is checking to see if you remember that instance and class variables are initialized to `null`. Line 6 throws a `NullPointerException`, making option D correct. If the array was initialized to `int[4][4]` or larger, then option E would be correct because the code would throw an `ArrayStoreException` on line 8.

38. C. This array has three elements, making `listing.length` output 3. It so happens that each element references an array of the same size. But the code checks the first element and sees it is an array of size two, making the answer option C.

39. B. `Driver`, `Connection`, `PreparedStatement`, and `ResultSet` are the four key interfaces you need to know for JDBC. `DriverManager` is a class rather than an interface. `Query` is not used in JDBC. Since only `Driver` and `ResultSet` are interfaces in the list, option B is the answer.

40. C. The class contains two security issues, making option C correct. First, line 23 returns a cached value without calling `checkPermission()` to ensure the user has permission to read it. Second, line 34 allows direct access to any system property the user passes, without validating the inputted property name. When invoking `doPrivileged()`, make sure there is no chance for a user to pass their own, unprotected values into the request.

41. C. All arrays are objects regardless of whether they point to primitives or classes. That means both `balls` and `scores` are objects. Both are set to `null` so they are eligible for garbage collection. The `balls` array is initialized to contain all `null` references. There are no objects inside. The `scores` array is initialized to all `0` values. Therefore, only two objects exist to be eligible for garbage collection, and option C is correct.

42. E. The code compiles without issue. The `main()` method creates a thread pool of four threads. It then submits ten tasks to it. At any given time, the `ExecutorService` has up to four threads active, which is the same number of threads required to reach the `CyclicBarrier` limit. Therefore, the barrier limit is reached twice, printing `Jump!` twice. While eight of the tasks have been completed, two are left running. Since no more tasks will call the `await()` method, the `CyclicBarrier` limit is never reached, and a deadlock is encountered at runtime, with the program hanging indefinitely. For this reason, option E is correct.

43. A,B,C All of the compilation issues with this code involve access modifiers. First, interface methods cannot be marked `protected`. This causes a compilation error on line h1, making option A correct. Next, lines h2 and h3 both override the interface method with the package-private access modifier. Since this reduces the implied visibility of `public`, the overrides are invalid and neither line compiles. Therefore, options B and C are also correct.

Note that the `RuntimeException` is allowed in an overridden method even though it is not in the parent method signature because only new checked exceptions in overridden methods cause compilation errors. Line h4 is valid. An object can be implicitly cast to a superclass or inherited interface. Finally, lines h5 and h6 will compile without issue but independently throw a `ClassCastException` and a `NullPointerException` at runtime, respectively. Since the question only asks about compilation problems, neither of these are correct answers.

44. E. The `public` modifier allows access from the same class, package, subclass, or even classes in other packages, while the `static` modifier allows access without an instance of the class. For these reasons, option E is the correct answer. Option A is incorrect because `class` is not a modifier; it is a keyword. Option B is incorrect because the `default` keyword is for interface methods and `switch` statements, not class variables. Option C is incorrect because `final` is not related to access, and package-private prevents access from classes outside the package. Finally, option D is incorrect because `instance` is not a Java keyword or modifier. Further, `protected` prevents all classes outside the package other than subclasses from accessing the variable.

45. C,D. Option A is incorrect because the peek() method returns the next value or null if there isn't one without changing the state of the queue. In this example, both peek() calls return 18. Option B is incorrect because the poll() method removes and returns the next value, returning null if there isn't one. In this case, 18 and null are returned, respectively. Options C and D are correct because both the pop() and remove() methods throw a NoSuchElementException when the queue is empty. This means both return 18 for the first call and throw an exception for the second.

46. A,E. In Java, a locale can be represented by a language code in lowercase, or a language and country code, with language in lowercase and country in uppercase. For these reasons, options A and E are correct. Options C, D, and F are incorrect because the lowercase language must be before the uppercase country. Option B is incorrect because the language is missing. Remember, the exam won't expect you to know which language and country codes exist, but it will expect you to know how to use them.

47. A,B,D. The unmodified code prints xxxxx, so you're looking for options that also print this value. Option A is correct because the labels are not referenced. Option B is correct because the outer while is broader than the inner while. If race.length() <= 4 is true, then race.length() < 4 must be true. The inner loop prints xxxxx, and the outer loop is not needed. Option C is incorrect because the outer loop only prints xxxx without the inner loop. Option D is also correct because a label is not used. Option E and F are incorrect because you cannot remove the while portion of a do/while loop.

48. C. While shoe3 goes out of scope after the shopping() method, the "croc" object is referenced by shoe1, and therefore cannot be garbage collected. Similarly, the "sandal" object is now referenced by shoe2. No variables reference the "flip flop" object, so it is eligible to be garbage collected. Finally, the Shoes object created in the main() method is also eligible for garbage collection, since there are no saved references to it. For these reasons, option C is correct.

49. A,C,E. A switch statement supports the primitive types byte, short, char, and int and their associated wrapper classes Character, Byte, Short, and Integer. It also supports the String class and enumerated types. Finally, it permits var under some circumstances, such as if the type can resolve to one of the previous types. For these reasons, options A, C, and E are correct. The other classes are not supported.

50. B. This code contains three stream pipelines for the price of one! Lines 16–17 are the first pipeline. They group the four Goat instances by the type of food they eat. This creates a Map with the elements {hay=[hay, hay], can=[can], shorts=[shorts]}.

Lines 19–22 are the second pipeline. This one starts by only including elements that have two matches, in our case hay. We then use the String key Goat. Finally, this pipeline partitions the single key based on whether it has any characters giving us {false=[hay], true=[]}.

On line 23, we get just one of the lists leaving us with [hay]. The final pipeline is lines 24–26. It sorts the single element in an attempt to confuse you and then prints it. Therefore, only one hay is printed, and option B is the answer.

Chapter 15: Practice Exam 2

1. D. Line 4 does not compile because enum constructors cannot be `public`. Line 10 also does not compile because a `case` statement must use an enum value without the type. In particular, `FALL` is permitted, but `Season.FALL` is not. For these two reasons, option D is correct.

2. B,F. The `LackOfInformationException` class does not compile, making option A incorrect. The compiler inserts the default no-argument constructor into `InformationException`, since the class does not explicitly define any. Since `LackOfInformationException` extends `InformationException`, the only constructor available in the parent class is the no-argument call to `super()`. For this reason, the constructor defined at line `t1` does not compile because it calls a nonexistent parent constructor that takes a `String` value, and option B is one of the correct answers. The other two constructors at lines `t2` and `t3` compile without issue, making options C and D incorrect. Option E is also incorrect. The `getMessage()` method is inherited, so applying the `@Override` annotation is allowed by the compiler. Option F is the other correct answer. The `LackOfInformationException` is a checked exception because it inherits `Exception` but not `RuntimeException`.

3. D. The code compiles, making option E incorrect. The key here is that the `AtomicInteger` variable is thread-safe regardless of the synchronization methods used to access it. Therefore, synchronizing on an instance object, as in `increment1()` or `increment3()`, or on the class object, as in `increment2()`, is unnecessary because the `AtomicInteger` class is already thread-safe. For this reason, option D is the correct answer.

4. B,E. The first two iterations through the loop complete successfully, making option B correct. However, the two arrays are not the same size, and the `for` loop only checks the size of the first one. The third iteration throws an `ArrayIndexOutOfBoundsException`, making option E correct.

5. F. A class can inherit two `default` interfaces with the same signature, so long as it correctly overrides them, which `Tree` does. It can also call an inherited version of the `default` method within an instance method, provided it uses the proper syntax. In this case, it does not. The correct syntax is `Plant.super.grow()`, not `super.Plant.grow()`. For this reason, this line does not compile. Since it is the only line that does not compile, option F is correct.

6. A,B. Lines g1 and g2 do not compile because these methods are available only in the `ScheduledExecutorService` interface. Since `s` is of type `ExecutorService`, the lines referenced in options A and B do not compile. Even if the correct reference type for `s` was used, line g1 would still fail to compile because `scheduleWithFixedDelay()` requires two `long` values, one for the initial delay and one for the period. Line g3 compiles without issue because this method is available in the `ExecutorService` interface.

7. A,D. Java methods must start with a letter, the dollar $ symbol, or the underscore _ character. For this reason, option B is incorrect, and options A and D are correct. Despite how option A looks, it is a valid method name in Java. Options C, E, and F do not compile because the symbols -, \, and # are not allowed in method names, respectively.

8. C,F. The javac command takes a --module-path parameter. You need to memorize that the short form of this option is -p. This makes options C and F the answer.

9. C,E. An overriding method cannot declare any new or broader checked exceptions as the overridden method. Option A is permitted because FileNotFoundException is a narrower exception than IOException. Options B, D, and F are permitted because new unchecked exceptions are allowed. Note that IOException is not required to be declared at all in the overriding method. Options C and E are incorrect because they are broader checked exceptions than IOException. Even if you didn't know Throwable was checked, you should have been able to solve this by process of elimination.

10. C. The code compiles and runs without exception, making options E and F incorrect. The question is testing your knowledge of variable scope. The teeth variable is static in the Alligator class, meaning the same value is accessible from all instances of the class, including the static main() method. The static variable teeth is incremented each time the constructor is called. Note that the constructor uses this to access a static variable, which is bad practice, but allowed.

Since teeth is a local variable within the snap() method, the argument value is used, but changes to the local variable do not affect the static variable teeth. The local variable teeth is not used after it is decremented, the decrement operation has no meaningful effect on the program flow or the static variable teeth. Since the constructor is called twice, with snap() executed after each constructor call, the output printed is 1 2, making option C the correct answer.

11. C,D. A fully modular application has all named modules, making options B and E incorrect. A bottom-up migration starts out with unnamed modules, making option C correct. By contrast, a top-down migration starts by making all modules automatic modules, making option D correct.

12. B,C,F. The ternary operator (? :) evaluates only one of the two right-hand expressions at runtime, so option A is incorrect. A switch statement may contain at most one optional default statement, making option B correct. The post-increment operator increments the variable and returns the original value, making option C correct. The logical operator (|) operator will evaluate both operands, while the disjunctive short-circuit (||) operator will only evaluate the right-hand side of the expression if the left-hand side evaluates to false. Therefore, they may produce different results if the left operand is true, and o ption D is incorrect. Option E is incorrect as the complement operator (!) is applied to boolean values. Finally, option F is correct and allows the assignment operator to be used in a conditional expression, such as part of a loop condition.

13. E. The code compiles, so option C is incorrect. The first two lines successfully create directories. The first move() statement moves a file from /flower/rose.txt to /garden, not /garden/rose.txt. There is already an empty directory there, but since the REPLACE_EXISTING flag is provided, the /garden directory is replaced with a file. The next move() statement throws an exception because there is no source file at /garden/rose.txt. For this reason, option E is correct.

14. C,D. To be a valid functional interface, an `interface` must declare exactly one `abstract` method. Option A is incorrect, because `CanClimb` does not contain any `abstract` methods. Next, all interface methods not marked `default` or `static` are assumed to be `abstract`, and `abstract` methods cannot have a body. For this reason, `CanDance` does not compile, making option B incorrect. Options C and D are correct answers because each contains exactly one `abstract` method. Option E is incorrect because it contains two `abstract` methods, since `test()` is assumed to be `abstract`.

15. D. The `execute()` method returns a `boolean`, not a `ResultSet`. This causes a compiler error on line 18, which corresponds to option D.

16. A,E. A Java file can have at most one top-level type and any number of package-private types. For this reason, options A and E are correct. Option B is incorrect because it can have at most one `package` statement. Option C is incorrect because it cannot have two `public` top-level classes. Option D is incorrect because the `package` statement must appear before the `import` statement. Option F is incorrect because top-level types may not be `private` or `protected`.

17. D. When the arrays are the same, the `compare()` method returns 0, while the `mismatch()` method returns −1. This narrows it down to option C or option D. When the arrays are different, `mismatch()` returns the index of the first element that is different. In our case, this is index 2, making option D correct. By contrast, the `compare()` method would return a negative number if filling in the third blank since `'i'` is smaller than `'o'`.

18. E. The code correctly creates a `LinkedList` with three elements. The stream pipeline does compile. However, there is no terminal operation, which means the stream is never evaluated, and the output is something like `java.util.stream.ReferencePipeline$2@404b9385`. This is definitely not one of the listed choices, so option E is correct.

19. D. Line `x1` does not compile because of an assignment and value mismatch. The `r1` variable is a `Runnable` expression. While there is an `ExecutorService.submit()` that takes a `Runnable` expression, it returns `Future<?>`, since the return type is `void`. This type is incompatible with the `Future<Stream>` assignment without an explicit cast, leading to a compiler error. Next, line `x4` does not compile. The `parallelStream()` method is found in the `Collection` interface, not the `Stream` interface. Due to these two compilation errors, option D is the correct answer.

20. A,E,F. Line `j1` should be verifying `read` or `execute` access to the file, not `write`, making option A correct. The system needs permission other than write to load a library. The rest of the lines are valid, making options E and F correct. While the user is free to pass in any value for the file, it is checked against a list of known files, thereby preventing arbitrary file access.

21. C. Lines 14 and 15 create `RemoveMe<Integer>` and `RemoveMe<Long>` instances, respectively. Since we are using generics, the method calls on lines 16 and 17 autobox the primitive values (1 and 1L) to the `Integer` value 1 and `Long` value 1L, respectively. Therefore, the method on line 11 removes the argument that matches this object value, and not the element at index 1, from the two lists. These are the two lines that print [2, 7, 8]. Line 27 is trickier. Since we are passing a primitive int, the index is used (and not an object matching the value) in the call to remove().This means line 28 prints [2, 1, 8], which is not what we are looking for. Since only lines 16 and 17 give us the desired output, option C is the answer.

22. C,E. The write methods are used as part of serialization, not deserialization, making options A, B, and D incorrect. Option C and E are correct because they use the correct method parameters and return types for readObject() and readResolve(). The method names used in options B and F, writeResolve() and readReplace() respectively, are not actually serialization or deserialization methods.

23. D. The second catch block in openDrawbridge() is unreachable since FileNotFoundException is a subclass of IOException. The catch blocks should be ordered with the narrower exception classes before the broader ones. For this reason, line 9 does not compile. Next, the local variable e is declared twice within the same scope, with the declaration on line 12 failing to compile. Finally, the openDrawbridge() method declares the checked Exception class, but it is not handled in the main() method on line 23. Since lines 9, 12, and 23 do not compile, option D is correct.

24. E. This is a correct module-info file. It exports the com.mammal.cat package to any modules that want to use it. By contrast, it exports the com.mammal.mouse package to only one other module. Finally, it demonstrates the uses directive. Since the code is correct, option E is the answer.

25. D. When converting an array to a List, Java uses a fixed-sized backed list. This means that the list uses an array in the implementation. While changing elements to new values is allowed, adding and removing elements is not.

26. E,F. Options B and D are incorrect because those flags do not exist on the jdeps command. Options A and C do exist, but do not include suggested replacements. Options E and F are correct as they will include a table of suggestions if any internal APIs are used in the JAR.

27. E. This code does not compile because the println() attempts to reference the sb variable. However, that variable is only in scope for the if statement. Since the code does not compile, option E is correct. If the println() were inside the if statement, option C would be correct.

28. A. This class is called with three command-line arguments. First, the array is sorted, which meets the pre-condition for binary search. At this point, the array contains [flower, plant, seed]. The key is to notice the value of args[0] is now flower rather than seed. Calling a binary search to find the position of flower returns 0, which is the index matching that value. Therefore, the answer is option A.

29. C. Line 4 is missing a type for the element. If a compatible type, such as int, was added before alert(), it would compile. An annotation element type must be a primitive type, a String, a Class, an enum, another annotation, or an array of any of these types. For this reason, line 6 compiles, and line 7 does not. Since lines 4 and 7 are the only lines that do not compile, option C is correct. Notice that lines 5 and 8 use a lot of extra modifiers, like public and abstract, that are usually applied implicitly.

30. D. This code is tricky. Java picks the most specific method signature it can find in an overloading situation. Normally, that would be the one with the two `int` parameters. However, that method is an instance method, and the `main()` method is looking for a `static` method. The next choice is the varargs one, making option D the answer.

31. D. The service provider interface clearly needs to be recompiled, since that's where the change occurs. The service provider also needs to be recompiled because it implements the interface. Finally, the consumer needs to be recompiled because it calls the interface. The service locator does not need to be recompiled as it only knows the service provider interface name rather than its method signature. Since three require recompilation, option D is correct.

32. A,D,F. `@Documented` can be applied only to annotations, not methods, making option A correct. If `@Override` is applied to a method that is not actually overridden, a compiler error will ensue, making option D correct. The `@SafeVarargs` annotation will trigger a compiler error if applied to a method without a vararg parameter or without a `final`, `private`, or `static` modifier, making option F correct. The rest of the annotations can be applied to methods without triggering a compiler error. For option E, the compiler might not recognize the cause (such as `magic`), but it will still compile.

33. B,E. The `Locale` class has a constructor taking a language code and an optional country code. A `Locale.Builder` is created only using a constructor. The `Properties` and `HashMap` classes are concrete types of `Map`, so they have constructors. By contrast, a `ResourceBundle` is an `abstract` class, and instances are typically obtained by calling the `ResourceBundle.getBundle()` method, making option B correct. Similarly, `DateTimeFormatter` is obtained using a `static` method, making option E correct.

34. A. The method reference on line x is supposed to define a `Function`. The `Shield` interface does define a single abstract method. However, that method has a `void` return type, which is not compatible with `Function`. Line y does compile since `addDragon()` has both a parameter and return type. Option A is the answer, since only line x fails to compile.

35. C,E. In option A, the assignment operator (=) incorrectly comes after the multiplication (*) operator. In option B, the short-circuit logical operator (&&) incorrectly comes after the division (/) operator. In option D, the equality operator (==) incorrectly comes after the multiplication (*) operator. In option F, the not equals operator (!=) incorrectly comes after the relational operators, (<= and >=). This leaves options C and E as the correct answers. For these answers, it may help to remember that the modulus operator (%), multiplication operator (*), and division operator (/) have the same operator precedence.

36. C. You can't use generics with a primitive, so it should be `Supplier<Double>`. This makes option C the answer. If this were fixed, option B would be the answer.

37. E. Line c1 correctly creates a stream containing two streams. Line c2 uses `flatMap()` to create a `Stream` of four `Integer` objects. The first problem is on line c3, which tries to use the numbers as if they are still pairs. Since we have a `Stream<Integer>` at that point, the code does not compile, and option E is the answer. Line c4 does not compile either as you can't call a `List` method on an `Integer`.

38. B. This problem appears to be about overriding a method, but in fact, it is much simpler. The class `CarbonStructure` is not declared `abstract`, yet it includes an `abstract` method.

To fix it, the definition of CarbonStructure would have to be changed to be an abstract class, or the abstract modifier would need to be removed from getCount() in CarbonStructure and a method body added. Since the only answer choice available is to change the getCount() method on line q1, option B is the correct answer. Note that the rest of the application, including the override on line q2, is correct and compiles without issue. The return types Long and Number are covariant since Number is a superclass of Long. Likewise, the exception thrown in the subclass method is narrower, so no compilation error occurs on q2.

39. A,B. First, they are both classes, not interfaces, making option A correct and option D incorrect. Next, while it is more common to use Reader for character data, InputStream and Reader are both capable of reading character data, making option B correct. Option C is incorrect, as both classes contain a read() method that returns an int value. As you may recall from your studies, neither use byte or char so that −1 can be returned when the end of the stream is reached without using an existing byte or char value. Option E is incorrect because neither contains a flush() method, while option F is incorrect because they both contain a skip() method.

40. A,C,E. Option B is incorrect as abstract classes allow any of the access modifiers. Option D is incorrect because interfaces do not have constructors. Option F is incorrect because neither abstract classes nor interfaces can be marked final. Options A, C, and E are true statements.

41. C. On the first iteration through the loop, the first five characters are removed, and builder becomes "s growing". Since there are more than five characters left, the loop iterates again. This time, five more characters are removed, and builder becomes "wing". This matches option C.

42. B,C,E. Options B, C, and E are valid statements about nested classes. An anonymous class can declare only one supertype, either a class or an interface, making option A incorrect. A member inner class cannot contain static methods, making option B incorrect. A local class can access only final and effectively final local variables, making option F incorrect.

43. E. DoubleBinaryOperator takes two double values and returns a double value. LongToIntFunction takes one long value and returns an int value. ToLongBiFunction takes two generic arguments and returns a long value. IntSupplier does not take any values and returns an int value. ObjLongConsumer takes one generic and one long value and does not return a value. For these reasons, option E is the correct answer.

44. D. The most common approach is stillMoreChoices(), which works for any SELECT statement that has an int in the first column. If the SELECT statement has a function like count(*) or sum(*) in the first column, there will always be a row in the ResultSet, so moreChoices() works as well. Therefore, option D is the answer.

45. E. This method does not set or return a value so it is not an accessor or mutator. Therefore, option E is correct.

46. E. Leaving it blank gives package-private access. This would be the correct answer if the code we wanted to receive access were in the same package. Since it is not, we would need modules in order to restrict the access and option E is correct.

47. E,F. To perform a concurrent reduction, the stream or the collector must be unordered. Since it is possible to use an ordered collector with an unordered stream and achieve a parallel reduction, option A is incorrect. Option B is also incorrect. While having a thread-safe collection is preferred, it is not required. Stateful lambda expressions should be avoided, whether the stream is serial or parallel, making option C incorrect. Option D is incorrect as there is no class/interface within the JDK called `ParallelStream`. Options E and F are correct statements about performing parallel reductions.

48. B,D. An `Error` indicates an unrecoverable problem. Options A and E are incorrect because the application could possibly recover. While it is possible to catch an `Error`, it is strongly recommended that an application never do so, making options B and D correct. Finally, options C and F are incorrect because `Error` extends from `Throwable`, not `Exception` or `RuntimeException`, although it is an unchecked exception.

49. D. Line 15 calls the method on line 9 since it is a `Watch` object, printing `watch`. Line 16 is a `SmartWatch` object. However, the `getName()` method is not overridden in `SmartWatch`, since the method signature is different. Therefore, the method on line 9 gets called again. That method calls `getType()`. Since this is a `private` method, it is not overridden, and `watch` is printed again, making option D the correct answer.

50. D. A `long` cannot contain a number with decimal points, preventing `min1` from compiling. When declaring multiple variables in the same statement, the type is only declared once. Therefore, `max3` does not compile. Underscores in numeric expressions are allowed as long as they are between two digits, making the line with `min5` and `max5` incorrect. Since three lines have compiler errors, the answer is option D. The `L` suffix is valid, as is having multiple underscores in a row.

Chapter 16: Practice Exam 3

1. B. The `hop()` method has `protected` access, which allows subclasses to call it, making line p1 compile. Additionally, code in the same package is allowed to access it, making lines p2 and p3 compile. The code compiles and runs without error, making option B the answer.

2. A,E. A `try` block can have zero or more `catch` blocks, and zero or one `finally` blocks, but must be accompanied by at least one of these blocks. For these reasons, options B, D, and F are incorrect, and option E is correct. A `finally` block must appear after the last `catch` block, if there are any, making option C incorrect, and option A correct.

3. C,D. Option A is incorrect because `Comparable` is implemented in the class being compared. To be useful, such a class must have instance variables to compare, ruling out a lambda. By contrast, a `Comparator` is often implemented with a lambda. Option B is incorrect because `compareTo()` is the method in `Comparable`. Option C is correct because these methods have different parameters but the same return type, with the same rules for ordering elements. Option D is correct because a `Comparator` doesn't need to be implemented by the class being compared. It can be passed to the `sort()` method as a parameter. Option E is incorrect because comparators are not required to be consistent with the equals() method. For example, two objects that are equivalent in terms of equals() may be sorted differently.

4.   B. This is a correct example of using lambdas. The code creates an ArrayList with three elements. Both lambdas are correct. The code removes any negative numbers and prints out the remaining two numbers, 0 and 5, making option B correct.

5.   D. Lines 2 and 3 do not compile because var can only be used for local variables. Line 6 does not compile because a single underscore is not permitted as a variable name. These three compiler errors cause option D to be the answer. Lines 4 and 5 use var correctly.

6.   B,F. A deadlock and livelock both result in threads that cannot complete a task, but only in a livelock do the threads appear active, making option A incorrect and option B correct. Options C and D are incorrect because they do not apply to thread liveness. A race condition is an unexpected result when two threads, which should be run sequentially, are run at the same time, leading to an unexpected result, making option E incorrect. Since livelock is a special case of resource starvation, in which a single active thread is perpetually denied access to a shared resource or lock, option F is also correct.

7.   B. Line 22 does not compile because a static interface method cannot call an instance-based abstract method. Since this is the only line that does not compile, option B is correct.

8.   E. The first time the inner for loop is executed, it calls exams.get(i) where i is equal to exams.size(). Since the maximum element is indexed as exams.size()-1, this results in an IndexOutOfBoundsException, making option E correct. Also, notice that there are no braces {} around the inner for loop; therefore, even without the exception, the most lines this code would print would be one, since there's only one println() statement executed.

9.   B. You are allowed to use null with instanceof; it just prints false. The bus variable is both a Vehicle and a Bus, so lines 18 and 19 print true. Then it gets interesting. We know that bus is not an ArrayList or Collection. However, the compiler only knows that bus is not an ArrayList because ArrayList is a concrete class. Line 20 does not compile. The compiler can't definitively state that bus is not a Collection. Some future program could create a subclass of Bus that does implement Collection, so this line compiles. Therefore, only line 20 fails to compile, and option B is correct.

10. A,E. Line 24 does not compile because arrays use length. It is ArrayList that uses size(). All of the other lines compile, making option A correct. It is permitted to split up the brackets, [], in the 2D array declaration on line 20. The code is also allowed to use crossword.length as the loop condition on line 22, although this is not a good idea for a nested array. Instead, the inner loop should reference crossword[i].length. The array starts out with all two hundred of the cells initialized to the default value for an int of 0. Both loops iterate starting at 0 and stopping before 10, which causes only half of the array to be set to 'x'. The other half still has the initial default value of 0, making option E correct.

11. C. Line 5 does not compile because the type of a variable cannot be inferred when the value is null. Line 8 does not compile because the type cannot be changed once the variable is declared. Therefore, option C is correct.

12. B. On line 10, `result` is first set to 8. On line 11, the loop is entered because 8 `>=` 7. On line 12, `result` is incremented to 9. Then the inner loop runs, decrementing `result` to 7. The inner loop is then broken by the `continue monitor` statement. The outer loop then evaluates the loop condition. Since 7 `>=` 7, it runs again ending with the inner loop setting `result` to 6. Since 6 `>=` 7 is `false`, the outer loop terminates after two executions and prints 6.

13. A,C,E. To start with, `bustNow()` takes a `Double` value, while `bustLater()` takes a double value. To be compatible, the lambda expression has to be able to handle both data types. Option A is correct, since the method reference `System.out::print` matches overloaded methods that can take `double` or a `Double`. Option E is also correct, as it's the equivalent rewrite of option A with a lambda expression. Option B is incorrect, since `intValue()` works for the `Consumer<Double>`, which takes `Double`, but not `DoubleConsumer`, which takes `double`. For a similar reason, option D is also incorrect because only the primitive `double` is compatible with this expression.

Option C is correct and results in just a blank line being printed. Finally, option F is incorrect because of incompatible data types. The method reference code is inside of a lambda expression, which would only be allowed if the functional interface returned another functional interface reference.

14. A,D,E. `Mixer` and `Spinner` are member inner classes that require an instance of `Kitchen` and `Mixer`, respectively, to instantiate. Since `bake()` is defined as an instance method of `Kitchen`, the `Kitchen` instance can be implied. For this reason, option D is correct. Options A and E are also correct and rely on a new instance of `Kitchen` rather than the implied one. Options B and C are incorrect because there is no instance of `Mixer` used. Option F is incorrect because the reference type `Spinner` is undefined without the names of the enclosing classes.

15. A. The service locator contains a `ServiceLoader` call to the `load()` method to look up the service loader, which is option A.

16. A,F. The `@Documented` annotation allows annotations to be included in generated Javadoc, while the `@Target` annotation determines the valid usage locations of an annotation. For these reasons, options A and F are correct.

17. C,E. The diamond operator, `<>`, is only allowed to be used when instantiating rather than declaring. In other words, it can't go on the left side of the equals (=) sign. Therefore, options B, D, and F are incorrect. The remaining three options compile. However, option A produces a warning because generics are not used on the right side of the assignment operator. Therefore, options C and E are correct. Option C is preferred over option E, since it uses the diamond operator rather than specifying a redundant type.

18. B,E. The original implementation compiles and prints 18. When using an `IntStream`, the `sum()` method returns an `int`. This makes option B correct as both an `int` and a `long` will print 18. By contrast, option A is incorrect because a `double` will print 18.0. Removing line 11 causes the code to not compile on line 13 since `mapToInt()` is not defined on `IntStream` (the stream is already made of `int` values), making option D incorrect. Removing line 13 causes the code to not compile on line 14, as `sum()` is only defined on primitive streams, not `Stream<Integer>`, making option F incorrect. Option E is the remaining correct answer. Running operations in parallel for such a tiny list is not helpful, but it does not change the result.

19. A. The `init()` method is accessible from the same package. The `race()` method is available from the same package or subclasses. Since `Tortoise` is in the same package, both methods are available and option A is correct.

20. B,D. There is not a `requires direct` directive, making option B correct. If the `requires transitive` directive where used in the answer options instead, option A would be the answer, since it represents a superset of the functionality. Additionally, option D is correct because `java.base` is implied whether you specify it or not.

21. F. When summing `int` primitives, the return type is also an `int`. Since a `long` is larger, you can assign the result to it, so line 7 is correct. All the primitive stream types use `long` as the return type for `count()`. Therefore, the code compiles, and option E is incorrect. When actually running the code, line 8 throws an `IllegalStateException` because the stream has already been used. Both `sum()` and `count()` are terminal operations, and only one terminal operation is allowed on the same stream. Therefore, option F is the answer.

22. B. This class is never instantiated, so the instance initializer never outputs 1, and the constructor never outputs 3. This rules out options A, D, and E. A `static` initializer runs only once for the class, which rules out option C. Option B is correct because the `static` initializer runs once printing 2, followed by the `static` method `callMe()` printing 4 twice, and ending with the `main()` method printing 5.

23. F. The `readObject()` method returns an `Object` instance, which must be explicitly cast to `Cruise` in the second try-with-resources statement. For this reason, the code does not compile. If the explicit cast was added, the code would compile but throw a `NotSerializableException` at runtime, since `Cruise` does not implement the `Serializable` interface. For this reason, option F is correct. If both of these issues were fixed, then the code would run and print 4,null. The `schedule` variable is marked `transient`, so it defaults to null when deserialized, while numPassengers is assigned the value it had when it was serialized. Remember that on deserialization, the constructors and instance initializers are not executed.

24. D. The `load()` method is on `ServiceLoader`, not `ServiceLocator`. Therefore, option D is the answer.

25. B. For this question, it helps to try all answers out. Most of them do not make any sense. For example, overloading a method is not a facet of inheritance. Likewise, concrete and abstract methods can both be overridden, not just one. The only answer that is valid is option B. Without virtual methods, overriding a method would not be possible, and Java would not truly support polymorphism.

26. D. This code actually does compile. Line `c1` is fine because the method uses the `?` wildcard, which allows any collection. Line `c2` is a standard method declaration. Line `c3` looks odd, but it does work. The lambda takes one parameter and does nothing with it. Since there is no output, option D is correct.

27. D. The code does not compile because the `Jacket` is marked `final` and cannot be extended by the anonymous class declared on line v2. Since this line doesn't compile, option D is correct. If the `final` modifier were removed from line v1, then the code would compile and print `Starting...Insulation:20` at runtime.

28. E. The `ResultSet` interface does not have a `hasNext()` method. Since the code does not compile due to a line without a comment, option E is the answer.

29. D. The code compiles without issue, so options E and F are incorrect. Note that line p2 accesses a `static` method using an instance reference, which is discouraged but permitted in Java. First, a varargs `int` array of `[0,0]` is passed to the `swing()` method. The `try` block throws `ArrayIndexOutOfBoundsException`, since the third element is requested and the size of the array is two. For this reason, the `print()` statement in the `try` block is not executed.

Next, since `ArrayIndexOutOfBoundsException` is a subclass of `RuntimeException`, the `RuntimeException` catch block is executed, and 2 is printed. The rest of the `catch` blocks are skipped, since the first one was selected. The `finally` block then executes and prints 4. Lastly, control is returned to the `main()` method without an exception being thrown, and 5 is printed. Since 245 is printed, option D is the correct answer.

30. B. Lines 10–12 created a map with two key/value pairs. Line 14 does not add to the map, since the key 2 is present. Line 15 adds a third key/value to the map. At this point, the map contains {1=4, 2=8, 3=9}. Line 17 replaces the values with one higher than the key, and the map contains {1=2, 2=3, 3=4}. The stream on lines 19–23 goes through the map and sorts ascendingly by key. It gets the lowest key from that sort, which is 1. Then it prints the value that goes with that key, which is 2. This makes option B the answer.

31. C. The `filter()` method passes two of the three elements of the stream through to the terminal operation. This is redundant, since the terminal operation checks the same `Predicate`. There are two matches with the same value, so both `anyMatch()` and `allMatch()` return `true`, and option C is correct.

32. E. Unnamed modules are always on the classpath. Both automatic and named modules are on the module path. Named modules always contain a `module-info` file, but automatic modules never do. Option E is correct as it meets both these criteria.

33. B. The code does not compile, so option E is incorrect. A variable declared before the start of a try-with-resources statement may be used if it is `final` or effectively final. Since s is modified on line 13, it is not either, therefore line 10 does not compile. Line 12 also does not compile. In a multi-catch expression, the two classes cannot be subtypes of each other. Other than lines 10 and 12, the rest of the code compiles, making option B correct.

34. B. When replacing a variable in a subclass, Java uses the reference type to determine the variable to use. Option A would be correct if the `size` variables were treated like method overriding, since all of the objects in the `main()` method are instances of `Light`. Instead, the reference type is used. The variables v1 and v2 are of reference type `Light`, so 5 is selected. Likewise, the variable v3 is of type `Wave`, so 7 is used. The output is 5,5,7, making option B correct.

35. F. A JDBC URL has three components separated by colons. None of these options uses the correct colon delimiter, making option F the correct answer.

36. C,D,E. A `static` interface method can only call other `static` interface methods, `private` or `public`, making option C correct. They cannot call `default` or `abstract` methods, making options A, B, and F incorrect. On the other hand, a `default` interface method can call all instance-based methods (`abstract`, `default`) and all `static` methods, making option D and E correct.

37. B,D. At the end of the method, `state1` and `state3` both point to `"water"`, while `state2` points to `"mist"`. Since there are no references to `"ice"`, it is eligible for garbage collection, making option B correct. However, garbage collection is not guaranteed to run, so option D is also correct.

38. D. In options A and B, the stream pipeline attempts to call `entrySet()` on the stream. However this method is only defined on `Map`, which makes these two options incorrect. Options C, E, and F are incorrect because the second to last line is `map()` instead of `flatMap()`. It doesn't make sense to sort the `Stream` generated by `map()`, and the code does not compile. By contrast, option D is correct. It creates a `Set` of matching `String` objects. It then builds a map where the key represents whether they match. Next, the code gets the list of all matching values, turns it into a `Stream` and uses `flatMap()` to turn it back into individual objects. Finally, the code sorts in descending order and turns the result back into a `String`.

39. B. This code is not a functional interface because it has three abstract methods: `fun()`, and `game()`, and `toy()`. Removing two of these three methods would cause the code to compile leaving it with a single abstract method. Note that removing the `@FunctionalInterface` annotation would allow the interface to compile, but not be implementable as a lambda expression.

40. F. The code compiles without issue, making options D and E incorrect. Applying the ternary `? :` operator, the variable `ship` is assigned a value of `10.0`. Both values are implicitly cast to `double`. The expression in the first `if` statement evaluates to `true`, so `Goodbye` is printed. Notice that there is no `else` statement on line g2; therefore, the second `if` statement is also executed, causing `See you again` to also be printed. Since two statements are printed, option F is correct.

41. A,D,F. The module system consists of a format for module jars, not a replacement making option A correct and option E incorrect. It also divides the JDK into modules, making option F correct. Since many modules are not part of the JDK, it cannot provide a complete list as suggested by option B. Modules can continue to use `jar` format or alternatively, use the JMOD format. Option C is tricky because `jdeps` was added. However, it is a command, not a file format. This does make option D correct.

42. B,C,E. The constructors declared by options A, D, and F compile without issue. Option B does not compile. Since there is no call to a parent constructor or constructor in the same class, the compiler inserts a no-argument `super()` call as the first line of the constructor. Because `Big` does not have a no-argument constructor, the no-argument constructor

Trouble() does not compile. Option C also does not compile because super() and this() cannot be called in the same constructor. Finally, option E does not compile. There is no matching constructor that can take a String followed by a long value.

43. C. The Function interface uses apply(), while the Consumer interface uses accept(), making option C the correct answer. For reference, get() is the name of the method used by Supplier, while test() is the name of the method used by Predicate.

44. B. The Roller class uses a formal type parameter named E with a constraint. The key to this question is knowing that with generics, the extends keyword means any subclass or the class can be used as the type parameter. This means both Wheel and CartWheel are allowed. The wheel1 declaration is fine because the same type is used on both sides of the declaration. The wheel2 declaration does not compile because generics require the exact same type when not using wildcards. The wheel3 and wheel4 declarations are both fine because this time there is an upper bound to specify that the type can be a subclass. By contrast, the super keyword means it has to be that class or a superclass. The wheel6 declaration is OK, but the wheel5 one is a problem because it uses a subclass. Since wheel2 and wheel5 don't compile, the answer is option B.

45. E. Since it's not a primitive stream, the underlying type is Stream<Short>, which means the data type of b is Short. On the other hand, the data type of a, c, and d is Integer. Because Short and Integer both define a doubleValue() method, these statements compile. The problem is with the return type of the two lambda expressions. The identity is set as 0, not 0.0, so the expected return type of each lambda expression is Integer, not Double. For this reason, neither lambda expression matches the method parameters of the reduce() method, and option E is correct.

46. B. Java starts out by looking for a properties file with the requested locale. In this case, the requested locale is the fr language, which it finds with toothbrush_fr.properties. For this reason, the default locale of es_MX is ignored, and the first value for color printed is violette. Next, it looks for a value for type property. Since it doesn't find it in the first properties file, it checks the default toothbrush.properties, where it does find it, and prints generic. For these reasons, option B is correct.

47. A,C,E. BooleanSupplier, DoubleUnaryOperator, and ToLongBiFunction are all valid functional interfaces in java.util.function, making options A, C, and E correct. Remember that BooleanSupplier is the only primitive functional interface in the API that does not use double, int, or long. For this reason, option B is incorrect, since char is not a supported primitive. Option D is incorrect because the functional interfaces that use Object are abbreviated to Obj. The correct name for this functional interface is ObjIntConsumer. That leaves option F, which is incorrect. There is no built-in Predicate interface that takes three values.

48. C. The method does not validate the input filename, which gives the user carte blanche to access the entire file system. The input should be validated in some way. One option to validate the data would be to check it against a list of known constants, making option C correct. The rest of the options do not improve security.

49. E. The Clownfish class contains an invalid override of the getFish() method. In particular, it cannot declare any new or broader checked exceptions. Next, there is an error in the main() method. Since v is a var, it is given a specific type based on the reference at compile time, in this case Fish. Fish is a supertype of Clownfish, so it cannot be assigned to a Clownfish reference without an explicit cast, resulting in a compiler error. Since the code contains two lines that do not compile, option E is correct.

50. A,D,F. This code uses try-with-resources to ensure all resources it creates are closed; therefore, it does protect from a denial of service attack, making option A correct. While it's preferable to declare the Connection inside the try-with-resources statement, it is not required, so long as there are no methods that can throw an exception between its declaration and the try-with-resources statement.

While this method uses a PreparedStatement, it does not bind the query parameter using setString(), so this code is at risk for SQL injection. For this reason, option D is correct. Finally, this code will always produce an exception at runtime, even if the database and related table are available, because rs.next() is not called before rs.getString(). For this reason, option F is correct.

Index

A

`abstract` classes, 44, 109, 112, 293, 407, 453, 470–471, 523, 555

`abstract` methods, 28, 37–39, 44, 50–52, 62–63, 65–66, 73–75, 81, 89–90, 92, 94, 100–102, 114, 119, 190, 361, 374–375, 380–381, 398, 405, 409, 432, 448, 451, 453–455, 458–463, 465–466, 468, 471–472, 491, 542–543, 546–548, 553–556, 562

`accept()` method, 190, 209–210, 436, 491, 499, 563

access control, 319, 531

access modifiers, 32–33, 67, 116, 245–246, 410, 450, 459, 472, 510, 556

accessors, 103, 468

accumulators, 199, 495

`add()` method, 158, 164, 177, 179, 481, 483, 487–488

`addFirst()` method, 182, 489

addition (+ or +=) operator, 218, 442–443, 501

`addLast()` method, 182, 489

`AddNumbers` interface, 92, 465

`addValue()` method, 282–283, 520

`adjustProperties()` method, 379–380, 547

`alert()` method, 405, 554

`allMatch()` method, 208, 226, 235, 429–430, 498, 504, 507, 561

`andCompare()` method, 183, 489

annotations. *See also specific topics*

  about, 354, 540

  defined, 354, 540

  defining metadata with, 378, 547

anonymous classes, 42, 86, 89, 93, 410, 452, 464–466, 556

`anyMatch()` method, 192–193, 196, 208, 226, 235, 429–430, 492–494, 498, 504, 507, 561

`apply()` method, 190, 209–210, 224, 436, 491, 499, 504, 563

`applyAsDouble()` method, 224, 504

`applyFilter`, 377, 547

`AromicBoolean`, 272–273, 517

array brackets ([]), 158–159, 162, 166, 174, 481–484, 486

array elements, 182, 185–186, 489–490

array initializers, 158, 481

array logic, 383–384, 548

array parameters, 103, 468

`ArrayDeque`, 182, 489

`ArrayIndexOutOfBoundsException`, 368, 393–394, 428–429, 544, 551, 561

`ArrayList`, 158, 162–163, 169, 176–177, 179, 184, 417, 481, 483, 485, 487–489, 558

arrays and collections. *See also specific topics*

  char, 294, 523

  elements of, 384, 548

  empty arrays, 175, 487

  indexing, 161, 164, 166, 178–179, 180, 182, 184, 482–484, 488–489

  in methods, 43–44, 452–453

  multidimensional, 162, 178, 482–483, 488

  sorting, 183–185, 369, 489, 545

`Arrays.asList()` method, 173, 486

`Arrays.compare()` method, 173, 486

`ArrayStoreException`, 176, 383–384, 487, 548

B

C

Online Test Bank

Register to gain one year of FREE access after activation to the online interactive test bank to help you study for your OCP Java SE 11 Developer certification exam—included with your purchase of this book! All of the questions and the practice exams in this book are included in the online test bank so you can practice in a timed and graded setting.

Register and Access the Online Test Bank

To register your book and get access to the online test bank, follow these steps:

1. Go to bit.ly/SybexTest (this address is case sensitive)!
2. Select your book from the list.
3. Complete the required registration information, including answering the security verification to prove book ownership. You will be emailed a pin code.
4. Follow the directions in the email or go to www.wiley.com/go/sybextestprep.
5. Find your book on that page and click the "Register or Login" link with it. Then enter the pin code you received and click the "Activate PIN" button.
6. On the Create an Account or Login page, enter your username and password, and click Login or, if you don't have an account already, create a new account.
7. At this point, you should be in the test bank site with your new test bank listed at the top of the page. If you do not see it there, please refresh the page or log out and log back in.

SYBEX®
A Wiley Brand